ONE WHO SURVIVED

Alexander Barmine

ONE WHO SURVIVED

The Life Story of a Russian under the Soviets

By

ALEXANDER BARMINE

With an Introduction by
MAX EASTMAN

G. P. PUTNAM'S SONS · · · NEW YORK

Fourth Edition

TO MÀRI

Contents

Illustrations

Introduction

THIS BOOK IS, in my opinion, the most important that could be written on the socialist experiment in Russia. Barmine is the sole man left in the world who can relate, and dares to, with the authority of theoretic understanding, intimate and diversified experience, unbroken morale, irreproachable integrity, and scientific detachment, the inside story of that experiment from the revolution to the great purge. He is the only man left to weigh in the scales of civilized intelligence the results as seen from the inside and the method as actually applied.

This will seem an extreme statement only to those who do not realize the extent of Stalin's extermination of the elite. There may be some precocious stenographer or confidential secretary, farsighted enough to have kept mum and retired into a cyclone cellar, who will crawl out with a true and significant memoir when the dictatorship passes. It is impossible not to hope for this. But so far as the thing could be accomplished with the help of research experts and the secret police, *incorruptible intelligence* combined with *inside knowledge* was exterminated in Soviet Russia, and in all its embassies and legations, with meticulous and ruthless care.

"When I work on my book," Barmine said to me, "I feel as though I were walking in a graveyard. All my friends and life associates have been shot. It seems to be some kind of a mistake that I am alive."

It *is* partly a mistake—a mistake of the G.P.U. in Athens who thought Barmine could be frightened into a trap, of the G.P.U. in Paris who thought he could be shanghaied with a crude trick. It is also partly pure accident—the accident of his being sent as a young man on important missions into the Western world, where his persistently inquiring mind could get a detached view of what was happening in his own country. It is astonishing that none of the Old Bolsheviks, internationalists though they were, tried to avoid the purge by escaping into a foreign country. With four exceptions—Barmine, Raskolnikov, Reiss, and Krivitsky—none even of those already serving abroad, so far as is known, refused to go back when summoned to almost certain death. Some of them perhaps did refuse and, lacking Barmine's good luck and highhanded manner of walking out, were secretly murdered—as in the end Reiss was, and Raskolnikov, and possibly Krivitsky. But in general the Old Bolsheviks seem to have walked into Stalin's execution chamber in a kind of wax-figure trance, as though the frustration of their highly cerebral motivation had left them deprived of the natural impulses of organic life. Undoubtedly Barmine's youth as well as his mental flexibility helped to distinguish him in this respect. He had gone Bolshevik as a mere matter of growing up, and without any real knowledge of what the doctrine was, or at least what any other doctrine was. He was thus still educating himself when the Marxist officialdom as a whole had stopped learning and ceased even to think.

By good luck, also, his tasks in the year or two before the purge were comparatively light. People who wonder why Lenin's pupils were so slow waking up to what was happening to the revolution under Stalin fail to realize the desperate pressure under which they worked. Life under the five-year plans, and even before that for the leaders, was a perpetual emergency. In the tension of the effort to build a new world there was no time, and the brain was too exhausted, to ask the complicated question: What kind of world is it turning out to be? That was Barmine's position before his appointment to a "diplomat's paradise" on the shores of the blue Mediterranean. There he found leisure to ask this question, and even begin to answer it.

More particularly his being in Athens may have played a part in differentiating his conduct from that of the more rigid Bolsheviks during the destruction of their party. His mind dwelt much in the Greece that is eternal, and I can think of no mental experience more wholesome to the rabid "Marxist-Leninist." Among lucky accidents, also, and very Athenian ones, we must place Màri Pavlides, the gifted architect with daring laughter and hair of "rosy gold," whose part in producing this miracle of survival was certainly not a small one.

Beneath it all, however, the basic cause is the man's excelling mind and character. The thoughtful reader will realize from his life story, though so modestly told, that Barmine's native gifts must have been unusual. He was one of those multiple-minded and resourceful Bolsheviks who could be thrown into any critical enterprise whatever and relied on to see it through to success. It is our good fortune that the one who survived should have had so varied an experience. Businessman, industrialist, soldier, diplomat, journalist—he gives us the firsthand testimony of four or five men in one. He is the kind of person to whom you can go for illuminating advice on almost any question.

But, besides that, Barmine belongs to a moral aristocracy that is rare in this turmoil of a world. I do not know, when I contemplate the life of this unbrushed, unmothered, unbrought-up, semi-orphaned, maltreated, runaway boy, who entered adult life almost as a tramp, where he got his high and fine standards of conduct. There is no need to stress his clear candor and truthfulness, for that is apparent in every page of his book. Victor Serge said, when Barmine's book of memoirs was published in Paris:

"There is no man in the world who will stand up and say: 'This is not true.' "

And, surprising as it is, that challenge was never taken up even by the Stalinists. Alexander Barmine's *Memoirs of a Soviet Diplomat,* written when he broke with Stalin and was sentenced to death in Moscow, and containing a most devastating exposure of the brutal counterrevolution in Russia, although published in both England and France, and although praised widely by other critics, *was never mentioned in the Communist press.*

The Party and its fellow travelers have had no lack of slanders for Walter Krivitsky, for Jan Valtin, and others who have told unpleasant truths about Stalin's Russia. They have demonstrated in the same breath that those authors do not exist and that they are notorious mountebanks. But about Alexander Barmine they never, for seven years, printed a word. In an earlier age one would conclude that these hell-demons of obscene vilification had recoiled before the man's simple moral dignity, the open and clear record of his soldierly service to the cause. The fact is, of course, that they could think of nothing effective to say. Their choice of silence, like their choice among slanders when they speak, is purely an expedient one. Its significance, however, is all the greater for that. It is a tribute to Alexander Barmine's character and position that no encomiums of mine could add to.

It is a tribute primarily, of course, to his reliability. And that is the main question. But such qualities do not come singly. It requires interior structure and organization to stand firm for the truth in a time of storm. In such storms as Barmine has gone through—the simultaneous sweeping away of his faith, his fatherland, his job, his friends, his place in society, the security of his person, everything that commonly holds a man up—it requires a highly integrated morale.

It is not related in this book that, when Barmine arrived in Paris "hunted and in despair," although his position and personality were such as could have been exploited in the world press with immense profit—and he was among other things a journalist—he declined every offer and opportunity of that kind. He did not once think of turning from the motive of social service to the profit motive. Nor did he think of retiring from the struggle for a better world. While earning his living working eight hours a day in a factory, he devoted his evenings to studying the new problems presented to humanity by the failure of the Soviet regime and to contributing his own reflections and experiences in a book. He was still supporting himself as a factory worker and still struggling nightly with those problems, when I first met him soon after his arrival in New York. To one who has watched, as I have, with sad amazement, the various forms of corruption and degeneration and awful intellectual debauch to which the debacle of socialism in Russia has given rise throughout the world, the steadfastness and courage and high persistence, the sense of an honorable obligation to mankind revealed by this shipwrecked Bolshevik have been reassuring.

I have found reassurance of another kind in the similarity, amounting almost to identity, of our political opinions. Barmine had read my *Stalin's Russia and the Crisis in Socialism* when we met, and his first words were: "You seem to have arrived by reflection at the same conclusions to which my experience has led me."

It is indeed remarkable, considering our diverse origins and the dissimilar paths we have traveled, how closely we agree on all phases of the Soviet experiment and its significance for socialist theory. Only once in reading this book did I run into an important opinion somewhat opposed to my own. I would not dismiss so lightly as Barmine does the mystery of the "Moscow confessions." I agree that demoralization under disillusionment and torment was the basic cause of this prodigy. I agree that the *hundred* who died without "confessing" to every *one* who "confessed" are the significant factor most often forgotten in discussing it. But I think the notion of serving the Party, or saving what might be left of the Revolution, played the part of a pretext, a loophole of self-justification, for these demoralized men. I also incline more and more to the opinion, especially since learning that Henry Yagoda, the head of the G.P.U. during the first show trial, was by professional training a pharmacist, that drugs played a part in the process of their demoralization.

Aside from that, I could sign practically every opinion expressed by the author of this book. Each day of our friendship has made it more clear that we have arrived by different roads at the same general conclusions.

MAX EASTMAN

March 1945

xiv

BOOK ONE

There is a charm in the name of Ancient Greece.
There is glory in every page of her history . . . and a sense of unapproachable beauty in her works of art.
There is a spell in her climate still, and a strange attraction in her ruins. . . .

ALEXANDER S. MURRAY

1. At My Post in Greece

GREECE IN EARLY SUMMER is a land of blue and gold, and that morning in June, 1937, was as lovely as any other under the cloudless skies of the Aegean. From the doorway of my small cottage at Kalamaki I looked down at the bright pink-and-white peasant dwellings scattered on a hillside draped with terraced vines. Below them the villas of the patricians bordered the bay. A few white yachts rocked gently to and fro on the blue water. Behind me the mountains were bleak and peaceful. Athens lay in a light haze ten miles away. It seemed a corner of the world that pain and misery and crime had left untouched. Could these things exist anywhere in the world?

Up from the road below came the water carrier's cry: *"Ne-rou-l-a-a-s!"* And close at hand I heard the gardener's daughter preparing my breakfast—coffee and cheese and unraised bread.

After breakfast I climbed into my Ford and took the road along the shore, past the Piraeus, past Hadrian's Gate and the Byron monument, into the heart of Athens. Beyond the huge oval of the new marble stadium I drew up at the gates of the legation.

The sumptuous building, which stood close to the royal palace, had been the Imperial Russian Legation, and we had inherited it. Everything here was going well. There was no reason for the U.S.S.R. and Greece to fear each other. Moscow was not concerned about Greece then. Athens was a peaceful and even a drowsy post. Acting as chargé d'affaires in the long absence of Minister Kobetsky, I had little to do but glance through the Greek, foreign, and Soviet newspapers, write a few letters, reply to an occasional memorandum from the Greek Foreign Office, and keep in contact with the diplomatic corps. The diplomat who serves his country in such a post should be the happiest of men. But I was uneasy, for I was conscious of a mysterious process developing in my own country. The Commissariat of Foreign Affairs seemed to be suffering from a strange torpor. For some months I had been left without instructions or information. Krestinsky, deputy to Foreign Commissar Litvinov, had just been relieved of his post. The signature of Stern, director of the German and Balkan Department, had suddenly ceased to appear on official documents. My dispatches remained unanswered. Something was going wrong at home.

This morning the letters on my desk were few; the news columns looked dull; their contents were soporific. Even the envelopes were stamped with the rubric:

Hellenes, sleep in peace: Hellas is strong.

IAN METAXAS

The telephone rang.

"The director of the Greek Press Agency insists on having a few words with you," my secretary told me.

I took up the receiver.

"We have just heard, sir, by radio from Moscow, that one of the Russian vice-commissars for defense has committed suicide. We did not get his name. Can you confirm this and tell us what lies behind it?"

I caught my breath. But my reply was quick and diplomatic. "I have received no such information from Moscow. Marshal Voroshilov, the People's Commissar for Defense, has four vice-commissars: Commissar Gamarnik, Marshal Tukhachevsky, General Alksnis, and Admiral Orlov. I trust that all are doing well. . . ." [1]

I hung up the receiver. Suicide? Who could it be? I hoped it was just another false story from the Nazi press. It was nearly five months now since the Piatakov trial, which ended in the execution of thirteen leaders. Arrests and disappearances were still probably going on, but in our remoteness we kept hoping that things were getting back to normal. It seemed likely after the nightmare of the first two Moscow trials that the leaders of the opposition had, at the price of extreme self-abasement and death, made it possible for Stalin to govern the country with a sense of security and let the terror subside. I tried to calm myself with this thought as I returned to my mail.

But two hours later a member of the legation staff burst into my office with an evening paper in his hand. His face was white.

"Gamarnik has killed himself," he said.

Neither of us betrayed our real emotion. Russians had learned in recent years, no matter what happened, never to express what they felt. We never broke this rule in any circumstances whatever. We could be sure of nobody, not even our family and intimate friends. I read the story and replied with as much calmness as I could muster:

"We must wait for news from Moscow. God knows what may be happening."

That evening the legation staff gathered as usual to hear the Moscow broadcast. We exchanged small talk and even tried to make a few jokes. Nobody dared mention what was uppermost in his mind. Over the air came the colorless voice of the Moscow spokesman: the subway was progressing nicely; a Party conference was in session. He read off figures concerning the housing campaign and the latest total of ore production. And then, without any change of tone: "Gamarnik, ex-member of the Central Committee of the Party, fearing that his anti-Soviet machinations would be unmasked, has committed suicide. Weather report: the Central Observatory forecasts for tomorrow . . ."

So the Commissar General of the Red Army was dead! An Old

[1] The three others were shot one after another, within six months of Gamarnik's suicide.

4

Bolshevik, whose long face with its fan-shaped beard was familiar to millions of Russians, Gamarnik had been a provincial leader in the October Revolution. Twice every week of late he had sat on the Central Committee in intimate consultation with Stalin, his comrade, who had now sent him to death. For I had no doubt that Gamarnik had chosen suicide as a way of escape from arrest and the inevitable firing squad.

". . . Moscow is expecting stormy weather," the announcer concluded.

I walked out into the cool night air. My hope had been vain that the purges were over, that my own doubts and questionings would be allowed to rest. Now, apparently, the whole agony was to begin again.

The next few days added to my feeling of impending disaster. Worse news came from Moscow. Marshal Tukhachevsky and seven of the most famous generals of the Red Army were suddenly seized. The communiqué added that they had been secretly tried, sentenced for high treason, and executed. We heard the voice of the Moscow announcer read out resolutions passed by numerous meetings of workmen, artists, scientists, and students, applauding the executions. Here were all the familiar phrases. The executed Red Army leaders were "fascist traitors," "mad dogs," "criminal scum of humanity," "stinking vermin."

I knew better. Most of the men who had been shot were known to me personally. Tukhachevsky, conqueror of Admiral Kolchak and brilliant generalissimo of the Polish war, had been in the last years my close friend. In Moscow I had worked in intimate collaboration with him. And I felt deep respect and affection for Uborevich, perhaps the most gifted in that galaxy of great soldiers. He had defeated General Denikin at Orel in 1920 and the last remaining White forces of the Far East in 1922. He had been the first to advocate mechanizing the Red Army.

Yakir also had been an Old Bolshevik of the underground days before the Revolution. While still a young general, he had won distinction by breaking through the iron ring the enemy had drawn round his troops in the Odessa neighborhood in 1919. Later he had become one of the best of our military leaders and was elected to the Central Committee of the Party.

There were others—Primakov, Eydeman, Kork, Feldman. All of them had won their spurs during the Revolution and the Civil War and the war against Poland. After the war they had thrown themselves into the task of building the Red Army, avoiding the turmoil of internal party struggles as much as they could. In 1928 they had stood by while Trotsky, founder of the Red Army and their former commander in chief, was sent into exile. Rather than risk the unity of their country, they had submitted to Stalin's decisions. Now Stalin accused them of treason, of having connived with Nazi Germany. I knew their

5

patriotism and old-soldier spirit too well to believe in these fantastic charges. They were gruesome and absurd, and were made more so by the fact that two of the eight generals, Yakir and Feldman, were Jews.

The most likely explanation was that the murdered generals had objected to the destruction by Stalin of the technicians and business organizers, the men of brains who could really run the country, with all the fatal consequences that this rash act would have for military defense. For these were the very generals, Tukhachevsky and Uborevich especially, who had mechanized the Red Army and prepared it, and all the national defenses, precisely for a war against fascist Germany. A few imprudent words, the mere fact of signing a protest to the Central Committee, would have been enough to make them dangerous in Stalin's eyes, and to bring their death warrants.

Some days later an official of the Foreign Office, an old friend of mine, arrived from Moscow. He told me of events that the press had not reported. I heard that General Hekker, chief of protocol of the Commissariat of Defense, had disappeared; that in headquarters alone some twenty younger generals, former classmates of mine at the Moscow General Staff College, had been executed; that hundreds of senior officers, associated with the murdered men by long years of collaboration, had been arrested.

The only military chiefs of distinction who now remained alive were Marshals Yegorov and Blukher, Admiral Orlov, General Alksnis, Chief of the Air Force, and Muklevich, former Admiral of the Fleet.[2]

In the days that followed the execution of the eight generals, no one at the legation uttered a word about what had happened. My colleagues as well as I merely let it be known that they accepted the Moscow stories. But I could no longer sleep. I have never lived under a darker sky than that bright blue sky of Greece. There was no longer any uncertainty in my mind. The earlier trials were only a beginning. Stalin, haunted by the revolutionary past in which he had played an undistinguished role, was determined to root out every trace of it. He could do this in only one way: by physically exterminating the "Old Bolsheviks" who remembered the events. By doing away with these men he would bury once for all the ideals for whose sake the Bolsheviks had endured his dictatorship and its disastrous results for years.

A few weeks earlier I had been talking happily with a young Greek woman, an architect of Athens, who was very dear to me— making plans for our future life in Russia. Now she saw me depressed and unable to speak. How could I break down her illusions about the beautiful new society we were going to join in building? How could I tell her that all my hopes were being blown away? The shots that

[2] All of them were shot or disappeared within a year.

rang out in Stalin's prisons ended the lives of thousands of innocents who had fought sincerely for Soviet Russia and socialism. This senseless terror had destroyed what was left of the faith that sustained me in my service to the Soviets.

The days that followed the execution of the eight generals were filled with a sense of disaster. At the legation no one said a word. Each of us felt stifled under the weight of private thoughts. An evening came when one of my assistants hung about my room, loath to leave. We exchanged silent looks, and then suddenly I committed the imprudence, perhaps the fatal imprudence, of saying:

"What on earth's happening there? This is too horrible. The best men—the flower of the army . . ."

I tried to regain control of my feelings.

"Come on, let's go for a walk."

We went out into the street. As we walked I told him everything I had learned from my friend in the Foreign Office.

I told him of Tukhachevsky's last appearance in public, six weeks before his death, at the May Day review in Red Square. Tukhachevsky had just learned that he was not, as had been announced, to go to London to attend the coronation of King George VI. Admiral Orlov had been assigned to replace him. For Tukhachevsky this was the handwriting on the wall. And everybody knew it. That May Day he had walked across Red Square, a tired man, with slow pace, his thumbs in his belt. He stood severely alone on the tribune reserved for the marshals at the right of Lenin's Mausoleum. Icy coldness surrounded him. None of the high officers present wished to risk disfavor by approaching the army chief who had fallen from Stalin's grace.

As he stood there, impassive, his fine pale complexion seemed grayer than usual. For the last time he was watching the troops of the Red Army, which he had helped to mold and had led to victories, file past him. He must have had a clear presentiment of what awaited him, for when an official in the U.S.S.R. falls from power, there is no return: disgrace is almost invariably the prelude to execution. Shortly after this the papers announced that Tukhachevsky had been relieved of his duties as assistant to Voroshilov and appointed military commander of the Volga District. As soon as he reached Saratov he was arrested and brought back to Moscow in a prison van.

Yakir, too, was removed from his post as military commander of the Ukraine, appointed commander of the Leningrad District, and then arrested, with his wife, as he passed through Moscow. Stalin was afraid to arrest these famous and loved commanders among their own troops.

He was afraid also to let them live overnight. According to the papers the eight generals were shot immediately after court-martial. Foreign papers printed a story that Tukhachevsky had been carried on a stretcher, wounded, into the courtroom. But this was probably invented. It was doubtful whether any trial took place. Stalin would hardly have dared to parade his victims before the eyes of their own companions-in-arms ordered to pass the sentence of death upon them.[3]

I also told my silent companion about other incidents of Tukhachevsky's downfall. His daughter, a child of twelve, had not been informed of her father's fate. On the day when the official communiqué was issued, she was greeted with abuse by her schoolmates: they would not sit in the same classroom with the daughter of a "fascist traitor." This little girl went home and hanged herself. Her mother, who was arrested the following day, became insane and was sent away to the Ural District in a strait jacket.

I related how, in the single military district of Kiev, six to seven hundred senior officers had been arrested for their association with Yakir during the Revolution or in more recent service. The manager of one of the Kiev movie houses was arrested for neglecting to censor a newsreel in which Tukhachevsky appeared. The directors of a radio station were put in jail for broadcasting a funeral march—probably by pure coincidence—on the day the generals were executed.

I knew Yakir's wife. She had been his constant companion for twenty years, sharing his early battles and later his studies and his periods of high office. As a courageous and well-educated woman, she had more than once been able to give him advice. The papers published a letter in which she blackguarded her executed husband whom she had loved so long, calling him an "infamous traitor." It was quite clear to me that she had been made to sign this document, either under threat or persuaded that by doing so she was serving the higher interests of the Party.

Izvestia announced that Marie Nicolaevna Tukhachevsky, the marshal's sister, was seeking permission to change her name.

The War Department, I explained, was not the only one affected by the bloody purge. The cyclone had also swept through our Commissariat of Foreign Affairs. Krestinsky, vice-commissar, old companion of Lenin, had been arrested. Dozens of leading ambassadors and chiefs of departments had been arrested and shot. The purge of the Foreign Department had been conducted by Korzhenko, a G.P.U.[4] man who had been made the new chief of personnel. Scarcely one head of a department had escaped. Yurenev, Rosenberg, Davtian, and other ambassadors had mysteriously vanished from their embassies abroad.

The same tragedy was being played out at the Commissariat of

[3] As I write this, Marshals Budyenny and Shaposhnikov are the sole survivors of the eight alleged judges. Marshal Blukher, Generals Alksnis, Kashirin, Dybenko, and others were shot or disappeared within the year.

[4] The G.P.U., all-powerful Soviet Secret Police (formerly called Cheka) was included in 1934 in the People's Commissariat of Interior Affairs (Russian abbreviation N.K.V.D.) and adopted N.K.V.D. as its official name. Since then it has experienced several changes of name, but it is still as often as not called G.P.U. and I shall for simplicity's sake retain this "popular" name throughout my book.

1933—"Long live the heroic Red Army, and its leaders—The Supreme Military Council!" *Stalin in his congratulatory message at the fifteenth anniversary of the Red Army.*

THE SUPREME MILITARY COUNCIL

1937—above, from left to right: Commissar Gamarnik—suicide; Marshal Tukhachevsky—shot; Marshal Yegorov—disappeared, presumably shot; General Khalepsky—disappeared, presumably shot; Admiral Orlov—shot; General Yakir —shot.

Below from left to right: General Kamenev—died of natural causes; Commissar Ordjonikidze—poisoned; Marshal Budyenny—alive; General Alksnis—shot; Admiral Muklevich—disappeared, presumably shot; General Eydeman—shot; General Uborevich—shot.

Maxim Litvinov, commissar of foreign affairs, later ambassador to U. S. A., with his two assistants. *Left:* Vice-commissar Gregory Sokolnikov, ambassador to Great Britain—condemned at second Moscow trial in 1937 to ten years in prison. *Right:* Vice-commissar Nicolai Krestinsky, ambassador to Germany—condemned at third Moscow trial in 1938 and shot.

© *International News Photos*
The first five marshals of the Soviet Union. *Sitting, from left to right:* Tukhachevsky—shot in June, 1937; Voroshilov—alive; Yegorov—disappeared, presumably shot in 1938. *Standing:* Budyenny—alive; Blukher—shot in 1938.

Foreign Trade. Commissar Rosengolz and his two assistants, Eliava and Loganovsky, with whom I had worked for years, had disappeared, dragging down into darkness all who had been connected with them by ties of either business or friendship.

Finally I told my assistant that our direct superior in the Foreign Office, David Stern, had been arrested and, like Krestinsky, had disappeared. He was director of the Department of German and Balkan Affairs, a German communist writer who had found a new home in the U.S.S.R. His wife and child had followed him, in tears, out of the apartment onto the landing, only to be beaten back by the police. Next day they were thrown into the street by the manager of the Foreign Office building, in which their quarters were situated. I had known Stern well. He was a young man of thirty-five, a writer of talent and an extremely hard worker, though bad health kept him most of the time in a sanatorium. Under the name of Georg Born, concealing his identity for diplomatic reasons, he had written a number of documented and rather colorful anti-Nazi novels. The best-known were *Notebook of an S.S. Man* and *In the Service of the Gestapo*. *Pravda* used to praise his books, which were published by the Central Committee of the Communist Youth in very large editions. But now *Pravda* contained an article by Zaslavsky on the German spy, Georg Born, "this degenerate product of the Gestapo, who at long last has been unmasked and duly punished." Zaslavsky did not make known the real name of Georg Born, and the diplomatic and newspaper colony never knew that his article explained the sudden disappearance of a prominent Soviet diplomat.

Thousands, in all branches of the government, had fallen victims to the fury of the purge. I knew many of them intimately. It was impossible to believe the charges of treason hurled by the Soviet press against these loyal workers. The whole thing was a nightmare.

While I was talking to my seemingly sympathetic colleague, I experienced a relief from the painful tension in my brain. But as I watched him disappear down the street and turned toward my own home, an uneasy feeling seized me.

"My friend," I said to myself, "tonight you have talked too much."

2. *The Trap*

A FEW DAYS LATER the assistant I had confided in that night was summoned home. We said our farewells in my office and made no reference to our previous conversation. I wondered if it was at his own request that he was being called back to report.

Soon after that my friends in the Foreign Office gave up writing to me. Minister Kobetsky, for whom I was substituting, died in a Moscow hospital. I sealed his desk and wrote asking what should be done with his papers, but Litvinov failed to answer. Then one day Lukianov, my code secretary, came into my room holding a telegram from Potemkin, Litvinov's assistant. He looked embarrassed.

"I have just had a personal order from Potemkin," he said. "I am to seal Kobetsky's papers and send them to Moscow. What shall I do about it?"

This order should have been addressed to me as the chief of the diplomatic mission. It was an unprecedented breach of procedure; and the breach could only be intentional.

"You must execute the commissariat's orders," I replied.

It was clear that Lukianov, who had a brother in the U.S.S.R. occupying the important post of secretary of the Central Committee of the Communist Youth, was receiving a special mark of distinction. Potemkin could hardly have guessed that within a fortnight, by the grim irony of the G.P.U., Lukianov's highly placed brother would be thrown into prison as an "enemy of the people."

By this time, I must say, I had lost all keenness for my work, and contact with the diplomatic corps and with Athenian society had become painful to me. I kept away from receptions and declined all invitations. If I had been able to bury myself in a desert, I would have done so. What could I say if some foreign diplomat asked me politely what was happening in Russia? I could give the stereotyped answer: "The Red Army is stronger than ever, now that the traitors have been weeded out. With a man of genius like Stalin, my dear sir, we have nothing to fear!" A *mot* of my friend Dovgalevsky, the late Soviet ambassador to Paris, came to my mind. "The diplomat differs in one way only from the witness in a court of law: he must tell the truth, and nothing but the truth, but he must never tell the whole truth." The truth! I could not tell any part of it.

It was no longer possible for me to serve abroad. I had to get out. I wrote to Moscow, asking to be recalled.

I prepared to meet my fate. Even according to Moscow's standards there was no conceivable evidence against me, but certainly something unpleasant would happen. Imprisonment? Or perhaps merely exile to some remote corner of Russia?

But here another problem presented itself. Could I take with me the woman I loved and who was to be my wife?

A wave of hatred and suspicion against all foreigners was raging in Moscow. The extermination of the whole foreign colony, of enthusiastic and loyal people who had come to Russia to put their knowledge at the service of the Socialist government, was proceeding with deliberate thoroughness. Hundreds were being imprisoned and executed or deported to Siberia. Having come under suspicion myself, I could do nothing to help her. Had I the right to sacrifice a human being who was dear to me, to take her with me along the road of privation and pain, simply because she believed in me and loved me?

She was in Paris at a congress of architects, and I wrote to her about my impending departure for the U.S.S.R., asking her to give up for the time being any idea of departing with me. I told her not to be surprised if I did not write to her. However long my silence, she must never lose faith in me. It might be years before we could join each other.

I wrote to my sons, who since the death of my first wife were living with my mother. They would once more see their father. I was bringing them, I said, bicycles, satchels, and some stamp albums—unbelievable treasure trove!

As the days passed without word from Litvinov, I began to grow nervous. There were, however, signs that Moscow had not forgotten me. One morning in July, arriving earlier than usual at the legation, I found a clerk going through my desk. His embarrassment was no less obvious than my own.

"I was looking for that telegram that came yesterday—the one about visas," he stammered.

"I should be obliged if you would conduct your search elsewhere," I said.

A few days later, on my way downstairs, I happened to glance through the glass door of my study and see Lukianov rummaging in my brief case. I turned sharply and entered the room. My private papers were in his hands. We stood there looking at each other. There was nothing to say.

The same day I received a letter from my son Boris, whom I always called the elder of the twins, because he was the bigger. He said that he was going with his brother and his grandmother to the south— "far, far, away to bathe in the sea." A little later on there was this passage: "Dear Papa, they read to us in school the sentence passed on the Trotskyist spies, Tukhachevsky, Yakir, Kork, Uborevich, and Feldman. . . ." (The child had got all the names right; obviously he had been made to learn them.) "Wasn't it Feldman who used to live in our apartment house?"

11

I remembered a poem written by a schoolboy of twelve published in the Moscow papers during the Zinoviev trial. Each verse had ended with the refrain:

"Like mad dogs we will shoot them all!"

What would my boys think if I should be imprisoned as the result of some vile, lying charge? They would believe the official communiqué. Nobody would dare speak for me, and I would never be able to clear myself. I would lose them as sons forever. I reflected that only by staying abroad could I possibly have a chance ever to tell them the truth and win them back.

With all these thoughts my state of tension became unendurable. To relieve it I arranged on Friday, July 16, to go for a fishing trip with my fiancée's brother George.

That same afternoon our commercial attaché telephoned me. We chatted a moment, and he said, quite casually:

"Well, Alexander Grigorievich, I shall see you soon on board, as agreed. May I call for you about seven?"

"On board what?" I asked. And to my amazement I learned from this third party that the Soviet ship *Rudzutak*[1] had just dropped anchor at Piraeus, and that, unknown to me, I had accepted an invitation to dine with the captain! By diplomatic custom the captain should have made it his first duty to call on me. Instead I had not even been informed of the ship's arrival.

"I'm afraid I won't be available," I told the attaché. "I have an engagement for this evening."

"But everything has been arranged—you are expected—you promised to come."

"I did nothing of the kind," I replied and hung up the receiver.

Ten minutes later the captain of the *Rudzutak* telephoned from the Piraeus. He apologized for not calling, explaining that he had been kept on board by urgent repairs, and begged me to come to dinner. He said that he wished to present his new political commissar and his new first officer. There were also several important matters he would like to discuss with me; and, besides, he had an excellent cook.

"Sorry, I'm going fishing at Voulagmeni," I answered curtly. "If you need to see me, you can come out there."

That evening about eight o'clock George and I started off, rowing briskly. The bay of Voulagmeni was idyllically calm; bright stars spangled the deep night sky. But I was far from enjoying the scene. I had other thoughts. I was trying not to draw the obvious conclusion from the eagerness of these men to get me on board their boat; it

---

[1] The ship was named after Jan Rudzutak, a vice-premier of the Soviet Government and close friend of Lenin, who was later declared an enemy of the people and disappeared.

12

seemed so unworthy of everyone concerned—of them, of my government, of myself.

Through the dusk we saw a car approach on the deserted road and draw up to the dock. Several men got out and scanned the waters of the bay.

"They're looking for us," I said. "Let's row ashore."

On the dock I found the ship's captain, accompanied by his two new officers, the commercial attaché, and a couple of members of the legation staff. We exchange greetings, and I invited them to a restaurant. At the table there was a feeling of forced cheerfulness. After dessert the captain suggested that we all go back to the ship and continue our party. Again I declined, wondering whether they were all involved in the plot.

One of the legation men stayed with me at the table after the rest had gone. I already knew the nature of his secret function, aside from his regular job in the legation.

We sat on the terrace overlooking the bay and faced each other across the table. The atmosphere was tense. A little incident put our nerves still more on edge. The waiter who had brought our tiny cups of coffee took the money with a trembling hand: his eyes stared vacantly from a bloodless face. Suddenly he collapsed in an epileptic fit, and our conversation was interrupted by the rat-tat of his head against a near-by table. While he was being carried out, my guest began to tell me a strange story.

"When I was in China," he said, trying to make his voice sound unconcerned, "I learned that a secretary of the consulate was making plans to quit the service. At that time I was acting as consul. I instructed him to take charge of the diplomatic pouch as far as the frontier. To avoid arousing his suspicions, I warned him not to cross into Soviet territory. The pouch would be picked up, I said, from the Chinese side of the border. There would be no need for him to have any papers."

My guest paused and sipped his coffee. He kept his eyes fixed on me. Perhaps he wanted me to ask: "And what happened then?" But I remained silent.

"The chauffeur stepped on the gas and did not stop until he passed the border and reached the G.P.U. outpost where they were waiting for our conspiratorial friend." He paused again. "The fellow tried to jump out when he realized that he had been tricked. But of course he wasn't alone in the car. He was lucky enough to get off with a few years in jail. . . .

"The story of the interpreter at the Peking Embassy is rather more complicated. He actually fled to Hankow. But our people got on his track, and two reliable Chinese were entrusted with the job of liquidating him. They managed to contact him and induced him to accept a dinner invitation. But he smelled trouble and did not show up at the restaurant. Next day they shot him in the street. By a miracle he escaped death. A car from the French Embassy happened by and picked him up before they could finish him off."

His fingers waved the subject away.

"But he had his lesson. I don't think we shall have any more trouble with him."

"Of course not," I observed.

His next words left no doubt as to his meaning. "You know," he continued slowly, "it wouldn't be difficult to get rid of a man in this country. There's always somebody willing to undertake a little job of that kind for five or ten thousand drachmas, and you can take it from me the police will know nothing." He turned his gaze toward the rocky shore. "An ideal place for that kind of operation."

"Surely," I agreed.

"Now, that reminds me of another story . . ." But I had had enough.

"No thanks," I said. "These gangster yarns aren't half so much fun as fishing." I shook hands with him and left.

That handshake with my potential murderer stays with me as a most unpleasant memory. But I probably owe my escape to such polite formalities. Without an overt act on my part it would be awkward for them to precipitate a breach. I no longer had the slightest doubt what they had intended to do on board the ship. Would they ever believe me if I told them that I had been merely awaiting a reply before returning to Russia of my own free will? My sense of personal dignity was revolted by the alternatives: to submit to kidnaping or to walk out. After the stories I had just heard, I knew what was in store for me. I had to decide where I would be of most help to the Russian people—perishing in one of Stalin's prisons or living as a free man somewhere in the world, knowing the truth and speaking it out.

The next morning I went to the legation as usual. In the course of the day I noticed that Lukianov had a keen interest in my plans for that evening. After work, chatting with me in an affable way, he suggested that we go for a walk. I declined. I was tired of this false friendliness.

"Are you sleeping at the legation or at your cottage in the country?" he asked.

"At the cottage," I told him.

But instead I stayed in town and went up for the night to a mountain hotel at Kefissia. When I came to my cottage next morning I found signs of nocturnal visitors on the sandy paths of the garden, wet with recent rain. And there were tire marks in the driveway leading to the house.

Well, I thought, if you came for me at that hour, you must be in a hurry.

There was no time for hesitation. I asked George to come to the

14

legation with me. Neither of us was armed, but it seemed a good idea to bring a companion. When I got to my office I drafted a telegram to Potemkin, informing him that I intended to take my annual leave immediately, and asking that arrangements be made for the attaché next in rank, who happened to be my table companion of last night, to take over my duties. I called Lukianov and ordered him to code and dispatch this message without delay.

George and I went up to the second floor, where I had a private apartment. In a few minutes there was a knock on the door. The attaché entered. Evidently he already knew about the cable. When he saw the two of us he recoiled visibly. His manner became solicitous. He had heard, he said, that I was going off at once on a holiday and had come to inquire after my health. I thanked him and said that I was feeling perfectly well. After an awkward pause he left.

I took my passport and some photographs and letters and glanced around the familiar rooms for the last time. My friend George was rather nervously following my movements.

Slowly we walked down the stairs. To all appearances this was merely a routine sortie of the legation head with a friend. No attempt was made to stop us. But I saw the frightened faces of some members of the legation watching our departure from behind half-closed doors. Obviously they thought we were armed to the teeth and ready to fight our way out. The doorman swung open the large double doors that led to the courtyard. He bowed, and I smiled at him. We got into my car and drove away.

My diplomatic career was at an end. Twenty years in the service of the Soviets were dead and done with. I was without a country. . . .

The city lay under a dead weight of heat. We drove up the Kefissia Road toward the mountains. There we stopped at a hotel.

After a sleepless night I nerved myself for the last effort. I sent a letter of outright resignation to Moscow. Then I asked George to book a seat for me on the Simplon Express. I went to the French Legation and was received with smiles by the friendly M. Pierrefitte, the young chargé d'affaires. We exchanged a few remarks about the latest political gossip of Athens. Then I mentioned casually that I was going on vacation and planned to visit France. Would he mind stamping my passport, which I happened to have with me? Of course—he would be delighted. The matter was settled in a few minutes.

The previous evening I had noticed that a couple of Greek "fellow travelers," who were good friends of the legation, never let us out of their sight. They had evidently volunteered their services as G.P.U. spies. They were still following us, at a convenient distance, when we left the hotel for the railroad station. They were on the platform when we got on the train. George, who knew them, waved his hand and shouted an exaggerated greeting to them as he went back to the buffet.

He brought a flask of brandy to my compartment. "Take a swallow:

it will do you good," he said. "Give my greetings to my little sister." We embraced and shook hands heartily.

The train pulled out, and I was soon looking back for the last time at my two years' home, at that sunny land of Greece, whose hospitable people, whose vine-clad hills and tranquil mountain slopes, far-scattered isles and azure waters, had grown so dear to me.

I cannot tell the reader what thoughts filled me as the Simplon Express sped like an arrow from my home in Athens, without explaining that I had come to that city lonely and disappointed in my life and had found love there. I had been guided in my travels through the country, and in making friends with its people, by one who both possessed and deeply understood its beauties. She had made it more than a land of legend to me. She had made it again, as it once was, a home for all that is clearest and best in the human mind. I was going to see her now in Paris, but only to seek her sure support through dark and ominous and perhaps very brief days. I was saying good-by for us both to the idyllic scenes of our romance.

When I joined her in Paris we both went into hiding for a time. My natural course would have been to announce myself to the French authorities, make public my resignation and my reasons for it, and ask for personal protection. So long as the affair was not made public, the efforts of Stalin's agents to destroy me secretly would be intense. If I were "liquidated" in time, no one would even know that such a thing had happened. I would merely have vanished from the earth as did Yurenev in Berlin, Davtian in Warsaw, Bekzadian in Budapest, and indeed nine out of ten of our ambassadors in foreign countries. I understood this perfectly, and yet I risked my life needlessly for four months through some feeling that I can only describe as total disgust, a feeling more than half composed of shame for my government. I felt that if the regime I helped to build had fallen to these savage depths, I shared in its guilt. I was not worth saving. Nothing was worth saving. It is not romance but the plain truth that only Màri's eager love and courage kept alive in me the will to live and fight.

3. In Hiding

THE G.P.U. AGENTS had apparently been nonplussed when I took the initiative and calmly walked out of the legation. However, they quickly set to work. First my mother-in-law-to-be was visited at her home in Athens by some friends of the Soviet Legation.

"Barmine is an enemy of the Soviet Union and will be severely punished," they told her. "He is finished. Write to your daughter and tell her to break with him. Give us her address."

My only crime at that time had been to hand in my resignation, but in the Soviet Union that was enough.

The poor lady was constantly harassed by such visits and by telephone calls. Eventually she was told that her daughter's life was in danger because I was already condemned. In order to save Màri she must give them her address in Paris. By this terrifying threat they managed to extort the address, but it was an old one. We had both changed our hotels.

In forty-eight hours Màri's mother was again visited by Soviet "friends." "The address you gave us is wrong," they said. Evidently the information obtained from her in Athens had been telegraphed to Moscow and relayed to Paris, where the G.P.U. agents made their investigation and reported back to Moscow that I had moved. Moscow then speeded a new order to Athens, and the Greek agents were again put on the trail. The G.P.U. worked extremely fast, cutting through the usual red tape and spending money lavishly, to get me before my story became known.

A new effort in Paris had more success. As a visiting architect Màri received her mail at the Maison de la Culture—a club of progressive intellectuals and artists. One day when she called for her mail she was told that the manager of the club, a M. Nicolas, was holding it for her, as he wished to see her. He asked her, when she entered the room, whether she had ever heard of an organization called "The Friends of the Soviet Fatherland"? Its president, M. Kovalev, had an important matter to discuss with her. Would she telephone him and make an appointment?

"What is this organization, and who are its members?" she asked.

"It's made up of people friendly to the Soviet Union. Most of them are former White Russian *émigrés*."

"But what has a Greek architect to do with White Russians in France?" she replied.

"Well—really they are not Whites any longer. They sympathize with the new regime and wish to go back to Russia."

"Then why don't they go back?" was her naïve question.

The French fellow traveler, inexperienced in such assignments, was floundering.

"You see—they first have to prove their loyalty by some activities here in France."

Having forced this admission out of him, Màri ended the conversation. "I'll think it over," she said.

In the letter of resignation I sent to Moscow from Athens I had given the Paris Central Post Office as my mailing address. If the Moscow authorities wished to contact me, the Soviet Embassy in Paris could write me a letter. But in preparing "wet business"[1] the official Soviet representatives were not to be compromised. It was left to the Soviet Fatherland's new friends to "prove their loyalty."

That night we decided that it would be unwise at the moment for Màri to meet M. Kovalev. But the next time she called for her mail the manager confronted her again. Why hadn't she seen M. Kovalev? He was very anxious to meet her, and the matter might be of serious concern to her also. She really ought to call him at once.

We thought it over again and decided that she had better see the man and get an idea of what was on foot. She phoned him and arranged to meet him the following afternoon in the Greek Pavilion at the Paris Exposition. She waited there the next day for three hours, but Kovalev did not come.

The newspapers of the same evening told why. They carried the story of the assassination of Ignace Reiss, former chief of the Soviet intelligence service in western Europe, who had become disgusted by the Moscow executions and broken with the Soviet Government. His letter of resignation was couched in virulent terms: "Let there be no mistake," he wrote. "Truth will prevail. The day of vengeance is nearer than those in the Kremlin think. . . . Nothing will be forgotten, nothing forgiven. The 'Leader of Genius,' the 'Father of his People,' the 'Sun of Socialism' will be called to account. All will give evidence against the tyrant, those who have been wrongly accused, those who have been shot though innocent; the workers of the world will see to it that their names are cleared forever. . . . Whoever holds his peace now is an accomplice of Stalin. . . ." Reiss had gone to Switzerland with his wife and son in the hope of finding safety and peace. An agent of the G.P.U. in Rome joined him there. Pretending to sympathize with his step, she lured him into a trap, and his body was found riddled with fifteen bullets on the road to Chamblandes. According to the papers the crime had been traced back to Moscow, to the office of Yezhov, chief of the G.P.U., who was in direct telephonic communication with Stalin's rooms. It had cost its organizers 300,000 francs.

In the morning Màri phoned Kovalev's office and inquired about the broken appointment. The secretary answered that Kovalev had left for an indefinite period on "an unexpected journey." But on the fol-

---

[1] Russian expression for a plot involving murder.

lowing day the newspapers published further reports of the investigation of the Reiss murder. One of the gang arrested was found to be a member of Kovalev's organization, and he had implicated other members. The French police searched Kovalev's office, but the men named had disappeared. They were finally traced to headquarters of the G.P.U. in Barcelona, where at that time they were safe.

I had never before heard of Ignace Reiss, but it happened that my letter of resignation and his letter breaking with Stalin's regime were mailed to Moscow on the same day. G.P.U. agents in western Europe had thus been simultaneously confronted with a double job of "liquidation." They could not find me, and so they dealt with the Reiss case first, an accident that probably saved my life. For their organization was now temporarily disrupted, and they were compelled to send the compromised agents into hiding and assemble a new gang.

It did not take the new agents very long to find my hiding place in Saint-Cloud. Whenever I left the house I was shadowed. My pursuers made no effort to conceal themselves. At times, in trying to hear my conversation, they would actually step on my heels. My tactic was to turn around and face them. They would then disappear, but soon others would take up the hunt. Thus the watch would have to be changed some days as often as four or five times. On the subway, in tobacco shops, going to and from restaurants—the shadows dogged me everywhere. Whenever I returned to Saint-Cloud a "death watch" would begin outside my windows. This little war of nerves was made more oppressive when I learned from my friends in Athens that the legation was maintaining complete silence about my disappearance. They want to get rid of me quietly, I thought.

One afternoon I rashly went for a walk in the woods of Saint-Cloud. I had intended just to stroll around the park. Suddenly I realized that my path was blocked by a big blond giant of Slavic type. I turned in the opposite direction; but there stood a wiry little French apache. The only route that was clear led deeper into the woods. My first reaction was to turn in there, but if I did so I would soon leave behind the strollers and loving couples in the grass whose presence was my protection. Boldness, then, seemed the only course. I turned sharply and walked toward the more crowded section of the park. With my hand significantly in my pocket I pushed by the little apache. He hesitated for a moment, glared at me, and then allowed me to pass.

During all this time the news from the U.S.S.R. continued the same: accusations, arrests, disappearances, executions. I shed my last doubts as to the fate I would have met if I had gone back. The whole world was learning now the destruction of our diplomatic corps by the G.P.U. Marcel Rosenberg, ex-ambassador in Madrid, was arrested; Leon Karakhan, ambassador in Turkey, was arrested and shot; Ustinov, minister in Tallin, died in suspicious circumstances; Constantin Yurenev, ambassador in Berlin, Davtian, ambassador in Warsaw, Boris

Podolsky, minister in Kaunas, Eric Asmus, minister in Helsingfors, Bekzadian, minister in Budapest, Yakubovich, minister in Oslo—all were recalled and had disappeared.[2]

Stalin was changing his staff—as a prelude, I thought, to changing his politics. I felt it my duty to raise my voice and try to save those of my colleagues who were still abroad from returning to certain death. I also wanted to arouse public indignation at the fate of the thousands of Stalin's victims in Russia. My silence seemed wrong, and I decided to come out into the open.

My first step was to publish a letter to the Central Committee of the French League of the Rights of Man and to the Committee of Inquiry into the Moscow Trials. I quote the essential parts of that letter:

December 1, 1937

Having just left the service of the Government of the U.S.S.R., I feel it my duty to bring to your knowledge the following facts, and to lodge with you, in the name of Humanity and of the Rights of Man, an indignant protest against crimes the list of which grows daily longer. . . . For nineteen years I have been in Soviet government service; for nineteen years I have been a member of the Russian Bolshevik Party. I have fought for the Soviet regime and dedicated all my energies to the cause of the Workers' State.

In 1919 I entered the Red Army as a volunteer, and six months later was appointed political commissar, first of a battalion, then of a regiment, in recognition of distinguished conduct in the field. After passing through the school for Red officers I held several commands on the western front. After the offensive against Warsaw, the Military Council of the XVIth Army detailed me to attend a course at the General Staff College. In 1923 I was retired with the rank of brigadier general. I carried out the duties of consul general of the U.S.S.R. in Persia during the period 1923–1925; for ten years I was on the roll of the Department of Foreign Trade; from 1929–1931 I held the post of director general of imports in France and Italy; in 1932 I was official agent for the U.S.S.R. in Belgium and a member of the government delegation to Poland in 1933; in 1934–1935, I was president of the central trust controlling the exportation of all products of the automobile and aviation industries—the Auto-Moto-Export.

Such, in short, was my record of service before my Greek appointment. Whatever my duties, my one object has ever been to forward sincerely the interests of my country and of Socialism.

The recent trials in Moscow have filled me with a sense of amazement and horror. I find it quite impossible to justify the execution of the old leaders of the Revolution, in spite of the con-

[2] Most of them were shot later without trial. Only the names of Karakhan, Yurenev, and Yakubovich were mentioned in public trials.

20

fessions which they have so lavishly supplied. . . . The events of the last few months have stripped me of my last remaining illusions. Trials widely and loudly publicized have been staged with the object of carrying out a mass extermination of the mainstays of the Russian Bolshevik Party; in other words, of the men who, in the old days, carried on agitation at the risk of their liberty, who made the Revolution and the Civil War, and who achieved victory for the first Workers' State. Today these men have been covered with mud and handed over to the executioner. It is quite obvious to me that a reactionary dictatorship is now in control of my country.

I have seen my leaders and my friends, all of them Old Bolsheviks, vanish behind prison walls where, probably, they have been executed or "suppressed." . . . I am convinced that their honesty and loyalty was beyond question.

I want to address to the general public an urgent, a desperate appeal on behalf of those who may still be living, and against the false and ignoble charges of which they have been made the victims. My mind is filled with thoughts of my friends who have remained at their posts in the various countries of Europe, Asia, and America, daily threatened by a similar fate. . . .

Had I consented to remain in the service of Stalin, I should have felt myself morally defiled and should have had to take a share in the responsibility for crimes committed daily against the people of my country. . . .

In breaking with the government I obeyed the dictates of my conscience. . . .

May my words contribute a little to the task of enlightening public opinion on a regime which has, in fact, denied the tenets of Socialism and the claims of Humanity.[3]

After mailing this letter I went to the leaders of the French Socialist Party, at that time members of the government. These busy men received me cordially and let their affairs wait for hours while I told my story. They acted swiftly. Marx Dormoy, minister of the interior, issued permanent resident permits to Màri and me. The prefect of police gave me a full-time bodyguard of two detectives and placed a police sentry before my house at night. Even more important

---

[3] F. Raskolnikov, minister at Sofia, heeded this appeal and fled to take refuge in France. There he was poisoned by the G.P.U. and died in the first days of the present war. My other friend, Ostrovsky, minister in Bucharest, was recalled to Moscow. Ostrovsky was distinguished as a Jew who had been accepted and tolerated as political commissar by the cavalrymen of Budyenny's army during the Civil War. This army, whose top commissars were Stalin and Voroshilov, was known for the frequent outbursts of murderous anti-Semitism in its ranks—a thing unique in the history of the Red Armies. Ostrovsky hesitated when summoned to Moscow, and even wrote to his friends in France inquiring about asylum there; but after receiving a personal letter, full of assurances, from Voroshilov, his old comrade-in-arms, he returned—and was arrested on the Soviet frontier. This trustful friend of Voroshilov was never heard of again.

than all this was the fact that our residence permits included the precious right, coveted by all refugees in France, to work and earn a living.

Now, instead of being alone, I found myself surrounded by new friends who trusted me and in whom I could trust. To my happy surprise some old friendships were renewed as well. I again met Victor Serge, the talented writer who had escaped by a miracle from Stalin's prisons. He told me that all his relatives in Russia, even his connections by marriage, were in prison; that his father-in-law had died as a result of the persecution to which he was subjected, and that his wife had almost entirely lost her reason.

My old friend from back in 1922, Boris Souvarine, author of a monumental biography of Stalin, came to see me. Fifteen years had passed since our last meeting, but we recognized each other immediately. Though his temples had grayed, his conversation was as full of life and as caustic as it had been in Moscow so many years ago.

"The young Red Army officer is fifteen years older and a good deal wiser." His smile was sad. "Well, so are we all. . . ."

I met for the first time Alexander Kerensky, former Russian Socialist premier; Miliukov, leader of the Russian Liberal Party; and Theodore Dan, leader of the Menshevik Socialists. I found these veterans most cordial and sincere, their warmth of greeting unspoiled by any satisfaction that a man who had recently opposed them politically was now disillusioned.

One day I was called upon by a young man dressed carelessly in the clothes of a Parisian workman, showing signs of premature exhaustion but full of vitality, keen-witted, and ready at any pretext to break into a hearty laugh. This was Leon Sedov, Trotsky's son, who had been condemned to death time and again in the Moscow courts. He was living on the sixth floor of a lodginghouse in an apartment filled to bursting with books and filing cases. Next door—as he found out later —dwelt a G.P.U. agent who watched every move he made.

Poor Leon Sedov! He was so bubbling over with activity, so rich in the possession of a unique experience stretching over thirty years, and he died so tragically. There is a mystery about his death that has never been cleared up. He had a chronic appendicitis and was seized with an acute attack. By an ominous coincidence he was taken to a private clinic, where he was operated on by a White Russian surgeon with suspicious connections. After the operation, when complications set in, he was left without any care and died.

Notwithstanding such somber experiences, we were gradually building up a normal life. Màri's mother came to Paris to attend our wedding. The ceremony was performed in the presence of a few friends. The Greek Orthodox rite calls for two best men. One was an old friend of Màri's family, the noted Greek leader, General Nicholas Plastiras.

The other was the tall white-haired Scot, Percy J. Philip, distinguished correspondent of the *New York Times,* a good friend and a most charming and intelligent person.

With the aid of French friends I got a job in the repair shop of the Air-France Company at Le Bourget Airport. At first the workers beside me could not help noticing that I had almost forgotten how to work with my hands. Their readiness to help me moved me profoundly. Although they knew nothing of me beyond the fact that I was a political refugee, they asked no questions. They showed more natural tact than I have sometimes found in the world of diplomacy.

I was at ease in my new job, but I soon found that my previous employers had not forgotten me. One evening I was accosted at the factory gate by the head of the union to which the men in my shop belonged. He asked how I was getting along and then informed me that he was recommending me for a higher-salaried position in the airport office. His interest surprised me. It was rather strange for the union leader to wait at the gate in order to offer a better job to a minor nonunion employee. It puzzled me still more when I learned that he was a Stalinist. But I took the necessary test anyway and was promoted to a good job in the traffic service of the airport.

A few days later I learned that the following week I would be on duty at night. This meant that for several hours I would be practically alone in the building. I happened to know that the Spanish plane for Barcelona left the airport at dawn each day. It would be easy for a few men to arrange matters so that I should find myself in Barcelona some fine morning—and in Barcelona the Russian G.P.U. had a free hand in dealing with anti-Stalinists of all nationalities. The French *commissaire* supervising my protection was deeply shocked when he heard that I had been assigned to night duty. "*Mince alors!*" he exclaimed. "We won't allow this!" He had a talk with the airport director, and I was excused from night work.

This proved exceedingly distressing to the head of the union, and I felt that the G.P.U. did not intend as yet to leave me in peace. Nevertheless it bored me to have two detectives accompanying me everywhere, and I told the *commissaire* in charge of my protection that I would take care of myself.

It was perhaps a rash step, for I very soon heard from Moscow again. One evening after work I called to see Percy Philip at the *Times* bureau in the Rue Caumartin. I often enjoyed sitting in a comfortable chair in the office of this wise Scotsman, listening to his witty conversation. I want to say here that, although many people were kind to me in France, I remember most of all the sympathetic and friendly welcome that Philip and the Paris staff of the *New York Times* gave me: George Axelson, a tall calm Swede; Lancing Warren, so phlegmatic that he looked drowsy, although he was always busy at a piled-up desk; the short, round Archambault, energetic and temperamental. I must express my gratitude to these men who helped me in those difficult days.

That evening Percy Philip's greeting was exceptionally gay.

"Hello, my young friend," he said. "Congratulations! I have a nice message for you from your government."

He picked up a file of dispatches and, turning to one from Moscow, handed it to me with comic solemnity. There, among the cables to appear in the morning news, I found one from the French press agency *Fournier*, dated March 9, 1939, and headlined: "The ex-Envoy of the U.S.S.R. in Greece to be judged *in absentia.*" It said that the Moscow Tribunal would shortly pass judgment on the former envoy of the U.S.S.R. in Greece, M. Barmine, together with five other functionaries of the U.S.S.R. who broke with the Soviets, and would *condemn him.*

"A very instructive example of Soviet procedure," Philip smiled. "In announcing a future trial they also announce the result!"

"Well, at least they're frank about it—I know where I stand," I said. "But this is rather a special distinction. Every Soviet official who stays abroad without authorization is automatically deprived of citizenship and condemned to death. Am I going to be shot twice? We did have a case of that kind. The Old Bolsheviks Drobnis and Kliavin were both shot by White firing squads during the Civil War and dragged themselves out of the common burial pit with several bullets in their bodies. Later they joined the Opposition and were shot again in 1937—this time by order of Stalin. This attention is certainly flattering. But I am afraid this trial will not give them much satisfaction. Contrary to the Moscow tradition, I feel no guilt and have no impulse to confess or praise the Leader for mass murders in the name of Socialism!"

"Don't get upset," Philip said. "You needn't waste your fire on me. Save it for a better occasion."

And as we left the office together he separated the dispatch from his file.

"Here, have this for a souvenir."

In the first week of May, 1939, after the dismissal of Litvinov, I received a call from Ronsac, director of the French literary agency *Opera Mundi. Paris Soir* wanted me to write an article on the meaning of Litvinov's fall for the special page, where foreign writers and statesmen regularly discussed world affairs. Ronsac promised world-wide distribution for the article. I warned him that my opinions would be in sharp contradiction to what the public expected, but he insisted, and I wrote the article. *Opera Mundi* mailed it throughout Europe and cabled it to America, but it did not appear in France or England. Ronsac was embarrassed when he saw me, and apologized: "The *Paris*

Soir people [was it Pierre Lazareff?] think you are crazy and they think I am too."

Here are a couple of sentences from that ill-fated article:

". . . There is every reason to believe that Stalin has long been seeking an alliance between the U.S.S.R. and the German Reich. If this has not already been realized it is only because Hitler does not want it. Yurenev, the Russian Ambassador, has been amicably received at Berchtesgaden, and the Georgian Kandelaki, Stalin's confidential agent, has been holding conversations with Hitler behind the official relations between the two countries. Negotiations between totalitarian states are conducted in the greatest secrecy, and the result may come as a complete surprise to everybody. . . ." And further, speaking of the territories east of the Curzon line: "These territories are inhabited by more than ten million people whom the U.S.S.R. would have the right, geographically and ethnologically, to claim as citizens, if she exacts payment for her benevolent neutrality in a European war through a partition of Poland."

I felt small satisfaction when, four months later, after the triumphant return of Ribbentrop from Moscow, several Paris papers dug up and printed my old article with such comments as the following: "This opinion is interesting because it was expressed four months ago, when a special plenipotentiary of the British Government was in Moscow and the idea of Stalin's *rapprochement* with Hitler appeared to Europeans unbelievable. Mr. Barmine foresaw the events, but his exposé was ignored. His article, written on May fifth, saw the light only in South America and Scandinavia. No English or French papers dared to publish it at that time."

Under these shadows a not unhappy year went by. I was with Màri; I was more or less safe; I had a job and friends. I was beginning to reshape my life.

But this was not enough for me. I needed something more than material security. I had spent my life working for a regime in which I had now lost faith. I needed a new "community of spirits" where I might play a part and have a responsibility. Living without a country for the rest of my life and being politely tolerated as a foreigner —this was unbearable to me, much as I loved and admired the French people. The more I reflected on it the more convinced I became that there was only one country in the world where I could rebuild my life as a free man and a citizen in the fullest sense of the word. That was the United States. That was a country made out of "foreigners," "outsiders," welded into a great national unity. I talked it over with Màri, and together we came to the decision to seek a new life in America.

In the spring of 1939 we went to the United States Embassy in Paris. The embassy officials listened attentively to our story. They were ready to help us, but told us that the law requires an affidavit from an American citizen sponsoring every immigrant. Luckily a cousin of Màri's was a prominent lawyer in New York, and he generously provided the affidavits and took charge of our case. After a few months we received our precious visas to enter the United States. These were our passports to a new and full life.

On board ship we searched the long horizon for the first signs of the country we were so eager to make our own. Like many other immigrants, we greeted the dim shore line with hearts full of enthusiasm. The city with its forest of skyscrapers was no longer a tawdry postcard chromo. Here it waited, a living reality, in the mists of a winter morning.

The immigration officer examined our papers and stamped them. We were admitted.

"Thank you," I said. I could hardly stem my emotion.

"You're welcome." He gave a routine reply, but we did not know that.

For us these conventional words were filled with meaning. They were an omen of good fortune in the new, friendly world we were entering.

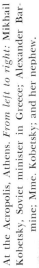

At the Acropolis, Athens. *From left to right:* Mikhail Kobetsky, Soviet minister in Greece; Alexander Barmine; Mme. Kobetsky; and her nephew.

Rushen Eshref Ünaidin, Turkish minister in Greece, now ambassador to Great Britain; his wife; Alexander Barmine; M. Kobetsky, Soviet minister in Greece.

Making a bonfire from the imperial golden eagles and crowns from the official buildings during the revolution of February, 1917. Petrograd, Russia.

BOOK TWO

They lived on glory, onward bound,
Barefoot, without bread.
And each man slept on the hard ground,
With a knapsack under his head.

Popular soldiers' song
of the French Revolution

BOOK TWO

4. Childhood

I NEVER KNEW my parents well and lived with them scarcely at all. On the occasions when we were together they left me severely to myself. It may well be that the impressions I gained from them in early life had a considerable influence on the development of my character. There was never a time when I was not familiar with difficulties, crises, and emergencies; and this fact, since the age was a restless one, no doubt made me receptive to revolutionary ideas. My case was not isolated: the life I led was that of many Russians of my generation. My story may help readers to understand what has happened in Russia.

My mother, one of a gamekeeper's eighteen children, had grown up in a village, knowing nothing but work and discomfort—though never actual shortage of food. She was always busy with her smaller brothers and sisters, keeping their bodies clean and their stomachs filled. The fact that all eighteen of them reached maturity shows that the conditions of her life, though straitened, were not desperate. When she was fifteen she worked on the estate of a Countess Brannitzkaya, pulling beetroot from dawn till nightfall in the fields for a wage of twenty-five kopeks (about twelve cents) a day. At seventeen she married a schoolmaster, a widower considerably older than herself, and the father of two sons. And I was her only child.

I can remember noisy quarrels between her and my father, shouting and slamming of doors in our little cottage. I can also remember days of terror when we were all expecting to be dispossessed for unpaid debts. In preparation for this terrible possibility my mother would spend the night packing various bundles, which she would get out of the house not by the door, but through the kitchen window opening on the orchard. When this happened I was taken to stay with some neighbors.

My parents would often go away and leave me for a long time and then come back for short spells in a slightly better mood.

At the age of six they sent me to live with my grandparents. I made the mysterious journey with my mother by train and carriage, through green lanes and past great fields and forests. We crossed several rivers on rafts. To me it was all new and exciting.

My grandparents lived in an old peasant house in the country, and when times were difficult for their children they would take in the grandchildren. There were always at least a dozen in the house. It was a white house, surrounded by cherry trees and situated some little distance from the small Ukrainian town of Uman with a mixed Jewish and Ukrainian population. This town was a gloomy place, though bathed in sunshine all through the summer and relieved with a few

29

gardens. It squatted on the bank of a river, was insanitary and often foul-smelling.

My grandmother spent all her time in the kitchen in front of a hot fire, surrounded by pots, pans, and dishes, and innumerable children. She managed to nurse them and keep them alive, but only by solving endless problems. I often used to see her with a pencil in her work-worn hand, doing her accounts aloud: "So much for cucumbers, so much for soap—and how much left for sugar?" She worked wonders. We did have sugar. And on special occasions we even wore shoes and clean blouses.

She had no time for discipline, and we formed a sort of independent republic, girls and boys of all ages, with running noses, dirty faces, ragged pants, and tangled hair. We spent our days outdoors, climbing trees, swimming, and exploring the countryside for miles around.

Rainstorms were our delight. As soon as we saw the clouds gather we got ready, and when they burst we rushed naked into the yard and screamed and danced like Red Indians while the rain poured off our bodies. After every heavy rain, like all the peasants around, we had to repair the clay walls of our house. Grandfather would clear a corner of the yard and fetch clay from the river bank. We children would go out and collect dung from the road. Clay and dung mixed with water, and pounded deliciously by our bare feet, made an excellent plaster for the walls. Grandmother took advantage of these occasions to renew the whitewash. Along the edge of the roof she would paint an ornamental border in blue.

The local market was another thrill. There were mountains of fruits and vegetables; there were fortunetellers and side shows, and stands where you could buy tops and gingerbread and rubber balls. Peasants from distant villages came with their horses and carts and shouted and argued over their business deals. We would stand, all eyes, in front of a booth on which were displayed marvelous little books with illustrated wrappers, containing collections of old Russian tales; or we'd hang around a stand with piles of hard candy, highly colored cakes, and cocks made out of barley sugar. I still remember how cheap everything was there. A bucketful of cherries, a sack of potatoes or pears cost little more than an American penny; for half a penny you could get a couple of huge watermelons. These prices sound marvelous today. Even so we were not always well fed, but sometimes lived for days together on thin gruel.

Grandfather would come back from work at nightfall and set off again at dawn. In the evenings he would do odd jobs about the house, splitting logs or mending the fence. We children enjoyed complete liberty on the condition that we did not whine or quarrel. If one of us came in complaining that someone had given him a black eye or torn his clothes, Grandfather would growl out: "If you can't stand up to them, don't fight. Go and wash your face." He was a sort of kindly patriarch who saw life in very simple terms. For grand offenses he believed in the salutary function of the slipper or birch rod. Naturally I got my share of that. One occasion remains vivid in my memory.

I happened to be very hungry. We were all seated round the table, a pack of little grubby creatures, our eyes bright with hunger and excitement. A steaming tureen of pumpkin porridge stood before us, and we were waiting with our wooden spoons in our hands until, as good manners dictated, Grandma and Grandpa should help themselves. (There was no room in our poor country life for individual plates, but I can assure you that we did not feel their absence.) So impatient was I that I was led to commit a grave breach of manners, and guilty conscience no doubt made me clumsy. I waited for nobody, but leaned across the table to take the first spoonful. Suddenly I slipped, and my hand plunged into the porridge. It upset the whole tureen and sent the scalding contents all over the legs of my young cousins. The disaster was complete. Cries of pain and horror bore witness to it. The porridge was lost forever. So terrified was I, realizing that I had been the cause of this, that I was quite unaware of my burns.

Grandfather got up with an ominous expression on his face. "Come with me," he said. Grandma put in a gentle plea for mercy: "Nikifor, don't beat the child." But Grandpa said nothing. He knew what he had to do. We went into the next room, and he shut the door. Then, sitting down, he took my head between his knees and administered to my behind a fiery walloping with his leather slipper. I made no sound and shed no tear. With flaming cheeks and ears I returned to the other room, not daring to look at anybody. Grandma bathed my burns with curdled milk and bound them up. A little later, when I was summoned to table to take my share of a new supply of soup, I burst into tears and refused to go. For years, whenever I thought of that scene, I was filled with a strong sense of guilt. I formed the habit of never taking my soup until everybody else had theirs—a habit that was to serve me ill in the rough life that lay ahead.

A day came when my mother arrived, looking young and pretty and dressed in city clothes of a kind we hardly ever saw. She had brought presents for everyone and had come to take me away to school in Vilna, where she lived. I distributed all my treasures among my cousins—empty matchboxes and cigarette packages, slingshots, knucklebones, stones of curious shapes, and nails. Our farewells were tearful.

No one was waiting for us at the Vilna station. My mother was living alone in a house with two rooms, tiny but clean. She replied evasively to my questions about Father. She was working in a hospital and would leave at seven in the morning and come home late at night.

I was a good pupil at school, though retiring and given to solitude. In my solitude I began to read avidly every book I could lay hands on—Fenimore Cooper, Jules Verne, Mayne Reid, Mark Twain, Steven-

31

son, Jack London, and Kipling. A little later I developed a taste for Pushkin, Victor Hugo, Zola, Tolstoy, and Dickens.

One day my mother found me deep in a volume of Maupassant. "Don't read that," she said sternly. "There are a lot of things in there you can't possibly understand." This was rather a shock to me, since I was at the age when a boy thinks he can understand everything. As a result I read Maupassant with increased attention, searching earnestly for some mystery I could not find.

Books gave richness to a life which, in material matters, was becoming more and more austere. I learned by chance that my father had "gone with another woman." He continued to contribute to my expenses, though at very irregular intervals. My mother suffered in silence. I understood her but said nothing. This attitude of reserve on both sides brought into our relationship a sadness which developed into a sort of estrangement. She reproached me with lack of affection, but I could think of nothing to say and dwelt with increasing bitterness in my own thoughts. In this way I lived until I was thirteen.

"Would you like to go and live with your father?" she asked me one day.

At the idea of getting to know a new town, a new world, of seeing my father again, I became so excited that I flung my arms around her neck.

"Oh, yes!" I cried.

I could see from her expression that I had hurt her, and I tried to make up for it. "But I'll come back, Mamma."

My father met me at the Gomel station. We went home to a comfortable house standing in a garden. No sooner had we arrived than he led me into his study, where he looked me over with an embarrassed air.

"You're quite a man now," he said. "I can talk to you openly. I have married again. You've got a little brother. You'll see him—and your stepmother." Then he called: "Katia!"

The woman who came in, carrying a child in her arms, reminded me of figures I had seen in reproductions of Dutch paintings. My "second mother" had a full face, a rather snub nose, and large, gray, laughing eyes. She was always cheerful, but I soon learned that beneath her comely appearance there was a mean and calculating spirit.

The first months passed agreeably enough, but before long I began to realize that I was in the way. My stepmother obviously regarded every mouthful that I ate as so much food snatched from her own precious infant. The small amount of pocket money my father gave me became a subject of bitter recrimination. He hit upon the ingenious plan of hiring me to do things so that he could plead as an excuse for his gifts that a laborer was worthy of his hire. I rolled cigarettes for him at the rate of fifteen kopeks a box. He taught me also how to use a saw and ax—accomplishments which were later to serve me in good stead. Hard work on the woodpile brought me a ruble a week, enough for the movies and candy.

My schoolwork was going well, but what was sooner or later bound to happen, happened. One day my father called me into his study and told me, with a good deal of hemming and hawing, that I would be better off with my mother, who was living too solitary a life.

"You are going tomorrow. I have announced your arrival by telegram."

Was there no place for me, then, anywhere? I made no answer to my father, but I was conscious of a feeling of despair—a feeling which, on no account, must I reveal to a living soul. I turned for comfort to daydreams. When I grew up I would be a sailor, an explorer, rich and famous. Then they would *all* want me to come and live with them. I would bring my mother and father together again. That would be my answer. Never again would I allow them to quarrel and sulk.

Another disappointment was awaiting me at Vilna. My mother, too, was thinking of getting married again. When she broke the news to me, I begged her not to do it.

"You'll only be unhappy again, Mamma," I said. "Let's live together, just us two. It'll be so much better."

On the day of her marriage—which took place while I was at school —we moved to new and much more comfortable quarters. It was with a feeling of sadness, however, that I entered my new room. My books, in corded piles, stood about the floor. They were all that remained of my previous life. Downstairs, the wedding festivities were at their height. Several times my mother came to fetch me, but I would not go down.

"You are grieving me deeply," she said. "Don't be so obstinate. Come along!"

But I was too occupied with my own sense of injury to listen to her. I lay down fully dressed on the bed and fell asleep in a state of confused and troubled sensitivity. When I awoke I found on the night table a few cakes and a plate of ice cream. The ice cream had melted and become a thick yellowish liquid. I suddenly remembered the festivities of the previous evening and broke into tears.

I have very few pleasant memories of school, where the dry, aloof attitude of the uniformed masters smothered any natural joy in learning. I should like, however, to mention one man who refused to wear a uniform and who exercised an influence on us in marked contrast to that of those drillmasters. He was a Protestant clergyman who taught us German by an extremely original method. It consisted of giving us as prizes candies which he bought with his own money. He was a cheerful, robust, boisterous man, with nothing of the professional solemnity of the ecclesiastic about him; and he always wore light-colored suits. Disregarding the rules of the school, he had us greet him each morning with a sort of chant in unison: "*Guten Morgen,*

33

lieber Pastor!" and the boys performed that exercise with a mighty will. The good man had only to put his face in at the door, and there would be such a celebration that serious work became quite impossible for a quarter of an hour.

It was due to a prize of chocolate given me by our *lieber Pastor* that I made my first friend, a boy named Kusskov. He was my unsuccessful competitor, and I shared the prize with him.

One day in the summer of 1914 I went to visit the cottage in the woods where Kusskov spent his vacations. I found it empty and gloomy, as only holiday houses can be when everyone is away. I waited in vain the whole of one day and the night following. My friend and his family never arrived. I was filled with anxiety. Then I suddenly remembered that at the station the newsboy had been shouting out something that I did not understand: "Mobilization ordered!" On getting into the train to go home I was struck by the strange looks on the faces around me, by the excited talk on all sides.

"What is happening, sir?" I asked the man next to me.

"My boy," he answered, "what's happening is that we are going to fight a war and give the Kaiser a sock in the jaw. Our Cossacks will be in Berlin in no time."

In books that I read, war was represented as something heroic and always victorious. I thought that from now on life would be like an exciting novel. Everyone seemed to be in the best of spirits, and I was, too, in spite of the fact that I had missed my friend.

The next day my stepfather came home with his eyes shining. "Thank God!" he said. "This means war! Russia will be victorious!" The streets were full of processions; the people carried tricolor flags, church banners, and portraits of the Czar framed in white embroidered towels. The air was charged with emotion. The crowds sang. Cossacks clattering down the streets on their horses were greeted with cheers and volleys of flowers. This was war!

At school our class uttered an "Oh!" of horrified surprise when the news came that little Belgium had been invaded by the German hordes. Never mind, our Cossacks would soon free Belgium!

Why wasn't I big enough to join the Army? Everything would be over long before I reached military age. Fate was unfair!

When the first German prisoners passed through the town, we ran to get a look at them. To me they seemed not terrible at all, but merely pitiful. Dirty and exhausted, they returned our stares with wan smiles. These invaders of Belgium looked as though they didn't much mind being taken prisoner! They made friendly signs to us and called out: "*Kinder, Kinder!*" It occurred to me that they, too, might have children just our age. One of my friends shouted, "*Deutsche Schweine!*" The prisoners looked away. Since we had no feeling of hatred in our hearts, we felt vaguely ashamed of what this boy said.

5. *War and Revolution*

THE WAR DRAGGED ON. We began to forget what peace had been like. Our army won several victories and took many prisoners. But there was no longer any talk of the Cossacks entering Berlin. On the contrary, the Uhlans entered Warsaw. The Germans occupied the whole of Poland and threatened Lithuania. It was all very difficult to understand. My elders put on smart uniforms and talked about what they were going to do. Nicolas and Gregory, my two half-brothers, went off to the front. They had been living with an aunt in Petrograd, but they stopped to see us on their way. They were as proud as peacocks of their golden shoulder straps. I looked on them with envy.

The younger, Gregory, aged nineteen, was killed on the first of August, 1915.

In the autumn my mother stopped going to work. "We shall be refugees," she told me. "They are evacuating the town. . . ."

I knew the dreadful fate of refugees and thought this was to be our fate, too. But evacuation, when it came, was carried out by train, in relatively comfortable conditions. Despite the confusion of the railroads and the chaos at the stations, we managed to take almost all our possessions with us. We were confined, however, in a freight car, and the journey lasted six weary days. Finally we reached the town to which my stepfather had been evacuated. It happened to be Gomel, and thus fate decreed the meeting of my two families.

This was a black period for me. There I was, between the two of them—my father with a new wife on one side, my mother with a new husband on the other. Nobody wanted me; I was left in an oppressive loneliness. Every word spoken wounded me; and some of the things said were really wounding. When, at mealtimes, my mother would pick out a piece of meat for me, her hand would tremble under her husband's disapproving gaze, for meat was scarce and expensive, and he thought that my own father ought to be responsible for my keep. His hostility kept me in a constant tension, and there were frequent angry clashes between us.

One evening, after a violent quarrel at the table when my stepfather tried to strike me, I ran out of the house and hid in a piano case in a near-by court. I stayed half the freezing night there, covered with straw, and then went to the railroad station and slept in the waiting room. I made up my mind that I would never go home again. I would look for work; I would no longer endure the humiliation of knowing that every mouthful I ate was grudged me. I went to school the next morning, and my mother found me there and tried to per-

35

suade me to come home. I refused absolutely. My friend Kusskov, who was also living at Gomel as a refugee, heard our argument. He told his parents, and they gave me shelter. To spare my pride they asked me to help their youngest daughter with her schoolwork. I thus became a tutor at the age of fifteen, and since then I have always earned my living. It was for me the end of my childhood.

Life in Gomel, as in the rest of Russia, was growing more difficult from day to day. Food prices rose, and some commodities disappeared from the stores. We heard bad news from the big cities, Petrograd and Moscow. Bread lines were forming, and there were occasional riots, which the troops put down. Wounded soldiers straggling in from the front filled the hospitals and overflowed into the school buildings, which had been taken over by the Red Cross.

The gay days of the early months of the war had disappeared. Instead, a weary mood, like creeping paralysis, painful yet lethargic, set in. Our armies were bogged down in muddy trenches, and the same monotonous reports filled the papers every day. Many were asking: "When will it end?"

On our rounds as volunteer collectors for the Red Cross we boys were not received so cheerfully as before. Some women who had lost husbands and sons in the war told us plainly: "We won't give—we haven't enough to live on! Tell them to give to us!"

One day the newspapers failed to arrive from the capital. Their place was taken by rumors. Someone said a revolution had broken out. Policemen disappeared from the streets. They remained indoors, and when they went out were careful to put on civilian coats over their uniforms. Public services slowed down; there did not seem to be any authority in the town. Then the newspapers reappeared, carrying word of the Czar's abdication.

Gomel tried to keep abreast of the times. The "Marseillaise" was played in the public squares, and young people walked about armed with rifles and wearing red sleeve bands with the letters V.M.—Volunteer Militia.

At school a few of the boys showed up with red ribbons. The principal tried to remove the ribbons on the ground that they were "a breach of the school rules." But he soon gave up the attempt, and that made us realize as nothing else could that big things were happening.

In the town garrison the weekly parade took place as usual, but the commanding officer wore a red rosette, and the band played the "Marseillaise" instead of "God Save the Czar." The troops took the oath of allegiance to the Provisional Government, and an eloquent gentleman made a speech about defending our liberty against the "Teutons" and carrying the war on to final victory.

But in the following days I learned that there were other viewpoints besides his. New and strange papers appeared. We heard the names

36

of political parties till then unknown to us. The town was humming with new ideas that flooded in from the north. The workmen and the soldiers of the garrison formed a *soviet,* the majority of whose members were Social Democrats. The older boys at school wanted to have a soviet too, and they demanded a relaxation of rules. What was better, a plan was set on foot to open a Youth Center, equipped with a library and reading room.

It was in this connection that I made my first acquaintance with a Bolshevik in flesh and blood. The word at that time was a term of abuse. These "Bolsheviks" were supposed to be dangerous enemies of our country who had passed through Germany with the consent of the Kaiser. They were opposed to continuing the war to final victory —opposed to that implacable war about which there was more talk than ever. During a debate on funds for our library a Bolshevik student named Model took the floor and began to object to the partisan way in which the money was being allotted. There were no copies of *Pravda* (the organ of the Bolshevik Party) in the reading room! His voice was drowned by shouts of "Kick him out, dirty Leninist!" But he kept to his point, demanded a vote, and got what he wanted. *Pravda* was added to our reading matter. His courage impressed me, and the name of Lenin stuck in my memory.

The municipality was preparing to issue bread cards, and assistants were needed. I wanted a more independent job and signed on. Besides this, I chopped wood for the neighbors. In the evenings my hands would be covered with blisters, but I would have earned good money. Very soon my savings amounted to the staggering sum of fifty rubles! What could I do with this sum except set out to see the world? As a result of my reading I had dreamed most often of Niagara Falls and the snows of Alaska, but, alas, the Revolution had brought them no nearer! It might be possible, however, to visit the Falls of Imatra, in Finland. On my way there I could see the two great cities, Moscow and Petrograd. My mother succeeded in getting me a free holiday ticket, as she was working as a nurse in the railroad hospital, and I started my adventure through a Russia beset with the turmoil of revolution.

I took with me a change of linen and a few cakes and apples, last-minute gifts from my mother. I found a comfortable place on an upper shelf of a car in which a lot of soldiers were playing cards. Looking back on that journey now, I realize that the train in which I found myself was in the true revolutionary tradition. At each stop the cars, already filled to capacity, were invaded by newcomers. Even the toilets were permanently occupied by four or five people. As for the corridors, it was impossible to squeeze your way through them. All the windows had been smashed, and people climbed in through the broken glass. Two soldiers pushed me firmly but not roughly against

37

the wall and proceeded to share my seat between them. Everybody was talking, swearing, elbowing, and smoking unimaginably rank *makhorka,* the crudest of Russian tobacco.

I tried to push my way into the next compartment, but that was even worse. Six unfortunate officers there spent the whole journey besieged by a violently hostile mob. The best that could be said for the crowd in my compartment was that quarrels were comparatively few and far between!

When we reached Moscow I learned that a number of people, mostly soldiers, had made the journey on the roofs of the coaches. They were tanned by the sun and black with soot and coal dust. Two soldiers had been killed through failing to duck their heads when the train passed under a bridge.

Moscow seemed to me a huge and dirty Babel. Every street corner was a debating hall. Everywhere you went pamphlets were thrust at you. Wherever you looked your eye was greeted by huge posters put up by the different political parties. Every square in the city overflowed with meetings, where soldiers, workmen, students, and townsfolk furiously argued the politics of the day. All work seemed to be suspended while people passed from one meeting to another. Words were in common circulation that I had never heard before: "bourgeois," "proletarian," "imperialist." Political passions were knife-sharp, and frequently a corner controversy ended in a brawl. The excitement was contagious. No one bothered to stop and eat; they just pulled chunks of black bread out of their grimy pockets and munched it while they talked. Children ran about, wild and unrestrained, as if it were a continual holiday.

I stayed with a friend of my mother's. Her husband, a railroad man, was a Bolshevik and spoke of Kerensky's Provisional Government with full-throated hatred.

"The politicians haven't had their fill of blood yet," he said to me, his face jutting forward grimly. "If the profiteers and capitalists want this 'final victory' of theirs, they'd better go and get it for themselves!" The bitterness that poured out of him was peppered with phrases from the Bolshevik press. The violence of his hatred staggered me.

But I had, after all, come to Moscow on vacation. So I went to see the famous monuments I had read about and spent a whole day at the Tretiakov Gallery, where I was deeply moved by Repin's famous picture of Ivan the Terrible embracing in despair the body of the son he has just killed.

So much for Moscow. The journey on to Petrograd was a replica of my other trip. But here was another great metropolis for me to see.

Despite the city's neglect, I was impressed by its spacious avenues and architectural beauties. The only thing that disappointed me was the equestrian statue of Czar Peter vanquishing the serpent. I had become familiar with the Bronze Horseman through Pushkin's poem, but it seemed to me much less imposing than the verses had led me to expect.

After I had my fill of sightseeing, I paid a call on some relatives. My cousins opened the door. They received me very kindly, offered to show me the city, and then suddenly burst out with:

"Your poor father! What a terrible thing for him!"

What was this terrible thing they were talking of? My aunt hastened to explain. My eldest brother Nicolas had just been killed on the Rumanian front. He had left a widow and a baby. I began here to understand the meaning of war.

Viipuri in Finland was the next city I visited. Russia belongs both to Asia and to Europe, but Viipuri is a European city. I found it a severe-looking place, with its house fronts of gray granite, and amazingly clean. The huge station was brightly lit, great crystal chandeliers illuminating tablecloths of a dazzling whiteness. Silver currency was still in circulation. It had long disappeared in Russia, its place taken by pieces of pasteboard looking like postage stamps and bearing the Czar's likeness.

Life in Finland was very calm, and its prosperity to me was disconcerting. The Russian conscription law did not apply to the Finns: the people were not involved in the war and apparently did not take the slightest interest in it. I was startled to feel myself so indubitably among foreigners, and not only because of the language barrier.

The Falls of Imatra did not live up to the dreams I had had of them. My imagination had conceived something more grandiose than this seething torrent which tumbled down to the little iron bridge where I stood. I had still to learn that power is not always to be judged by its external signs.

My money was almost gone now, and I hurried back to Petrograd to take the Gomel train. At one station we passed through I saw the women's battalion, which was soon to be the Provisional Government's last line of defense against the Bolshevik insurrection. The soldiers on the train stared with undisguised hostility at these beardless, over-smart warriors, who were carrying out the minutiae of army life with a sort of musical-comedy meticulousness. The women, however, pretended not to hear the coarse oaths that broke out all around them.

I got back to Gomel with no adventures more serious than a petty theft. One night I had gone to sleep hungry, wondering whether, when I woke, I should spend my last coin on a newspaper or a roll. But I found in the morning that my purse had vanished, and with it my problem. I felt sorry for the thief, whose disappointment must have been greater than mine; but for the whole of the last day of my journey I ate nothing at all. I was so hungry when I arrived in Gomel that I ran all the way home.

I had to have a job now for the rest of the summer, and I joined up with a gang of lumbermen. "No pay," they told me, "but you get your keep." Well, that seemed good enough.

We traveled by boat up the Sozh River. When we reached the forests we had to build living quarters for ourselves; and then the real work began. We worked in three shifts and had to cut a set quantity of wood each day. At first this job took each shift ten hours, and when our turn for rest came our hands were raw and bleeding. By degrees, however, we got used to the rough labor and reduced our time to six hours.

The trees, with their load of leafy boughs, fell beneath our strokes with the noise of breaking waves; the dense foliage was filled with the scent of sap. When work was over I used to roam the countryside with a friend, while the young workmen went off courting the girls of the neighborhood—and often returning with scarred faces and black eyes.

My friend was always urging me to go with him to Kiev. His idea was that we should stow away on some steamer bound for that wonderful city. We started out according to plan, but were foolish enough to go ashore with the regular passengers at one of the stopping places. It proved impossible to get on board again. Luckily we had left no baggage on the ship!

Here at Loyev, where the Sozh joins the Dnieper, we found a barge whose crew was willing to take us along. The skipper of this boat was a jolly old peasant who teased us a lot about being so young and slim, and grumbled into his beard:

"I'd like to put you to work as stevedores!"

We took him at his word.

"All right," we answered. "Wait till we get there and you'll see."

When we got to Kiev we started unloading sacks of flour. And devilish heavy they were; they covered us with white powder from head to foot and almost broke our backs! I never knew before how exhausted the human frame could be. The attitude of the regular stevedores was hostile at first, but our manifest good will soon made them friends.

I worked at many jobs while I was growing up. I exchanged dockside labor for a grubby spell mending old tunics in a secondhand uniform shop, after which I did some minor clerical work for the municipal authorities. All this while, however, I kept on cramming for my school studies. As my father was a schoolteacher, I was lucky enough to be admitted free to one of Kiev's *gymnasia* (high schools).

After the fall of the Czar, the Ukrainian nationalist movement, long persecuted, came out into the open. Its parties formed committees which assumed power throughout the Ukraine. The central authority in Moscow gradually lost all but nominal control here. By the autumn of 1917 the Ukraine had a self-proclaimed nationalist government of its own that was to all intents and purposes independent. It was known as the Rada, and its first president was the writer Vinnichenko.

He was later replaced by Simon Petlura, who had been one of his assistants.

Kiev was chosen by the Rada as the Ukrainian capital. But, owing to the colonization policy of the old regime, Kiev, like almost every other large town in the Ukraine, contained an overwhelming majority of Russians. The supporters of the Rada were therefore in a minority; the Russian section of the population was strongly hostile to it. The workers, because of their sympathy for the Bolsheviks, disliked the Rada; whereas the officials and wealthy Russian merchants and industrialists hoped for a nation-wide counterrevolution that would restore "One and Indivisible Russia" and do away with separate republics. The large number of middle- and white-collar-class Russians in the town were opposed to the Rada because the policy of Ukrainianization had reduced them to the position of a group with questionable rights and an insecure status.

Once more revolution burst upon us. One afternoon in November, 1917, as we were seated in the classroom, we heard the droning of an airplane overhead and the sound of gunfire. These were still unfamiliar sounds to us. When school was over we found people gathered in excited groups on the street. The news was passing through the city like an electric current:

"The Bolsheviks have started an uprising to establish Soviet power in Kiev. They have seized the arsenal. . . . The Ukrainian Rada troops are surrounding them. . . . In Petrograd the two German agents, Lenin and Trotsky, have attempted an insurrection and set up some sort of a government. . . . Kerensky is massing troops in the suburbs of the city. . . . Order will be restored in a few days. . . ."

Such were the rumors in Kiev during the days when the Bolsheviks seized the power in Petrograd.

The attempt of the local Bolsheviks to capture the arsenal failed, but the atmosphere remained tense. The municipal employees, of whom I was one, even declared a strike, and this "white-collar" movement was the butt of many jokes. The Rada was making a violent effort to organize an army of *gaidamaks* (Ukrainian Cossacks), and improvising uniforms for them, based on the traditional costume of the countryside—wide trousers and Cossack fur caps tricked out with yellow and blue. We boys were full of admiration for this military finery. But one of my classmates was always making sarcastic remarks about these new uniforms. He was a serious young fellow with a shock of fair hair; without much reluctance on my part he undertook to educate me politically. His name was Levine; I did not know at the time that he was a member of a Bolshevik organization.

41

6. *Invasions*

WITH THE COMING OF WINTER our privations increased. The Bolsheviks had now been in power in Russia for three months. From day to day we expected to hear that they had been overthrown. Trotsky was negotiating with the Germans at Brest-Litovsk. We young people discussed the situation among ourselves, and it seemed to us very odd. The Russian Revolution was bringing great difficulties to the Rada government in the Ukraine, where the Bolshevik Party was very active in the industrial east. The Bolshevik miners of the Donets Basin had revolted and seized power and were organizing Red troops. In Kiev, factory workers were talking openly of getting rid of the Rada and setting up a Soviet government.

There was always a strike in some plant. But in the middle of January, 1918, work suddenly came to a standstill all over the city. The Rada published communiqués announcing that the *gaidamaks* were successfully resisting the Red troops. But there were contrary rumors that they were retreating before the Red troops advancing from Donets. Once again there was a Bolshevik outbreak at the arsenal. The revolt spread quickly through the city. The rattle of rifles could be heard on every street corner. From some remarks dropped by Levine, I gathered that the local Bolsheviks were attempting to prepare the way for the approaching Red Army.

When we heard fighting, we rushed out into the streets. The whine of bullets and their dry clatter against the brickwork kept us glued to the walls. I caught sight of my landlady, her eyes red with weeping. "Where is Vassili Petrovich?" she asked plaintively. Her husband, a workman employed at the arsenal, had not come home. He never did come home.

Everywhere in the city housewives were sticking strips of paper over their windows to prevent their being shattered by the vibration from the big guns. Bullets were flying all over the place, though no one knew where they came from or who was firing them. They did not keep people from collecting in crowds before the bakers' shops. There was a rumor that armed men were looting houses in the street next to ours. That night the doors were barricaded, and a system of sentries was set up. It was impossible to get into a house without first being carefully scrutinized through a peephole in the door. That done, a couple of old people armed with ancient revolvers would open it just enough to let you slip through.

On the fifth day the fighting stopped as though by magic. The sudden silence seemed strange and sinister. I heard somebody say: "The Bolsheviks have been smashed!"

We went out again and started exploring the city. Some disemboweled horses were lying at a near-by crossroads. But the first corpse we saw was stretched out on the pavement. It was the body of a young soldier. His face was a greenish color, and his head had been crushed. His brains lay scattered on the asphalt. Somebody had removed his boots, and his naked feet looked blue. We gave this body a wide berth.

Near the station we noticed some abandoned military trucks. Children were clambering over them, hunting for cartridges and small shells: they would take the powder from them and use it for making fireworks, which they let off in the narrow alleys.

My landlady returned, worn out and with puffy eyes. Fifteen hundred Bolshevik workmen had been massacred at the arsenal. The workers' suburbs were in mourning.

After a few days the guns started booming again on the other side of the Dnieper. The Red Army, led by Muraviev, was drawing inexorably nearer to Kiev. The workers at the arsenal had planned their rising a week too early. Six days later they could have seized the city without bloodshed. I remember a woman coming to the house and saying: "The Petlurians have cleared out!" Simon Petlura, a Nationalist schoolmaster, was then head of the Rada of the Ukraine. His government and the remainder of its troops fled to the Austrian frontier. They wandered about to such an extent that soon even the schoolboys were joking about it:

> The Government is on the train;
> Underneath is its terrain.

"Let's go and see whether the Reds are here yet," I said to Levine.

In the Kzeshchatik, chief street of the city, a crowd mostly composed of working people was wandering about, vaguely waiting for something to happen. Then horses' hoofs sounded in the distance, and a squadron of cavalry, without any distinguishing marks and dressed in the long gray cloaks common to all these armies, came suddenly in sight, advanced as far as the public square, and beat a hurried retreat. An armored car with two turrets followed them. It halted in the square, and two sunburned men, wearing red brassards on their sleeves, got out. The Reds! The Reds! The crowd swarmed round them. A few women cried: "Do you know what happened at the arsenal? Shot, the whole lot of them!" Horsemen came galloping up, and then a meeting was improvised round the pedestal of a statue. A man, bareheaded, with a forceful bearded face, clambered up and started shouting harsh phrases that went straight to the hearts of his listeners.

"Comrades, Kiev has been freed by the Red Army of workmen and peasants who have risen in revolt. Comrades, the power of the Soviet brings you . . ."

43

It was only later that I heard that this was Skrypnik, a member of the Bolshevik Central Committee and commissar in Muraviev's army.[1]

A little farther on, parties of Red soldiers were engaged in scrutinizing the papers of those going toward the suburbs. We were shocked to see the following scene: A couple went up to one of the Red patrols. The man was dressed as a workman. His papers were in order. They moved on, but the patrol commander, who had been following them narrowly with his eyes, called them back. Very roughly he tore open the man's sheepskin overcoat and revealed a pair of golden shoulder straps. These were the symbol of the hated enemy of the revolution; they were the death sentence—the man was lost. "Take him!" the commander growled, and two soldiers led him off, while the woman, not yet understanding, cried out: "What's the matter, dear?"

We stood horrified, two boys of eighteen confronted for the first time by cold-blooded violence.

Four hundred officers were shot at the arsenal as a reprisal for the massacre of the workmen. Blood calls for blood. This was merely a beginning.

At the end of five weeks Muraviev's Red Army had to retreat before the advance of the Ukraino-German forces. For the Rada, driven almost completely out of the Ukraine, had asked for German aid; and the Germans had come with thirty-three divisions, more than 200,000 men. The resistance of the Red Army was broken. The Germans advanced with lightning speed: Kiev was occupied on March 16, Poltava on March 30, and Kherson on April 10. By the end of April, 1918, the Kaiser's troops had occupied all of the Ukraine and entered the Crimea.

Kiev was quickly emptied of Soviet troops and changed hands without a shot being fired. At school an awful rumor went round: "The Germans are here!" There was something impressive in the thought that, after fighting for four years against the whole world, they had now penetrated into the heart of the Ukraine.

That day I noticed an extraordinary change in the railroad station. Ever since 1917 it had been dilapidated and incredibly filthy. But now parties of German soldiers were busy scrubbing the floors, wiping down the walls, and pasting up new notices in Gothic print. Everything smelled of soap. People gazed with stupefaction at this incredible phenomenon. Many odd things had occurred since the Revolution, but nothing so odd as this sudden attack with the scrubbing brush! When a helmeted officer came on the scene with buttons bright and boots shining, the soldiers, washrags in hand, saluted him—a surprise to us. Sometimes in the streets we would catch sight of the *Hetman*, Pavlo Skoropadsky, ruler of the new monarchist Ukraine, a protégé of

[1] Skrypnik, who later became one of the most influential of all the People's Commissars in the Ukraine, and a faithful collaborator of Stalin, fell into disfavor and committed suicide in 1934.

the Kaiser, passing in his grand official car. He was a man of mature age, dressed in a dazzling white Cossack uniform and wearing the cross of St. George, a decoration of the czarist regime. The local illustrated papers were printed in Berlin, and a quantity of Ukrainian banknotes, also produced in Berlin, were in circulation.

To keep me going until my schooldays ended, the principal found me a position as tutor with a tavernkeeper called Petrichenko. My job was to coach his son, a pale, shifty-eyed youth, in his schoolwork, in return for which I got my board and lodging.

My pupil at first showed signs of a strange stupidity. One day, when he came home with his usual bad report, his father took him into the stable and gave him a terrible beating. From my room at the other end of the yard I could hear the wretched boy's cries. I realized later that his backwardness was a form of unconscious and passive resistance to this brutal treatment.

Petrichenko said to me, "Don't spare the rod. Just you tell me, and I'll give him a good hiding whenever he needs it." But I replied that if he wished me to continue as tutor to his son he must give up his supplementary ministrations. "I'll answer for him," I said; and my pupil, who developed a sort of grateful passion for me, set himself to justify my confidence. We worked hard together. As soon as his fears were removed, his report card showed a marked improvement.

The family regarded me with the deepest respect, though not, unfortunately, to the extent of providing me with a new pair of shoes. The whole drama of that winter is summed up for me in my old shoes, which left my feet at several points in contact with the mud and snow. However, Petrichenko fed me, and, thanks to his soup, I managed to pass my final examinations with the other boys of my grade.

There were the customary festivities, the usual distribution of graduation pins stamped with two dates: June, 1918, and June, 1928. We all took the solemn oath to meet again at Kiev, in the school buildings, in ten years' time and relate our experiences. But this meeting never came off. The boys who left school in 1918 were drawn violently into opposing channels; they had little chance of meeting again, except, perhaps, as enemies. A few graduates of my year ended up in the Red Army, but more of them joined the Whites, whose recruiting agents were very active in Kiev.

I myself went to live with my Bolshevik friend Levine, who had startling pamphlets in his room, dealing with every subject under the sun. We spent whole nights in argument. The complete reorganization of mankind, on a basis of equality and freed labor, seemed to him to offer no difficulties whatever. Communism was the only salvation for our starving peasants. "Suppose," he would say, "just for the sake of argument, that you have three muzhiks. One has a horse, another a plow, the third a sack of seed. Divided, they cannot even sow their own strips of land; united, they can manage perfectly well.

45

"If we want to get rid of poverty, injustice, and war," he went on, "the only thing we've got to do is to abolish private property."

"Well," I told myself, "in that case I'm with the Bolsheviks, too!"— so triumphant did I feel at having followed the argument. It all looked extremely simple. All we had to do now was to fight those who wanted to prevent the workers from reorganizing the world.

One night our conversation was interrupted by the brittle rap of rifle butts on the door.

"Who's there?" Levine and I stood tense.

"Open up!" came the command.

Levine kicked his pamphlets under the bed. I opened the door, and in rushed a Ukrainian gendarme with several German soldiers.

"What do you want?"

"Shut up! You're under arrest."

The two of us were escorted out to the Lukianovka barracks, where "unreliables" were being temporarily interned. As I walked by Levine's side between the soldiers, I felt excited. I glowed with a feeling of comradeship for everyone, far and near, who was joined with us in the struggle for a happy new world.

We were never told why we had been arrested—but doubtless someone had informed against us. We were thrown into the prison camp under guard of German soldiers, and we got our daily rations of black bread and coffee from the German military kitchen. We spent our time lying on straw mattresses in a corner. We had no idea how long we would stay there.

Levine had told me about revolutionists exiled to Siberia in the Czar's time, and how they had escaped.

"Not even thousands of miles of wasteland could stop them," he said.

Well, in our miniature Siberia all we had to do was to climb a wall, race across several patches of garden, and be off.

I pointed this out to Levine, but he wasn't enthusiastic.

"No," he said. "The chances are that we won't be here very long, and if we try to escape we'll only be jumping from the frying pan into the fire."

I was getting restive at our monotonous existence. Only Levine's conversation made it bearable.

I had observed that during the distribution of coffee the guards were all concentrated in one corner of the courtyard. The other side remained unguarded. I decided I'd risk it. I told Levine what I planned to do, but he hedged again.

"Let's wait awhile and see what happens."

"No," I said. "I've had enough. I'm going."

At seven o'clock that evening, when the men lined up for coffee, I took a place near the beginning of the line. I passed the huge pot, and the guard ladled some of the muddy liquid into my cup. Then I sauntered off to the other side of the guardhouse. As I rounded the corner I tossed the cup into the bushes and started to run. The way was clear. I reached the wall which surrounded the camp. I knew the place where the bricks were chipped and I could get a foothold and climb over. I dared not look back.

No sooner had I placed my foot in a crevice and made the first jump than I heard a raucous shout behind me. I looked back, terrified. A stocky German guard was rounding the corner.

But I had a place to hold onto, and I did not mean to give up. I strained upward. Bricks crumbled under my foot. As I clawed at the top of the wall I could hear him cocking his rifle.

My fingernails were broken and bleeding, but I was at the top. In a second I'd be over the wall. I did not dare to look at the guard again. There was no time for the delicious parting insult I had planned. A shot rang out suddenly and loudly. I was sure I was killed as I rolled off the wall into the bushes on the other side. But I had no wounds. I jumped up and ran across a number of small gardens, vaulted some easy fences, and found myself in the street. There I felt for the moment safe.

Toward night I took refuge with a friend in the suburbs and kept close to my room. Apparently my escape did not bother my captors— they had more important worries. The following week Levine was released. He had been badly frightened on my account and on his own. "When I heard the sound of that rifle," he said, "I thought it was all up with you."

"So did I," I replied, and we both laughed.

7. *Wanderings*

I HAD NO DESIRE to be re-arrested, and since there was no special reason for my remaining in Kiev, I left town. Of the ensuing events I remember little. My idea had been to reach the district of Cherkassy, where one of my uncles was living. Unfortunately, while still in the freight car in which the journey was made, I fell ill and was soon delirious. Fever kept me in a state of complete exhaustion; first I shivered with cold, then I stifled with heat. A kindly peasant managed to get from me, during my mental wanderings, the name of my destination; and when we arrived he saw me off the train and had me put into a wagon and driven to my uncle Peter's home.

47

I regained consciousness in what seemed to me paradise itself. Actually it was the hospital of a small obscure market town. The room was white, an open window gave onto a garden full of flowers, and an elderly nurse, dressed all in white, was near at hand with a bowl of *kissel*.[1] I learned that I had just had a bad attack of Spanish influenza, that disease which so many were to die of in 1918.

The clean, methodical Germans instituted a pitiless system of requisitions. A tragic incident occurred in the village of Vissky, where my uncle Peter lived. Some German soldiers, out on a plundering expedition, had been beaten and disarmed. The German commander issued orders for the arrest of ten peasants and imposed a heavy fine on the village. The following night a German sentry was killed. The Germans, finding some rifles with sawed-off barrels hidden on one or two farms, straightway arrested a dozen more young fellows and then shot all the prisoners. A handful of youthful peasants put up a fight in the park surrounding the manor of the Countess Brannitzkaya, which the Germans had taken back from the peasants and restored to her. They set fire to the superintendent's house and then fired point-blank at the soldiers who were trying to escape from it. Twenty Germans, including an officer, were killed.

I did not take part in what was happening, but it was becoming dangerous for me to stay in the village. I was already regarded with suspicion, and I knew what it meant to get on the wrong side of the authorities. Two weeks before, my uncle had sent me to a refinery for some sugar. This refinery stood close to the railroad station, a few miles from Vissky. I happened to be in the station waiting room when the bell announcing the departure of a train began to clang. A peasant woman, towing a little girl after her and bent double under the weight of a sack, was dashing for the platform. But the door was guarded by a gendarme, who pushed the woman brutally back. The little girl fell down and began to cry. The poor woman begged the man to let her pass: the train was already moving slowly. I picked the child up and said to the mother as I did so: "It's no good speaking to him, you can see he's just a brute."

I had hardly uttered the words when I was knocked down with a head blow from the flat of the man's sword. With a volley of oaths the gendarme went out onto the platform. I can see myself now, scrabbling on the dirty floor for my spilled sugar, the bluish white chunks of which were stained with red, for I was bleeding profusely.

An old countryman waiting for me outside with his cart asked me what had happened. I said nothing. I forced myself to remain calm despite the pain and my sense of outrage. For I knew I had to keep still unless I wanted to land in jail.

This incident, coming after what had occurred in Kiev, classed me among the "dangerous elements." Now that we were living more or

[1] Cranberry starch pudding.

48

less in a state of siege, it looked as though I might have to pay dearly for what I had done. One night Uncle Peter came for me.

"You'd better clear out," he said. "I think the Germans are going to shoot anyone they're at all doubtful about."

That night I left Vissky with two young neighbors.

After a hike through the woods we reached the banks of the Dnieper. There we separated. My companions were going to join the *Ataman* Mazurenko, who was gathering peasants to fight against the *Hetman*. I decided to return to Kiev. I went on foot along the river bank, spending the nights in melon gardens and subsisting on watermelons and cantaloupes. After ten days I reached Kiev.

The city was decidedly safer, although street fighting was still sporadically breaking out. I managed to find a job giving lessons to the daughter of a doctor with monarchist sympathies. The old man's hopes were dashed to the ground when the newspapers published telegrams from Germany announcing the military collapse of the various fronts, the Armistice, the Kaiser's flight, and the Revolution. A peasant revolt flooded the Ukraine. Bands commanded by local *atamans* were closing in on Kiev. The Germans were withdrawing their forces in the face of the peasant upsurge. The army of the Rada was advancing from the west.

By December, 1918, the *Hetman* of the Ukrainian state held no more than a few villages in the immediate neighborhood of besieged Kiev. It was then that I got my second view of him. I happened to be passing the great Cathedral of St. Vladimir. A few coffins—about fifteen of them—draped in the colors of the old Russian Empire, had been laid in front of the church. Some military units commanded by officers in Czarist uniforms paid the final honors. The *Hetman* dismounted from his horse and advanced beneath an archway of Czarist tricolor flags; he was wearing the same uniform as his officers. The Nationalist blue and yellow colors had completely disappeared.

So the Ukrainian pantomime is over, I thought, amazed by this sudden change in the appearance of things. A few idlers watched the ceremony from afar, but there was not a single cheer. The troops were tired and few in number—no longer an imposing sight. "Let the dead bury their dead," I said to myself.

An attempt to bolster up the bellicose spirit of the few remaining detachments of officers and students who still wore monarchist badges was made by the publication of communiqués to the effect that the French were disembarking at Odessa! The reaction, grasping at a straw, hurriedly transferred its loyalty from Germany, now in the throes of revolution, to the victorious Allies.

The German soldiers formed councils and demanded in their meetings an immediate return home. Their vaunted discipline vanished. The German High Command hastened to evacuate the disaffected troops. On the last day of the evacuation the *Hetman* Skoropadsky, disguised as a wounded German officer, was carried from the palace on a stretcher. He escaped from Kiev and any possible vengeance on the last train out.

The sound of cannon, familiar for weeks in the suburbs of besieged Kiev, now ceased. The remnants of the *Hetman's* troops retired to the center of the city, threw down their rifles, and dispersed. Not a single German soldier remained. So ended the *Hetman* state. The next day Petlura came back. The Nationalist Rada republic was once more in control of Kiev.

Early that morning Levine broke into my room. "They are on the move," he exclaimed.

"Who are?" I asked sleepily.

"Come and see," he said.

I dressed quickly, and we went to the hill which overlooked the Bibikov Boulevard. I expected to see squadrons of cavalry in Ukrainian uniforms, but instead I found myself gazing with surprise at thousands of sledges and carts accompanying what appeared to be a people in revolt. Crowds of peasants mingled with nondescript soldiers without any identifying insignia. With their belts stuck full of grenades and their bodies crisscrossed with cartridge belts, they were armed with the most miscellaneous collection of weapons it was possible to imagine, ranging from muskets to primitive pikes; and occasionally a machine gun would go by, mounted on an old peasant wagon. Many of them were accompanied by their wives and some by their children, and they sang to the music of accordions as they marched. Some were in gay spirits, others solemn. Among the flags they carried, the Ukrainian yellow and blue was far outnumbered by the red. As we saw this torrent flowing through the streets of Kiev, we realized that it was more than the entrance of Petlura. The peasant revolution was on the march.

Levine said to me: "Piatakov[2] has set up a Bolshevik government on the left bank of the Dnieper. We've got to get through the lines. Our place is with them. Are you coming?"

"You bet I am."

We started next day with a crowd in a train that seemed to trundle along without any fixed destination. We were jammed in a freight car without partitions, and all of us ran the risk of being suffocated if we built a fire on the floor or of freezing to death if we didn't. Suddenly the train came to a halt. Self-appointed delegates ran along the cars crying: "Citizens! The engineer won't go on unless we give him two bottles of vodka—dig out what you can!"

In order to pass Petlura's sentries it was necessary to have some excuse. And we boys, with our school diplomas, said we were going

---

[2] A leader of the Bolshevik revolution in the Ukraine, one of the most gifted and influential men in the Central Soviet Government. He was condemned an "enemy of the people" in the Second Moscow Trial in 1937 and shot.

home to our parents, who were waiting for us on the farther side of the moving battle front.

We covered the next thirty miles on a locomotive. It was moving in the direction of the front, where everyone wanted to go. Some lucky people had foreseen the circumstances and had paid the engineer for the privilege of hanging onto the sides of the engine; but Levine and I could find room only on the cowcatcher, just over the lamps. We suffered tortures from the cold wind and the heat of the engine. Our legs were half-frozen, our chests lacerated by the icy wind, and our backs burned owing to the proximity of the boiler. The snow lay desolate around for miles. It was a terrible journey.

At the last station a Petlura officer halted the whole crowd of us. "Get the hell back!" he ordered. We sought another way, through country roads remote from the fighting lines. Here we fell in with a group of petty traders who were also trying to cross and return to their villages.

We traveled with them in sledges along the deserted roads. Toward the end of the fifth day we passed Chernigov and drew near the zone occupied by the Reds. Faces darkened with anxiety. But suddenly someone cried: "Soldiers!" And a number of very young peasants, fully armed but in civilian clothes and riding bareback, galloped up to us.

"Give up any arms you've got!" shouted one of them, who seemed to be in command. "Anyone who hides a weapon will be shot!"

We had no weapons. They took a hurried look at our baggage, but no one was searched.

"Who are you?" we asked.

"Red partisans!" [3]

The regular Red Army was still far away. On the thirty-first of December we came up to it—once more in my familiar town of Gomel. A young man in a leather jacket scrutinized our papers in a small guardroom in a suburb. They were not very convincing—nothing but our diplomas. Suddenly he looked up.

"Alexander!" he cried.

It was my old school friend Model, who had once fought so hard to have *Pravda* distributed in the reading room. That had been only eighteen months ago!

Model was soon to rise high in the ranks of the Bolsheviks. But I met him fifteen years later in a Moscow street, his face lined with despair, and furtive caution stamped all over him.

"What are you doing?" I asked.

"Just keeping alive," he answered. "I was turned out of the Party, on the ground that I belonged to the Opposition, and lost my job. Come to see me, and I'll tell you about it."

He gave me his address. When, a few days later, I knocked at his

[3] Guerrilla fighters.

door, it was opened by a terrified old woman who said he was no longer there, that she could tell me nothing, that she didn't know him. I asked no questions. It was 1935.

8. Civil War

I RAN STRAIGHT to my mother's house, hoping to greet the New Year with her, but a stranger opened the door. My mother had left a letter for me. She was working in a hospital a hundred miles north. She wrote that my father had died during the summer. I went to see his wife, whom I found depressed and aging. Her house was sadly dilapidated. The front doorsteps were in ruins, the ceilings sagged, and the kitchen, once spotless, was littered with neglected crockery. As always, she joked with me, but her laughter was halfhearted. I could find no words and left in a gloomy mood.

Then began for me a chaotic year of journeys, fights, and adventures of every kind. I was instructed by the Soviet military committee to carry a message through the enemy lines to Kiev. Since I knew the district well and could speak Ukrainian, the task was not too hazardous. I recrossed the lines hidden in a train packed full of German soldiers being repatriated. Their stove saved me from freezing to death.

I arrived in Kiev two weeks before it fell to the Bolsheviks, when Petlura and his Rada fled again. Antonov-Ovseenko, in command of a small army composed of Donets miners and workmen from Red Kharkov, seized the town in February, 1919, and established with Piatakov an all-Ukrainian Soviet government. But the Soviet power was actually installed only in the towns; whereas bands of peasants, led by *atamans,* held the neighboring countryside. The Petlurians were engineering a rising in Podol, a suburb of Kiev; the Poles were in Korosten, eighty miles west of Kiev. The *atamans*—Stroug, Zelyoni, Sokolovsky, and others—were massacring Jews in the villages; Makhno and Grigoriev were leading bands of anarchists; General Denikin was starting an offensive in the south. Such was the state of the Soviet power in the Ukraine when Christian Rakovsky arrived to take charge.

In all this turmoil my line of reasoning was simple. I wasn't going on with my studies while the power of the Soviets was in danger and our country was attacked by enemies from all sides. I must take my share in saving it, defend it with rifle in hand. I decided to volunteer as a private in the Red Army, and I took my application to the military commander of the Kiev district. He listened to me with geniality and sympathy and then ordered his secretary to enroll me.

"Are you a Party member?" he asked as I was leaving. "You must join the Party now. The Red Army needs conscious fighters. You will be doubly useful to us as a Party member."

In the evening I told Levine that I had volunteered in the Army and what the commissar had told me. My friend backed up his advice vigorously.

"The commissar was damned right," he said. "You should enter the Bolshevik Party right now. You've already worked hard for the Soviet cause, and now you're off to fight at the front. No one can stay in a halfway position in this crisis. You must go right along to the end with us. I'll recommend your name to the Kiev Party committee."

At this time the procedure for becoming a member of the Bolshevik Party was long and formal. References from two Party members were necessary. There were two preliminary stages, each of six months, during which one ranked first as a "sympathizer" and then as a "candidate." Only after passing through both successfully could one enjoy full membership.

Levine took me to see Mikhail Tcherny, secretary of the Kiev organization. In a room filled with clouds of cigarette smoke I saw an amiable man with a high forehead and curly hair, dressed in an embroidered blouse. He looked at me for a moment with a smile on his lips.

"Since you have twice crossed the lines in the service of the Soviets," he said, "I am going to admit you without the usual preliminaries. And remember this: the Bolshevik is before all things a fighter; next after that, he is an agitator; third, it must be his constant endeavor to set an example."

So now I was a Bolshevik.[1] I was proud that I had been found worthy of trust. I was to count for something in the Revolution. I felt that I was on the threshold of a new life which promised to be full of exciting danger.

Tcherny shook my hand warmly, and we left his office. I never saw him again. When General Denikin's White Army occupied the city, he remained behind to take charge of an underground organization. He was captured, bore himself courageously at his court-martial, and was hanged.

Upon my enlistment in the Red Army I was attached to a special training battalion. We were told that we would shortly join the new regiments to be sent into the country to suppress peasant uprisings. I had some trouble reconciling this necessity with the words of the slogan inscribed over the door of the War Commissariat: "Peace to the

[1] At this time the Party was called "Russian Social Democratic Workers' Party (Bolshevik)." Later in the year, at Lenin's suggestion, the name was changed to Russian Communist Party.

peasant huts, war to the palaces." But we have to be realists, I was told. How could we let the peasant counterrevolution go on massacring the Jews, starving the cities, floundering along in an indiscriminate slaughter dictated by fifty different leaders of lawless bands?

Our battalion was quartered in a "school for young ladies of noble parentage." Until we came, the Revolution had left this school untouched. Cut off from their parents, the girls were living their cloistered lives under the supervision of elderly spinsters as if nothing had been changed. The Bolshevik commissar, seeking quarters for us in the crowded city, had come upon this little island surviving from the old regime and decided to requisition it. But the pleas of the principal, who pointed out that the girls had no place to go, led him to a compromise. The girls would move to the two upper floors while we occupied the ground floor. When we were drilling in the courtyard, the sound of someone practicing on the spinet would float down from the upper floors. Sometimes we would see the girls taking a morning walk, two by two, dressed in tippets and white collars. First they would turn stiffly from the overfriendly winks of the young soldiers. Later we would see them gathered in small clusters watching us. Before we left, they were conversing with us, and some of their conversations concerned rendezvous. Nature did not find it hard to bridge the gap between the young revolutionary soldiers on the ground floor, with unshaven faces and crude army boots, and these delicate daughters of the aristocracy taking their lessons above.

Party members from our battalion were assigned to various regiments of raw conscripts. It was our duty as Bolsheviks to form the backbone of these new formations. I was not long in the battalion before I was assigned, with a number of comrades, to a newly formed regiment of Volga peasants. They were sent to the south of Kiev, where the peasant guerrillas were making headway, and they had very little enthusiasm for fighting in the Ukraine.

I received my baptism of fire in a protracted battle against the bands of the two *atamans,* Stroug and Zelyoni. The Bolshevik Skrypnik was in charge of the operations whose object was to surround the district of Tripolye. Two months earlier Zelyoni had surprised a regiment of Young Bolsheviks there and killed them almost to a man. The boys were sleeping in a group of whitewashed cottages when Zelyoni's carts burst into the town. (The *atamans* conducted their campaigns in carts and carriages, which gave them the mobility of cavalry.) The prisoners were lined up on the high cliff overlooking the Dnieper and swept by machine-gun fire into the river.

At our approach Zelyoni retreated toward the Dnieper and transferred his headquarters from Vasilkov to Tripolye. In the evacuated headquarters we found a number of papers and some proclamations bearing his signature. These called upon the peasants to liberate "the Ukraine, our Dear Mother" by cutting the throats of all Jews and Communists.

The battle began against an invisible enemy, and was at first more difficult than dangerous. When I heard the bullets whistling about me, my chief fear was of being afraid. We were told to dig trenches with our hands and bayonets. In these trenches we were bitterly cold at night; in the daytime, hot, hungry, and thirsty. For we remained in the front line for four days and nights without, naturally, any proper organization of rations. So famished were we on the last day that, in spite of scattered rifle fire, we attempted a raid on a field of peas lying between the two positions. A hail of bullets drove us off. Nothing I ever ate has seemed as desirable to me as those inaccessible peas.

At dawn on the fifth day the signal was given for a general assault, and we rushed forward without meeting any immediate resistance. Apparently the enemy had fled. Suddenly, however, I saw my companions diving into a ditch beside the road and running. There was a shout of "Look out! Cavalry!" and a cloud of dust could be seen moving rapidly in our direction. All were soon in the ditch. But I had taken a good look at that cloud of dust and thought it looked more like sheep than cavalry. I did not have so much as a stripe, but I became so furious at the sight of soldiers running terror-stricken from a flock of sheep that I found myself shouting, waving my arms, and swearing as though I were the officer in command. I even went so far as to fire over the heads of those who were running away.

"Get back into line, you cowards!" I yelled, "or I'll shoot the lot of you!"

I appealed to my fellow Communists to get back on the road and help me. We dragged the fleeing soldiers after us.

"It's nothing but a herd of sheep, you damned fools!" I shouted.

Together we rounded up the company, and I took command forthwith, getting the men into some sort of order so that when the officer in charge came up he found us holding the position.

Without realizing it at all, I had accomplished a very distinguishing feat, and I came near getting shot for it. An official inquiry was held, as a result of which it was found that our troops as a whole had made a very bad showing. Certain detachments, attacked unexpectedly, had permitted the enemy to make a break in the ring drawn around him. As a result of a faulty liaison, my own company was out of its place in the fighting line. Skrypnik was impulsive to the point of being slightly crazy. "Shoot the Communists as an example to the others," he ordered. My commanding officer pointed out that, in our company, two of the Communists had given an admirable example, having succeeded in checking a rout. "All right then," Skrypnik decided, "we will promote them. Make them commissars!" Thus it happened that I became the political commissar of a battalion.[2]

[2] In the Civil War the Bolsheviks were constrained to make use of former czarist

We finally occupied Tripolye and found in the village only women, children, and a few old men. The younger men had all gone into hiding. Not a cow, not a chicken, not a scrap of bread was to be seen anywhere. With amazing skill everything edible had been concealed. It made us realize that we had to reassure the peasants, who had been told that the Reds seized all they could find and paid for nothing. To accomplish this our High Command issued an order that any looting would be punished by death. A few looters were shot, one of them for having helped himself to a single suckling pig. The sight of us in the flesh did more than these measures to reassure the peasants. My ability to coax in their native Ukrainian helped persuade them to bring out bread and eggs from their hiding places. At last even a few chickens appeared, and we felt that confidence was being restored.

This happy state of affairs was ruined when the authorities issued a mobilization order, instructing all men of military age to report within three days under threat of severe punishment. A crowd of women surrounded headquarters, shouting angrily: "You can't have our men! We'll never see them again! If you want to shoot them, you'll have to find them!" The women were quite ready to tear us to pieces, and the battalion commander promised to do what he could to get the mobilization order postponed.

While attending to a conference of commissars held on a flight of garden steps at the Central Committee building in Kiev, I saw for the first time Christian Rakovsky.[3] He was still in his early youth, a man with keen, smiling eyes, an energetic face, and a gift of persuasive eloquence. As head of the Soviet government of the Ukraine, he was the heart and brain of a whole region—torn as it was by internal quarrels, utterly chaotic, and constantly on the point of collapse. His reputation as an old leader of the Rumanian Socialist movement who had escaped from Jassy prison and joined our revolution, endeared him to us. He told us that the world situation was hopeful, for mutterings of revolution could be heard in every country of Europe. The immediate local situation, however, was grave in the extreme. Petlura and Denikin were marching on Kiev at the head of numerically superior forces, and the *atamans* were in control of the villages.

officers. Many of them served sincerely and well, but in order to assure their reliability, the Bolsheviks appointed a "political commissar" to each command. The duties of these commissars were varied. They shared authority with the military officer, but in a crisis their authority superseded his. They took over all political functions, such as dealing with a recalcitrant peasantry and keeping up a Bolshevik morale among the troops.

[3] Christian Rakovsky was later Soviet ambassador in London and Paris. Exiled to Siberia for his participation in the Trotskyist Opposition, he was one of the last to recant. During the Moscow trials he was arrested along with Bukharin and a number of others, charged with having been a fascist spy. He confessed to innumerable unbelievable crimes and was sentenced to twenty years' imprisonment.

Next day I went back to the front, but I found my regiment already in retreat before Petlura. Under Pavlov, head of the military council of Kiev, we tried to make a stand in the southern suburbs of the city. But meanwhile Denikin was approaching from the east, and on August 30, 1919, we had to evacuate Kiev to avoid being cut off. We took refuge in the forest regions to the north.

Pavlov was a levelheaded soldier whose air of quiet confidence never diminished, however precarious the situation might be. He was one of those men who seem destined always to save what can be saved out of the very jaws of defeat. I can see him now standing on the roadside, watching the march-past of regiments reduced to a few hundred men each. "We must reorganize," was all he said. In 1927 Pavlov became one of the advisers of Chiang Kai-shek and was drowned in the course of a difficult retreat in south China. From his staff I learned that Yakir, a young commander of the Forty-fourth Division, surrounded in the neighborhood of Odessa, had broken through the iron ring of the White Armies and was fighting his way northward to help us.

Amid these events my personal existence became so varied and so filled with complex and exciting incidents that, were I to narrate them, this chapter would fill my book. I confine myself to certain happenings which influenced my future.

The first was a delicate mission into the countryside: My regiment was called upon to provide three squads to requisition food from the peasants. Each squad consisted of one commissar and four soldiers. The first squad set out in charge of a fiery Georgian commissar and never returned. Doubtless it was massacred. The second managed to find its way back, but without weapons, having been kicked and clubbed out of the villages. My squad was the last to go. We entered a large village on a moonlit night. The slender spires of two churches were silhouetted against the starry sky. We knocked at a door. A very old man opened to us.

"What is your government here?" I asked.

"Government? There isn't any, thank God," he answered slyly. "We're getting along nicely without one."

In the morning I called a meeting of the village. Nobody came except a few women. I pointed out that we needed food, and that it would be bad policy on the part of the peasants to drive to desperation a regiment of eight hundred soldiers camped less than thirty miles away. I added that, provided everyone did his best, we would be content with very little. We would not enter the houses. Each family would contribute equally. Receipts would be given for everything contributed. There would be no arbitrary requisitioning. . . .

I awaited anxiously the results of my exhortation. There was a buzz of excitement in the village, and I could see the peasant women making mysterious visits into the woods, but nothing was brought in. I wondered if my diplomacy had failed. I decided to wait another day.

57

Finally an old woman showed up with a sack of potatoes, two loaves of bread, and a small bag of flour.

I took out a notebook, wrote down the nature and amount of her contributions, and asked her name.

Her eyes bulged out of her head with surprise. When she went back, she held before her like a flag a signed receipt for what she had given.

The news spread very rapidly that I was not going to sack the village, as others had, and by afternoon contributions were arriving in a steady flow.

The total exceeded my wildest hopes. One after another, the farmers' wives turned up, bringing bread, flour, and potatoes. "The village elders would like a word with you," one of them said to me. "They're coming to my house for a glass of tea this evening." This might, of course, be a trap, but I decided it would be better to go alone and with no weapons showing. Our conversation lasted far into the night, and I departed with their blessing. The only credit I can claim is that, instead of threatening, I explained things to them.

My regiment had given me up for lost and was preparing to decamp when I made my appearance with thirty cartloads of food. They received me and my four soldiers with cheers, for supplies had practically run out. The commander surveyed the haul with his hands on his hips. His only comment was: "Well, I'll be damned!"

Soon after my promotion, a problem arose that troubled me: As a commissar in the battalion I was paid 3,000 rubles a month, the salary of a battalion commander. The first time I received this sum, my conscience, as an enthusiastic newcomer to the Party, stirred uneasily. Could I accept such a privilege when the ordinary soldier was getting only 150 rubles? I had no difficulty in persuading the other Communists in my regiment that it was our duty publicly to refuse this favoritism. The political commissar of the brigade, however, reprimanded us for questioning the policy adopted by the Party toward specialists. "Wait a few years," he told us. "When we've trained a corps of Communist officers and put the Socialist regime on a firm footing, then we will introduce equality." Alas!

This little misunderstanding—which was soon dissipated, for the mere whisper of the words "Party discipline" overcame our scruples—did not bar my promotion to be commissar of a regiment. It was a new regiment formed from the remnants of three others, which had been disbanded after the evacuation of Kiev. Some of them were from Yakir's forces, which had now joined us—but in what condition! Two men in every three were without boots and were dressed in nothing but rags. Though I had been through a great deal less, I was not, despite my high office, much better to look at. My boots were almost worn out, my knees were coming through my trousers, and my tunic had lost its color, if it ever had any. I matched the regiment.

In the course of several months of uninterrupted fighting in retreat in the forests north of Kiev, our division lost half its men, and the Red Command ordered us transferred to central Russia for reorganization. By this time my service as commissar in a fighting unit had made me conscious of a vast military ignorance. Trotsky, head of the Red Army, just then issued an appeal for candidates to receive special training as Communist officers. He hoped in this way to remedy the state of dual command, the division of authority between commissars and old "regular" officers. This dualism had resulted, as I have already said, from the necessity of having the former czarist officers watched by Communists, and, on the other hand, of giving them, in the field, the support of men invested with the authority of the Party. Trotsky's idea was that, when the Red Army should have developed its own politically trained officers, the commissars would disappear, and the unity of command so necessary for efficiency in war would be re-established.[4]

Trotsky's appeal came home to me. I had had enough experience as commissar to appreciate the disadvantages of divided authority. I asked to be relieved of my duties as commissar of the regiment and sent my name to headquarters as a candidate for the School of the Red Officers. The political commissar of the Army granted my request.

So now another journey lay before me, this time by barge upstream on the Dnieper. My life had not been lacking in uncomfortable expeditions, but I remember the nights on that barge as the nearest thing to hell I have ever known. The hold, which was the only shelter available against the cold night air, was filled like a bag of peas with lice, bedbugs, and fleas. I would awake from a brief doze to find myself being devoured by insects from head to foot. I would rush up on deck like a madman, only to discover that my clothes were loaded with them.

At midnight the barge drew up to shore. A fire was built, and in the flickering shadows everybody, from cook to commander, jumped about naked, shaking his clothes over the flames to rid them of these vermin that dropped crackling into the fire. I finished my trip literally sick.

By a strange coincidence my destination once again was Gomel, for the Minsk Infantry Officers' School to which I was assigned had been

[4] This aim was achieved at the end of about ten years, and the better state of affairs lasted until 1937, when Stalin, after destroying the High Command, found himself faced with the necessity of attaching to the Communist officers formed by the Revolution new political commissars entrusted now with the duties of secret police. It is well known that this step led to the almost total destruction of the middle and upper ranks of the Army. Two years later, in the autumn of 1939, when the liquidated Red Officers' Corps had been replaced by fledgling juniors whose loyalty to Stalin had been insured by rapid promotions, privileges, and honors, the Russian dictator again did away with the institution of commissars. He restored it again in the attack on Finland, abolished it after peace was achieved, and restored it once again for the critical period of the war with Germany. He restores it when from a military point of view it is most vicious and abolishes it when it is comparatively harmless. This is because, after his purge of the officers, he has no confidence in the loyalty of the Army to his own person.

transferred there owing to the advance of the Polish Army. I expected to see my mother in Gomel, but hardly looked forward to it, for while I was at the front she had written me a dreary letter. She could not understand me. Instead of being proud of a son who was fighting with the Red Army and had already been made a commissar, she scolded.

"Stop playing the fool," she wrote, "and come home. Your two brothers have been killed. Don't you think that is enough? You will die for no good reason at all, and I shall be left without support. You ought to think a little of me...."

I replied hotly that my two brothers had fallen in the service of imperialism, waging an unjust war in the ranks of an army of oppressors, while, if I should spill my blood, it would be in the Red Army of the workers, fighting for the liberation of all the oppressed of the world. If death overtook me, my life would have been given for a glorious future. I asked her to try to understand and to join wholeheartedly in the cause of the Revolution.

I was only nineteen.

9. Red Cadets

THE BATTERED MILITARY TRAIN was still rattling on behind me as I left the Gomel station. I walked out around the big square in the best of spirits, whistling jauntily.

I had no knapsack and no baggage of any kind, not even a change of linen. I wore a leather coat and a revolver at my belt. On my cap was the five-pointed red star; in my pocket were a few Kerensky banknotes, worth less than half their printed value; in my wallet I had a small scrap of paper authorizing me to enroll in the School of Infantry Officers of the Red Army of Workers and Peasants. That was the sum total of my belongings.

But I had all the future before me—unless, of course, some stray bullet finished me off. Should that happen I would die gloriously, though without realizing it, for the Revolution. What a blessed destiny it was not to be at the mercy of events but to have at the end of the stretch of years one goal and one goal only—the conquest of the world for the proletariat. Young men like me would be needed, both dead and alive, before such a victory could be attained. Meanwhile it was the duty of each one of us to do his best.

I turned off through the narrow shabby streets to visit my mother. Here was the house. The windows were empty; something was changed. I knocked on the door, but no one came. The neighbors told me that my mother had got a nursing job with some army hospital unit: no, they couldn't say which, but it had gone off by train a few days before. So I was not to see her. But there was no time for sentimentalizing about that.

The School of Infantry Officers was lodged in spacious buildings which had formerly housed a theological seminary. I was delighted, almost amazed, by the cleanliness and order everywhere. Real beds with real sheets! That meant a lot to me, for I had not known what it was like to have a change of linen for over a year! The walls of the lecture rooms were hung with diagrams of gun mechanisms; there were racks of carefully waxed and polished small arms; and the sentries on duty at the entrance, unlike the battered soldiers I had been accustomed to, were smartly dressed. They did not carry their rifles slung casually from the shoulder by a piece of cord.

I was pleased at the change in my own appearance after I took a bath and had my head shaved and received a new uniform and a military greatcoat. Besides, my arms were filled with textbooks on such subjects as topography, tactics, and army regulations.

Most of my memories of this infantry school are pleasant. Despite the chaotic situation, despite the fact that it was located in a small town besieged on three sides and resisting only because of lack of unity in the enemy ranks, despite a general lack of everything, it managed to carry on its good work in an atmosphere of calm confidence.

Gomel, a forest-girt city of western Russia, had a population of about 80,000. For the most part this was made up of Jewish petty merchants, artisans who now had almost nothing to produce and sell, and workers in the wood and match industries and railroad shops. Seen on the map, the country around Gomel formed a sort of enclave between two battle fronts—Denikin's White troops in the east and south, and General Haller's Poles in the west.

The Red lines of defense round this region were scattered and highly vulnerable. The Red Army High Command had concentrated every good unit on the approaches to Moscow and Leningrad. Only a small number of battle-weary and demoralized detachments of the Twelfth Army held our lines. It would have been tempting to the Poles to push through these hungry and dispirited troops to Gomel. Our one comfort was that the Poles were not at all anxious for the success of Czarist generals who were fighting in the name of "Russia, One and Indivisible," and who therefore must be opposed to an independent Poland. For that very reason Denikin sent his crack Cossack forces to the northeast to fight their way to Moscow and held back from giving Haller adequate support in the west. Between two hostile forces we, a handful of four hundred students, thus received a breathing spell in which to master the rudiments of the art of war before having to fight both of them.

It must have taken an enormous amount of tact, energy, and ingenuity to run the school successfully. The teaching staff was composed of officers of the old regime, who were probably at heart opposed to Bolshevik ideas and who were certainly of an entirely different mentality from the students they had to train. They had been induced to take on the job by an appeal to their professional pride and sense of duty. Trotsky, with Lenin's support, was successfully putting into action his pet scheme of building up a Red Army with the help of professional soldiers. The scheme resulted in some cases of treachery and costly failure, but on the whole they were few. What was really remarkable was the amount of courage, devotion, and loyalty shown by these men of the old army officers' corps.

Very slowly the czarist officers were won over to the Red Army. Among them, the officers promoted during the World War who came from the middle classes found it easiest to join the Bolsheviks wholeheartedly. These officers at first had watched doubtingly while Trotsky and his aides reorganized the Russian Army. But now they were becoming convinced that the Reds were determined to fight. Trotsky showed them that, if they helped, their authority over the men would be supported. Finally, Pilsudski's march on Russia roused their national feeling. If they were not eager to fight alongside the Bolsheviks, they were at least ready to defend their country, White or Red, against the Poles.

The director of our school, an old officer of the Imperial Guard called Ryazhsky, was very proud of our smart appearance, though he adopted a rather skeptical attitude to the task demanded of him, which was no less than to turn a lot of young peasants and workmen into infantry officers in six months! With his turned-up mustache, military boots, glaring eye, and Russian blouse he was almost a caricature of the Imperial Guard type. While he did not regard the past with any special affection, he made no pretense about concealing his irony toward those in power. But he was excellent at his work, and he seemed happy enough, provided he could control his apprentice officers more efficiently than the People's Commissars were controlling the Republic.

Two Communists had been assigned to assist him—both valuable men, one by reason of his shrewdness, the other because of his wide political knowledge. Gayster, the latter, who was in charge of political training, filled many important positions in the district and ended up as undersecretary to the Central Commissariat of Statistics.[1] His companion was Commissar Michael Ivanovich Blukhov, one of the best examples I ever came across of a simple man of steadfast revolutionary faith.

Blukhov was tall, and he owed his success as a soldier to the fact

[1] His last days were spent in prison, for no very clear reason. I remember seeing his name, in 1937 or 1938, cited in some connection at one of the Moscow trials.

that he had been born with a snub nose. This had led to his being enrolled as a private in the Pavlovtsi Regiment of the Imperial Guard, formed in memory of the Emperor Paul I, for this regiment consisted entirely of men with snub noses like that of the murdered Czar. The Pavlovtsi happened to be in Petrograd during the 1917 crisis; and Blukhov, snub nose and all, heard Lenin speaking from a balcony and believed in bolshevism from that day.

The large classrooms were filled with students. There was a sprinkling of young Communists, but most of them had been recruited from the surrounding countryside. They were tall, husky peasant lads who knew nothing of military tactics and very little of bolshevism. The Bolsheviks had promised to make officers out of them—an almost unheard-of opportunity for peasants reared in the czarist caste system. They had come to college willingly enough, though not too confident in their future.

There were also some young industrial workers among them. These had been recruited by the local Communist Party from the Gomel factories. They were very enthusiastic, and more politically conscious than the peasants. Then there were some rank-and-file soldiers who had been selected from Red Army units at the front. And finally there were some high-school youths from the middle class and the intelligentsia who had defied their families and volunteered. This diverse assortment was welded during the training period into a unified, energetic, high-spirited whole. The peasants brought their health and stamina to it, the workers their agility and awareness, the soldiers their experience in military life; and the intellectuals helped all the others in their unaccustomed studies.

We lived in large, clean dormitories where everything was kept in perfect order. The winter is very severe in that region, and for days the temperature would be fifteen degrees below zero. In the barrack rooms the water would freeze in the copper buckets. Wood was very scarce. Only with the greatest difficulty could we get some logs to the school over the snowbound roads. But occasionally we were lucky enough to find an abandoned house in the outskirts of the city, and we would tear it down. Fortunately the High Command supplied us with adequate clothing. We had good greatcoats and boots and woolen underwear. We often slept fully clothed, even to our sheepskin caps. If some companions were absent on guard duty, we covered ourselves with their mattresses as well.

Our food—more or less the best that was to be had—consisted of black bread full of lumps and always moldy, frozen potatoes that were sickly sweet, and a pot of herring soup every other day. There were no fats in our diet, since the small amounts available were reserved for the hospitals and the children of the town. Once in a while the peasant father of a student would visit the school. Overwhelmed by the cordiality of his reception, he would return with gifts of butter or eggs "for the boys." Our hospitality paid dividends! At such times we would build a special fire and have a feast. Our frozen potatoes would be garnished with melted butter, a sliver of salt pork, or a bit of egg yolk. No French chef was ever so ingenious as we were with our concoctions of new dishes out of a few scraps.

Our day began at five o'clock in the morning and lasted until late at night. Five hours would be spent in the classrooms. The first weeks were indeed trying for teachers and students alike. The peasant youths scarcely knew how to read or write; they would gaze perplexed at the diagrams and mathematical symbols on the blackboards. A teacher would start off by posing an artillery problem and then find that he had first to teach his students the rudiments of arithmetic. Before they could understand the riddle of topography they had to learn some elementary geography and drawing. The officer who was explaining the mechanism of arms first had to coach his class in handling the parts of a gun without dropping the tiny pieces to the floor.

I remember the intensity with which the student body of peasants and young workmen tried to grapple with the art of military tactics. Their very willingness acted like a tonic on the skeptical and overburdened instructors: the teachers' mood changed gradually from resignation to active interest. Before long the wheels of education were grinding slowly but surely.

After work in the classroom we went out into the open, where we would spend two or three hours drilling in the bitter cold. The people of the town found this rather surprising, since formal drill of this sort had not been seen since the Revolution. They had become used to the dreary parade of listless men back from the front. But to see freshly uniformed troops, smartly performing the manual of arms or walking through the streets making maps, seemed to improve the morale of the entire town. Things might not be so bad after all.

Some mornings we had shooting practice, and after hard drilling this was almost a pleasant sport. Our instructors had devised an excellent system: If a man was a good shot, he was allowed to go back to the barracks earlier than the others, and so get his soup fairly hot. Thus encouraged, I quickly became as good a shot as I was a student— and it was not difficult to excel there, for I was one of the few who had a high-school education.

At the end of an afternoon of military maneuvers in the open country, when we came back tired but marching briskly and singing at the top of our voices, the townsfolk greeted us with cheers. They accepted us as their own and took pride in our appearance.

In addition to our military studies, we also had a political course, using the famous textbook of Krylenko. The committee of the local Communist Party sent their best theoreticians to take charge of this course. These homespun Marxists taught us the Party program, the principles of Soviet government, and a few elementary Marxist theories. Having some political experience, I assisted the teachers. At this time everything else was scarce, but books were plentiful. The presses

64

in Moscow and Petrograd were working overtime, and stacks of Party literature followed in the wake of the Red Army. The students responded quickly to the Bolshevik teachings. After all, they themselves were an example of how Lenin and Trotsky were building a world that would belong to the toilers. Formerly they could look forward to nothing but drudgery; now they were studying to be officers.

One day Commissar Blukhov came into the dormitory where I was assembling a rifle.

"Alexander," he said, "tonight you will have to prosecute Lenin and Trotsky."

"Prosecute Lenin and Trotsky!" I exclaimed, leaping up. "What do you mean?"

"Well, that's just what Moscow wants us to do," he replied, his eyes twinkling. "It's a new teaching method. We've been talking and talking in our political classes, and the students take it in. But we must teach them how to speak and argue for themselves. We must make them political fighters for the Party and the Army. Tonight you'll attack Lenin and Trotsky just as if you were a monarchist, Kerenskyite, and Menshevik rolled into one. We'll have a mock trial and see how well our students can argue for the Bolsheviks."

So that evening I assumed the role of prosecutor. The commissar was on the judges' bench, while the crowded hall served as a jury box. I leveled the familiar charges against the Bolshevik leaders. They were paid German agents sent into Russia to foment discontent. They were responsible for the Civil War, the thousands of deaths, the food shortage, and many other crimes.

First my audience was amused by the show, but as I warmed to the theme they became restless. A peasant lad wriggled in his seat and suddenly stood up.

"That's a lie!" he shouted. "Lenin and Trotsky are devoted to the people. We trust them. The Whites are to blame for all those things." Other students stood joining him, forgetting that it was make-believe. They stood up and shouted their answers to my "arguments." For a moment I felt that the play was becoming a little too real, and I nervously eyed the commissar. He had forgotten to bang his gavel for order. He was happily surveying the shouting students who had been galvanized into revolutionary agitators. Well, anything for the cause. . . . I continued my diatribe.

The meeting was a huge success. The "vindicated" Lenin and Trotsky were solemnly proclaimed "not guilty" by the unanimous audience, and I gladly quit my role as prosecutor and voted with the rest. Little did we think that one day a Bolshevik by the name of Stalin—then unknown to us—would turn the charges of "German agents" and "Imperialist spies" against all the leaders of the Revolution and adapt our innocent educational method to the uses of mass murder.

In the little spare time we had, we attended to our duties as Soviet citizens. As soldiers of the Red Army we had full civil rights and participated actively in the political life of the town. The local Soviet in Gomel—the municipal authority of our besieged city—was trying, in spite of the state of siege, to continue its work. Our military school was entitled to three delegates in the Soviet. Along with our commissar and a non-Party officer I was elected to serve. In the Soviet I was appointed to the credentials committee.

The overwhelming majority of the delegates were Bolsheviks. But some Menshevik Social Democratic workmen had also been elected, and several members of the Jewish Socialist Bund. There was a good deal to discuss at the sessions. We debated the food scarcity and the military situation. The Bolshevik deputies quite openly criticized the handling of affairs. The Menshevik delegates supported the criticism but held the Soviet power responsible.

After a few days the Bolshevik leaders in the Soviet received from Moscow an order to exclude the elected Mensheviks as enemies of the Revolution. Esther Frumkin, who was then a leader of the Socialist Bund, protested vehemently against this attack on working-class democracy.[3] In those days I was not very clear in my mind about what was happening. This step did not seem quite fair to the workmen who had elected them. But we were told that such was the decision of the Party. The Menshevik deputies withdrew in a dignified manner, little suspecting that their party had been outlawed for good. I reflect with regret now that one learns only too late the full significance of what is done in the heat of a political moment.

At the officers' school we first had only a small Communist "cell" of a dozen members. The Gomel Communist Committee used some members of our cell for propaganda work in the factories, to maintain morale. In school also we had to "show an example." We tried hard to keep near the top of the class in our studies and help in the political development of our non-Party comrades. That was a large task, since there were almost four hundred students to be won over to an understanding of Bolshevism. But exploding events suddenly swelled our Communist cell.

The winter of 1919 became the time of gravest danger for the young Soviet Republic. A White Army, under the command of General Yudenich, completely equipped with English arms, was marching on Petrograd. The "Volunteer Army" of General Denikin was advancing on Tula and Moscow, after occupying Orel and the whole of the Ukraine. General Miller, with the assistance of English and American troops, held Archangel and the coast of the White Sea and was trying to descend to Vologda. Admiral Kolchak was threatening the Ural districts and the Volga. Winston Churchill had proclaimed a crusade of fourteen nations against the pest of bolshevism, and the blockade of the Allies was slowly tying the loop of famine around Russia.

When things looked blackest, the Central Committee decided to

[3] She later joined the Bolsheviks and became one of the militant leaders of the U.S.S.R. before ending her days in prison during the purges of 1937.

launch a recruiting drive on behalf of the Party. The idea was a good one; anyone who joined us now, at a time when it was more likely that a Communist would be hanged or shot by the Whites than rewarded with a government job, had some claim to be regarded as sincere. The Party committee mobilized all the members of our cell for the campaign. It was the first occasion on which I spoke at a big open meeting.

The meeting was held in a movie theater. I was terrified when I was told to go in front of the curtain and face an auditorium thick with faces peering through a cloud of tobacco smoke. I tried to work up the necessary self-confidence by putting my hands in my pockets. The Red Army was then everywhere in retreat, and I compared it to a coil which will spring out farther the more it is compressed. I spoke hotly of our fight for victory. The applause that greeted my well-meaning efforts was rather mild at first, but my nervousness vanished, and I did pretty well.

We went campaigning everywhere, into factories, offices, hospitals, and schools, saying in substance: "Join a party which offers you neither privileges nor advantages. If we win, we will build a new world; if we lose, we will sell our lives dearly. Who is not with us is against us!" From that small town alone our desperate cause drew 1,500 new recruits. Our military school joined to a man. Our cell increased from 15 to 370 members. Among them were a number of our teachers— former officers of the Imperial Army. This recruiting campaign, conducted throughout Russia, resulted in the formation of a party of hundreds of thousands of fighters pledged to conquer for the Soviets or die. It was the survivors of this heroic period whom Stalin and his henchmen exterminated during the purges of 1937 and 1938.

Hunger, cold, and typhus were raging in the little town. The local authorities tried desperately to keep life going, although sometimes it seemed impossible. Everyone of military age had already been mobilized. The very young and the very old who remained were not getting the solid food necessary for some of the heavy tasks that had to be performed, and they deserted to the country. The public services almost vanished. Our military school was the only organized force capable of emergency action.

Thus we were called upon at all hours of the day and night for special duty. We would be awakened in the bitter cold to fight a fire in a remote section of the town. The fire-fighting equipment had to be dragged to the scene by hand, since there were no horses. At other times the hospitals demanded our services. We could do nothing about the hundreds who were dying for want of medical supplies, but we could go into the forests to get firewood to keep them from freezing to death. For this work we tried to get the help of peasants in the neighborhood. We combined this wet wood from the countryside with the dry wood from abandoned houses which we ourselves pulled down. Sometimes, when a high Red Army officer was killed at the front,

67

we would have to act as honor guard and escort the body from the railroad station to Soviet headquarters, and then to the cemetery. When it was necessary to mobilize the remaining townsfolk capable of work for unloading a train or for other purposes, we would be sent to organize the job. Sometimes after a snowstorm the railroad tracks would become encased in ice, and we would be summoned to chop it away so that traffic could be resumed.

Every day the few remaining horses could be seen laboriously dragging through the streets to the cemetery those who had died the evening before. The bodies were laid out in the cold sunlight, dressed in shirts or covered with ragged sheets—for there was a shortage of linen and of clothes of any sort—and enclosed in long dry-goods boxes, which were the nearest we could come to coffins. There were too many corpses and too few men to bury them. A thaw might come at any moment, and that would mean a recrudescence of epidemics. At times the whole military school was detailed for cemetery duty. We had to dig great ditches a yard deep in the frozen earth and throw into them all these human remains, many of them covered with wounds, yet some retaining in death a curious appearance of purity.

Despite these burdensome extra duties and the misery of an exhausted city, we were of good cheer and slowly but persistently made progress in our studies. We were not only dealing with an imaginary foe on the blackboard. There was nothing academic about our training. So practical was it that a good third of our number never finished the course but were killed in battle in midsemester and buried with a thin show of military honors—if there happened to be place and time for such things. Thanks to the excellence of our organization and our conscientious discipline, we formed a sort of shock detachment that was pushed into every critical point of the battle front. Such was the destiny all over Soviet Russia of the *Koursanti,* or student officers.

In the midst of Civil War, Trotsky found time to establish more than sixty of these Red military schools all over Russia—five times as many as had existed under the Czar. He knew the value of the *Koursanti* as the best-trained and bravest of the Red forces. It was the *Koursanti* who counterattacked against the British-made tanks of General Yudenich outside of Leningrad and halted the panicky retreat of the Red troops. They faced the tanks with their naked bayonets, and, while hundreds of them fell, others succeeded in prying off the thin armor, like lids from preserve jars, and reaching the occupants within. It was the *Koursanti* who were thrown into the breach when Wrangel tried to pierce the region of Kakhovka in the southern Ukraine. In two weeks of some of the bitterest fighting in the war, the *Koursanti* halted Wrangel and broke the back of his offensive. And in 1921 it was the *Koursanti* again who were sent across the ice in the face of the fortress artillery of Kronshtadt to break through at all costs.

We in Gomel had our share in these trials. In little more than six months at school, our studies were interrupted four times by a call to battle.

10. Lessons under Fire

OUT OF OUR four hundred students, a hundred and fifty were killed in "front practice." Of the thirty men in my own class, fifteen were to perish within four months. The first duty assigned to us was particularly disagreeable. A unit of mobile troops on the south front had mutinied and refused to go into the line. We were sent for. We surrounded and fought the mutineers, arrested the commanding officer and the commissar, and disarmed the disaffected soldiers. Both leaders, together with several others, were immediately court-martialed and shot. We returned from this expedition embittered and without much glory but having learned something essential to the soldier's duty.

On another occasion the city was suddenly threatened by a Polish offensive. General Haller was approaching from the direction of Rechitza, a place lying on the Dnieper some thirty miles west of Gomel. We were called upon to bar his way, but this time we remained in the lines without any major fighting. The Poles were merely trying to sound out our resistance.

My chief memory of this incident is a grueling walk in the dawn along a bitterly cold, empty road fringed here and there with birch trees. I had been dispatched to the neighboring unit to establish contact on our left flank. I was so worn out that I almost slept as I marched. I was quite alone and trudged on mechanically, trying to find the first outposts, which lay hidden in the snow.

We stayed only ten days at the front and went back to our studies with only a few casualties. The whole Polish drive petered out after a few days.

In December, 1919, our school joined with Yakir's troops in an attack on Kiev. This was a more serious matter. Yakir sought to take advantage of General Denikin's reverses on the Moscow front by launching a surprise attack on Kiev, which was weakly fortified. He asked the command of the Twelfth Army for support, and our school was sent to help him. By a forceful thrust we succeeded in piercing the enemy line and reaching the center of the city.

In Krestchatik—Kiev's main street—we had our first experience of street fighting. Here the Civil Guard and hostile residents helped the Whites by firing at us from windows and throwing down anything that came to hand—stones, scrap iron, bits of furniture, boiling water. After furious fighting we were forced to retire.

A day or two later some White armored cars appeared suddenly in a village we were occupying ten miles west of Kiev. Rifle fire broke out from every direction. We retreated toward a small river, hoping to

69

cross it on the ice, but it was too thin and gave way. It was only with the greatest difficulty that we managed to scramble ashore. My legs were stiff, and, though I had been in the water only a few minutes, my greatcoat of cheap felt was frozen so hard that I could snap off pieces of it. One of my legs had been struck twice by bullets. I now began to feel the weakening effect of a long diet lacking in fats. Though my wounds were slight enough in themselves, they would not heal, and I had to go to the hospital and thus paid a visit to a corner of hell which Dante seems not to have explored. Never shall I forget the operating room where, in an oppressive stench of rotting flesh, rows of groaning men had been laid out naked on tables, presenting every imaginable variety of torn bodies and gangrenous wounds. The hospital was crowded, badly equipped, and in want of the most elementary essentials, such as anesthetics and disinfectants. The sight of so much black and green putrescence made me so sick that I forgot my own pains.

In March, 1920, by a sudden push, Haller was able to occupy Rechitza and cross the Dnieper. Gomel was just about to fall into the enemy's hands when Trotsky arrived. Already the convoys of refugees, their miserable carts piled high with boxes, papers, and odds and ends of possessions, were dragging their way along the roads leading to Novozybkov; already the local authorities were on the move in their cars. There was nothing left at the station but the last armored train, a sort of forlorn hope, commanded by a fanatical ex-sailor. Then everything suddenly changed, and the tide began to turn. Trotsky's arrival meant that the city would not be abandoned, and he brought with him teams of disciplined organizers, agitators, and technicians, all animated by a spirit of dauntless determination.

The Fifty-eighth Division, reduced to a few hundred bayonets, had just retreated before the oncoming Poles. In the morning, through the windows of our classroom, we had watched these relics of the Red front straggle through the town. Were these the Red troops? We could scarcely believe our eyes.

An hour later our commander confirmed it.

"Our lines have collapsed," he told the assembled school. "The Poles are moving up, but they have not yet learned the true state of our defenses. There are a few hours left to close the breach. We are the only force that can do it." He turned to the officers. "Prepare your companies to leave tonight. We shall counterattack at dawn."

We made preparations to leave. Guns were examined and cartridge pockets filled. The rolling kitchens were wheeled out. Supplies were loaded on the two-wheel military carts. In a few hours we had done what was necessary and were lined up in company formation awaiting the order to march. The president of the Gomel Soviet bade us farewell. He spoke a few grave words. It was our duty to hold the line. The republic had entrusted to us this part of the front for the next few days.

Our commissar replied briefly on behalf of the students. The school would hold the line or die, but it would not surrender. Looking at all the calm, unmoved faces of the *Koursanti*, it was difficult to believe that these speeches were regarded as more than formal expressions of sentiment. But the fighting of the next week showed how seriously they were taken. Many of those who listened so calmly were never to return from this battle.

Our school arrived at dawn to take up a position at a bridgehead on the Dnieper outside Rechitza. The battle that ensued was the bitterest in my experience. We delivered a bayonet charge against a number of marksmen hidden behind a hedge and sending a deadly fire into our ranks.

One of the old officers, Kasimir Tomachevsky, a Pole by birth, led us with the utmost coolness, revolver in hand. He was the first through the hedge. This commander was a man of few words. Unlike certain of the other czarist officers, he made no attempt to curry favor among the *Koursanti* by mouthing Bolshevik phrases, and we eyed him with some suspicion. Silently, and a little unexpectedly, he had joined the Communists during our recruiting drive. But he had remained the same severe, somewhat aloof officer. Several months later he left the school for service at the front and was killed in the fighting near Warsaw at the head of his unit.

We followed Tomachevsky, and the hand-to-hand fighting began. This was war in its most primitive form. Our military theory and months of study converged in a single bayonet thrust. We fought desperately, but the favorable position and superior number of the enemy finally told. Our left flank was bogged down in the swamp, as we were forced back under fire.

We were charging this time against veterans of the Great War, who had gained their experience on the fields of France and Germany. It was our worst battle. Out of 240 of us, more than 100 were left on the ground. But, although our attack failed, General Haller's troops never got through. They had sworn to reach Moscow!—so we were told. Those of us who survived the day said: "They shan't even see Gomel!" And they didn't.

Commissar Blukhov's brother, one of our students, was killed. I brought the sad news to Michael Ivanovich. His gray face set slowly in a hard expression. He could find nothing but the most simple remark to make: "Good-by, little brother. You gave your life for the Revolution." Then after a moment of silence he went on discussing the operations.

Trotsky paid a visit to the front lines. He made us a speech. We were lifted by that energy which he carried wherever a critical situation arose. The situation, catastrophic but twenty-four hours earlier, had improved since his coming as though by a miracle. In fact, the only miraculous thing was the perfectly natural effect of organization and the resolute courage of men.

71

For a long time I kept among my papers a copy of Trotsky's speech —dedicated by him to our school and its heroic battle for Gomel— typed out in his train. Those few pages of grayish paper were a very precious memento of the school to me. Did the G.P.U., I wonder, find them twenty years later among my things in Moscow and file them as evidence of my complicity in the "Trotskyist treason" of 1919? Why not? Every standard of good sense has gone down in chaos with the mingled truths of history. . . .

Among the men dressed in black leather who accompanied the inspirer of the Red Army on his visit to our trenches was a young fellow of whom I took no particular notice. Trotsky's son, later known as Leon Sedov, at that time about fifteen years old, was with his father. I have already mentioned meeting him in Paris, when, like me, he was exiled and a Soviet outlaw. Together, a few days before his sudden death, we lived over again this earlier memory of the battle for Gomel.

Our six months' course, which had been lengthened to eight by fighting intervals, drew to an end. Raw peasant youths who had never handled a gun became in that short time passable soldiers with at least the rudiments of military tactics. Boys who could scarcely use a pencil when they joined the class now knew the mysteries of the compass and the science of geometry. They could take apart, put together, and operate a machine gun, and they understood the elements of artillery and fortification. They had learned something also of military organization and the command of men.

They made good officers in spite of the extraordinary conditions of our student life—or perhaps because of them. This unprecedented undertaking of Trotsky's succeeded. Our class passed its examinations, and we were assigned to commissions at the front.

Thus the day came when I left the school in a new rig, my chest adorned with crossed straps, and a short officer's sword, symbol of military authority, knocking against my knee.

Carrying a small khaki suitcase, I got into a railroad car reserved for soldiers—one of those "comfortable" cars of the fourth or fifth class, where the occupants lived in common and slept on straw around a small iron stove. I was en route for Mogilev's command, where I would be at the disposal of headquarters for the Sixteenth Army, at that time commanded by Kork.[1]

It so happened that our train stopped at a crowded little station. It was a sunny morning in the month of May. I got out to buy some food from the peasant girls who were running up and down the platform offering—at ridiculously high prices—milk, potato cakes cooked in sunflower oil, and even little rolls with golden crusts, baked in some village that had escaped the horrors of famine. I bumped against a nurse dressed in white and wearing a starched cap. We stopped dead,

[1] One of the eight generals shot with Tukhachevsky on June 11, 1937.

both of us. It was my mother. We were overcome by emotion and amazement. She was hurrying back to her hospital train, which was almost due to start in the opposite direction. We had time only for a few words and a quick embrace. Our meeting was all the happier for being unplanned and unexpected.

11. We Did Not Take Warsaw

AT ARMY HEADQUARTERS I was received with a certain amount of suspicion. Of what use could a young officer be after a six months' training at the hands of a lot of political agitators? The old officers here, recruited as specialists by Trotsky, asked this question of themselves. They put me through an examination from which I emerged satisfactorily. Another was given me by the political commissar. This was more difficult, but he had to admit that, though my Marxist knowledge might be imperfect, there was no doubt of the excellence of my intentions.

I was assigned to a reserve regiment of infantry commanded by a former noncommissioned officer named Illyuchenko. He had to take on two of us new graduates. He was a large, ruddy-faced man with a great sense of his own importance. In order to stress his rank he always went from his lodgings to both army and regimental headquarters in a carriage, though the distance was no more than a few hundred yards. He took a spiteful pleasure in appointing me to the command of the last platoon of the last company, which was the ninth of the third battalion. Since the regiment was "dressed" in order of size, I found myself in charge of the smallest men on parade, though I happened to be one of the tallest officers there. Still, if I had had nothing more than the purely decorative aspect of my command to worry me, I could have been happy enough.

In the spring of 1920, Soviet Russia offered peace to Poland, but Pilsudski was bent on conquering the area "from sea to sea"—all that was Polish before the partition of 1772, when Poland had included East Prussia, Lithuania, White Russia, half of Latvia, and a part of the Ukraine. On April 22 he signed a military agreement with Petlura, leader of the Ukrainian Nationalists. This agreement virtually made Petlura's government a puppet in the hands of the Poles. Within two weeks Pilsudski had defeated two Red armies and entered Kiev.

Tukhachevsky, the commander of the western front, was now planning a large-scale offensive against Warsaw. This was to be undertaken because Lenin wished, by this move, to begin the march of the Red Army on Europe. Trotsky, on the other hand, raised objections against advancing beyond the ethnographic border and crushing the Polish state by force of arms.

We knew nothing of what was happening in the higher ranks, but we felt that the Sixteenth Army was destined to a feverish existence. Every day it had to absorb new draftees—that is to say, a mob of men drawn from the woods, fields, and villages. These must be transformed without delay into soldiers worthy of the mighty army whose duty it was to liberate Poland from capitalism and Germany from the Treaty of Versailles. A large number of these men were deserters who had been lying hidden for months, perhaps years, in the forests and villages of Russia. Several extraordinary commissions were appointed to round them up systematically, condemning them to "conditional execution" [1] where necessary, granting amnesties where advisable, organizing drives into the heavily wooded countryside. Some of these deserters had remained concealed since the beginning of the World War and had never been in the Red Army at all. Our regiment received several hundred of them. Their arrival was the occasion of my next promotion. The commander put me in charge of a company that would have delighted the heart of a stage director wanting to introduce some comedy into a tragic play.

The new recruits were an incredible mixture of men—wretched scarecrows of all ages, filthy dirty, dressed in every variety of peasant costume, uniform only in their raggedness. They loafed along, hung about with sacks and packages, scratching themselves, swearing softly, suspicious, hostile, intimidated, and apparently determined to do as little in the soldiering line as possible.

I approached them in my brand-new uniform, and never had the smart little sword knocking against my knee seemed so laughably ineffective. For a moment I despaired of ever being able to do anything with such material. Then I told them to fall in. Once drawn up on parade, any men cease to be merely a mob. The degree of discipline involved is small, but it is enough. One feels immediately that one is in control. I made them a short speech.

"Comrades, from this moment you are soldiers of the Red Army. You must be keen and you must obey! I am your commander. I need noncommissioned officers. I rely on you to supply them. Those who have ever had a stripe in the old Army, say so!"

No one answered. There was a general air of mistrust.

"Former noncommissioned officers, two paces forward, march!"

Not a movement. I felt my fledgling authority seriously compromised. I walked down the line, carefully looking at the faces, ques-

[1] An alarming phrase which saved them from actual punishment at the moment, but meant that they would be shot if they did it again.

tioning the few who seemed to be a little more military than their fellows.

"Here, you! You've been a sergeant, I can see that. Step forward!"

The man stepped forward. I put him through one or two evolutions, noting his responses. He shammed awkwardness, pretending not to understand the words of command. I ordered him back to the ranks and tried one or two others with as little success. Two hundred pairs of eyes watched the scene, missing nothing. Finally I addressed an undersized recruit clothed in pitiful rags. He won the day for me by admitting that he had been a sergeant. In fact, he knew all about the Army, he said.

"You are promoted," I announced. "And now, jump to it!"

He helped me to find others, and himself became one of my most valued collaborators, energetic and resourceful.

The next thing I had to do was to get my men clean and exchange their rags for uniforms. I arranged for the public baths to be reserved for them on the following Wednesday afternoon. I drew a supply of underclothing, soap, disinfectants, and even new shoes and leggings. But new tunics and trousers would not be available until Thursday. I couldn't let them come out of the baths and put on their awful lice-ridden clothes. Well, war is war! When they had finished washing, their rags were nowhere to be found, and they had to be content with undershirts and underpants.

Thus clad, they fell in behind me in fours, and we marched through the town singing and trying to look as soldierly as possible—two hundred poor devils in shirts and underpants headed by a Red officer very much on his dignity, but secretly rather embarrassed. Mogilev, formerly the headquarters of the Imperial Army, had a tradition of smartness which it did everything to sustain. Our march caused general stupefaction, and the worst of it was that my men, as is usual on such occasions, sang well together but knew only the songs popular before the Revolution, and had a weakness for the least refined! As these songs had the merit of evoking the soldierly spirit of pre-Revolutionary days, it would have been foolish to check them. So here were my two hundred trouserless soldiers yelling at the top of their voices words which would have "made a Comanche blush"! A crowd of approving urchins swarmed around us.

In addition to directing their military training, it was my duty to imbue my ex-deserters with the rudiments of civil, political, and moral knowledge. I borrowed my arguments from Krylenko's *Political Manual,* a little book bound in red which the Party Bureau of Propaganda issued to all young officers. It was a sort of encyclopedia of bolshevism, written with spirit and passion.[2]

[2] At the end of the First World War, the Old Bolshevik, Nikolai Krylenko, was a sublieutenant at the front, when suddenly he found himself appointed by Lenin and Trotsky commander in chief of the Russian armies faced with the duty of

I did my best to deliver a number of lectures. It happened that one of my colleagues, a shrewd old captain who was usually drunk when he was not on parade, came in while I was delivering one. He looked at me with a grin on his face.

"Rather heavy going, isn't it?" he remarked somewhat tactlessly.

"Not at all," I replied. "You hit on an awkward moment, that's all. . . ."

There were a good many awkward moments. My men had a way of listening to me in silence, lost in a sort of gloomy boredom, resigning themselves to my eloquence as they might to a prolonged drizzle of rain.

I made friends with a Communist officer, a former sailor of Tartar origin, who had been a member of the Party since 1918. We agreed to share lodgings. He was a phlegmatic fellow, good-tempered and slow of speech, who gave me the feeling that he could be relied upon in any circumstances. On taking up my quarters with him, I was surprised to discover that he was living with two young women—little more than girls—and that all three slept in the same bed. The sounds of laughter at night made it clear that they were on most excellent terms.

"I picked them up on a retreat," said the sailor, as though that explanation was quite adequate. "They had lost everything. I gave them food, and they sort of clung to me. What was I to do? I couldn't very well kick them into the street."

The situation became complicated when his wife arrived, a militant Party member, who had been on an assignment in the Far East. He was very fond of her and had great respect for her character, saying she had "made a man of him" and taught him the real meaning of the Revolution. She was small and serious, with close-cropped hair, and she went about in a man's cap and tunic with a brief case under her arm—a typical example of the female agitator so common at the time.

Nothing dramatic happened; the whole business was settled in the most peaceable fashion. The two waifs took to sleeping together on the floor in one corner of the room, surrendering to the official wife any claim they might have to the conjugal bed. Although it was so many years ago, I can still picture the little group gathered together of an evening and hear the two girls, one slim and fine-featured, the other

breaking down the resistance of the former General Staff. Later, he became attorney general of the republic, and finally People's Commissar for Justice, a post which he occupied until 1937.

Every summer Krylenko went mountain climbing, and he carried Stalin's bust to the top of the highest peak of the Pamirs. But that did not save him. Holder of several Soviet decorations for conducting a number of the most publicized of the political trials, he disappeared in 1937. His successor referred to him in the columns of *Pravda* as "a miserable traitor."

76

plump and fresh-complexioned, whispering together. At the time I viewed the situation with mixed emotions. Brought up as I was on Dickens rather than Maupassant, I regarded love as something secret and dreamlike. I had not foreseen what would happen to it in times of civil war, with all the terrible simplification of human needs that such times bring.

My orderly at this time was a young soldier of about seventeen called Prosorovsky. He was a bright lad with a leaning to the arts. I have forgotten now why he left me, but I know that some years later, in one of the smartest streets of Moscow, I met a young man with dark rings round his eyes, dressed with elegance, who shook me very effusively by the hand. It turned out to be Prosorovsky. He was studying the art of the cinema and was on the way to establishing a reputation. He had already won recognition with two films, *Bella* and *Princess Mary*, in which he had realized for the screen, in slightly Byronic vein, some of the inventions of Lermontov. A few years later I met him again in the Caucasus, where he was living with his wife in one of the G.P.U. sanatoria. So far as I could make out, he had made a double career, being at once artist and agent of the secret police. In November, 1935, at a small watering place in the Caucasus, we ran across each other for the last time. He was still going around with a number of secret-service men. Within a few months of this meeting I heard that he had committed suicide. Spy mania had already become rampant all over the country. Prosorovsky's name was Polish; nothing was known of him before his war record. It seems to me not unlikely that he was given a revolver with the words: "Do it yourself; it makes less trouble all round, and your relatives won't suffer so much."

Commissar Blukhov, the snub-nosed ex-member of the Pavlotsi, had rejoined our regiment. A conversation which we had at this time was to be a determining factor of my future, little as I knew it then. We had just read the news that Raskolnikov, in command of the Red fleet, had appeared before Enzeli, a small Persian port on the Caspian. He had delivered an ultimatum to the authorities, seized two old Russian gunboats stranded there, and landed a detachment of men, who, according to *Pravda*, "were received with popular acclaim." Commissar Blukhov and I looked at each other, moved by the same tremendous idea. We were about to liberate Persia! To start the Socialist Revolution in Asia! At our approach all the oppressed peoples of the East would rise!

I may not be able to revive the naïveté of our optimism, but I can give a pretty true version of our thought process. How, we asked ourselves, were the great imperialist powers to be fought? How could the peoples of the East be aroused? And we answered the question by deciding to learn oriental languages, disguise ourselves as merchants, penetrate into the heart of Afghanistan and India, and there prepare the national revolution. Fantastic as it may seem for one minor officer lost in the middle of a great war, this idea took sufficient possession of me, as you will see, to change the direction of my life.

A day came when the troops were solemnly assembled on parade, and the officers commanding the various units read to their men the orders issued by Tukhachevsky as commander in chief on the western front, and by Kork, the Sixteenth Army commander. Tukhachevsky concluded with an inspiring battle cry: "Forward, to Vilna, Minsk, and Warsaw!" Kork reinforced it with another: "For the liberation of the workers and peasants of Poland—forward, the Sixteenth Army!"

Our orders were countersigned by the political commissars of the front—Unschlicht and Smilga.[3]

In the battle of Warsaw our armies were led by brilliant commanders, original, daring, and with substantial victories behind them. Tukhachevsky, the commander in chief, who came from the Czar's guard, had risen rapidly in the Red Army and assisted Trotsky in its organization. Trotsky has written that the young strategist "displayed extraordinary talents." In his *Memoirs,* Marshal Pilsudski, Tukhachevsky's adversary in this campaign, wrote: "His fine quality of leadership stamps him forever as a general with daring ideas and the gift of putting them into vigorous execution."

At this time Josef Pilsudski was assisted by General Weygand, the head of a French military mission in Poland. Pilsudski could not have asked for a better adviser. Weygand was to play an important role in his success.

Pilsudski had transferred a large part of his army to the south of the Ukraine in order to wipe out Budyenny's cavalry. He calculated that he would be able to defeat Budyenny in ample time to reinforce the army about Warsaw before Tukhachevsky could launch an offensive. But on July 4 the Red armies of the western front began to move. The Polish front crumbled under the strong attack of superior numbers, and the Red Army surged through Vilna, Minsk, Grodno, and Ossovetz. We advanced so rapidly that our supply trains were sometimes as many as seventy or eighty miles in the rear. The opening offensive was crowned with success and pushed forward with such enthusiasm that the reserves rushed in without awaiting orders—a breach of discipline which merrily confused the operation.

The enemy avoided an engagement. The population of the regions we occupied remained hostile. It became increasingly difficult to get supplies. At times our artillery was without ammunition. Our trains stayed at Vilna; our armies were stretched out like loose strings along the roads leading to Warsaw. It was fairly obvious that our communications were in danger of being cut. Meanwhile French artillery manned by French officers were being massed before Warsaw.

[3] Both were well-known Bolshevik leaders; later they disappeared during the years of the purge.

Tukhachevsky advised Moscow to stop the offensive on the line of Brest-Litovsk, to reorganize the lengthened armies, to bring up reserves and supplies. It was wise strategy, but Lenin wanted to take the risk. He hoped that the conquest of Warsaw would break the Polish resistance and open the way for the Red Army to the fields of Europe to meet the mounting German revolution. And indeed Warsaw seemed already in our grasp; we were only thirteen miles away. Pilsudski has related his impressions of our approach. "This unceasing, wormlike advance of a huge enemy horde," he wrote in his *Memoirs*, "which went on for weeks, with spasmodic interruptions here and there, gave us the impression of something irresistible rolling up like terrible thunderclouds that brooked no opposition."

At this moment Weygand unleashed a lightning bolt against the stretched-out Red troops. He threw his army against our left flank in the direction of Brest.

Tukhachevsky now counted on the army of Budyenny, who had Stalin at his side as commissar, to come to the defense of his open flank. Had this been done, the battle of Warsaw might have had a different end. But instead of moving north to aid Tukhachevsky, these forces continued west in the direction of Lwów. Pilsudski and Weygand were left free to launch their counteroffensive.

Why did Budyenny's cavalry fail to guard Tukhachevsky's flank? The answer to this question gives a clue to many things. Stalin and Voroshilov were political commissars of Budyenny's army, which received the orders of Tukhachevsky, its commander in chief, to move north and advance on Lublin. Stalin was not disposed to take orders from Tukhachevsky. He decided that an independent advance of the army with which he was connected, and a capture of Lwów, would add to his prestige.

It is not difficult to understand Stalin's psychology at this time. Overshadowed by more brilliant men, he wanted to gain a place in the limelight. He had long been resenting the secondary role he was playing in military affairs. He resented the leadership of Trotsky and of newcomers like Tukhachevsky. For these reasons he attempted to maneuver without reference to the main army and win a little victory of his own. The result was two defeats and the loss of the war.

The Polish attack on our left flank began on August 16. Few of the Red troops were in a position to offer resistance. Even after this fact and the strategy of the enemy were clear to all, Stalin instructed Budyenny to continue his attempt to capture Lwów. Thus while in the south Budyenny's army was futilely kicking away at the Lwów defenses, the Poles sliced their way through to Brest-Litovsk and Bialystok. Meanwhile a second attack reinforced by French artillery was developing against our front.

Thus from two sides Pilsudski hammered at our forces. The barrage laid down by the French artillery outside Warsaw was of truly World

War character. Our men fell by the thousands. The push of our army was broken beneath the walls of Warsaw. Tukhachevsky ordered a retreat. We poured homeward along the way we had come, fearful of finding our communications cut.

What is there to say of the retreat? I saw this campaign much as Stendhal's soldier saw the Battle of Waterloo, in terms of forced marches first toward Warsaw and then away from it.

The return was complete chaos. Transports, staffs, hospitals, fighting troops—all the various arms became involved in inextricable confusion. The artillery, by this time quite useless, was merely in the way. There were times when the retreat became a rout. Direction was lost. We marched on, ignorant of where we were going—especially when darkness fell—through forests and marshes, hungry and exhausted, stopping at every crossroads to await instructions. Everywhere was a babel of shouted orders. Most of the time, as far as I remember, I was half asleep with fatigue. Suddenly, in some clearing of a nightmare wood, our torches would reveal a confusion of cars and wagons that had lost their way. . . . The countryside was bleak and devastated.

At Bobruisk, headquarters of a proposed "Red Army of Poland" which never quite got born, I happened to see three young Polish Communist officers bending over a map. I was to meet them the next winter at the General Staff College, where we all took a course. One of them, Loganovsky, subsequently entered the diplomatic service and was secretary of the embassy at Warsaw, where he directed the underground work of the G.P.U. and the Comintern, and later at Vienna. I saw him again in 1924 on my way through Austria. Clever, and gifted with great strength of character, he was made privy to the most secret and dangerous activities of the Soviets abroad. For some years he was a member of the G.P.U. staff, and then he became assistant to Rosengolz, the People's Commissar of Foreign Trade. The day after Tukhachevsky's execution he was arrested. Some fools or crooks swore to the fact that for twenty years he had been a Polish spy—he, who for ages had snapped his fingers in the face of the Polish police. That was his end.

During the march on Warsaw I had occasion to meet a strapping, bearded commissar, notable for his coolness in moments of danger. This was Radin, chief political commissar of our division. In 1936 I saw his name in a list of persons designated as "enemies of the people" and denounced by the press at the same time as Zinoviev.

Our armies lost nearly all the territory taken from the Poles. Stalin had the satisfaction of seeing his old rivals, Trotsky and Tukhachevsky, defeated. In the Party discussions that followed Stalin was held responsible for the blunder. He never forgave Trotsky and Tukhachevsky for his own failure. The seeds of the Red Army purge which Stalin carried out in 1937 were planted in those early conflicts between himself and our best military commanders. As long as they lived Stalin knew that he could not completely obliterate the history of his own shabby role.

On October 12 Soviet Russia and Poland concluded a peace. The war in the west had come to an end.

12. *The War College of the Red Star*

AT THE END of the Polish campaign the Military Council of the Sixteenth Army detailed me to take a course at the newly constituted General Staff College for senior officers. I set off for Moscow. Instead of the small lieutenant's rectangle which I had worn when I joined the Army, I now displayed on my sleeve the four golden squares of the commander of a regiment.

In the autumn of 1920 Moscow looked like a city that had lost 50 per cent of its population. The place was half vacant, miserably poor, and melancholy. Scarcely a single automobile was to be seen. A few cab drivers still managed to pick up a living; their droshkys were drawn by wretched old bony horses with stomachs swelled out from hunger. Life at the fronts had been feverish and active; in Moscow it dozed its days away in dismal lassitude. Only in the Kremlin Lenin, the brain of the Revolution, worked on without pause, with a calm courage which at times seemed to express fanatical ardor, at others despair.

The Red Square was still bare, badly paved, and dominated, from behind the Kremlin walls, by a number of chapel towers which have since been swept away. It was reached through the Iberian Gate, now vanished, where stood a small shrine, now also gone, containing a miraculous icon of the Virgin Mary.

But the real center of Moscow, completely strange to us army Communists, was the Soukharevka Market. It was always filled with people, though its trade was wholly illicit. Men in gray uniforms strolled about. Crowds of women, some of them in from the country with little bags of farm produce to barter at famine rates, others from the city offering for sale the heterogeneous relics of former prosperity, surged through the square. They were happy if they could display two scraps of sugar on a saucer, and I confess that my feelings were more often moved by such pathetic traffic than by the forced sale of ancient coral necklaces or of complete leather-bound sets of the works of Verbitskaya—that once famous female novelist who had drawn tears from a generation of young ladies.

The district commander gave me a card entitling me to stay at one of the hotels reserved for military use. It was situated near Nikitskie Vorota (the Nikita Gates), on one of the circular boulevards. The tiny square, adorned today by a crude monument to the famous Darwinian scholar Timiriazev, was, at that time, extremely picturesque. The whole central part was filled with crumbled masonry—the remains of houses destroyed by artillery fire during the October insurrection. A huge building near by, situated right on the boulevard, had been burned, and nothing but a tall skeleton framework was now left. At the far end of the square the house fronts still bore the scars of street fighting.

My hotel was a two-story affair, never a first-class establishment. But the chief thing, after all, was to have a roof over me and a table at which to work for my entrance examinations. My room seemed more suitable for a transient love affair than for military study. That, however, did not prevent my setting to with zeal. I could not get any of the books I needed from the nationalized bookshops, and I was reduced to pursuing my courses in geometry, algebra, and history with the help of multigraphed lecture notes. However, I was glad to be able to have even these.

The district commander supplied me with both physical and spiritual sustenance. The physical part of his bounty consisted of bread—black, of course, but there was enough of it. My food cards assured me a supply of thin soup and a ration of potted meat amounting to about one-fifth of what my appetite demanded. His spiritual fare took the form of theater tickets.

I found in the next room to mine an old schoolmate from the early days in the Gomel high school, who now offered to guide me around the town. He was an odd creature. I remembered him as red-haired, pock-marked, cross-eyed, slightly lame, and always sponging and driving petty bargains. When I met him again in the capital of the Revolution, he had become quite a fashion plate, never going out without a starched collar, swallowtails, and carefully pressed trousers. This made him a strange sight on the street, grotesquely out of harmony with the severe appearance of the city. He minced along, cane in hand, among men dressed in military boots and leather jackets with revolvers in their belts, and women drawing behind them small sleds containing their rations. He would pass unnoticing a flock of vultures tearing the frozen entrails of a dead horse lying on the pavement.

His name was Shura Richevich, and he was secretary to the Arts Commission. I suppose he was still driving petty bargains, but on a scale more in keeping with his changed position. Since money was practically worthless, artists and entertainers exhibited their talents in exchange for bags of flour, sugar, potatoes, or butter, and it was Shura's duty to arrange these exchanges. Although it was illegal, he managed to exact a commission in foodstuffs for himself, and so he was fairly well supplied. He had a supply of saccharine and used to make sweetened "tea" for me—a rare luxury, an infusion of dried carrots. He even pushed his attentiveness so far as to initiate me into the mysteries of musical comedy.

Our harassed divisions were returning from Poland, pursuing General Wrangel's White Army, or driving the *atamans* out of the Ukraine. In the Kremlin Lenin was meditating the problems caused by the famine. Trotsky in his war train was rushing from one battle front to another. Each night the Cheka was dispatching to the next world its regular installment of counterrevolutionaries, or of innocent wretches arrested as such. But still the theaters played the *Cloches de Corneville* and the *Geisha*, in which pirouetting midshipmen in glittering caps, unknown to any navy of the world, went three by three into tea gardens to be welcomed by little geisha girls bowing and fluttering their fans, and everyone spoke or sang completely idiotic sentiments that had nothing on earth to do with anything. In the cold theaters the actors' breath would vaporize ludicrously in contrast with the cherry-blossom scenery of summer in Japan. But this worried no one in the audience, neither the soldiers fresh from yesterday's battle and ready in a few hours to set off for tomorrow's, nor the girls beside them. At first I clapped like the rest, finding the geishas charming and not giving a thought to the disemboweled horses that had marked the retreat along the roads of Poland, or the ambulances floundering in swamps. But these shows began to get on my nerves after a while. The examination was near, and the last few days I buckled down to work till late in the night.

The General Staff College was situated in Vosdvizhenka Street, a building formerly belonging to the Hunt Club. The great staircase was flanked by two stuffed bears holding card trays. The walls were adorned with antlers and other trophies of the chase. It was in this unsuitable setting that the chief of the college, old General Snessarev, once an explorer of Central Asia, received us with meticulous politeness, and I imagine with considerable curiosity.

The college could not boast one instructor of good revolutionary color. The whole staff consisted of former generals of the Imperial Army, famous, decorated, and sometimes well known even outside their own profession—men such as the two Novitsky brothers; Neznamov, author of several major works on strategy; Verkhovsky, who had been war minister in the Provisional Government of 1917; Martynov, who had fought against the Japanese in 1905; Velichko, who had been responsible for the fortification of Port Arthur and was known as "Kuropatkin's evil genius"; Gatovsky, expert in cavalry tactics; and Svetchin, the brilliant theorist and historian of the art of war.

In the whirlwind of extraordinary and sometimes incomprehensible events, most of these men accepted their lot with the calm philosophy of professional soldiers. They were ready to work for any government which seemed able to rebuild collapsed Russia. Many of them were skeptical about the ability of the Soviets to do this, but they responded loyally to the appeal of Lenin and Trotsky to build a new army and were willing to give what help they could. Their work went a long way toward giving the Red Army its new General Staff and qualified senior officers. It is only fair to give them credit for what they did.

The pupils of the college provided an unusual contrast to the teaching staff. All had fought in the Civil War, all knew well what war meant, and more than one had gained distinction as tacticians and strategists, although completely ignorant of the theoretical side of the job. Some of them were nearly illiterate, but that did not alter the fact that they had done wonders as cavalry leaders, defeating generals no less expert in the theories of Clausewitz and Napoleon than their present teachers.

These far-from-ordinary pupils were ready at a moment's notice to leave their school benches and go to the aid of the republic on the battlefield. The professors, too, would have their educational duties interrupted, perhaps three times a year, when they were given short terms in the prisons of the Cheka as hostages or suspects. Each time the internal situation took a turn for the worse, they would find themselves behind bars. Such interludes came as no surprise to them; it was even said they kept satchels packed in readiness.

Life at the War College was reduced to the roughest essentials. No one should imagine that we enjoyed anything like the comfort of students at Oxford or the Sorbonne. The Republic looked after our interests, it is true; but what it gave was at once much and little— board, lodging, and uniform. This latter, at least, was not without a certain magnificence. Many of us wore striking cavalry breeches of dark red, decorated with yellow braid. Great, strapping, sunburned fellows strode from lecture room to lecture room in all the bravery of green and blue bemedaled tunics and high boots, carrying textbooks and loaves of black bread under their arms. Together with the former generals of the Imperial Army who were their teachers, they would wait patiently in the corridors for the daily distribution of rations. By two o'clock, as a rule, we had eaten the day's issue of bread and drunk our soup (it was not the kind one remembers with pleasure!); from then on there was nothing we could do to stave off the pangs of hunger but drink unsweetened tea.

The Levada Hotel, where we lived, was not heated. In our rooms, next to the useless radiators which evoked memories of a vanished civilization, we constructed a kind of stove made out of bricks, with a chimney sticking out of the window. These bricks we collected from the ruined houses that littered the most frequented thoroughfare of Moscow. Each man made his stove in the style, shape, and size that suited his taste. But that done, the question arose, what could we burn in these variegated contraptions? When the cold was intense we used anything we could find, even valuable furniture. My friend Pomerantsev invented a method of procuring fuel which deserves commemoration. The manager of the hotel kept a close eye, as was right, on the general maintenance of the place. One day, examining Pomerantsev's room, he got the surprise of his life. He discovered that the furniture, the floor, and, in places, the walls, had a merely superficial solidity. The bureaus had only false fronts, the shelves and backboards had vanished from the insides of the wardrobes, squares had been removed from the floor where the furniture covered it, whole sections of paneling had been taken from behind pictures. And this was not the only room where such things had happened. Everything had become two-dimensional, as in a movie studio.

The college was divided into three classes—junior, middle, and senior—and there were in all about six hundred student officers. We worked in groups of five, each under the direction of its own tutor, an officer of the Czarist General Staff.

One day I read with pleasant surprise the announcement of a special faculty of oriental languages to be conducted jointly by our War College and the Foreign Office for students from both institutions. My old dream of serving the Revolution in the East, although I had almost given it up as hopeless, still lived. I applied for courses in the oriental faculty, in addition to my military work, was admitted, and tackled three languages simultaneously—Persian, Hindustani, and Arabic.

The head of the oriental faculty was a czarist naval officer of noble family, a brilliant linguist named Dolivo-Dobrovolsky. Vladimir Zuckerman, director of a department in the Foreign Office, was the political commissar. (He was shot on December 16, 1937, at the same time as Ambassador Leon Karakhan and Yenukidze, secretary of the Central Executive Committee.)

For the opening of the faculty of oriental languages we gathered in the great hall of the General Staff College—about seventy students, half officers, half civilians from the Foreign Office. We were addressed by the head of the college himself, General Snessarev, who had passed a good many of his forty years' service in the Orient as an officer of the Czarist General Staff. The old man, in a vigorous speech, gave us his idea of the purpose of our work in the border countries of the Middle East where the Russian and British empires meet.

"I am myself," he said, "going to conduct the course in the military geography of Sinkiang, Tibet, Pamir, northwest India, Baluchistan, Afghanistan, and Persia, whose roads I have traversed many times on foot. I have lived with the native people in these countries and spoken their languages. I shall tell you all you need to know about these countries as Soviet General Staff officers and diplomats.

"Since the time of Peter the Great the Russian Empire has been irresistibly drawn toward warm seas and the Indian Ocean. And Russian expansion in this area has always been blocked by the British.

"In 1716 Peter the Great sent armies under Prince Cherkasky in an unsuccessful march against Bokhara and Khiva, intending to open the way to India. Emperor Paul I, for the purpose of seizing India from the British, in January, 1801, ordered the *Ataman* Orlov and his Don Cossacks to cross the border and attack the British. For more than a month, in the middle of a severe winter, twenty-five thousand of these troops were on the march with their artillery. They had already crossed the Volga and advanced deep into the steppes of Turkestan when Paul was assassinated in St. Petersburg as the result of a plot of which the British ambassador to the Russian Imperial Court was one of the instigators. The expedition was immediately recalled by the new emperor, Alexander.

"In the nineteenth century the road to the Persian Gulf and Arabian Sea, those outlets on the warm waters which are indispensable to us, were blocked again and continually by the British. We waged several wars in Persia and Central Asia in the effort to open it, but the British Empire stood always behind our adversaries. The victories of the Russian armies in the Balkans were also always frustrated by British intrigue.

"You will ask me why I am telling you all this when the Soviet Revolution has cast out imperialism. It is true that the Soviet Republic has no imperialistic aims. The purpose of the Soviet Revolution on a world scale is to liberate oppressed peoples everywhere from imperialistic exploitation, and especially to bring freedom to the peoples of the Orient. But the most serious obstacle in the way of this liberation is still British imperialism. If we want to give the peoples of Asia their freedom, we have to break the power of British imperialism. It is still our deadliest enemy and theirs. Here is your task, and you will need to learn from us and our experiences how to deal with it.

"I personally went over the entrance examinations of every one of you, and I am certain that in you we selected, on the one hand, those student officers who are most capable of assuming the double work of study in the General Staff College and in the faculty of oriental languages. On the other hand, we have made the same careful selection from the Foreign Office. The General Staff, together with the Commissariat of Foreign Affairs, will from now on watch your work and decide how you can best be used in the coming years."

As he spoke I looked around at my fellow students. Most of them were young and tough and seemed sure of their own force. General Snessarev's prediction about them proved in large measure accurate. This double course of study required intense work, and a few had to drop out in order to keep up with their courses in the General Staff College, but each year a fresh group was chosen in the same way.

Many of those who sat listening with me were to rise high as Soviet diplomats and military leaders. Five years later, when I was leaving

Persia after serving for two years as consul general, more than three-quarters of the Soviet diplomatic and consular corps in the Near and Middle East were graduates of the faculty of oriental languages. And this remained true in these countries, and also in China and Japan, for many years after. Among those present at the inaugural address were the future Ambassador Pastukhov to Persia; Slavutsky to Japan; the Minister Khakimov to Arabia; and the Consuls General Sharmanov, Sarkissbekov, Khassis, Batmanov, Zaslavsky, Mamaev, Melzer, Levitsky and others; also a score of young generals who later served as advisers to Chiang Kai-shek or as military attachés in the countries of Asia. Most of them were purged in 1937-38. Of the tragic deaths of Khassis and Blumkin I have written elsewhere in this book.

While at the college I made the acquaintance of several commanders of the Red Army, who had come there as students. There was Gay, formerly a public-school teacher, gifted cavalry general, rival of Budyenny, fresh from Germany, where he had been interned upon retreating to the German frontier after the battle of Warsaw; ex-tailor Shchadenko, later chief of the political department of the Red Army; and the former Cossack privates Zotov and Matuzenko, lieutenants of Budyenny, whose bravery was celebrated by Babel in his *Red Cavalry* and whose fame at this time far eclipsed that of Voroshilov, Budyenny's commissar.

Another colleague of mine was Bubenetz, son of poor peasants and former private of the Czarist Army, made famous as the aide of Chapayev in Furmanov's novel about that commander. Chapayev himself passed some months in our college but departed for the front to begin his heroic fight against the White Cossacks of the Urals, where he was killed. Then there was the ex-sailor Dybenko, a genial giant renowned for the part he had played, as leader of the Baltic fleet, in the events of 1917-18. He had just contracted a much talked-of marriage with Alexandra Kollontay, well-known Bolshevik leader. (Dybenko disappeared in 1938.) With him were his companions Uritsky and Fedko. In 1938 Fedko was appointed vice-commissar for defense after the mysterious disappearance of several former holders of that risky post. Before that he had shared with Marshal Blukher the command of the special Far East Army. (He also soon disappeared.) Uritsky, brother of the president of the Petrograd Cheka assassinated in 1918, became chief of the intelligence service of the Red Army. (He disappeared in 1937.) Another of our students, Stetsky, turning to Party work, was appointed director of agitation and propaganda of the Central Committee and became, in 1935-37, the principal spokesman of the Party. (He was later arrested.)

Another friend of mine, Ventzov, was military attaché in France at the time of the signing of the Franco-Soviet Pact. (He was later recalled and has disappeared.) Another, Alksnis, was political commissar of a division at the time when he came to the college, and he later became Chief of the Soviet Air Force—an exceptionally brilliant career. He too has vanished. Most of the students of the General Staff College were to rise high in military and Soviet ranks, and most of them were to perish in the purges.

Three remarkable men sat for their entrance examinations at the same time as I—Savitsky, a member of the War Council of the Ukraine; Kovtiukh, the hero of the Kuban campaign so powerfully described by Serafimovich in his *Torrent of Steel;* and Dimitri Schmidt, perhaps the most remarkable of the three, whom I met for the first time on the steps of the college in September, 1920. His energetic face was clean-shaven, but he wore a fringe of beard under his chin in a former naval fashion, which, in our day, was made popular by Radek. He had thin lips and hot, piercing eyes. He wore a fur cap set at the rakish angle one associates with the cavalry of the south. His uniform consisted of a blue blouse adorned with two medals of the Red Banner —a very rare distinction in those days, even among the seasoned warriors of the Red Army—a Caucasian belt hung with metal ornaments, and a great curved saber in a patterned scabbard. He limped from a wound not yet completely healed and supported himself on a stick. He moved slowly and obviously felt out of his element in the capital. He was the typical commander of the revolutionary years: intense, an incarnation of energy, stretched taut like a strung bow.

Like many others, Schmidt had emerged from an obscure harried village existence to first rank in the revolutionary army. He was the son of a poor Jewish shoemaker. If it had not been for the Revolution, Schmidt, like so many others, might have followed in his father's footsteps, expending his vast energy in minor pranks and village enterprises. The social upheaval had unlocked stores of talent that no one dreamed lay hidden among the masses, enabling thousands of them to apply their gifts of leadership on a national scale.

At the beginning of the Revolution, Schmidt joined the Navy. When half of the Russian fleet was frozen in the Baltic, and the other half scuttled in the Black Sea in 1918 to keep it from the Germans, the sailors turned into soldiers. Schmidt became a leader of one of the shock troops that harassed and tormented the White armies. Naked to the waist, their chests crisscrossed with cartridge belts, they marched upright into the heaviest gunfire, hurling insults and hand grenades at the enemy. They became the terror of the Whites, who nicknamed them the "Red Devils." Schmidt finally decided to turn his sailor-soldiers into cavalrymen, and his detachment became famous throughout the Ukraine. Young peasants flocked to join him, and before long he was at the head of a regiment and soon of a brigade.

At his entrance examination Schmidt was quite hopeless and rather touching. A board of three old generals put the candidates through their paces. The senior member of the board was Martynov, famous for his book on the Manchurian campaign of 1905 and for his addic-

© Acme

Fedor Raskolnikov, former commander in chief of the Red Fleet, later ambassador—recalled in 1938 from Sophia and fled to France; died at the Côte d'Azure in 1939.

© Wide World

Christian Rakovsky, former premier of Soviet Ukraine, later ambassador to Great Britain and France—condemned to twenty years in prison.

Nikolai Krylenko, the first generalissimo of the Russian Army after the Revolution, later attorney general of the Republic and commissar of justice—accused as a traitor and disappeared in 1936.

General Dimitri Schmidt, former Red cavalry commander in Ukraine, twice decorated for bravery, accused of terroristic plot, shot in 1936.

tion to philosophy. The generals carried their tasks through without enthusiasm, putting to these commanders of brigades and armies of the Civil War exactly the same questions they would have put in the old days to young officers who had merely studied their textbooks. We were told, for instance, to write an essay on "the importance of the war with Sweden and the victories of Peter the Great to the newly established Russian Empire." Luckily our examiners were indulgent!

At the *viva voce* interview which followed, Schmidt was the first to be called up. Dragging his wounded leg, his great saber clanking at his side, he advanced slowly to the table.

"What are the dates of Peter II?" he was asked.

"I have no idea," he replied dryly, speaking with a slight Ukrainian accent which gave the words a quite unintentional note of insolence.

"Name the wars of Catherine II."

Schmidt gave a sidelong smile as though he knew the examiners were mocking him.

"I don't know them."

The three generals glanced at one another. Martynov pressed his point.

"Tell us when the Empress Catherine reigned and the date of her death."

"I was not born at the time, and she doesn't interest me."

He tapped nervously with his stick on the floor. Martynov burst out:

"This is intolerable, gentlemen! I refuse to put any further questions to this candidate."

Here the political commissar of the college intervened, and this brilliant cavalry leader was admitted to the War College on condition that he would promise to pass the examination later on when he would have leisure to study history—which, of course, meant never. But Schmidt did put in two years of hard work at the college.

We became great friends. He was absolutely brave, very simple and very determined, given to mockery and to spells of almost childish sentimentality. His character had been formed in the hard school of war, and he kept that mold to his dying day.

We used to spend long evenings together in his little room on Tverskaya. His wife, Valentina, young, charming, and, like him, steeped in the events of the time, served us with tea and the unforgettable objects which, in those days, did duty for cakes. Dimitri Schmidt would recount the epic careers of the men who had fought with him, sailors turned cavalry soldiers to fight the Germans, the Whites, the Petlurians, and those warrior bands which did not know exactly whom they were for.

In 1919, when Kamenets Podolsk, near the Austrian border, was surrounded by marauding guerrillas, Schmidt broke through to the town and determined to defend it at all costs. He billed the walls with manifestoes couched in mingled phrases of threat and encouragement. They were signed: "Comrade Schmidt." He held the town. While at Kamenets Podolsk, he received a visit by airplane from Tibor Szamuely, People's Commissar for War in Soviet Hungary, who was on his way to Moscow. This may have had something to do with his subsequent appointment to the command of a body of shock troops assembled to force the Polish and Rumanian frontiers and come to the support of the Hungarian Soviets. The idea of fighting his way into Hungary did not dismay him at all. I am certain that he has always regretted the order was never given. Red Budapest fell too quickly.

Once in the Ukraine, accompanied by only two aides, Schmidt rode into the camp of the *atamans* commanding a band in arms against him. They were too surprised to seize him; and, when negotiating proved difficult, Schmidt as a last resort, by the light of a bivouac fire, shot down his opponents with his revolver. His brigade had meanwhile surrounded the camp, and the band surrendered.

Some years after he left the War College, and while he was stationed at Minsk, I heard of Schmidt again. One of the senior officers had insulted his wife. Schmidt sent him tumbling downstairs with a bullet in his guts. But the man was not killed, and the affair was hushed up.

During the period 1925-27, Schmidt joined the Opposition. He had just arrived in Moscow at the time of the Party Congress of 1927, when the expulsion of the Trotskyist Opposition was announced. He was clad, as usual, in the uniform of his division—a great black Caucasian riding cloak, a jangling belt with silver ornaments, a great curved saber, and a fur cap cocked over one ear. Coming out of the Kremlin in company with Radek, he ran into Stalin. Political feeling was violent just then. Stalin was in full career as a conspirator within the Party, but had not yet brought the Party to heel.

Schmidt went up to him and, half joking, half serious, began to blackguard him as only an old soldier can—that is, in terms which have to be heard to be believed. As he finished he made a gesture as though to draw his saber and told the secretary general that one day he'd lop his ears off.

Stalin listened without saying a word, but his face was dead white and his lips were drawn in a tight line. For the time being he chose to treat Schmidt's insult as beneath his notice, but there can be little doubt that he remembered it ten years later in the purges of 1937. Dimitri Schmidt was the first Red Army officer to disappear. He was accused of terrorism. No confession was forced from him. He was executed without trial.

When I think of Schmidt I think also of a great bear of a fellow with curly hair, sharp eyes, and the voice of a fanatic. This was Savitsky, a member of the War Council of the Ukrainian Republic. He had a wife and child whom he adored. Everything he did, he did with his whole heart. We lived together on the same floor for three years, helped each other pull home through the streets little sledges piled with flour and potatoes—rations for the student generals of the Red Army. We hunted together for old bricks among the rubbish covering the spot where now rises the magnificent Central Telegraph Office. We shared the same chair when warming ourselves before the stove, bent together over the same tactical problems and the same French grammar. Once he brought me triumphantly a Ukrainian translation of Bukharin's and Preobrajensky's *A.B.C. of Communism*. As an old member of the Ukrainian Socialist Left, he was filled with pride at having got this book published in the language of his native country. Ten years later I met Savitsky again in Moscow, where, as a lieutenant general, he was acting as chief of the Red Army personnel. Together we paid a visit to one of the former estates of the Czar's family at Archangelskoe, where he had organized a rest house for senior army officers. Still burly, still eager, he had changed scarcely at all. He showed me over the spacious palace, richly furnished with *objets d'art,* suffused with the reflected light of peaceful snowfields. Our generals came here occasionally for a few days to enjoy a little rest . . . until the years of the Great Purge, when Stalin sent nine-tenths of them, including Savitsky, to an eternal rest.

13. *The College in Time of Crisis*

IN 1920 the Party cell in the college—about 80 per cent of the students—took part in the violent discussion on trade unions. What form should the unions take in a Soviet state? Lenin, Zinoviev, and Rudzutak favored subordinating the unions to the Party and yet allowing them a measure of independence in defending the interests of the workers. Trotsky wanted to see the unions more and more incorporated into the state. A workers' state, he said, required no special organs for safeguarding the economic interests of the workers. Bukharin tried to make a compromise. The Workers' Opposition, on the other hand, believed that the trade unions should control production themselves without state interference.

The controversy was extremely sharp. Spokesmen from each of the four groups came to the War College to speak. We heard Alexandra Kollontay defend the Workers' Opposition in a fiery speech. She was still a beautiful woman and came in a costume of black with a high collar up to her chin, combining sophisticated simplicity with natural elegance. She was pale, showed no sign of age, and was in full possession of those great gifts that made her an orator of the first rank. Even in those days she was denouncing the prevalence of bureaucrats in the Party and demanding a return to working-class democracy. She impressed us deeply, and we listened attentively. The fact that she was married to one of our students, Dybenko, made us receive her with especial warmth.[1]

When the moment for voting came, out of 300 Communist students of the college, 13 sided with Trotsky, 32 with Lenin, and 250 with Kollontay and the Workers' Opposition. The Party thus expressed itself fraternally and in complete freedom. Although the authority of Trotsky, our commander in chief, was very great in my eyes, I thought he was mistaken in this matter and voted for Lenin's platform.

During the period of my studies at the War College I saw Lenin several times at Party and Soviet congresses. He was in a very real sense the heart as well as the brain of the Revolution. A stocky man, suggesting force as well as intellect, he was simple and utterly without affectation. Like any other delegate, he could be found sitting on the tribune steps scribbling his notes. When it was his turn to speak he would mount the tribune and wait, slightly annoyed, for the applause to subside. To the delegates, often enough confused by the profound and pretentious "dialectics" of such brilliant debaters as Zinoviev, Kamenev, Bukharin, and Radek, the appearance of Lenin on the platform was a relief. Now we would hear a simple, direct talk giving us the facts of the case, and everything would be clear. The audience leaned over expectantly as Lenin began. When he got well started, they relaxed. Now they knew where they were going.

I stood near the platform when he made his last speech, toward the end of 1922 at a conference of the Moscow Province. He spoke as if under a great strain, but it did not occur to any of us that it was his last speech. We took it for granted that Lenin would always be there to explain things in his short and simple sentences. But we did see beads of sweat forming on his brow while he talked, as though thought itself or speech were a vast effort, and he was breathing heavily, as though in pain, when he sat down. Other leaders of the Bolsheviks were respected and admired, but Lenin was loved. Nothing was further from him than the thirst for personal power.

While Stalin was intriguing, as he was even then, to get the threads of power into his grasp, Lenin was working to build up an informed and able citizenry "so that any cook could run the state." During Lenin's time, opposition outside the Party was not yet as rigorously

[1] Alexandra Kollontay later became the first woman ambassador of the Soviets, serving in Mexico and Scandinavia. For some unaccountable reason she accepts the dictatorship and remains in Stalin's good graces.

denied expression as it was later "in the paramount interests of the Revolution," and the internal functioning of the Party was democratic. Discussion on all questions was free and open. There was no fear yet of reprisals if one happened to turn out on the wrong side of the fence.

In this connection I want to recall an incident of 1919, the most critical year of the Civil War. I was sent to Simferopol with a Red Army mission to contact the staff of Dybenko, who was in command there. One of our mission, Maxim Stern, was a member of the Central Committee of the Menshevik Party of the Ukraine. Although Simferopol was then under siege, and the White armies of Denikin, holding the eastern Crimea, were only fifty miles away, Stern requested the use of the Simferopol city theater for the purpose of a political meeting. The theater was turned over to him gratis, and he held a mass meeting composed of citizens and Red Army soldiers, to whom he expounded with eloquence the Menshevik point of view and his basic opposition to the principle of one-party dictatorship. In the manner of a town-hall meeting, and with the same good feeling, I myself and two other Bolsheviks replied to him. The discussion was hot, but never passed the bounds of courtesy. Although he had all the time he wanted and said everything he had to say without mincing words, the audience voted by a large majority for our resolution.

I recount this incident because there is a tendency now among critics of Stalin's murderously repressive regime to imagine that something similar dates back to Lenin and the first years of the Revolution.

Trotsky was very different from Lenin, and in some respects complemented him. Where Lenin was informal and genial, Trotsky was formal and a little aloof. I remember when he first addressed us at the Staff College. The meeting had been announced for eight o'clock, and generally, in the traditional Russian fashion, a meeting so announced would start at nine or ten. Trotsky, however, ascended the platform exactly as the clock was striking the hour. That was his custom, and it had a strong effect upon the minds of us Russians. His entrance was imposing, in spite of his plain uniform, devoid of insignia. His pointed beard, flashing eyes, and broad shoulders gave an impression of angular force which, when he spoke, was emphasized by his sharp gestures and metallic voice.

Unlike Lenin, who rarely resorted to passionate diatribes, Trotsky hurled a fiery flow of invective against Churchill, Poincaré, and the other imperialists who were trying to strangle the Revolution by blockade. His bitter irony and assurance carried us with him. But as soon as he had finished he left the hall. There was no personal contact in the corridors. This aloofness, I believe, may partly explain Trotsky's inability as well as his unwillingness to build a large personal following among the rank and file of the Party. Against the intrigues of Party leaders, which were soon to multiply, Trotsky fought only with the weapons he knew how to use: his pen and his oratory. And even these weapons he took up only when it was too late. With his proud passivity and quixotism it was easy for the unscrupulous and relentless Stalin, a master of intrigue, to outmaneuver Trotsky.

Early in 1921 an internal crisis, far more serious than any threat from outside, began to imperil the existence of the regime. The chief cause was a shortage of food, owing to the using up of reserves during the Civil War and to the policy pursued toward the peasants, a policy which can be summed up in the single word—requisitions.

The peasants, having received nothing for the crops that had been seized, were unwilling to sow more. Until they could get the necessary manufactured articles from the cities again, they saw no reason to part with their grain. The cities, on the other hand, were facing famine, and production had fallen almost to zero. Hungry and exhausted, the workers were losing faith in the promises of the Bolsheviks. Rumors of discontent and even of revolt were spreading. It seemed as if the working masses had shot their bolt and were ready to give up. The atmosphere in Moscow was very tense. Unrest was reported in certain regiments of the Army.

The student body was suddenly ordered not to leave the college building day or night. We were armed with rifles and slept in lecture rooms transformed for the purpose into dormitories. Karl Radek came, on behalf of the Central Committee, to explain the situation to us. We assembled in a state of tension. Radek, thin, pale-eyed, ugly, sagacious, spoke for three hours to an absorbed audience. His Polish accent was frightful, but at the end of the first fifteen minutes we had forgotten it, so completely did his earnestness and the frank seriousness of his explanation impress us.

He made no effort to conceal from us the extreme danger of the situation. Kalinin, president of the Republic, had been greeted in the factories with catcalls, boos, and cries of "Give us bread—we've had enough talk!" Bolts and wrenches had been thrown at him.

"The Party," Radek said, "is the politically conscious vanguard of the working class. We are now at a point where the workers, at the end of their endurance, refuse any longer to follow a vanguard which leads them to battle and sacrifice. . . . Ought we to yield to the clamors of workingmen who have reached the limit of their patience but who do not understand their true interests as we do? Their state of mind is at present frankly reactionary. But the Party has decided that we must *not* yield, that we must impose our will to victory on our exhausted and dispirited followers. Grave events are impending. You must be ready. . . ." This meant that we might have to use our weapons not against the counterrevolution, but against the masses who had been the support of the Party.

This is precisely what happened at Kronshtadt a week or two later—in March, 1921. The Tenth Party Congress was in session in Moscow when the garrison and civil population of that chief fortress of the

Republic, on which depended the safety of Petrograd, rose in insurrection. A mortal danger thus threatened the Republic just when food was most scarce and the spirit at its lowest. The reactionary forces hoped to take advantage of this revolt to renew the Civil War.

In a period of general exhaustion this might prove an entering wedge for counterrevolution. All the elements fighting against the Bolsheviks took on new heart. The monarchists, the followers of Wrangel and Denikin, dispatched emissaries to Kronshtadt to win over the rebels. The Bolsheviks feared that, starting under the Soviet flag and with the slogan "Soviets without Communists," Kronshtadt might soon become a starting point for the complete defeat of the Revolution and the restoration of capitalism in Russia. Had the situation been less pressing, there might have been time to debate the issue with the rebels. But the gravity of the moment compelled the Soviet Government to act at once.

The Party Congress decided in these circumstances to put an end to internal discussions. The Workers' Opposition was solemnly dissolved. Dissident groups and movements were forbidden. The delegates departed by hundreds to fight on the Kronshtadt front. One whole class of our college was sent to strengthen the command, among them Generals Dybenko, Fedko, and Uritsky—three inseparable friends— Stetsky, Borshchevsky, Turchan, and others. The Supreme War Council appointed Tukhachevsky to conduct the operations. Trotsky hurried to the scene. One artillery unit of the Petrograd garrison declared itself for the Kronshtadt rebels, and a number of its leaders were shot.

After two weeks my friends returned from Kronshtadt, victorious but bitter. Turchan had been in command of the first brigade of *Koursanti*—students from the military schools—to attack across the ice. They started from the north shore of the Gulf of Finland, only to be broken by the artillery fire of the rebel forts. Whole masses of ice had cracked up under fire, and hundreds of the cadets had been drowned in the freezing water. The second attack was hurried forward for fear of a thaw, which would permit the insurgents to use the fleet. This time the assaulting troops—two divisions led by Dybenko and Fedko—started from the south shore. The men made their way across the lumpy ice, wearing white smocks for camouflage. The orders were to reach Kronshtadt at any cost. The guns of the fortress killed great numbers of the attacking troops and halted them for a moment within a short distance of the island. Two soldiers, mad with fear, took shelter in a barge frozen into the ice and refused to return to the line. Borshchevsky, commanding this regiment, shot them both under the eyes of his troops, whom he then led forward. Suffering heavy losses, the Soviet troops succeeded in reaching the fortress. Fighting continued in the streets for one or two hours. By nightfall the revolt was suppressed. The loyal Communists held prisoner by the rebels were released. I give these details as they were told me, in a saddened mood, by my friends.

In the midst of my studies a letter arrived informing me that my mother, as a result of two attacks of typhus, was lying miserably sick in a field hospital. I asked for leave of absence to visit her. A few months previously in a small wayside station I had parted from a woman of forty, upright and in the full vigor of life; I found her thin, wrinkled, bent, and looking twenty years older than she was. Her hair had been cropped, and her mind was wandering. I took her back to live with me. Each day we shared my pound of bread, my handful of buckwheat, and two or three herrings. This modest ration little by little restored her strength.

Although our situation was no worse than that of the majority of Muscovites, my mother was bitter. She stormed against the Bolsheviks and accused me of having thrown my life away for an evil cause.

"You've fought for two years—there's been all that death and suffering—what for?" she asked. "So that commissars in the Kremlin can wallow in luxury while we starve."

It was no use telling her that our leaders lived quite modestly. I kept my patience for a long time, but one day I answered back:

"You sweated at twenty-five kopecks a day for the Countess Brannitzkaya. We are suffering, too, but in order to build a new society with abundance and happiness for all."

One of my student friends, whom I will call Tarikov, had a wife, a pretty little Tartar woman named Khadidje, who took an interest in our unhappy household. She was charming. She came in once in the midst of an argument like this. I was despondent. I had been unable to convince my own mother of the justice of our cause. Perhaps I was to blame. Tarikov's wife came up to me where I sat with my head in my hands. She bent over me.

"Don't be sad, Alexander. What can you do? The old people are all alike."

Suddenly she kissed me and ran out.

As I watched her little figure disappear through the door, I forgot my sorrow over my mother. I was deeply perturbed. We met often again after that and took long walks in the streets of the city. I was soon passionately in love, and so apparently was Khadidje. Although we lived in neighboring rooms, she would write me long letters, the style of which at first surprised and then enchanted me, such magic lay in her language. I found out later that this eloquence was made of metaphors borrowed from the lyric poetry of the Orient.

The ardor of her epistolary style, however, did not prevent Khadidje from remaining attached to her husband, a Tartar like herself, who probably understood her a great deal better than I did. She was evasive when I urged her to leave him. He learned of our meetings and asked me for an explanation. The standards of the Party were strict in such matters, but they were based upon an attitude of wide tolerance. We felt that we should reach a rational solution in a friendly way. I have an impression that most of the militants of my generation were scrupulous in affairs of the heart and careful always to respect the woman's sense of dignity. We agreed, in a calm and friendly discussion, to let Khadidje decide between us.

It was a blow to me when Khadidje chose not to throw in her lot with mine. To make matters worse, I saw, by accident, a correspondence, quite as lyrical as ours, which she was conducting at the same time with another officer. I did not let her know what I had found out, but I felt very bitter. Disillusioned, and quite sure that I knew all that was to be known of the perfidy of the female heart, I decided to take the first opportunity that offered of going to some far-off place.

When spring came, my mother left for the Ukraine to resume her hospital work, and the opportunity I was looking for came soon. On his appointment as Soviet ambassador to Bokhara, Yurenev asked the General Staff to let him have some officers with a knowledge of oriental languages. The General Staff passed the order along to the college, and five students were selected, I among them, to go to Bokhara as military attachés to the Russian mission.

Before the Revolution, the Emirate of Bokhara, in Central Asia, had enjoyed the official status of a Russian protectorate, similar to the Indian principalities of the British Empire. Its feudal organization had been left untouched. In 1917 a Young Bokhara Party had been formed, which drove the Emir from his country and declared its adherence to the Russian Revolution. The leader of this movement, Fayzoulla Khodjaev, was said to be an astute and able man who thought in terms of the future. Bokhara remained independent with a government of its own, and Moscow had an ambassador there, Aprelev. Upon his sudden death, Yurenev was chosen for the post.

The Emir had fled to Afghanistan, whence he was carrying on his fight to regain the throne. The British, worried by the advancing Red wave which had swept to the very edge of India, assisted him. At one point only a ten-mile strip of Afghanistan territory separated Bokhara from India. Detachments of British and Red troops faced each other across this narrow strip. The Soviet Government had sent some troops to help Bokhara, but friction had developed between the native soldiers and the Red Army. Yurenev was taking us along to serve as liaison officers and advisers.

He received us at the old Hotel National, which was being used at that time as a home for high Soviet officials. He was a thick-set little man with a pugnacious face and was dressed in a military tunic.

"We are going to make an effort," he told me, "to establish a real Soviet regime in Bokhara."

Leon Karakhan, assistant to Foreign Commissar Chicherin, signed our diplomatic passports.

14. *The Bolshevik Missson to the Feudal Orient*

IT WAS a curious expedition, rather like those which during the Middle Ages used to be sent to unknown kingdoms. The embassy staff numbered forty-six. We filled a whole train—a hospital train temporarily put at our service, with a first-class coach attached. Apart from the civilian personnel, which included a cook and a number of typists, we took with us a detachment of Red soldiers, a quantity of food, medical supplies, weapons, articles for barter, and some presents. The married members of the mission brought their families.

In normal times the journey would take five days; we were on the road twenty-four. The sun poured down its burning heat on the steppes and wastelands through which we traveled; the stations were in ruins; but it was a gorgeous trip. Men, and sometimes women, lay half-naked on the carriage roofs, reveling in the hot sun. We all felt at the top of our form, conscious that we were on the way to adventure, with a great mission to accomplish, and enjoying meanwhile an unexpected rest cure.

An unknown woman occupied a reserved compartment in our first-class coach. She was said to be the widow of a Bokhara diplomat, and I expected to see a small, Asiatic woman with a dark, suntanned skin. To my surprise I was introduced to a young and beautiful girl of the purist Russian type, who appeared to carry the weight of her sorrow with much lightness of heart. She was, in fact, the widow of the former Soviet ambassador, Aprelev, whose death I have already mentioned. She was going back to Central Asia to escape the Moscow world, to avoid inevitable social triumphs for which she had no heart, and take up a solitary and self-sufficient life. As our journey dragged out she found in us a miniature Moscow world. Most of the men were at her feet. Occasionally she would accept their company as a form of distraction, but would relapse later into a state of discontent with us and with herself. She confided to me one day her desire for solitude. I answered her in something like the following words:

"If you really want to be left alone, I think I can offer you a solution of the problem. So long as you remain unattached, a beautiful and desirable young woman, you are bound to receive the attentions of a lot of young fellows whose lives are thick-set with dangers. I have myself just suffered a profound disappointment, and as a result can regard you with detachment: women do not interest me any more. I offer you a purely nominal marriage. Officially you will be my wife; actually you will be completely unfettered. We shall both consider ourselves entirely unbound by the marriage contract. How does this idea appeal to you?"

Olga Fedorovna laughed gaily as I unfolded the scheme. But when she realized that I was quite serious, she reflected a moment and then said:

"I accept. We shall be married as soon as we get to Bokhara."

We announced the good news to our companions. I responded to the congratulations showered upon me without batting an eye.

On the way to Bokhara our diplomatic train stopped at Tashkent, a city combining occidental modernity with oriental languor. A marvelous sun heightened every color, increasing the delights of perception and quickening the blood in our veins. Yurenev told me to go with him to the headquarters of the commission in charge of Turkestan affairs—a body known as Turkkommissia. To avoid the heat of the day we started early. Our way lay along broad, quiet streets, lined with gardens and made pleasant by the sound of irrigation streams and singing birds. We came to a small, white-painted house, apparently wrapped in slumber, with a simple signboard over the door and a drowsy porter. This was our goal. As the gate stood open and the porter seemed incurious, we entered without ceremony and found ourselves in an outer hall. I pushed open a door, lifted a curtain, and we saw a bare room in which two men were lying asleep on mattresses and cushions spread out on the floor. At our entrance they jumped up.

"What's the matter? Who are you?"

"The Soviet Embassy to Bokhara has arrived. We are looking for the Turkestan Commission."

"That's us."

They spoke no less than the truth. I recognized them from their portraits as they stood half-dressed before us, one a tall fellow with spectacles and curly hair, his strong features set in a round face; the other smaller, with cropped head and a large nose, his upper lip marked with a faint mustache. For both were well-known members of the Central Committee of the Party, and collaborators of Lenin. Indeed, it was because he had vaguely opposed Lenin's policy in the matter of the trade unions that the shorter of the two had been appointed to this distant mission. He was Tomsky, president of the Central Council of Trade Unions, a lithographic worker, one of the oldest members of the Party and president of one of the first Soviets ever founded—at Reval (Tallinn) in 1905.[1] His tall bespectacled colleague was Rudzutak, later to become a member of the Political Bureau.[1]

After we had adjourned to the office (distinguished from this room by maps, telephones, and typewriters), the famous Asiatic green tea was brought in and the Turkkommissia gave us the details of a situation in Bokhara which could not, without exaggeration, be described as bril-

[1] Charged with working against the Party and its leaders, and hunted by the G.P.U., Tomsky committed suicide in 1937. Rudzutak also disappeared in the purge, as noted before.

liant. The military front in this region was constantly shifting, and the Red troops, consisting of widely separated detachments, suffered more from malaria than from the enemy. This malaria was of a peculiarly virulent type, and no one could resist it long. Moreover, the *Basmatchi*, anti-Soviet peasant guerrillas and champions of Mohammedanism, held most of the country, drawing their supplies from Afghanistan, Persia, and India. The Emir of Bokhara had renounced none of his claims. At present he was hiding in the mountains. The peasants, discouraged by armed invasions and requisitions, had left most of the land uncultivated. There was already a shortage of food. There would soon be famine. The Civil War had devastated all the eastern part of Bokhara. The Young Bokhara Party, just renamed Bokhara Communist Party, did not inspire much confidence. It was divided into two groups based on political and blood affiliations—the Khodjaev, led by Fayzoulla Khodjaev, and the Mukhedinov. The Khodjaev seemed to be the more modern in outlook and more inclined to be loyal to us.

As to the work beyond the borders, the Pan-Hindu Revolutionary Committee, created and supported by the Communist International, was agitating with a certain degree of success. A school of Hindu officers was functioning under its protection, training the future leaders of an Indian Red Army designed to carry the revolution into India.

I secured the address of this Pan-Hindu Committee, hoping to learn more about it and incidentally to show off my knowledge of Hindustani. At the address I found an ordinary single-story building with not even a signboard over the door. On the doorstep a bootblack was dreaming away the hours.

"Can you tell me," I asked him, "where the Pan-Hindu Committee has its quarters?"

He could tell me nothing. He was not interested in revolutionary committees and had no special desire to conquer India. In trying to make him understand me I had raised my voice. An angry face with large eyes and a little black beard appeared at a window just above our heads. Its possessor laid a finger to his lips when he saw me and made me a sign to enter by a neighboring door. I obeyed. He came into the hall to meet me.

"This is it. This is the committee. But why the hell are you shouting so loud? The committee doesn't exist officially. The government has promised the English to dissolve it."

Such a promise had indeed been given in response to an ultimatum from Lord Curzon. Despite the great demonstrations in the streets of Moscow and Leningrad against the "insolence of the British imperialists," the Soviet Government had decided on a policy of appeasement. But it had not given up its plans of carrying the revolution to the East, and the Pan-Hindu Committee did little more than take in its signboard, rename its publications, and give its military school a more innocent name. I recall this incident when American political writers solemnly discuss the "dissolution" of the Comintern.

The bearded man introduced himself to me as Tivel, an Orientalist, former secretary to Zinoviev, now president of the Pan-Hindu organization. His two colleagues, sent with him from Moscow, were named Goldberg and Friedland. So much for my hopes of displaying a knowledge of Hindustani! Tivel, with his lusterless skin and coal-black eyes, might in a pinch have passed for a Hindu. He made me at least a present of a Hindustani grammar. (I was to meet him again in Moscow in 1935, where, with Radek, he was at the head of Stalin's private foreign information bureau. Not long after that he was accused of having plotted the death of the dictator and was shot.)

From Tashkent to Bokhara is not over three hundred miles as the crow flies, and a little less than six hundred by train. The train takes you through mountains full of flowers and sunshine—one of the garden spots of the world, were it not ravaged by wars and tyrannies. Bokhara itself is surrounded by medieval walls of clay. Sentinels watch from the towers; others guard the gates. Just outside are spreading orchards, full of apple trees and apricots and thick, luxuriant grass.

The Soviet mission made an impressive entry into the city. Light four-wheeled carriages drawn by thoroughbreds rushed us at full speed, with whips cracking and coachmen shouting, through streets so narrow that the pedestrians had to flatten themselves against the walls to save their lives. It seemed a miracle that we trampled nobody in our furious charge.

The natives wear *khalats,* long and wide varicolored garments like dressing gowns, the women concealing their faces behind thick black veils. No windows open into the narrow alleys. The houses, constructed around interior courtyards, are shut away from the world, with which they communicate through old gateways, sometimes decorated with carvings and never without a knocker for the use of visitors. From these half-sleeping narrow streets, heated like furnaces by the blazing sun, we dashed headlong into the refreshing shade of a vast covered market, a whole darkened city divided into alleys and swarming with humanity and flies and filled with every kind of merchandise.

It was like a scene from the *Arabian Nights.* The shops spilled over onto the footway. One could sit down and drink a cup of coffee, or squat, bargaining, on a carpet among a crowd of Parsees, Hindus, Turks, Uzbeks, Greeks, Chinese, Russians, Jews. All the riches of Asia were here, stuffed in sacks, chests, and gourds, displayed in baskets and trays, or hanging from the ceilings. Wandering peddlers circulated among the crowd vending sweetmeats and cool drinks. The place was a jumbled motley of the secret East. The women, from under their black veils, stared curiously at us. And then, in a flash, our carriage dashed through a gate, and once more the blaze of the deep blue sky was an almost physical weight upon our heads.

At the Soviet Embassy we found our colleagues, on whom even quinine had ceased to have any curative effect. Everyone was down with fever—that savage type of malaria peculiar to Central Asia which kills as often as not, and when it does not kill leaves the victim sucked dry of energy. We found ourselves about to relieve an office full of ghosts.

Olga Fedorovna, my prospective bride, had a good friend, Marusya, in the embassy staff, who greeted her joyfully on the steps. She was a middle-aged woman of determined mien, overflowing with an energy that even malaria could not kill. She decided it was her duty to take care of the young widow. She undertook all the preparations for the marriage, and did so with enthusiasm, quite ignorant of the fact that the ceremony was to be a mere formality. Yurenev lent us his private carriage for the occasion, and it arrived filled with flowers. When we reached the city hall we discovered that we needed another witness besides Marusya. I caught sight in the street of one of my colleagues, our consul in Sinkiang who had traveled with us, and pressed him into service.

Before entering the registration office Olga turned to me with a challenging smile:

"Are you still willing to go through with it? Don't you think we're taking the whole thing too lightly?"

"There's no reason to back out," I answered.

Nothing is simpler than the registration of a marriage. We signed our names, and the witnesses theirs.

"Be happy," said the Soviet functionary, closing his ledger. And that was all.

The four of us repaired to a little Georgian restaurant of the kind that all over eastern Russia enjoys almost a monopoly of serving *shashlik* and sweet and dry wines. The proprietor paid us the usual compliments. He was a fat, smiling Georgian, wearing a purple velvet cap and embroidered slippers.

When darkness fell, we returned to the embassy, and I wished my wife good night before retiring to the terrace where I slept in the open air.

At this point our friend Marusya became upset and indignant. Wasn't she in part responsible for the happiness of this newly married couple? She had worked hard to make everything a success. And now the quiet explanations that we gave her seemed insulting. The whole thing was a sham, was it? We had made a fool of her. We had made fools of everybody. In a burst of disappointed anger she told us we were two idiots and retired to her room.

I spent that night and many others alone upon my terrace underneath the stars.

We set to work to learn the details of the local situation. Bokhara, notwithstanding the two clans of Khodjaev and Mukhedinov, was in form a People's Republic ruled by a Council of Nazirs—who corresponded vaguely to our People's Commissars. The Nazirs were all men of importance and members of the Young Bokhara Party, composed of the younger generation of enlightened merchants, who drew their inspiration from the Young Turks and were dreaming of a national renaissance. The term *Showra* (Soviet) sounded strange in a country possessing neither modern technical equipment, modern industries, nor a working class.

Since the fourteenth century the Khans of Bokhara have been petty despots living secure and independent existences behind the defense provided by their deserts. The last Emir—he still held his court somewhere in the eastern wilds of the country—had waged a long struggle against the revolutionary influences coming from Russia. He had imprisoned members of the Young Bokhara Party and condemned many of them to torture and to death. Fayzoulla Khodjaev had emerged from hiding to place himself at the head of a group of artisans and merchants who had staged an insurrection on the approach of a detachment of the Red Army during the previous September (1920). The Russian artillery had decided the issue.

A local Soviet government was formed and the Young Bokhara Party, renamed the Bokhara Communist Party, given the standing of "sympathizer" in the Communist International. The property of the Emir and of the great nobles was confiscated, but not a finger was laid upon that of the merchants and farmers. A Cheka was installed under the control of two Russian "advisers." It arrested suspects but shot nobody. The new government carried on its work in exactly the same way that governments of Bokhara had for hundreds of years. I would see a Nazir, or minister, squatting on a carpet and dictating decrees to a scribe, who would write them in old Persian characters on a board balanced on his knees. While this was taking place there would be a coming and going of young men with almond-shaped eyes, some of whom had put on leather jerkins and strapped revolvers to their hips without managing to give themselves the slightest suspicion of a martial air. I was told that the Emir had taken his harem with him but left his "male favorites" behind, and that several of these latter, having attached themselves to the officials of the new regime, had in some cases achieved official posts.

The new masters of Bokhara may have needed our assistance, but at heart they regarded us as enemies. The power of the Soviets was still, for them, the power of Russia; and they feared it. We meddled therefore as little as possible in their internal affairs, of which, as a matter of fact, we knew almost nothing. We knew at least that the Bokhara "Communists"—merchants in the daytime—held their party meetings quite incidentally in the evening after business hours. Their feelings were more nationalist than revolutionary, and they really leaned to the conservative Mukhedinov clan. Were it not for the ceaseless energy of our friend Fayzoulla Khodjaev, the pan-Islamic sympathies of the rival Mukhedinov group would long ago have won the day.

Fayzoulla Khodjaev, called "the Lenin of the Uzbeks," was small, wiry, and full of consuming energy, in spite of the malaria which often gave his face a greenish tinge. He enjoyed life and could laugh gaily beneath a crushing load of work. He knew his people, was a great orator and a clever politician, and was much loved. He alone was capable of devising a language in which the little revolution of Bokhara and its big brother of Russia could understand each other. Later he helped the Central Soviet Government reshape the frontier of his country. In the new republic of Uzbekistan he united the Uzbeks of Bokhara with those of the old Russian Turkestan. He became head of this new republic and one of the seven presidents of the U.S.S.R., having equal formal status with Kalinin, the head of the Russian Republic.[2]

I went to see Khodjaev several times. After crossing the inner courtyard of his house, I would enter a huge room absolutely empty and painted white. To reach his office at the opposite end I had to go fifty paces across a carpeted floor. His appearance was sickly, but there was a forceful look in his face, and his eyes were piercing. He wore a simple military tunic, though when he appeared in public he always put on a turban and draped himself in a flashing silk *khalat*.

When I visited his rival, Mukhedinov, an Oriental of the traditional type, I found him squatting on his heels in a dark little room of the Emir's palace, dressed in native robes. To reach him I had to pass under a number of ruined arches flanking a memorial tower, cross gardens which were full of golden pheasants and peacocks, and skirt the barred windows of the former seraglio.

A contingent of Russian troops held the strategic valley of Harm in eastern Bokhara, known as the "valley of death" because of the fevers that haunted it. Ninety per cent of our men fell victims to these fevers. The garrison had to be relieved every two months. Quinine was useless.

As military attaché and liaison officer I had to travel through the length and breadth of the country. The modern settlement of New Bokhara, European in appearance and without much interest, stands about five miles from Old Bokhara. A little nearer is a Jewish city, a sort of Eastern ghetto, where for centuries there has lived a Hebrew type of great racial purity and of a beauty worthy of its Biblical past. I shall never forget the impression made upon me by the women and children I saw in the poverty-stricken alley of this ghetto. Under the Emir's rule the Jews had to wear round their waists, as a sign of servitude, a rope instead of a girdle. After the Revolution, those who could afford it bought belts and sashes and wore them with a proud air.

[2] He was condemned as a fascist spy with Bukharin, Rykov, and others, at the third Moscow trial and was shot in March, 1938.

Shulamites, whose praises old Solomon would have delighted in singing, came to their doors and smiled a welcome to us.

Soon almost the entire new staff of the mission succumbed, in its turn, to malaria. Some days all of us were in bed, and the embassy had to close its doors.

Olga Fedorovna was also taken ill with fever. Our attitude to each other was one of politeness slightly modified by familiarity. I would sometimes go and put a few flowers on her bedside table and inquire after her health, after which I would mount my horse and set off on my round of inspections. I don't know how it was that things began to go wrong between us. But a day came when she reproached me with a lack of attentiveness, though I had been priding myself on handling a delicate situation with great tact. I remember that, on one occasion, after an exchange of sharp words, I hastily withdrew. Riding through the streets, I dug my spurs into my horse's flank and set off at a gallop at the head of my party. I was the only trained rider, and I led them in a mad race, jumping streams and dashing through a number of gardens at top speed. Yurenev was nearly thrown. I made no reply to his curses. Our furious ride continued. My companions all risked their necks. Finally Yurenev got so angry that he drew his pistol and told me to pull up.

"Damn you," he said later, when he had recovered his composure. "If you hadn't obeyed, I swear I'd have shot your horse."

At regular intervals attacks of fever kept me tossing and turning on my bed. I would be visited at such times by my new friend, a sailor from the Red flotilla on the Amu Darya River. That flotilla was an extraordinary collection of old hulks which still continued to play a considerable part in the events of that region. Micha brought with him his wife, a little Russian peasant woman who shared her husband's liking for cognac. I had some bad moments as a result of attempts to check my fever with swigs of Micha's brandy. Olga Fedorovna, from her room below, could hear them drinking, laughing, and singing. She felt offended; I felt snubbed. We had put ourselves in such a position that neither could express such feelings to the other. At last she made up her mind to go back to Russia, and I carried her bag to the carriage —the same carriage that had taken us to our wedding. We exchanged a few last words fraught with a half-hidden sadness.

15.   *From the Afghan Frontier to the Café de Pegasse*

THE SITUATION in eastern Bokhara was growing worse and worse. The *Basmatchi,* partisans of the deposed Emir, were getting out of hand. Reports from that region were vague and contradictory. Soviet agents sent to purchase wheat from the peasants disappeared. It was clear that the local military and civil authorities could not handle the situation. The Soviet consul kept asking to be recalled, reporting that he was seriously ill with malaria. Yurenev appointed me consul general and military resident of eastern Bokhara, and I left immediately for Karshi, the administrative center of the region.

Karshi was a small, half-abandoned town at the foot of the mountains, less than 150 miles from the Afghan frontier. The troops there, consisting of a brigade of Soviet infantry, were decimated with fever. The native Communists divided their time between trading, praying in the mosques, and attending to municipal business. Relations were strained between them and ourselves, they being unwilling to supply us with food, we being driven to requisitions.

"The Red Army must live," I told them. "Don't forget that if we go, the Emir's *Basmatchi* will come and cut all your throats."

My argument, however sound, did not make them let go of their sacks of flour and rice. The town had already been looted twice by bands of *Basmatchi.* A third of the houses were in ruins, their occupants having fled to the mountains or been murdered. It was sad to see the dilapidated shells of houses standing there in the sunlight, surrounded by unguarded vineyards full of plump sweet grapes.

The soldiers led a tiresome life. The *Basmatchi* would make occasional sorties into the town at night. They would raid and loot and be off before the soldiers could appear. The climate was hot and exhausting. Each week we buried a number of men dead of the fever. Our intelligence service kept us badly informed of the movements of the *Basmatchi,* who were in close touch with the English. Several English patrols wandered about among the enemy tribes lying between Afghanistan and the wild mountains of the Pamirs, "the roof of the world," buying food and paying for it with gold and silver.

I stayed at Karshi only about two months, but that was long enough to ruin my health. Fever was not the only trouble. I suffered from chronic ulcers of the foot—a common ailment among Europeans of those subtropical regions. I used to dictate my orders and letters lying in bed, my feet stretched out toward a stove which stood in the middle of the room. I received my visitors in the same posture. My left foot was so covered with sores that I could not wear a boot on it but had to go about with one foot in a Turkish slipper.

A colleague of mine named Khassis from the General Staff College was a little farther north at Fergana, commanding the Red division quartered in this part of Turkestan. He conceived the happy idea of sending us poor exiles in Karshi several barrels of a peculiarly aromatic and health-giving wine. . . . Alas, pledge though it might be of brotherly affection, this wine did not succeed in putting me on my feet.[1]

Though I bore the title of consul, I had practically no consular duties. My actual functions were those of a superior officer commanding the troops in a district under Russian protection. Our troops were fifty miles east, and my only companion was a Lett, brought to this country by a series of fantastic accidents, and now acting as commander of the Bokhara militia—a picturesque agglomeration of turbaned and ragged ruffians, most of whom had been *Basmatchi* in the past or were certain to be in the future. This Lett used to spend his evenings with me on the flat roof of the consulate, a huge house depressingly empty of all furnishings except a few lonely rugs. Many of the neighboring houses had been abandoned. From our roof we looked down upon deserted courtyards and narrow streets in which nothing moved save an occasional jackal prowling for food. We could see the shadows of these animals crouching in the magic brightness of the moon. On these lonely evenings I thought wistfully of my unreal marriage and its colorless ending. My Lettish companion tuned his guitar and tried to relieve our solitude with a romantic song that never varied:

> Everything in life is lived,
> Everything in life is vain.
> Love, longing, betrayal—
> It is all a trifle.

My work was rather irregular. Our officers would come from the front with complaints about rations and requests to be allowed to requisition food from the inhabitants. Native officers of the Bokhara militia would come for advice, or to get me to explain their orders from the Central Command, or to plan their defense and prepare instructions for their troops. At five o'clock a bout of fever would seize me and never leave me till darkness fell. Then I would rise from my couch, quite exhausted.

Nothing broke the monotony of my days except on one occasion a visit from a member of the Mukhedinov family, who, to appease the clan, had been made president of the republic, and Arifov, his minister of defense. They were on their way to meet the *Basmatchi* chiefs,

[1] Khassis, a capable officer, was later sent as consul general of the Soviet Union to Canton. In December, 1927, when the Chinese Government crushed the Canton Communist uprising, Khassis, with four other members of the consular staff, was taken out of the consulate and summarily shot.

ostensibly to patch up one of those peaces which had not even the authority of a truce but allowed an opportunity for a lot of dishonest bargaining and backstairs intrigue. They had broken their journey at the house of a rich merchant of Karshi and were holding a reception for me on the roof of his house.

It was a solemn reception. The master of ceremonies provided a feast of roast mutton and rice, after which a party of Uzbek musicians set their instruments twanging and whining to an accompaniment of thudding tambourines. This music, so different from our own, has an exotic charm. The two government officials had brought with them their "boy favorites," graceful young adolescents of twelve or fifteen who looked odd in uniform. They danced for us, and danced admirably, for they had been trained to the art since infancy. Since the Revolution, Arifov had put these unemployed boys on the government payroll by making them into a band of musicians for his commissariat.

I could not help feeling a little suspicious of allies who traveled with such a ménage. But since I had to show them some courtesy in return, I arranged for a party at the consulate. While it was in progress the President and the Minister of Defense continued to perform their official functions. They would interrupt their drinking of green tea or wine to take out the seals of state from some inner pocket of their *khalats* and, after spitting on them to moisten the ink still adhering, would apply them solemnly to various decrees, rescripts, and judicial decisions. . . . So much for justice in Bokhara!

Because of the sudden cold of the evenings, these two gentlemen borrowed my best uniform greatcoat and my carriage—at that time the only four-wheeled vehicle in eastern Bokhara—and departed after a formal exchange of courtesies, sped on their way by almost lyrical good wishes on my part. I never saw them again, for they deserted to the enemy, uniformed "favorites," guitar players, scribes, and all, including my brand-new greatcoat. The carriage, being of no further use to them after they got to the end of the road system, was returned to me. How right Fayzoulla Khodjaev had been, I thought, to warn us against the Mukhedinov, with their feudal traditions, and advise us to trust only the men whom formerly the Emir had condemned to the bastinado.

Malaria had drained me of all energy. The old military doctor attached to the infantry brigade, who was usually drunk, tried to persuade me to take "a course of vodka." But I preferred to wait for a different sort of treatment. At the end of October, 1921, the General Staff College recalled all its absent students for the new year's course. I handed my affairs over to my secretary and mounted my carriage with a feeling of relief. I took along a considerable fortune, consisting of a sack of white flour, a sack of dried raisins, two silk *khalats,* a gift of the Republic, and a cotton blanket four inches thick. During the journey I had to sleep with one eye open, for all this wealth was a great temptation to marauders.

The Volga District was still suffering from famine. Some instances of cannibalism had been reported. The stopping places were either completely deserted or swarming with poor creatures in the last stages of despair. The American Relief Administration, under Herbert Hoover, was offering a helping hand. I was rather astonished at this. I had understood that the capitalist world wanted nothing better than to see the collapse of Communist Russia. The famine, we felt, was partly a result of their own blockade. The charity of the American Relief Administration suggested that there were some people on the outside whose hearts were still warm—or was it simply capitalist hypocrisy? I could not be sure.

There was a shortage of food in Moscow as well, but that was no new thing there, and rationing was organized. There were fewer deaths: suffering was longer drawn out. The Civil War at last was over, and the situation full of hope, at least for militants of my generation.

Moscow was filthy with an autumn thaw when I got out of the train, laden with all my sacks and still wearing one high cavalry boot and one varicolored Turkish slipper. There were no horses to be seen. I managed to get hold of a sort of coolie with a hand sledge onto which I packed my treasures; then I limped off toward the Hotel Levada. Money was valueless, and I paid my porter with three pounds of flour.

The General Staff College had undergone a Communist *chistka* (cleansing). The Communist Party, which had entered the Civil War with a few hundred thousand members, had at present a couple of million. Now that the chief danger was over, the Party was taking account of its new members. The officially declared purpose of the *chistka* was to weed out adventurers and socially alien elements and those who had joined out of personal interest.

I had experienced such things before, having been present at two *chistkas* in Gomel during the Civil War. After each danger was past and the enemy quelled, the Party would call its members together and ask them what they had done and where they had been during the emergency. From those who had lain hidden, no explanation was accepted: they were quickly detected and deprived of their membership cards.

The first man to be called now before the control commission in our college was Tukhachevsky, who had just then been appointed head of the college. The room was filled with students and with officers of the Moscow garrison. Tukhachevsky already enjoyed a great reputation as a result of his twelve daring attempts to escape from prisoners' camps in Germany during the World War, his loyalty to the Revolution at its most critical moment, his victorious campaign on the Volga, and his offensive in Poland. We all knew that in 1918 he had been one of the first to command Red Army units worthy of the name. He was the first commander of the famous First Iron Division and the victor over Admiral Kolchak.

A young man with a square-cut, energetic face, he took his stand before the judges, dressed in a private's tunic, dignified, unconcerned, with not the least suspicion of pose. The sole decoration he wore was the recently instituted Order of the Red Banner, given only for valor on the field of battle. The simplicity of his appearance pleased us, for we had already had enough of amateurs in resplendent uniforms among our colleagues and in the higher ranks of the Army.

It was in a tone of almost complete detachment and in brief sentences that Tukhachevsky spoke of his past record to an absorbed and silent audience.

". . . Entered the Red Army in 1918; parentage aristocratic; formerly subaltern in the Imperial Guard; captured by the Germans; escaped. While in the Red Army commanded first a division, then an army on the eastern front. By special order of the day of Comrade Trotsky, President of the Revolutionary War Council, was decorated with the Order of the Red Banner for having inflicted a decisive defeat on Kolchak. Was later commander in chief on the western front. Before joining the Communist Party had been a member of no political organization. Since joining the Party had been subjected to no disciplinary action. . . ."

The members of the commission put a few questions which Tukhachevsky answered in the same laconic manner. One or two nods were exchanged, and then the president announced the board's decision: "Michael Tukhachevsky, a member of the Party since 1918, and head of the General Staff College, is declared worthy of his membership."

Tukhachevsky then came down from the platform amid general applause.

The next student to be called was a large-shouldered man with a clean-cut profile, who held his head proudly. This was Jacob Blumkin, who, if only he would give rein to his natural eloquence, could have unfolded one of the most romantic life stories imaginable.

"By birth I am a Jew and a bourgeois. After passing through college I became a professional revolutionary and was formerly a member of the Social Revolutionary Party, left wing. Acting on instructions from the Central Committee of my Party, I killed Count Mirbach, the German ambassador, in July, 1918. I organized and directed clandestine groups in the rear of the White armies in the Ukraine. I was attached to the command of the guerrilla troops and carried out several confidential missions in the course of which I was more than once wounded. As a member of the Central Committee of the Communist Party in Persia, I took part with Kutchuk-Khan in the revolution in that country. . . ."

Blumkin too was declared "worthy of the high distinction of membership in the Party of the Proletariat." [2]

[2] In 1929, for having secretly visited Trotsky at Istanbul and carried a letter to Trotsky's friends in Moscow, Blumkin was shot on Stalin's order without trial. Then for the first time blood was spilled in the internal struggles of the Party.

Iuri Sablin ascended the platform next. He, like Blumkin, was formerly a leader of the Social Revolutionary Party and had been largely responsible for the success in Moscow of the October insurrection. In the Civil War he commanded a division and was wounded twice. He was a man of rare courage. It is worth recalling that there were four former members of the Executive Committee of the Left Social Revolutionary Party among the Communists in our General Staff College—men who only three years before had been fighting against the Soviet Government in the Moscow revolt of 1918.

My colleague Briquet was excluded from the Party, though I jumped up on the platform to speak hotly in his defense. He came of a bourgeois family, and the commission decided that his record of active service left a good deal to be desired. He was "excluded as a careerist." I knew that he had behaved at the front with conspicuous gallantry and that he was a loyal Communist. This unjust decision was ultimately reversed; but until it was, Briquet suffered from a severe sense of shock.

Tukhachevsky was not destined to remain head of the college for long. The government put him in charge of troops sent to suppress a peasant rising in the Tambov District, led by an ex-Social Revolutionary schoolmaster called Antonov. The Army handed over the headship of the college to another senior officer named Hekker, whose acquaintance I made in the following way.

We students had all assembled in the great hall of the college to hear the new chief's inaugural address. I sat down at a table beside a man older than I, rather small, with curly auburn hair, a thin mustache, and delicate hands.

"Too bad Tukhachevsky's going, isn't it?" I said. "I don't suppose the new man's as good, do you?"

"Well, we'll see," he smiled.

A moment later the chairman said, "The head of the college will now address the meeting."

My neighbor rose and walked quietly to the platform.

The amusing nature of this first meeting created a bond between us. Hekker, who always referred to me as "the Benjamin of the college" because I was the youngest student, was more than my senior officer—he was my friend. In later years he became military attaché, first in the Far East and then in Turkey, and afterward chief of protocol on the staff of Voroshilov, the People's Commissar for Defense. He will come into my story later.

During the *chistka*, in defending my colleague Briquet I had made two friends—himself and his young wife. She was at that time pursuing her studies at the main academy of the Party, Sverdlov University or, as it was commonly known, "the Republic of Sverdlovia." A remarkably original republic it was, composed of young enthusiasts drawn from every corner of Russia, who had come here to have their fill of "ideas." The Republic of Sverdlovia took a passionate interest in everything having to do with politics, in Marxist theory, in the events of the day, and in the new poetry. It had its cliques and its crises. Groups of us—officers from the War College and "Sverdlovian" students—used to meet in my room or the Briquets', shivering with cold, to drink the boiling water which we called tea, although not a tea leaf ever got anywhere near it. Dried raisins from Karshi were our only snacks, and, since there was an entire absence of sugar in Moscow, they were a precious dainty.

The room would be full of young men and women sitting cross-legged on the bed, the divan, and the carpet. We would discuss an article of Bukharin's, or a poem, or debate some subject of the day. Once one of the girls flung open the window, though outside it was fifteen degrees below freezing, because she needed air, she said, since the poem she was about to recite demanded as background a sense of space and a murmur of city streets. Then she delivered, in a deep man's voice which made the passers-by stop to listen, verse after verse of Mayakovsky's "Keep to the Left," with its "brazen note of bugles from the barricades."

In the general poverty of those times the War College enjoyed certain advantages which permitted its members to play, to some extent, the part of patrons. Our club became one of the best in Moscow. The most famous actors, the most celebrated poets declaimed before us. Not only did they find us an appreciative audience, but we helped them keep alive by paying them in food instead of money. After an evening dedicated to Art, I used to see some of these famous performers and writers going home in carriages belonging to the college, or dragging out of the entrance hall hand sledges on which were piled generous sacks of provisions. Nejdanova, Sobinov, Petrov, the leading singers from the Moscow Opera; Mordkin, the famous ballet master; Tretiakov, Asseev, Mayakovsky, best known of contemporary poets, would shower their talents on us and receive in exchange rice and barley, sugar, herrings, and even butter.

Meyerhold would sometimes entertain us in his theater. That amazing producer had just put on Mayakovsky's *Mystery-Bouffe,* part epic, part tragedy, and part satire, the scene of which is set half in heaven and half on earth. It was Mayakovsky at his best, handled by Meyerhold at his most brilliant, and I wonder whether the audience of those days, made up of soldiers, students, workmen, and intellectuals of the Revolution, starving perhaps but rich in hope, was not the best that those two men of genius could have found anywhere.

We would sit in our overcoats, for the theater was unheated, and watch them perform. Meyerhold, thin as a rake, his head bare and his hair flying, the collar of his coat turned up to his ears, jumped about the uncurtained stage, rushed into the wings, now giving a push to some theater mechanic, now shouting last-minute instructions to some actor petrified with fright, who in a minute or so would appear from the skies on top of a symbolic scaffolding and denounce the inhumanity of war. Mayakovsky, from his place in the audience, would frequently leap to his feet to shout something in his tremendous voice. It was so cold that you could see the steam coming out of their mouths. When the show was over we would walk home all together through the empty streets, swinging rhythmically over the glittering snow, repeating with all our lung power lines from poems or scraps of verse.

Meyerhold was subsequently imprisoned, his theater closed, and his company disbanded. He himself was dubbed clownish and condemned as incapable. Where he is now I do not know. As to Mayakovsky, it is some years now since he put an end to his own mystery-bouffe by blowing out his brains—although posthumously Stalin recognized him as the greatest poet produced by the Revolution.

Moscow at that time enjoyed a rich and endlessly experimental intellectual life. Most of the great thinkers of the immediate past either had emigrated or were spending their time grumbling at the new regime. Young people were swarming in on every side, filled with a fiery enthusiasm unlike anything ever known before. Revolutionary Marxism, with its spokesmen, Lenin, Trotsky, Bukharin, Preobrajensky, Riazanov, Lunacharsky, and Karl Radek—that pleiad of brilliant men of action, theorists, thinkers, politicians, and moralists—was questioning every human value and projecting the foundations of a new world.

There was an answer to everything, and if often the answer was too categorical, it was at least vital, stimulating the mind and setting the imagination on fire. Into international politics, law, military tactics, ethics, sexual problems, literature, painting—into everything a new light was being poured. What a contrast to the gray sterility of the U.S.S.R. under Stalin, where without a glimmer of originality the reactionary features of czarism are being step by step restored, where no one dares do much more than paraphrase the mediocre speeches of the Dictator, where poets can only sing his praises in verse and essayists in prose!

Under the patronage of Lunacharsky, Moscow, at the end of the Civil War, was a promised land for poets and artists. The painters invented new movements: constructivism, suprematism; and the poets also: imagism, *nitchevoki* ("neant-ism"), etc. In the cafés at the center of the city, wretched co-operative affairs where we could only drink coffee made from chestnuts and tea brewed from carrots, sweetened with saccharine or with microscopic pieces of sugar, one could always be sure of hearing poets of genius like Yessenin, Mayakovsky, Selvinsky, Tretiakov. When they had finished declaiming their verses, we would club together and offer them a cup of ersatz coffee and a cake.

This was no organized Bohemia, no commercialized Montparnasse, worked up by a lot of picture dealers and proprietors of cafés like the Dome and the Coupole, a Bohemia that for the most part is a bogus hodgepodge of disgruntled foreigners. It was the real thing, where

113

despair was genuine, extending to suicide; where enthusiasm was authentic, rising to masterpieces. There are still men alive who can remember that time.

One of the most popular of the cafés frequented by the poets was that known as the "Stall of Pegasus." I remember the winged steed painted on the wall spreading his golden pinions above an unshaved poet dressed in a peasant's blouse, who shouted:

> Spit, wind, your bunches of leaves!
> I am a hooligan just like you. . . .

One night as I reached home after a romantic evening of this kind, the sleepy porter handed me a tiny square letter that had come by post. It was an event, for I was out of touch with my mother and was carrying on no correspondence with any friend. The handwriting was that of Olga Fedorovna, my legal and unreal wife, now living with her father in the Tambov Province. I opened the letter, I must confess, with my heart beating faster than our formally defined relation justified. It was, alas, a coolly reasonable letter, suggesting that, since the circumstances no longer required it, we should end this paradoxical situation by securing a divorce. I answered in the same vein. But, owing to the fact that she was living in a province and I in Moscow, there were difficulties. We had to write more than once. Her subsequent letters were equally formal and polite, but in one of them a more personal postscript informed me that she was still suffering from malaria. I was then undergoing treatment for the same trouble at the Institute of Tropical Diseases. The doctors had promised me a complete cure in three months. I hardly believed it, and in fact it did not happen; but nevertheless I wrote to Olga Fedorovna insisting that she see my doctors. I asked myself while writing whether my sole concern was for her health. I was not sure.

A week or two passed without answer. I was working one evening alone, preparing for my examinations. The Tartar officer who shared my room was in the hospital fighting for his life against typhoid. I had taken him downstairs on my back a few days earlier and put him in an ambulance. Suddenly there was a knock at my door. It was snowing outside. Olga Fedorovna entered, swathed in furs, her color heightened by the cold; and joy entered with her.

What was it she had come for? Was it the medical treatment we should discuss first or the divorce? We sat there smiling at each other. Hadn't we been foolish long enough?

The next day I appeared before General Martynov, the professor of military history, to be examined on the Russo-Japanese War. Martynov knew that I had mastered the subject and put me a routine question or two on the defense of Port Arthur.

Port Arthur? I couldn't remember a thing about it!

"What's the matter with you?" asked the old general. "Where are your brains?"

Martynov was kind enough to give me another five days in which to prepare the subject. When I appeared before him again my answers were satisfactory. And that evening I took my wife to the Stall of Pegasus.

16. The Beginnings of Soviet Diplomacy

ABOUT THIS TIME Yurenev suggested that I might, while still continuing my studies in the General Staff College, take a job under Chicherin in the Foreign Office. The People's Commissar for Foreign Affairs was a mighty worker and exhausted the efforts of half a dozen secretaries to keep up with him. As he slept little and did his best work at night, he had to have a complete staff available at any moment of the twenty-four hours. There had to be always two secretaries on duty. I signed on for night work.

The Foreign Office was already, even at this early date, installed in the building it occupies today on the Kutznetsky-Most. The secretariat was in charge of an athletic Greek with the classic features of an Apollo, whose name was Kanghilari.

Chicherin was a man whose peculiar habits had to be respected. His workroom was completely buried in books, newspapers, and documents —as was his writing table. Beside the latter stood a smaller table on which were a bottle of brandy and some glasses. When, toward dawn, he felt he could no longer keep awake, George Vassilievich used to refresh himself with a glass of Martel. The room next door was empty and opened into an anteroom occupied by the secretaries. It was our job to open all letters, telegrams, messages, and reports and sort them on a large table. We never disturbed Chicherin by taking his mail to him. What he wanted he came and got. He used to patter into our room in his shirt sleeves, wearing a large silk handkerchief round his neck and slippers adorned with metal buckles on his feet. These buckles, which, for comfort's sake, he never troubled to fasten, made a clicking noise on the floor. The first time he saw me on duty he did no more than peer inquisitively at me over his spectacles. Then he took a bundle of dispatches which was lying on my table and trotted out again, his little pointed beard sticking out in front of him.

The notes sent out by this foreign minister of the Socialist Revolution gave endless trouble to the chancelleries of Europe. He composed them himself with great care, aided by a disconcertingly retentive memory. In his rare moments of leisure he composed songs or wrote verses or played brilliantly on the piano. An old bachelor, he lived in an apartment in the Foreign Office building and was looked after by a Swiss couple with whom he had long been on terms of friendship. His way of living was very simple. He paid no attention to decorum, to personal comfort, or to the normal conventions, whether in dress or anything else.

He had a warm, paternal feeling for his staff, which was at times both touching and comic.

Handsome Kanghilari, the head of the secretariat, was a great success with women. Unfortunately his attentions turned to the wife of one of the secretaries. One day this secretary burst into Chicherin's office and sobbed on the chief's shoulder.

"Kanghilari is making love to my wife!"

Chicherin was indignant. When the secretary left, the old man walked into the anteroom, grabbed the first person he met by the lapel, and exclaimed plaintively:

"This Kanghilari is impossible! He has disrupted the family life of my entire staff!"

Notwithstanding this exaggeration, he straightened the situation out by assigning the aggrieved secretary to a post abroad. The secretary departed well placated, his wife on his arm.

Chicherin's favorite time for seeing foreign ambassadors was midnight. Count Brockdorff-Rantzau, the German ambassador, his head held stiffly in a starched and shining collar, rubbed shoulders in the anteroom at this unheard-of hour of the night with plenipotentiaries from the Baltic and Asiatic states—for now, while the great Western powers were keeping us in quarantine, these alone had representatives in Moscow. It was a real event when one day we received a telegram signed by Poincaré—relating to an exchange of prisoners—and still more an event when Soviet Russia was invited to take part in the Genoa Conference.

European correspondents and sympathizing foreigners would often visit Chicherin between three and five o'clock in the morning. At about five I would take the chief's Rolls-Royce and set off to the other end of Moscow to fetch his confidential typist. At six he would start dictating his mail to her. The letters would be brought to my table. They had to be entered in the register, numbered, sent off, and the copies filed. George Vassilievich used to come and help me affix the red seals to secret documents intended for Lenin, Trotsky, and other leaders.

"Be careful!" he would mutter, hopping about. "Do be careful, you'll burn the paper."

This done, I had a quiet hour which I spent reading copies of the more important messages, the very headings of which were enough to

George Chicherin, commissar of foreign affairs—died in 1936 of natural causes.

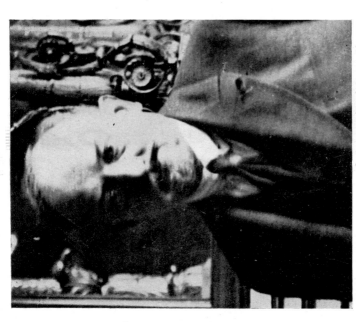

Constantin Yurenev, former commissar general of the Red Army, later ambassador to Germany—in August, 1937, called to report to Moscow and disappeared, presumably shot.

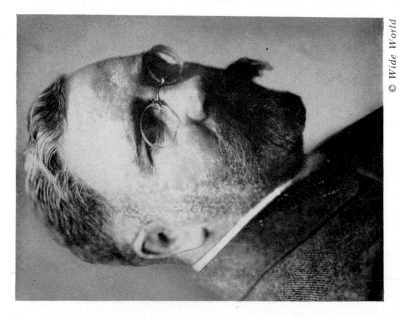

© *Wide World*

Leon Kamenev, member of Politburo, vice-premier, president of Moscow Soviet—shot in August, 1936.

© *Wide World*

Gregory Zinoviev, member of Politburo, president of Leningrad Soviet, president of Comintern—shot in August, 1936.

fill me with awe. "The People's Commissar for Foreign Affairs to the President of the Council, Vladimir Ilych Lenin. . . ." The education and insight I was gaining in this hour was my reason for keeping an exhausting nighttime job at the same time that I was continuing my studies.

I remember a scheme outlined by Chicherin in one of these letters. Like Lenin, he had no sympathy whatever for the League of Nations, which he regarded as a thinly disguised coalition of the victors against the vanquished. He proposed to set up, under the protection of the Soviets, a League of Peoples, in which the wronged, the oppressed, the exploited, and the members of ethnic minorities should be included on exactly the same footing as the dominant powers. In contrast to the League of Nations, this League of Peoples was to become a center of international justice between nations.

On one occasion Chicherin's typist, in a moment of carelessness caused by fatigue, committed an error which in the Moscow of today would almost certainly be punished as an act of sabotage and counterrevolution. All messages to Lenin finished up with the conventional phrase: "Communist greetings." Instead of this, she sleepily wrote: "Capitalist greetings"!

I noticed what she had done as I was going through the copies. The bicycle messenger had already left. I telephoned the guardroom at the Kremlin, only to find to my dismay that the packet had already gone through. I called Lenin's office, and a member of his staff told me that the dispatches were now lying on Vladimir Ilych's desk and that nobody could touch them. What would be the result of this unfortunate "capitalist greeting"? Actually, nothing happened, but the wretched typist went quite green when I showed her the copy. George Vassilievich laughed into his beard: the Revolution would not be deeply compromised. Nobody dreamed at that time of putting down such mistakes to sabotage or counterrevolution.

Almost all the men who worked with Chicherin have now disappeared—either shot or imprisoned. As I call their names to mind, I feel almost as though I were moving in a world of ghosts.

There was Fechner, a young civil servant of pleasant manners and considerable ingenuity, who after fifteen years of devoted labor became chargé d'affaires at Lithuania. We always said he'd never be anything but a big child—but that didn't prevent his being suspected of unimaginable crimes and thrown into prison in 1937. Many other names come back to memory: Zuckerman, methodical worker and sincere Communist, who was later to be director of the Near Eastern Department—shot without trial on December 16, 1937; Sandomirsky, formerly an anarchist who, in czarist times, had served a sentence of hard labor for revolutionary agitation and was in charge of our Balkan Department—deported to Siberia in 1935 and believed to have been shot; Ganetsky, a veteran of the Social Democratic movement, once vice-commissar of foreign affairs, transferred to the department in charge of circuses and music halls—and imprisoned in 1937.

Most of Litvinov's secretaries met the same fate. With few exceptions they disappeared in the prisons or in the cellars of the G.P.U. One of his favorites, Divilkovsky, avoided that fate only because he was killed in an automobile accident a year or two before the purges began. Another favorite, his private secretary, Eliena Krylenko, the sister of the Commissar of Justice, escaped for a more happy reason. She married Max Eastman, and when he published his historic book, *Since Lenin Died,* giving the first prophetic analysis of the rising dictatorship and disclosing the existence of the sensational document called "Lenin's Testament," she was serving as head secretary of the Paris Embassy. When peremptorily ordered to return to Moscow, she wisely declined.

The most distinguished of the victims was Karakhan, vice-commissar of foreign affairs and the closest collaborator of Chicherin, whose name headed the list of those shot on December 16, 1937.

Leon Mikhailovich Karakhan, in contrast to Chicherin, used to turn up at the office about eleven o'clock in the morning, freshly shaven, impeccably dressed, complete with gloves and polished spectacles, looking, in his well-fitting suit, like a matinee idol. He had charm, engaging manners, and a happy share of oriental good looks; his pale skin showed to advantage in contrast with the little pointed black beard he wore. Our young staff gave him unstinted admiration, amazed that humanity could produce such perfection. He had a purity of profile such as is seen, as a rule, only on ancient coins; he carried himself well, had a gay temperament, and was a master of persuasive speech. He was a born optimist, a conscientious worker, simple in his dealings with others, and was always ready to give a helping hand to his younger colleagues. No one could have been better suited by nature for a brilliant diplomatic career, nor more ideally equipped for training diplomats.

After serving his apprenticeship at the Brest-Litovsk negotiations, Karakhan was sent as Soviet representative to Peking where he had the job of reopening diplomatic relations with China. Later he was appointed ambassador to Turkey where he was accredited to Mustapha Kemal's government. His signature appears on many treaties. Nobody knows why he was shot. The execution took place under conditions of utmost secrecy, and his memory was brutally blackened during the Trial of the Twenty-one, which followed. He was very attractive to women, and I have an idea that, in connection with this trait, he got on the wrong side of the Dictator, who never forgives a slight. I cannot help thinking that some trivial matter of this sort contributed to his fall, though there were other reasons, the chief of which was his high standing as an individual.

He married the première ballerina of the Moscow Opera, Marina Semenova. On the eve of his execution she was offered the chance to divorce him and resume her maiden name and retain her status in the theater. She continues to dance for the pleasure of the men who sent her husband to his death.

At the time of the Genoa Conference I made the personal acquaintance of Christian Rakovsky, then also vice-commissar of foreign affairs, who was then in the prime of life, always smiling, and in touch with everything that was going forward. I also met Bekzadian, president of the Council of People's Commissars of Armenia. Both accompanied Chicherin to Genoa. Bekzadian was the unfortunate Soviet ambassador already mentioned who disappeared from Budapest at the end of 1937.

The proposed trip to Genoa kept all the junior members of the staff, both men and women, on the *qui vive*. They all wanted to go, and George Vassilievich, driven frantic by their endless flow of requests, rushed into my room one night and said:

"Put up immediately a notice forbidding anyone to mention the Genoa Conference!"

In high good humor, I decided to take the chief's outburst of temper seriously. As a soldier, I knew how to carry out orders. Savoring in advance the surprise of my colleagues, I affixed the following to the bulletin board:

THE PEOPLE'S COMMISSAR HAS GIVEN ORDERS THAT NOBODY IS TO SPEAK TO HIM OF THE GENOA CONFERENCE.

"Ah," said Karakhan later with a smile, "that will greatly simplify my task."

Chicherin peered vaguely over his spectacles at my notice and allowed it to remain in position for several days. But an English journalist took the joke seriously and cabled it home as evidence that, so great was the excitement produced by the prospect of a reconciliation with the capitalist countries, that the foreign commissar was literally beseiged by important men of state.

With the approach of summer my studies at the War College became so intense that I had to quit my post at the Foreign Office. The next year I saw Chicherin intermittently in connection with various diplomatic matters. I saw him for the last time at the Fourteenth Party Congress in the Kremlin in 1925.

He had a broad grin on his face: he had just been elected to the Central Committee of the Party. It was probably the last great pleasure of his life. The Litvinov group had fought bitterly against him for control of the Foreign Office, and had set themselves to bring to nothing every decision he made. Chicherin declared finally that he found it quite impossible to work with Litvinov, and openly called him his "antipode" at the Central Committee Conference. He was then a very sick man and soon went on leave to Wiesbaden, where he was sorely tempted to settle down. Long and tedious negotiations were necessary before he could be induced to come back to Moscow, although he was still officially People's Commissar for Foreign Affairs.

Karakhan went to Wiesbaden to persuade him to return. He was brought back, however, only so that he might be replaced without a scandal. Litvinov quietly stepped into his shoes, and Chicherin vanished from the political scene—forgotten even before he was dead. But being overridden in this way was only one of his grievances, for he was a victim of gross ingratitude and negligence on Litvinov's part. The foreign minister of the Revolution, to whom the Soviets owed so much of their safety, was condemned to live in a wretched little lodging, without heat and without sufficient food—until finally the Central Committee intervened and saw that he was properly looked after. He spent his last years in complete retirement, occupying incognito a modest apartment in one of the narrow streets near the Arbat and relieving his melancholy with music, for he was a fine pianist. He saw no one except a couple of his former secretaries. When he died he was denied burial in the Kremlin Wall, and his remains lie in the monastery of Novo-Dyevichii.

While I was working as Chicherin's secretary I often met Litvinov, who was then his second assistant. Quite stout and impressive, he was very serious, though at the same time a pleasant companion. He was merry at the table and remained a good dancer until past sixty. Not very scrupulous in his personal relations, but exacting in his work, he had a special talent for worming his way into high places. In a few years he was able to replace Chicherin, who was not touchy and had a wholly disinterested passion for his work.

Litvinov, born Meyer Vallach, had entered the revolutionary movement early. In 1901 he was a member of the underground Socialist group in Kiev. He was arrested for concealing arms and printing equipment, and sentenced to five years in Siberia. But he escaped from the prison in Kiev. During the revolution of 1905 the Party confided to him the important mission of transporting arms and literature into Russia. In 1907 the Bolshevik "expropriators" of the Caucasus, who included Stalin, then known as Koba, bombed a carriage bearing currency, and Litvinov took part of the funds abroad to be changed. When arrested by the French police, on information of the czarist secret police, he was found in possession of these funds and expelled. He went to London.

He returned to Russia during the Revolution, and in 1918 was named plenipotentiary to Britain. But his mission collapsed—London preferred to boycott bolshevism—and he returned to Moscow. It was Litvinov who carried through the job of rehabilitating Red Russia in the eyes of the world. The climax of his career was that day in Geneva when the delegates of the Soviet Union were admitted into the League of Nations. Litvinov, followed by his secretaries, entered the conference hall amid general applause, and this signified that bolshevism had "grown wiser" and that Russia would henceforth be allied with the Versailles policy.

These last years he has lived in constant danger, inexplicably surviving all his friends and collaborators. Stalin still has need of him. Litvinov is a good poker player. He smiled enigmatically when he traveled abroad after the purges, and continued to do so even when his children were no longer allowed to accompany him—even when his wife was sent from Moscow to the Urals to live.

The leaders of the Party were shot first, and that is understandable. It was necessary for Stalin to begin with the thinkers. Then followed the generals, the marshals, the industrial chiefs, and, at about the same time, the diplomats. Two of Litvinov's four assistants were executed, the third was put in prison, and the fourth disappeared. His old friends and personal protégés, Ambassadors Yurenev and Rosenberg, disappeared also. Almost all the heads of departments of his ministry and the leading diplomatic personnel abroad, gathered and trained by him over fifteen years, were shot. But Litvinov continued to smile enigmatically. "They were traitors; all is well!" Was he so confident because he deemed himself indispensable, or did he have to keep a good face because his family were held as hostages?

Stalin discarded this faithful retainer on allying himself with Hitler. Litvinov was the last Jew, with the single exception of Lazar Kaganovich, who remained in the upper ranks of the Soviet Government at that time.

During the next two years Litvinov sometimes appeared on the official tribune for special occasions, his clothes well pressed and his flabby face clean-shaven. To all appearances he was living a normal life. But no one knew whence he came or where he went or what he was doing. At each appearance the diplomatic corps in Moscow gazed in amazement to see him still alive. He was brought out from his mysterious place of confinement at the outbreak of the German-Soviet war, when he made a radio address to the English, asking them on behalf of Russia to invade the Continent, and again when he attended Stalin's conference with Harriman and Beaverbrook. In November, 1941, he was taken out of cold storage and appointed ambassador to the United States.

What will be Litvinov's fate in case of some new unpredictable turn in Soviet policy? No one knows. But one thing is certain: No political figure in Stalin's Russia who has been privy to many state secrets, secrets stranger than the fictions of novelists, has ever been able to resign and end his days in a quiet retreat. There are in totalitarian states no quiet retreats for men who have served the dictator and been thrown off.

While our diplomats were away negotiating with the powers of

Europe, I put in a period of field work with the General Staff College at Khodynka Camp near Moscow. We spent our time making topographical surveys and engaging in tactical exercises.

One day when I was coming back from Khodynka, Yurenev met me in the street as I was dismounting from my horse with my surveys, maps, and topographical instruments.

"I want you," he said. "I have just been appointed to Riga, and I'm going to take you with me. Do you agree? Good! Be ready by the end of the week."

With Yurenev pushing, things moved fast. I had my appointment as secretary of the legation in Latvia, and was on the train to Riga in forty-eight hours.

Russia was slowly recovering from her wounds. Famine was still rife in certain parts of the country, and everywhere there was a shortage of food and much poverty. But the whole picture changed when we crossed the frontier. Except on my trip to Viipuri in Finland in 1917, I had never before seen a city so clean, so well kept, so comfortable as Riga, with its attractive shop windows, neatly paved streets, and bright-colored cottages. The legation was equipped with mirrors and expensive furniture—a regular bourgeois interior. The first morning we were brought a breakfast such as we had never even dreamed of. I tasted my first cup of *café au lait,* a luxury that I was to enjoy with mixed feelings, a little worried, a little sad.

A few days later I went for a walk in the public gardens, wearing my Soviet insignia in my buttonhole. I had an angry encounter with a White Russian officer, who accosted me with "Take that off!"

I answered him in the same tone, and after one of those arguments in which men behave so much like roosters, he, learning that I held a diplomatic passport, retired. But Yurenev, when I told him of this incident, said:

"You'd better not wear that badge. If you got your neck broken, all my help couldn't bring you back to life. Much as I might like to, I couldn't treat the occurrence as a *casus belli,* though it might indeed put us in a very awkward position."

I protested but had to obey orders.

Our government had established a rest house for senior officials at Mayorenhof, quite close to Riga, realizing that small rest was to be had on Russian soil. The Lettish police kept a strict eye on this holiday place where commissars, journalists, and members of the Central Committee would spend their evenings singing revolutionary songs. Like all policemen, they had a taste for plots, and they convinced themselves that this singing was evidence of an extremely dangerous one. We at the legation were constantly being bombarded with questions on the subject.

At Mayorenhof I saw Litvinov, who was bringing his family from

London; Stryeklov, editor of *Izvestia* and future biographer of Bakunin (what, I wonder, has become of him?); Sukhanov, one of the Menshevik leaders of the Petrograd Soviet in 1917, a historian of parts, who was sentenced in 1931 to ten years' imprisonment; and once more Fayzoulla Khodjaev, whom I had last seen wearing a turban and over his uniform a silk *khalat*. He accompanied me on a trip to the seashore in a raglan coat and felt hat, his complexion yellower than ever and his head stuffed with projects for the reorganization of Central Asia.

I returned to Moscow on the eve of the Fourth Congress of the Communist International, accompanied in the diplomatic coach by several foreign delegates—Clara Zetkin, still full of fight though now an old woman; the Czech Bohumir Smeral, a fat man in spectacles, the greatest opportunist of all the Communists up to then existing in the world; the Pole Valetsky; and the Hungarian professor Varga. Finally, there was Boris Souvarine, who had come to represent the French Party.

Two of these foreign delegates showed the most revolting lack of consideration in their dealings with us. Varga and Valetsky maintained that they had a right to a private compartment, though the car was so full that it was obviously impossible for me to give them one. I also could not give them mine, as I was bringing, concealed in my compartment, a fugitive who had been condemned to death in Riga. Souvarine supported me wholeheartedly in the discussion that followed. The two members of the Comintern executive threatened to make a complaint about me in high quarters, and did in fact do so when we arrived in Moscow. Surely an old revolutionary like Valetsky ought to have been content with a berth in a first-class sleeper—and so ought an ex-member of the Red Government of Hungary like Varga. The little luxuries of power go to men's heads.

A few days after my return to the college, our political commissar, Muklevich, summoned me to his office. The complaint of these two men was lying on his table, and he reprimanded me for my lack of courtesy. I appealed to Souvarine to confirm my version of the incident. He defended me in a strongly worded letter, in which he had a good many unflattering things to say of his colleagues. Muklevich quietly suppressed the complaint.

Souvarine and I became friends. At that time he was a member of the Executive Committee of the Comintern, and I paid several visits to him in his modest room at the Lux Hotel, which was the headquarters of the delegates of the International.

I take this opportunity of saluting the memory of Muklevich, who was one of our really great soldiers and is certainly no longer alive. Fat and sturdy and round-faced, this Old Bolshevik had all the quiet confidence and also the appearance of a born leader. At one time a simple sailor, like Dybenko, he rose to be commander in chief of the Soviet fleet and assistant People's Commissar for Defense, then was placed in charge of war industries and naval construction, and disappeared suddenly in 1937. He was the kind of man whom Stalin does not willingly let live, even behind bars.

17. *Mutterings of the Storm*

WITH THE CLOSE of the Civil War the changes in our life were very marked. The Revolution had been through some bad times and suffered several military shocks, but it had never doubted its strength. The Party's internal quarrels had been conducted in a mood of confidence in the future. This was so even at the time of the Kronshtadt rising, when the Republic was dangerously near to destruction. But now, with the end of the fighting, a new danger to the Revolution arose—a danger of defeat on the economic field.

Even before Kronshtadt the conflict about the trade unions had made the Party realize that it must make momentous decisions in this field. At that time the difficulties had been shelved rather than solved. Now we must choose definitely the lines along which the economy should develop. Lenin announced, to our astonishment, his New Economic Policy, opening free markets to the peasantry. This policy very soon showed its fruits in improved conditions of living. Food was better and more plentiful; the standards of production rose everywhere; there was, throughout the country, an undeniable sense of lessened tension. But money had reappeared; money was once more becoming the touchstone of social life.

We young Communists had all grown up in the belief that money was done away with once and for all. It had never occurred to us that the near-suppression of currency in the time of the Civil War had been not so much the expression of steady progress toward a socialist ideal as an expedient due to devaluation and the impossibility of a free exchange of goods produced in small numbers and of bad quality. The real truth was that it had been both an expedient and a long-time policy—a policy devised by the best economists of the Party—Lenin, Bukharin, and Preobrajensky—and intended to be a stage in the development of the socialist experiment.

At the end of the Civil War, inflation had depreciated paper money to an enormous extent. And this inflation was increased by the policy of making certain services—railroad travel, streetcars, postal services, plays and movies, medical treatment, etc.—free to the toiling masses. A pocket handkerchief was worth more than a banknote stamped with a dozen rows of zeros. The state printing house no longer took the trouble to number or divide these banknotes: we got them in huge sheets, like postage stamps, and I have more than once seen these sheets used as wrapping paper or wallpaper in peasants' cottages. A further difficulty arose from the fact that there would soon be a shortage of paper—even for the printing of money!

And now, under the N.E.P. with its revival of freedom of trade and payment of taxes in kind—both designed to bring about a reconciliation with the peasants—money began to regain a definite value. Everything, from now on, had to be paid for. The handsome winter equipages so loved by the Muscovite heart began to make their appearance —elegant sleighs drawn by thoroughbreds. Several restaurants opened, and as we walked down the streets we could hear the blare of their orchestras, but they were beyond the reach of most of us. We had to pay for the smallest ration of food, pay for baths, pay for a moment's amusement.

The men of the Revolution, young and old, suddenly discovered that they needed money and had none. It had never occurred to any of them to bother with making it. A few lucky devils had an extra pair of boots, and that was about all. Official Communists, even the highest-up, received a salary of some 200 rubles a month—that is to say, the wage of a skilled workman. If money was reappearing, wouldn't rich people reappear too? Weren't we on the slippery slope that led back to capitalism? We put these questions to ourselves with feelings of anxiety.

Dressed in the uniform of the General Staff College, decorated with medals won at the cost of their blood, the heroes of the Civil War discovered in their wanderings about Moscow that everything was beyond their reach, that the profiteers could snap fingers at them with impunity; and they began to wonder whether they had fought in vain.

I remember one evening when a few of us from the War College walked for hours along the Tverskoy Boulevard, back and forth from the Pushkin monument to the statue of Timiriazev. We were discussing what had happened to the Revolution. We felt as though the Revolution had been betrayed, and it was time to quit the Party. "Capitalism is returning. Money and the old inequality that we fought against are back again."

In the end our decision was: "We don't know why the Central Committee is doing this, and, while it seems bad to us now, we must have faith." Our confidence in the leaders of the Party, in Lenin, Trotsky, Bukharin, Zinoviev, made this possible for us—or so we convinced ourselves. They knew where they were going, they knew where they were leading. They might be defeated, but they certainly would never betray us.

I found our college full of new problems and in a mood of bitter grievance. The Civil War was over; our seniors had finished their courses. What was to become of them now? Most of the important posts were occupied by generals of the old regime, professional soldiers who had rallied to the Soviets and helped win the war. Trotsky's policy toward them had contributed to the victory of the Revolution. But what now? The college began to talk of the necessity for reorganization, for injecting new blood into the senior ranks of the Army, for preparing the next war in terms of the Marxian military doctrine—of which Tukhachevsky had become the unexpected theorist. Our general attitude was expressed in the simple slogan: "Make room for the young Red generals!" Tomorrow the Dybenkos, the Ventsovs, the Fedkos, the Uritskys, the Gays were going to graduate. The old generals calmly proposed to relegate them, for a time at least, to the lower commands. After leading armies on active service, they were to find themselves in charge of battalions and companies! The situation gave rise to an ironic song—"Ode to the Company"—written for the graduation dinner by a student. There was ambition in this as well as concern for the Revolution—justifiable perhaps, but still ambition. Why not call it by its proper name and simply say "careerism"? This, too, was to be an element in the process of building the Army anew from top to bottom.

The political problem was further complicated by the fact that the head of the Red Army, the member of the Party who had gained most glory by the recent victories and was most admired for the energy he had displayed—Trotsky—seemed to consider that the old professionals still had a part to play. The former generals Lebediev, Brussilov, Novitsky, Vatsetis, and Kamenev were still collaborating with him, and, although the War Council was made up of proved revolutionaries, our graduates were suspicious of the influence wielded by this overdecorated staff.

A sort of underground opposition to Trotsky began to show its head both in the Party and in the Army. Its rallying points were Stalin and Voroshilov. They knew that as long as Trotsky remained at the top there would be no room there for them. They therefore took advantage of the discontent of the young officers to lead a movement against the old generals. The movement set its face not only against the trust placed in "professionals," but also against the policy of centralized command.

Naturally the War College was divided on these questions. A sort of clique came into being, led by an Old Bolshevik—old merely in terms of his Party career, for he was under thirty—a man decorated with the Order of the Red Banner, full of energy and possessed of a demagogic gift of oratory. This man, Kruchinsky by name, fomented the existing discord with considerable skill. He was supported by several students—Dybenko, Uritsky, and Fedko—who were moved to this by Voroshilov. He was opposed by a few of the younger men, myself included, who had had enough of quarrels and personalities. We managed to defeat his candidacy to the executive board of our Communist cell despite an imposing pressure. To the general surprise he disappeared, "withdrawn from circulation" by the Cheka, which had found out that he was nothing but an adventurer. His claim of long membership in the Party was a bluff, and he was no more entitled to the glory of his alleged exploits than to the decorations which he sported on his shirt.

The Central Committee, no doubt remembering how the students had voted on the trade-union question—the majority declaring for the Workers' Opposition against Lenin, Trotsky, and Bukharin—decided that the college must be subjected to a special "cleansing." This new *chistka* descended on our heads like a cloudburst. It was administered relentlessly by a commission enjoying full powers and acting in secret. Among its members were Bubnov, who later became People's Commissar for Education, and Skliansky, Trotsky's assistant, who died three years afterward in Chicago. The commission had been proposed by Trotsky and approved by the Central Committee.

The commission sentenced men to exclusion from the Party and the college, or both together, giving any reason that seemed good to it and often giving none at all. In this way it threw into the street, without employment and with their reputations compromised, a number of officers who had done splendid work at the front and had just finished their military studies. Several of these outcasts committed suicide. My friend Gaevsky, who, as I knew well, deserved his reputation for utter fearlessness under fire, was expelled from the college. He was tall and thin and had been a jolly fellow, but when next I saw him he was a broken man, indignant and despairing. We met in a corridor close to the director's office. Gaevsky was carrying a letter to Trotsky to which was attached something that glittered. He said bitterly: "If I am unworthy to be a member of the college I don't know why I was given the Order of the Red Banner—they can have it back!" He was reinstated, for this error of judgment had been too flagrant. Later he became a well-known organizer of industry. In 1936 he was charged with "terrorism" and vanished, branded as an "enemy of the people."

Another of my friends, Itskovsky, son of a poor Jewish tailor, who, in the old days, had been a long-time guest in the czarist prisons and had fought with Piatakov in Kiev early in the Revolution, was expelled on the motion of Bubnov, with whom he had shared a mattress in a Kiev prison and whose colleague he had been in the Ukrainian government. Bubnov, meeting him one day after that, offered him his hand; Itskovsky refused it with a smile:

"I don't shake hands with a son of a bitch," he said. I can see him now, cheerful when things were going wrong, saying with a broad smile that there was worse to come. Where did he get that happy temperament? When the Revolution broke out he was released from a prison where, for five years, he had been living in solitary confinement, loaded with chains. It must have been there that he trained himself to smile no matter what happened. The commission reinstated him in the War College, and later he attained a high post in the Commissariat of Foreign Trade. He disappeared in 1935, accused of "Trotskyism." And Bubnov followed him in 1937.

While I was ill with an attack of malaria in the hospital I, too, was sentenced to expulsion from the college. The commission had examined my case in my absence, and all I knew was that I had been dismissed—a few months before entering the senior class—on the ground that I "was too young and in poor health." I decided to appeal to the Central Committee of the Party.

Vyacheslav Molotov, then secretary of the Central Committee, was available for interviews any day. I went to a two-storied, yellow-painted house in Vosdvizhenka Street, not far from the Kremlin. My Party card gave me admittance. "First room on the right," I was told. The room was huge, badly kept, and poorly furnished. There was a table in the middle surrounded by chairs. Several people were waiting, seated near the door. At the far end, in front of the window, was a smaller table, covered with papers and with several telephones. Molotov sat there talking with a workman. He had a very large and placid face, the face of an ordinary, uninspired, but rather soft and kindly bureaucrat, attentive and unassuming. He listened to me carefully, made one or two notes, asked a few questions, and said, stuttering slightly: "All right. I'll do what I can for you."

Four days later my sentence of expulsion was reversed. The authorities made a good many mistakes in those days, but some of them were thus quickly repaired. The democratic spirit of the Party then still revealed itself in direct contact between members and officials, and also in a simplicity of manners which at times came near to crudeness.

About this time I met a very unusual man whose end was singularly tragic. He was a young Red officer from a rich Jewish family, twice decorated for bravery in the field and a talented painter and caricaturist on the side. His name was Byelotsky. Byelotsky was determined never to become a high official but to remain in close contact with the masses. He declined a high military career and went down to the rural organizations of the Party to teach and work as secretary of village cells. For eight years he labored as a Party organizer in different villages of the Kirghiz Republic. He was one of those men who will adopt a country with passion and devote himself entirely to its interests. He knew every detail of the Kirghiz countryside. Finally, from a small Party worker he rose, in spite of himself, to be secretary of the Central Committee for Kirghizistan—that is to say, the *de facto* ruler of this autonomous republic. This man, one of the few Bolsheviks who had revived the old Narodnik idea of "going to the people," was denounced in 1937 as "an enemy of the people," and he disappeared.

When the Civil War ended, certain White generals of Denikin's army, who had recanted, were appointed to teach at the college. With a feeling of some curiosity I attended the course of lectures in strategy given by "Comrade" Slashchev, an elderly officer with a scarlet face, a large red nose, and hair cut stiffly *en brosse*, who used always to appear in a green tunic still showing the marks of his torn-off epaulettes. We gave him the title "comrade" out of respect for the authorities who had appointed him. Slashchev always referred to himself as "Slashchev of the Crimea," having been responsible for erecting a series of well-nigh impregnable defenses at the neck of the peninsula —which the Red battalions captured by an overpowering thrust. He had been with Baron Wrangel, by whom he was appointed to the command of the White Army in the Crimea. At Djankoy he won considerable notoriety by hanging from the lampposts all the members of an organization of Young Communists—workmen and students, boys and girls alike. After that he was known all over Russia as "Slashchev the Hangman" until the day when, having betrayed Wrangel at Constantinople, he came over to our side, carrying with him a good many documents of value.

One day, when he was illustrating a lecture by analyzing the battle of Perekop, a member of my class said: "I beg your pardon, Comrade Professor, but I was in command of a division at that battle, and I can assure you that we never had against you that many troops."

"Quite likely," answered the ex-hangman politely. "I have not been through all the reports—and the Soviet troops made up in valor for what they lacked in numbers."

Notwithstanding such tributes to his new employers, Slashchev was shot dead in the street one day by a Young Communist, the brother of one of his victims.

At the end of 1922 the Soviet Government invited the representatives of Poland and the Baltic States to a disarmament conference in Moscow. The Foreign Office detailed me to act as one of the secretaries. Chicherin did not appear, and Litvinov was in charge of the Soviet delegation.

Poland was represented by Prince Radziwill and Lukasiewicz, later ambassador in Paris, and they managed to persuade Finland, Latvia, and Esthonia to follow Poland's example and send delegates. Lithuania, though she had severed diplomatic relations with Warsaw since the Vilna affair, seemed anxious to achieve a *rapprochement* with us and also participated.

At the gathering in the hall where we stood talking before the opening of the conference, Prince Radziwill, tall and imposing with his long beard, noticed the enameled badge—red flag with hammer and sickle—on my lapel. I was amused when with true diplomatic courtesy he remarked:

"That's fine work. Where was it done?"

I lifted the lapel, and it was his turn to be amused, or rather surprised. The manufacturer's address proved to be Warsaw. (Since Russian craftsmanship in this line was not up to par, we had had a number of such badges made in Poland for use by Soviet representatives traveling abroad.) The Polish aristocrat raised his eyebrows and changed the subject. Prince Radziwill's second visit to Moscow took place eighteen years later, in 1939, when he was brought as a prisoner, his family having been seized by Red troops during the Nazi-Soviet invasion of Poland. He was later released at the request of the Pope and King Victor Emmanuel and permitted to go to Italy.

The crowded hall included a Lithuanian general whose uniform was very handsome and resplendent, with more crosses, stars, and ribbons than that of the most famous victors in the Great War. Very tall, and broad in proportion, General Radus-Sincovichus stood for me as the true prototype of all musical-comedy commanders. He figured in an episode which became for us a matter of heated discussion.

The assembled delegates were awaiting the delayed arrival of the Russian representatives. A double door was flung open, and General Novitsky, former vice-minister of war in the czarist government, member of the Red Army General Staff, came modestly in, wearing a uniform that could boast neither decorations nor badges of rank, a faded tunic, and clumsy, yellowing high boots. Novitsky, one of our professors for whom we felt a real respect, was small and rather thin. He bowed to the room in general, and suddenly found himself face to face with the imposing figure of Radus-Sincovichus. To our consternation the two men embraced like long-lost brothers.

Radus-Sincovichus had been a member of the Czar's War College before the Revolution. As a commissioned officer in the Army of the Czar he had been Novitsky's brother-in-arms. But how could a leader of the Red Army of Workers and Peasants show such affection for an officer in the service of a capitalist state? Ought he not to have ignored the past and concentrated solely on the problem of disarmament? We were all shocked at first, but some of us finally laughed at our implacable comrades who continued to frown on this very human act. At least they did not go so far as to accuse dear old Novitsky of conniving with the enemy of the Soviets!

Nothing more came of this disarmament conference than of the many which followed it. But it was a means of bringing us into closer contact with our neighbors.

18. *Born into Sorrow*

IN THE COURSE of these last two years, ideas and manners in Moscow had undergone a serious change. I was profoundly influenced by these changes. My idea in taking up the study of oriental languages had been to devote myself later to propaganda in the East. Was not the revolutionary spirit rising both in Persia and in Afghanistan? I had imagined myself traveling through those countries disguised as a merchant, though really acting as a revolutionary.

But now the revolutionary spirit was in a period of decline. The Soviet Republic was living on neighborly terms with countries untouched by revolution. Instead of preparing secret revolutionary activities fraught with peril and interest, I found myself moving toward a career in the diplomatic service. Instead of an agitator and organizer of insurrection, I was to be a state official. The Foreign Office was keeping open for me a job as consul in Persia. It was agreed that immediately after graduation I should leave with my wife for that country.

During the third and last year of my studies, my wife and I still lived at the Hotel Levada. My mother-in-law shared our room, which was large enough to permit a screened-off corner for her bed. The rations issued by the military authorities would have been quite sufficient if only they had been allotted in a sensible manner. We had the right to so many pounds of meat a month, but it was all delivered in one installment. Since it was impossible without ice to keep it, whether raw or cooked, in an edible condition, we used to gorge ourselves sick for a week and then do without for the rest of the month. The quartermaster's store was short of ice chests; besides, it was constantly waging war with other institutions and had to take what it could when it could.

That autumn Olga Fedorovna found herself pregnant, and very soon after that her health gave way. The effects of malaria, of years of undernourishment, of exhaustion and emotional excitement had taxed her powers of resistance. Her condition now caused her acute discomfort. She found it almost impossible to take food. She had periods of violent nausea and was confined to her bed. A doctor whom we consulted advised her to have an abortion. A disappointed expression came over her face when she heard him pronounce that word. We decided, therefore, to try another doctor. She went with her mother to see him. I had been at the college, and when I came back I found her once more in bed, with a high color. I was so anxious that I dared not ask her what had happened and spoke of other things in a tone of assumed indifference.

"Don't you want to know what he said?" she asked me reproachfully.

The doctor, it seemed, had been willing for her to bear a child, had prescribed a diet, and promised that her condition would improve. In the period that followed she did, in fact, seem to become more normal, though she remained very weak and grew continually thinner. We decided that she had better go home to her father in the country and not come back to Moscow until ten days before the date of her delivery. Her father, a retired clerk, lived in a village of the Tambov Province called Rasskasovo, where there was plenty of vegetables, milk, and white bread. Olga would be assured of fresh air, quiet, and good food. The summer months in that gentle flat countryside are mild, and I was delighted at the thought of sparing her the exhausting life of the capital. I set to work for my examinations with a good will after she had gone.

I had to pass simultaneously the examinations of the General Staff College and of the faculty of oriental languages. Since 1921 I had given up my study of Hindustani to concentrate on a more complete mastery of Persian. The musical tongue of Saadi appealed very forcibly to many of us. The old scholar Mirza Djafar Khan, our professor, finding me so keen, offered to give me special lessons without extra charge. I was soon able to take notes of his lectures in Persian.

On July 10, 1923, I passed the last examination with honors. I was now the possessor of a *summa cum laude* degree. Olga's pregnancy was drawing to its close, and I expected every day when I got home to find a letter saying that she was coming back at once, for we had decided that the child should be born in one of the good Moscow maternity homes. This night a telegram was waiting for me at the hotel: "Twin boys. Olga doing well. Father."

My delight was tinged with some anxiety, for the twins must have been born prematurely. Two days passed. On the twelfth of July the hotel porter handed me another telegram which contained two words only: "Olga died."

Mechanically I climbed to our fourth-floor room and sat down on the divan, twisting in my hands that odd strip of paper, reading and rereading the incredible words that it contained. Everything round me was in its customary place: Olga's clothes were hanging on the pegs, her glass and toothbrush were on the shelf. I could not understand. I was too young. Never before had irreparable disaster struck me like this in the face. I was familiar with death on the battlefield, but the death of a person so dear to me, of one so young, so vital, and in the act of giving life—that was more than I could take in. I was stunned. My throat and my eyes were dry.

Some friends came in, talked to me, sat beside me—and no doubt I gave them answers. The first thing to do was to go to Rasskasovo as soon as possible. The formalities took three days—getting leave, procuring a military railroad pass, furnishing myself with the necessary papers. I have no idea what went on in my head during all that time. I know only that I refused firmly to believe that Olga was dead. It must be a mistake, a nightmare from which I should soon awake, since everything around me went on as though no tragedy had happened, and since I was so soon to see Olga again.

I made the journey in the same state of mind. It was stronger than any grief. At the little station I looked around for Olga. Of course she would be there, just to assure me that what had happened was nothing but a bad dream. But she was not there, nor did I meet her on the footpath that led through cornfields to the house. Surely she knew what time the train arrived? Ah, of course, it was too soon after her lying-in for her to be up.

The house had an air of melancholy. The trees surrounding it looked mournful in the sunshine. My father-in-law came out to meet me and pressed my hand in silence. I went in. Two bundles of white linen were lying on the bed, and a sound of weak whimpering came from them.

Were these two little scraps of complaining flesh all that remained to me of the being so full of life? I looked at them with resentment. It was because of them that Olga had died.

My father-in-law said very quietly, "She named them Alexander and Boris. She held them in her arms. She was happy."

Olga had been on the point of leaving for Moscow when her pains began prematurely. She had had a terrible time. Her labor had continued for two days. The second of the twins had had to be delivered with forceps. The doctor who had attended her seemed quite incapable of dealing with such a case. Exhausted by hemorrhage, she had managed to struggle on for forty-eight hours after the birth.

"Where is she buried?"

It was only when I stood beside the newly dug grave in the village cemetery that I really understood. Her old father and I walked back through the fields. Death had become a reality. At home the two scraps of flesh and blood continued to whimper. Life, too, was real.

My father-in-law leaned over them with his faded beard and gently gave them swabs soaked in milk to suck. The hungry little mouths ceased to complain. A doctor came to see them.

"Born prematurely—too weak," he said. "They're only six days old, but they've got gastritis already, both of them. No use making them suffer unnecessarily by trying to keep them alive. This one will probably go any minute now; the other may hang on for a day or two."

Olga had died in order that they might live, and now they were to die, too. As the thought came to me, the two little shapeless bundles became suddenly strangely dear—and I was seized with a determination to protect them and to save them. I leaped into the saddle and galloped to the next village, where I found another doctor who was well spoken of.

"Come back with me, now, at once!" I cried. "There are two babies who've got to be saved!"

A bumpy little carriage took us back to Rasskasovo along sunny roads between woods and fields of corn.

The doctor was a long time examining them.

"It looks as though my colleague were right—there's not much chance of saving them. Still, we can try. This cow's milk is what is killing them—they must have mother's milk."

He prescribed a drug, prepared in infinitely small doses, which was to be given them once every hour. Their grandfather took charge of it. There was nobody else in the house.

Meanwhile I mounted my horse again and rode about the near-by hamlets hunting for a wet nurse. People looked at me suspiciously when I stopped them to ask if there was a young mother in the neighborhood. My uniform frightened them. I had to make explanations. When they heard my story they became more friendly, and I was finally directed to a farmer's hut. I knocked at the door. To the woman who opened it I argued at length, promising all my future food ration as a senior officer—promising anything she wished to ask. At this period it was not easy to find a peasant who would voluntarily take a job in the cities, and there was throughout the countryside a certain amount of hostility toward uniforms. My offers were politely refused. Were the two little babies to die, then, just because I couldn't find them a nurse?

I was returning in despair when on an impulse I entered another farmhouse and found a young mother who consented to nurse them. She came with me at once, bringing her own child, too.

She was a robust peasant woman, and her presence filled me with hope. Still, every time I entered the house I would be torn with anxiety, and I was always surprised to hear that they were alive—sickly, only just breathing, but still alive. On the tenth day the doctor expressed a surprise even greater than my own.

"If it weren't for the fact that we no longer believe in miracles, I should say this was one," he said. "Those kids, just the same, will be bowled over by the slightest shock. There's nothing more I can do for them. If you can get them to Moscow and find special treatment for them, they may survive. But the risk of a journey is immense."

It might be so, but, after hesitating all through the night, I decided to take the risk. We were driven to the station at dawn in a light trap. The nurse, of course, took her own child to Moscow, too. So there I was, in charge of three newborn babies. There were no reserved compartments on this local line, and the train was packed with peasants and their sacks and bundles. They spent their time smoking a rank, coarse-cut tobacco. Those lying in the upper berths dangled their great boots over the edge just above the three fragile little heads wrapped in white linen. The atmosphere was thick with human stench, and the carriage was so full that it was impossible to move about. Even the corridor was crowded.

It took us thirty-six hours to reach our destination. The twins kept up a ceaseless whimper, but at least they were alive. They were alive, and I began to believe in their future. Olga's sacrifice had not been in vain.

In Moscow it was raining. I left the nurse and the three babies in a crowded waiting room and ran to the Public Health Department. An official informed me that the Clinic for the Newborn was full and nothing could be done. I rushed to the Foreign Office. Leon Karakhan received me with open arms.

"We're thinking of sending you as consul to the Khan of Maku. He is, you know, a Persian feudal chieftain in insurrection against the Shah, a sort of bearded despot. Do you think you're up to dealing with his tricks?"

But Karakhan saw from my expression that I had not come to ask him for a better job in the service.

"What's the matter?" he asked.

As soon as he heard my story he lifted the phone and called the vice-commissar of public health. They told him they'd find room somehow—that I could take my babies to the clinic. The nurse and I climbed into an old open droshky—nothing else was available—and, while the rain still poured down on us, with the babies wrapped in my uniform greatcoat, we drove to the Clinic for the Newborn, in charge of Dr. Speransky. I had to summon the great man from his office before I could prevail on the officials to cut short the formalities and admit us.

Once inside the building, a nurse put my two bundles—now frighteningly quiet—on a padded table in the entrance hall. One of the two, Boris, had a little froth at his lips. Obviously he was at his last gasp. A woman doctor immediately gave him artificial respiration. He was literally at the point of death. Some hours later, however, my two sons were lying in an incubator, assured of a chance to live. They remained delicate but gave evidence of considerable powers of resistance. Today they are twenty-two, and I dare say they need those powers more than ever!

The graduation of my class was marked by a party at which the stars of the Moscow Ballet came and danced in the great hall of the War College. There were speeches. The Central Committee distributed among the graduates twenty places at its new rest house at Marino. One of them fell to me, and I was glad of the opportunity for a change. My room at the Hotel Levada had become intolerable.

Marino is a huge estate, once the property of a prince, the sort of feudal domain which Turgenev so well described. Prince Bariatinsky, the conqueror of the Caucasus, had once lodged there his prisoner, the Tcherkes's Imam (Prince of the Church), Shamyl, the hero of the

Caucasian struggle for independence. The palace stood in a great park some of the vistas of which had been modeled on those of Versailles.

The Central Committee's instructions to the director, Strizhak, were that his guests should be made comfortable and given, above all, plenty of good and varied food. Strizhak carried out their orders, but only by dint of overspending his budget. As a result he was placed under investigation and finally committed suicide.

I was dazzled by so much comfort and splendor. The rooms were furnished in rare woods, gold-tinted Karelian birch and tropical mahogany. When I first entered the great dining hall, with its crystal chandeliers and its side table loaded with fruits, and heard the excited talk and happy laughter, I could think only of the hardships through which we had passed during the preceding years. If a little of that fruit had been available for Olga, she might still be alive. And she was not the only one. Thousands of other women had died, like her, from sheer exhaustion. My personal tragedy was just one incident in the great tragedy of my country.

As I remembered the rations we had drawn as much-envied students of the War College, and the wretched meals with which Olga and I had had to be content, all this fine food provided by the Central Committee turned bitter in my mouth. I could not eat it. I pushed away my plate. I felt a sort of morbid hatred for the handsome dining hall. I asked to be allowed to take my meals in my own room, and I felt some quiet only when surrounded by my books and listening to the wind in the old trees.

BOOK THREE

Of Christ's twelve apostles, Judas alone proved to be a traitor. But if he had acquired power, he would have represented the other eleven apostles as traitors and also all the lesser apostles, whom Luke numbers as seventy.

From *Stalin*, by Leon Trotsky

19. *At Grips with Diplomatic Problems*

IN OCTOBER, 1923, Moscow was in the throes of violent excitement. I began to be sorry that I had not studied German instead of Persian. We were preparing for the German revolution, every detail of which had been organized by the Communist International under the direction of Zinoviev.

Radek gave a series of lectures on the subject at the War College. He spoke to packed benches, and we felt that his whole being was dominated by the anticipation of what was to happen. He initiated us into the economics, history, psychology, and opposed ideologies of the German people, one section of which, the workers, was about to impose its will on the other for the salvation of the country and the progress of mankind. Radek was, as always, eloquent. He spoke with his usual heavy Polish accent, but intelligence and fire were dominant in him. He never uttered a dull phrase, never let the attention of his hearers droop, was always at grips with reality, which he held, as it were, in the pincers of his logic.

A slender young woman with auburn curls and the beauty of a Minerva without her helmet, who stood leaning against the frame of the door, seemed to be drinking in his words. This was his future wife, Larissa Reisner, who had been at nineteen a fighting soldier in one of the first Red battalions of the Volga, and who was now a writer of vigorous and vivid books. A few days later she would be following, hour by hour, the abortive revolution in Hamburg, an experience out of which she afterward made a moving volume.

At the last moment before that revolution, Zinoviev wrote a series of articles in *Pravda,* defining in advance the foreign policy to be pursued by the German Soviet Republic. Despite my confidence in the German proletariat, I could not help thinking that he might possibly be counting his chickens before they were hatched.

The Foreign Office had put me at the disposal of Boris Shumiatsky, who had been appointed ambassador to Persia, and at about this time he sent for me. For two years I was to work with this remarkable man. An old militant Socialist, organizer of a rising and of a Soviet at Krasnoyarsk in eastern Siberia during the 1905 revolution, and an erudite student of Marx, he was a Jew about forty years of age, with a massive face, wavy hair, and a deep, commanding voice. Gifted with astounding energy, capable of working all day and all night, eager and uncompromising, he was of the stuff of which leaders are made. He was to be trade representative in Persia as well as ambassador. (He was denounced as "an enemy of the people" during the Great Purge and disappeared.)

He told me that I had been appointed consul general in Ghilan, a province of northern Persia lying along the Caspian Sea and the economic center of the whole country. The consulate was situated at Resht, the commercial capital. Strategically and economically, however, the port of Enzeli (now Pehlevi), also under my jurisdiction, was of prime importance for our influence in Persia. The region is a very unhealthy one. There is a Persian proverb which says: *"Morg mikhakhi, Ghilan berow"*—"If you want to die, go to Ghilan."

I had traveled with Shumiatsky and the embassy staff. We had two unexpected companions as far as Baku: my War College friend, Jacob Blumkin, and the famous poet, Sergei Yessenin. They got along well together and never went to bed sober. Yessenin made a painful impression on me. He had been torn between town and country in his youth, and between Bohemia and the Revolution in young manhood. Now he was suffering from overindulgence in alcohol and women and from the orgies to which he would treat himself in the intervals between his poems—which are, nevertheless, some of the most moving in the Russian language. The handsome young genius had turned into a sot. His face was pale and puffy, his eyes tired, his voice husky. He gave the impression of being completely demoralized. Blumkin, whose soldierly temperament always saved him from excesses, had saddled himself with the job of "pulling Sergei together." It was more than anyone could do!

In Moscow a little later Yessenin met and married Isadora Duncan. She had come to the land of the Soviets to spread the new dance form of which she was the originator. The Soviet Government had placed at her disposal a children's school. Yessenin was intrigued by the great dancer and thought he saw in her a mate with whom he could share a life of artistic creation. But their marriage was not a happy one. Instead of the heavenly dancer he had envisioned, Yessenin found Isadora a fading woman, well past middle age, who encouraged him to drink by drinking with him. In Moscow everyone knew that their days were passed in drunken desperation. After traveling together in the United States and several European countries, they were divorced.

A lyric poet in the most exquisite tradition of Russian peasant poetry, Yessenin was unable to adapt himself to the mechanistic heroics of the revolutionary period. The poetry of revolution, which came naturally to such city poets as Mayakovsky, was alien to Yessenin. Alone, embittered, he turned to rowdyism and practically stopped writing. He became involved in a number of unsavory brawls for which the Soviet press rebuked him. One day he wrote a few words of farewell in his own blood and hanged himself in a Leningrad hotel. Mayakovsky addressed to him a famous poem: "It is easy in our times to die, Sergei; it is harder to live. . . ." A few years later Mayakovsky shot himself. It is easy to die. . . .

Shumiatsky insisted, for the sake of prestige, on crossing the Caspian

Sea in a warship. The destroyer supplied to us for this purpose was an old vessel, but it looked well with its high, spare lines. There was a big sea running. Our steel ship literally "lay over" on the rollers. Every member of the embassy staff was seasick. It took me several days to recover. The solid ground of Persia seemed to me to be suffering from a rhythmical movement caused by invisible waves. The local authorities received us with a solemnity which suggested that they at least were on solid ground.

Although proclaiming a new policy of fraternal equality toward Persia, and an end of extraterritorial concessions, the Soviet Government, when brought face to face with realities, adopted a course little different from that pursued by the old Czarist Empire. The diplomats of the former regime had systematically prepared, chiefly by economic penetration, for the ultimate conquest of Persia. The Persians were forbidden by treaty to maintain armed ships on the Caspian. Russia, on the other hand, kept two gunboats anchored at Enzeli. The difference now was that the gunboats belonged to the Soviets. Russia was in control of the fishing grounds of Ghilan and Mazanderan, and a Russian company held a concession which included the only road linking the north coast to Teheran, the capital.

To be sure, by a treaty signed in 1921 the Soviets had agreed to abolish the system of concessions and had surrendered most of the advantages enjoyed by the former Imperial Government. But the clauses of this treaty were far from faithfully observed. Our authorities administered the fishing rights, and the harbor also was in our hands. We were afraid that if we withdrew, the whole district would fall into the hands of the English, who were extremely active and enjoyed the support of the party of the powerful War Minister, Reza Khan.[1] This man was later to become absolute ruler of Persia and win her a position of real independence, imposing upon her people a number of reforms imitating those of Mustapha Kemal of Turkey. He had a profound knowledge of the Russians, drawn from a period when, as a noncommissioned officer, he had served with a Russian Cossack regiment stationed in Persia.

My consulate general was thirty miles from Enzeli, where I maintained a vice-consul and often visited myself. I arrived at Resht on the same day as the newly appointed British consul, Mr. Trott, but a few hours earlier, a fact which was to have unexpected importance later. My headquarters was situated in a comfortable and spacious building which had once been a merchant's house. My staff consisted of two Russian secretaries and two Persian clerks. All five of us were men between the ages of twenty-three and twenty-five, all unmarried; and, as we worked late and rarely went out, the consulate soon won the nickname of the "Russian monastery."

[1] Deposed and exiled when the English and Russians entered Iran in September, 1941, he died in exile three years later.

Two old Persian servants, who had served the consuls of the Czar, surrounded us with attentions and never let us forget the ceremoniousness of oriental life. Their clothes were rather shabby, and this fact, living as they did in a country where dress plays a great part in social matters, gave them a jaundiced view of life. It so happened that my British colleague, whose house was opposite, had just fitted his servants with brand-new uniforms. My two *gulams*, desolated by the news, respectfully laid their grievance before me. Were we going to allow the glorious flag of Russia to be humiliated in the eyes of all Persia? Their elbows were coming through their sleeves. My first act as consul was to bring happiness to these excellent old men. I ordered them new black liveries adorned with red braid and silver buttons. I had a man make these especially for us and decorate them with the hammer and sickle. The same device was sewn on their caps, which were of traditional local pattern. Their display of solemnity, braid, and silver was far greater than that put forward by Mr. Trott's people, and thus our national prestige was saved, though I question whether the "foe" realized it!

My conscience as a Communist was very soon put to the test. When the concessions had been in force, it had been the habit of astute Persians of wealth to become Russian subjects, and thus be assured of consular protection for their properties. These men now came to me with requests to renew their passports. In our eyes they were just a lot of capitalists to whom we owed no consideration whatever. But Shumiatsky's instructions were definite. The passports must be renewed; every protection must be afforded our fellow citizens in Persia, even though they *were* capitalists. Through them we might be able to extend our influence. It was the thin end of the wedge.

Part of my duty was to pay official visits to the military and civil governors as well as to a number of local bigwigs. Among the latter were several *mullahs*, priests of the Moslem faith, who, in central Asia, were as often as not the prime movers in organizing civil war against us. But necessity knows no law. I was polite; so were they. One of the *mullahs*, an old and influential man, made a profound impression on me by the simple dignity of his welcome. He received me in a huge, dilapidated building where he lived all alone. The court of honor was completely bare of furniture; so were the various rooms, in the last of which this aged ascetic squatted on a carpet. His last feeble spark of life seemed to be concentrated in his eyes, which expressed shrewdness and humanity. He had the reputation of being a sort of saint, and Reza Khan corresponded with him and always came to see him when he was in Resht.

Reza Khan had probably decided to see how far he could go with the new Soviet ambassador, for it came to my ears that the local authorities were seizing, on one excuse or another, the lands belonging to our protégés. It made my position extremely delicate. I addressed immediate and sharp protests to the governor, and the seizures stopped. But that was not all. Some detachments of Persian police established themselves on the edge of the fishing grounds which we controlled and were quite obviously preparing to occupy them with a surprise attack. In great haste the members of the concession posted sentries and began to erect barbed-wire fences. The tension increased from hour to hour. I wired to Teheran for instructions. Shumiatsky's reply was: "Whatever happens, don't permit occupation of fishing grounds. Two gunboats at your disposal." At the same time Foreign Commissar Chicherin, seriously alarmed at what was happening, sent me a personal code telegram: "At all costs you must avoid an armed clash, which might compromise our whole foreign policy in the East. . . ."

Whether I yielded, therefore, or whether I resisted, I would be the goat. The question was, how could I avoid yielding and yet not resort to arms? An attempt to surprise the defenses was, indeed, made, but luckily resulted in no bloodshed or fighting. For our sentries gave the alarm, the personnel took fighting positions, and Reza Khan's men showed no wish to expose themselves to fire.

I decided to play the strong-man act ostentatiously, ringing up the officer in command of the flotilla, telling him to prepare a landing party in case of necessity and be ready to cover them with gunfire should they be attacked. The guns were in fact manned and aimed threateningly at the shore. Then I went to the Persian military governor and told them that I reserved to myself complete liberty of action and was determined to defend our inalienable rights. The whole thing, of course, was a bluff. I would never have given the order to open fire. But the military governor withdrew his men, and the war of nerves was won. From that moment our relations began to improve.

In order to break down British influence, our people in Moscow, after their attempt in 1920 to provoke a Persian revolution failed, had decided to strengthen the hands of the central power so as to weaken the influence of the local nobles and feudal princes, who were always susceptible to British money. Their plan, in brief, was to promote the establishment of a modern centralized state, with which they could maintain friendly relations based on trade. It was a long way from those days in Tashkent and Bokhara when we had dreamed of turning Asia upside down! Our present aim was to encourage the growth of national sentiment and favor the building up of a national power composed of traders and bureaucrats. I received instructions couched roughly in the following terms: "Suggest the advisability of forming a National Party. . . . Get the leading men of the country to telegraph to the capital demanding a progressive Nationalist government. . . ." Unfortunately we had no money and little as yet to export. Our hands, consequently, were tied.

My personal idealism, at this time, suffered a number of shocks. I learned the part played in politics by money. For instance, a Seid asked me for an audience. What he said was, in substance, this:

"I have permission to start a newspaper." (That he had permission may have been true; but he had not yet decided what the policy of the paper should be.) "Now, I am a proved friend, my dear sir, of your great country. Lenin is the greatest man who has appeared in the world since the Prophet, and I should like to produce a journal of strong Russophile leanings. The English are intriguing against you. Mr. Trott is animated by the blackest intentions. What I need is a sum of three hundred *tumans* a month. . . ."

I thanked this well-wisher and promised to think it over.

Another rather unusual visitor was a Kurdish warrior who had held some official position but who was now out of a job. He was richly dressed and, in true mountain fashion, carried a dagger and a pistol stuck in his sash. To put the interview on a friendly footing he graciously laid the pistol on my office table. On the pretext of offering him a cigarette I opened and failed to close the drawer in which I kept a gun of my own. In a quiet voice he pointed out that it was no uncommon thing for a man to have enemies. Husbands, he said, are sometimes troublesome; servants are not always trustworthy; the authorities may, at times, show an ugly temper. Anything, in fact, may happen, and it is always well to have at one's disposal a discreet assistant who, in case of need, can be relied on to get rid of the awkward husband, the embarrassing journalist, the disloyal servant, without undue fuss. He assured me that there were a number of influential persons who were not above making use of him. . . .

I showed him the door as politely as I could.

Some days after arriving, I decided to take a walk and look at the city. I picked up my hat and started down the stairs. But one of the servants confronted me at the door with a very respectful bow.

"His Excellency the consul is thinking of going out?"

"Yes—I'll be back soon."

"But His Excellency the consul intends to go to the city?"

"Why, yes. What's the matter?" I realized that he was looking a little agitated.

"A thousand excuses for presuming to trouble His Excellency, but His Excellency really should not do that."

"First, please don't call me 'Excellency' any more. And what's all this about, anyway?"

"But His Excellency—excuse me—the esteemed consul cannot do it."

I was getting really irritated now.

"Look here, are you crazy?"

He could not bring himself to explain, but begged my permission to bring up the clerk of the consulate, who would clear up the point for him.

144

The clerk, when he came, was even more embarrassed. But he managed to tell me that the Russian consul could not go about like an ordinary person. Prestige in the Orient was everything. The Russian consul had always been the leading personage in this northern province. He would ask even the governor to call when he needed to talk with him, and the governor would have to wait in the anteroom if he was busy. People, of course, must never see him walking in the streets! If I wished to see the city, the carriage could be summoned in less than a minute, and the two footmen would be in attendance.

"But that's nonsense," I said. "We aren't czarist consuls. We don't need all that folderol."

He made a last appeal.

"Your immediate predecessors observed this convention," he said, "and I am sure our ambassador knows about it. May I humbly suggest that you take this matter up with the ambassador before you break the tradition? In the eyes of the Persians there has been no change; you are still the consul of the Great Northern Neighbor. And I assure you, people in the Orient like an imposing departure. Their respect depends upon it."

His anxiety was so sincere that I gave in for the time being, and he summoned the carriage.

It arrived at once, a gleaming victoria with a liveried driver and two solemn-faced footmen who took up their positions, one beside the driver and the other behind me.

The driver lashed his horses and we raced at full speed through the crowded streets, the footmen shouting and bellowing to the public to get out of the way. My first impulse was to tell them to stop this noise and drive slowly so that I could see the town. But, no, to hell with it, I thought, this also is probably part of my prestige. I saw practically nothing and lost all interest in this excursion I had planned so differently for myself.

At my first visit to Teheran I took the matter up with the ambassador. I told him that in my opinion there was a better way for Soviet consuls to gain prestige. With my ability to speak Persian fluently, and my long studies of the customs of the Orient, I believed I could go among the people like a human being and make friends with them. I was sure that in this way our influence would be greater, and the true character of the new Russia would become known.

Shumiatsky gave me a free hand in the matter, and then I really began to enjoy myself. I explored the city on foot, and in my own way, taking a long walk almost every afternoon, stopping in the market place, lingering over the bric-a-brac and bookstalls, talking with the merchants and their clients. Sometimes I would travel by public bus out into the suburbs. The busses would be filled with women—veiled, as they always were in Persia then, and supposed to be silent in public. But, when the male passengers had got off, these women, hearing me speak Persian with the driver, would grow so inquisitive that the taboo was forgotten, and they would begin to chatter like magpies, over-whelming me with questions! What was I doing in Persia? Where did I come from? Was I a soldier or a merchant? Was I married? How many children had I? Was my wife pretty?

Other afternoons I would pass my time in the barbershops or visit the public baths, where, in an atmosphere thick with steam, I would listen to excited discussions like those at a town meeting.

At first people would point at me, whispering: "Look at that for a Russian consul!" But little by little they got used to me, and I made friends. I realized how many friends, and what an innovation it was, at the official reception on a Soviet holiday, when I saw my clerks gazing with consternation at the huge crowd that swarmed the rooms of the consulate to shake my hand.

20. *Persia Will Not Be a Republic*

EARLY ONE MORNING in January I was awakened and called to the telephone. I heard the vice-consul at Enzeli speaking in a voice shaken by emotion.

"Vladimir Ilych is dead.

"What?—Lenin?"

"Lenin is dead."

I sat stupefied at my desk. We had all forgotten that he was mortal. We knew, of course, that he was ill. What would happen to the Party and the Revolution without him? The overwhelming, terrible news was like an angry gust blowing through the open windows of the house. There was no time to think, no time to realize the immense signifi-cance of what had occurred. I had to telephone to Teheran for instructions and issue them to my assistants; to send telegrams to Mos-cow; to assemble the members of the Communist cell; to summon all the Soviet citizens to a meeting; to inform the Persian authorities; to receive the hundreds of Persian visitors who began to pour in; to organize some sort of ceremony for them and for the Russian colony.

This ceremony took place that same day in the Court of Honor of the consulate general, across which were stretched the usual red streamers bearing slogans written in Russian and Persian: "Workers of the World, Unite!" "Oppressed of Every Land, Unite against Imperialism!" A platform had been erected beneath these slogans, and from it I read the official communiqué and spoke a few words. Before me on a carpet stood the civil governor, the military governor, a much-bemedaled *sartip* (general), the *mullahs* of the principal mosques, and the heads of the chamber of commerce. All wore formal mourning: some of them may have been genuinely touched, for Lenin had become a symbol of liberation to the whole of Asia. Mohammed Saed, the Persian consul at Baku, later ambassador at Moscow, and then Persian prime minister (eased out by Stalin in November, 1944), represented the Foreign Office on this occasion. I thought suddenly of the rather inappropriate slogans displayed behind me. Ah, well, I reflected, they are honoring Lenin, and Lenin has produced some slogans they would like even less!

Night came. Exhausted by the labors of the day, I retired to my living quarters—a succession of almost empty rooms occupying the whole of one floor. I sat down, my head in my hands, thinking of nothing. Then gradually I began to reflect. The lives of even the greatest individuals must end sooner or later, but the life of the people goes on. Before my eyes hung the official portrait of Lenin. It seemed to me that until then I had never really seen it. Tears poured from my eyes.

For a long time, in the darkness of the night, I paced up and down the empty rooms in solitude. My mind went back to the days when I had stood beside communal graves where soldiers who had been my friends but a few hours before, full of life and enthusiasm, had just been briefly buried.

What was going to happen to us now? Who was to take the wheel of this great ship with its course set to the future through unchartered seas, with its amateur crew, its battered machinery, its young and daring engineers? A few brilliant men remained: Trotsky, Tomsky, Piatakov, Rykov, Bukharin, Radek. . . . I scarcely thought of Stalin. He was very little known, and, back there in 1924, it seemed unlikely that he would ever play a leading role. Undoubtedly Zinoviev and Kamenev would dispute with Trotsky the moral right to be Vladimir Ilych's successor, but for the men of my generation they had no claim to it.

The year 1924 saw a sudden change in our international position. Great Britain recognized the Soviet Union, reopening relations which had been in abeyance since 1918. Many of the other great powers followed suit. Soviet opinion counted this a considerable success and saw in it a guarantee of peaceful development in the years to come. In the microcosm of my consulate general these changes expressed themselves in terms of my relations with Mr. Trott. We used to meet occasionally, and we knew each other well by sight, but we were not friendly because our countries were not. Ought I to go now and congratulate him on what had happened, or was it for him to come to me? I telephoned Teheran for instructions. The embassy told me to wait until these weighty questions of procedure could be thoroughly examined. The embassies of both countries were studying the matter at Teheran. The various ranks of the diplomatic and consular officials concerned, and the dates of their arrivals at their posts, were being made the object of a scrupulous investigation. It developed eventually that I could claim a slight seniority over Mr. Trott in the official hierarchy on the ground that I had arrived in Resht a few hours ahead of him. It was his duty, therefore, to pay the first visit. He did so, and I returned it the same day.

Mr. Trott was not very fluent in French but knew Persian well, and we conversed in that language. He showed me with great pride his garden, which was heavy with the scent of roses, and he carried friendliness so far as to stick one of his finest red blooms in my buttonhole. Since his own coat was adorned with a white one, we had a little joke about the "War—or shall we say Peace?—of the Roses." In Mr. Trott's flower-surrounded consulate I also met Sir Percy Lorraine, the British minister in Persia, on his way to Teheran. I had thereafter many pleasant conversations with Mr. Trott in which the subject of politics were studiously avoided. Should these lines come his way, I should like him to know that I have a pleasant memory of those occasions. My delight in establishing cordial relations with him was all the greater since, shortly before our arrival in Resht, there had been a theft of documents from the British consulate, in which a servant working there had been suspected. The dead body of this servant was found later in a well. Rumor, of course, said that Russians had paid for the documents, and that vengeance rather than a guilty conscience was the cause of this death.

During the period when Mr. Trott and I were at Resht no such gruesome international events took place, but there was one little two-sided intrigue that may now be brought to light.

One day Mamed Aga, the secretary of my consulate, came into my private office with a worried and mystery-laden look. Mamed was a Tartar by origin, brought up in the Moslem faith—a non-Party member, but all the same a devoted Soviet employee who had worked in the consulate some years. On the previous evening, he told me, as he was sitting over a cup of *mokka* in a coffee house, a *munshi* (Persian secretary) from the British consulate had come and sat down beside him. After the usual flowery oriental approaches, he had come to the point in this fashion: Was not Mamed Aga a son of the Moslem faith? And didn't he know that the Bolsheviks threatened to destroy all religions, including that of Allah and his Prophet? Of course, Mamed Aga had to earn his living; but shouldn't he do something to make up for the sinful way in which he earned it—something for those who respected religion and defended the Moslem world?

With that, the *munshi* briefly conveyed to my surprised secretary a personal offer from his superiors in the British consulate that he supply them with copies of my weekly reports to Moscow and Teheran,

148

which it was his job to type out. They were certain he would consider it his duty as a devoted Moslem to do this. But to make it even more pleasant, they would pay him twenty-five *tumans* (about twenty-five dollars) for each report.

Mamed Aga had deferred his answer and come to ask me what he should do.

I congratulated him on his loyalty and on his tactics. Every week after that, when each report was finished, we would give free rein to our imaginative powers for the benefit of the British consulate. We produced some delightful and on the whole harmless fiction, and every week Mamed Aga brought me the twenty-five *tumans* which he had received from His Majesty's treasury.

I wrote to Shumiatsky, telling him the story and asking how I should use this unexpected income. I suggested that, as the only progressive nationalist weekly in Resht was badly in need of funds, I might turn over the money to them. Shumiatsky approved, and so every week one of my staff members would make a generous contribution of British money to this newspaper, which was agitating for national reforms and against the British imperialist influence in Persia.

This lasted for several months. But one day Mamed Aga waited in vain at their meeting place for the British *munshi*. An official of the British mission in Teheran had come just then for a brief stay in Resht. Perhaps he found our literary exercises less edifying than the local officials had. Perhaps our inspiration was failing. Anyway, this source of income was cut off.

Persia at this time was passing through one of the decisive periods of her history. Little by little Reza Khan was getting all the power into his hands. As prime minister and minister of war, he was putting his men in key positions, reorganizing the Army, and reforming the tax system. The Shah, who was already little but a figurehead, had gone to Europe on a semi-voluntary pleasure trip. Reza Khan's idea was to convert the country into a strongly centralized republic, with a constitution on the Turkish model, and become its president for life. Upon the Shah's departure, as though at the wave of a magic wand, a republican movement came into being. Republican newspapers sprouted full grown from the ground. Down with the dynasty! Down with the monarchy! Long live progress! Such was the tenor of hundreds of messages sent to Reza Khan by various groups of merchants. At the same time the civil governors found themselves possessing less and less authority. The real power passed into the hands of the military governors, the men of Reza Khan.

It was amusing to see how these monarchist generals on the order of their chief clumsily took the reins of republican agitation into their hands. But the agitation went a good deal further than had been intended. Peasants staged manifestations at Resht demanding the land of the feudal estates. Workmen and fishermen, mindful of the insurrection of 1920, created new disturbances at Enzeli and displayed the Red flag. At this point—just as suddenly as it had arisen—the anti-monarchist wave subsided. Reza Khan had changed his plans. He let two years pass with the Shah in Europe and himself in the place of power. Then he deposed the Shah and founded a dynasty of his own.

He decided upon this change of plan under the influence of the British, who thus outmaneuvered us. For we had favored the republican campaign and had planned to make Reza another Mustapha Kemal. In some Foreign Office circles our ambassador, Yurenev, who followed Shumiatsky, was held responsible for this failure. Yurenev was an avid hunter and spent many days in the chase. He was, in fact, absent during the decisive period. However, in personal letters I had from him in Moscow, he denounced that "chicken-brained bunch around Litvinov in the Foreign Office" for giving silly instructions which aroused the suspicions of Reza Khan and spoiled their friendly relations and our plans.

The customs of the Persians were ripe for a radical change. Besides having to wear a veil, women were excluded from the movie houses and the city parks. I saw them, at the unveiling of a monument to Reza Khan, sitting like crows on the edge of the sidewalks, their feet in the gutter, because the sidewalk belonged to the park, which they were forbidden to enter.

When I gave a reception, at which I intended showing a number of films, the religious authorities insisted that there should be a special session for women in a locked hall. And they took great care to arrange matters so that the mechanics in the projection box should not be able to see this female audience. We showed the tragic film of the funeral of Lenin, with its shots of the little snow-covered house in Gorky where he died, the Russian crowd waiting in below-zero cold to file past the bier of Vladimir Ilych, the guard of honor round the uncovered coffin —Zinoviev, Kamenev, Rykov, Bukharin, Tomsky—watching over their friend, the masses of men and women in deep mourning moving to the light of torches along the black and white streets. My Persian guests were deeply moved and felt that the scene being enacted before them was no less than the death of the great Prophet of Russia.

My contacts, too, with the townfolk left me with the feeling that I was dealing with a people in need of reforms. The procession of the *Shakseivakhsei*, a celebration commemorating the death of Hussein, the descendant of the Prophet, contained an element of barbarous crudity. On this occasion the fanatic believers crowded the streets, wailing and mutilating themselves. The men, some with manacles on their limbs, gashed their bodies and faces with daggers, swords, and scimitars. They were soon dripping blood all over. Some carried children on their shoulders and slightly cut them, too, and covered them with blood. The glaring white of their clothes, the dusty sunlight, the rags, the agonized face, the general sense of exaltation, fatigue, and pain, the sight of fresh blood mingled with sweat and dirt—all these things together gave an impression of unbridled savagery. Believers who were rich enough came through the ordeal without a scratch, having satisfied their craving for martyrdom and the demands of tradition by hiring some poor devil to lacerate himself in their stead. They walked beside their proxies very proud of their sacrifice and sure that it was equal to that of the less fortunate.

In order to strengthen our commercial influence, Shumiatsky was establishing a number of mixed Soviet-Persian companies in conjunction with native businessmen. They were financed by a Soviet-Iranian bank set up on his initiative. This bank was administered by a young Jewish Communist named Arkus, an exceptionally able financier. In accordance with Party rules then still in force, we of the service received salaries of not more than $250 a month. On the boards of these mixed companies, however, the Soviet directors were paid the same as their Persian colleagues, so that their incomes were two or three times as big as ours. Arkus was the only one of them all who turned over the difference to the Party treasury. He later became vice-president of the State Bank in Moscow. His name figured among the "conspirators" mentioned in the Zinoviev trial. But he himself never appeared in court, and no "confession" was ever produced. Undoubtedly Arkus spoiled the best part of the show by refusing to testify to money transfers which had not taken place. He was never mentioned again and was doubtless secretly shot.

Karim Khakimov, my friend and predecessor in Resht, passed through one day on his way to take up a new appointment as consul general in Meshad. He was a workman, a miner of Tartar origin, a true child of the Revolution. A Moslem who had become a Communist, self-educated but well-read and gifted with the tact of a natural diplomat, he had marvelous success in dealing with his coreligionists. Some years later he became the first Soviet ambassador to Arabia, and as a Moslem he was permitted to reside at Mecca—a concession of high importance. He came home to study at the Communist Academy under Bukharin, after which he returned to Arabia.

During the purge of the diplomatic corps in 1938, Khakimov was recalled. Paris newspapers published a report that he had disappeared from his ship at Alexandria. Let us hope that he lives—that he availed himself of the anonymity of the Orient to escape the clutch of the G.P.U.

I had just been offered the post of first secretary of the embassy at Teheran when malaria once more laid me low. So bad was my health that I went into the hospital at Enzeli. My colleague, Slavutsky, then consul general at Tabriz, was appointed in my place. He later became our ambassador to Japan. He was one of the two who graduated with me from the class in Persian at the faculty of oriental languages. The other was Pastukhov, who later became our ambassador to Persia. Both disappeared in the purge.

21.   Teheran—Athens—Rome—Berlin—Moscow

AT THE END of 1924, when I left the hospital, Shumiatsky gave me a leave of absence; and Yurenev, then ambassador in Rome, invited me to spend my holiday with him.

I turned over my post to Levitsky, who ranked as an Old Bolshevik, his Party membership dating from 1909. He joined the Opposition later and disappeared in the purge of 1938.

Before leaving for Italy I went to Teheran to see Shumiatsky, making the acquaintance of his commercial assistant, Mayers, an *émigré* lately returned from America. He was a thoroughly Americanized businessman, given to swift decision and no talk, and later became a director with Dybets of the Soviet automobile industry. Both disappeared in the purge. Mayers had a very beautiful wife who afterward married Valeri Mezhlauk, vice-premier of the Soviet Government—well known in America, where he went often on special missions. Mezhlauk also fell victim to the purge.

Shumiatsky, seeing that I had recovered, almost spoiled my vacation by recommending to the General Staff that I take the post of assistant to our military attaché, General Bobritshev, who invited me to make with him a tour of the nomadic tribes of southern Persia. But I declined the offer and left for Italy. I went across the Caspian Sea and through the Caucasus, and embarked at Batum for Naples on an Italian steamer. Its comfort, cleanliness, and good meals offered a strong contrast to life in the Orient.

The boat followed the coast line of Anatolia, putting in for a day each at Trebizond, Ineboli, and Samsun, pretty little Turkish towns of white houses standing on the terraced slopes of green hills. We visited the small cafés where real Arab coffee could be got. It took us a week to reach the Bosporus.

I will not attempt to describe the lights of the Golden Horn and the magnificence of Istanbul. In the huge building which had been the Imperial Russian embassy and was now the consulate general of the U.S.S.R., my colleague, Vladimir Potemkin, gave me a warm welcome. He was an ex-professor, a man of bourgeois origin, and, though a

Party member, wielded little influence at that time because he was thought of as a man who joined the Party only when victory was assured.[1]

Greece, of which I got a glimpse on this voyage, was both gay and tragic. As a result of its defeat in Asia Minor, the little country had had to provide asylum for a million and a half Greeks driven from the region of Smyrna by the victorious Turks. That enormous number equaled one-fifth of the whole population of this small country already exhausted by a war.

Athens, however, looked radiant. I spent a week there. Madame Ustinov, our minister's wife, a simple and charming woman, gave up several days to showing me round. We visited the museums, the Acropolis, the island of Aegina, Eleusis, and Sunium. At Sunium I saw with deep emotion the name of Byron cut into the white marble of a temple column. Gazing on the blackened letters, I recalled the great poet's melancholy lines:

> Place me on Sunium's marbled steep
> Where nothing save the waves and I
> May hear our mutual murmurs sweep;
> There, swanlike, let me sing and die!

Ustinov introduced me to the diversions of the Western world, and for the first time in my life I visited a dance hall. He paid our bills with halves of banknotes, for the government had hit on the ingenious idea of having them cut in two and thus reduced their value by 50 per cent. That some such drastic method of solving the fiscal problems had been necessary was obvious from the number of barracks filled with refugees which met the eye at every turn.

A passenger of renown left the Piraeus on the same ship with me, the Belgian Emile Vandervelde, a leader of the Second International. I had very mixed feelings about him. Wasn't he the leader of that "reformist socialism" which had done so much to block the Revolution in western Europe? I discussed this point at length with a young Belgian socialist, Van der Ginst, who accompanied Vandervelde. We walked up and down the deck in heated argument, the placid beauty of the sea and the sky serving to keep us friendly despite the clash of our views. I belonged to a generation of Russians reared under the dictatorship of the proletariat, familiar with no ideas, no doctrines, no convictions but those of bolshevism. I had grown up hearing nothing else, convinced that we were the guardians of the ultimate truth, and that no adversary had anything to teach us. And here I found myself face

---

[1] Potemkin was later ambassador at Rome and Paris and assistant to Foreign Commissar Litvinov. Subsequently he was appointed commissar of education. His survival is probably explained by the fact that during the Civil War he was a member of Stalin's personal staff.

to face with a young Westerner, a socialist like myself in ideals, who offered for my contemplation a totally different, but strongly constructed, system based on political democracy. He questioned all of my values, many of which he categorically rejected. My own judgments were simple and admitted of no appeal. The Reformists, because of their willingness to compromise with the bourgeoisie and their horror of the necessary violence, had betrayed the working class, which, having learned wisdom from its mistaken trust in them, would end by joining us.

"Well, all I can say is, look out!" remarked the young Belgian. "By giving a free hand to violence, bolshevism has provoked a reaction which no respect for human dignity will serve to check. The answer to Red revolution is fascist revolution. The dictatorship of the proletariat has brought into existence the compensating phenomenon of a dictatorship of the reactionaries. What good is all that to mankind? Recourse to violence means the liquidation of just those liberties which are the most valuable today—and on which socialism must rely."

This way of thinking seemed to me at that time the product of a sort of cowardice typical of middle-class intellectuals. These cultivated and well-meaning people lacked the guts to take those decisions essential to a struggle which could be won only by a tactic of implacability. We Bolsheviks took for a starting point the energy of the proletariat. That was the gist of my reply to Van der Ginst. Seven years later we were to take up the argument again, but our roles were to be rather different. To that I shall return. But the question then debated was never thereafter long out of my mind. I brooded over it in solitude; I talked it out with many different people. I must admit that my viewpoint, so securely grounded in youth, faith, and fanaticism, was at last cruelly shattered by historic events and by my own experience.

At last we entered the Bay of Naples, where the light and the colors are so dazzling that the traveler feels he has lived until that moment in semi-darkness. Forgetting that I was expected at Rome, I spent two weeks exploring the Bay of Naples and the near-by country, causing Yurenev no end of anxiety and elaborate efforts to find me. The wealth of Italy's historic past went to my head. I wandered among her ruins, visited her museums, gazed at her monuments. I climbed Vesuvius. I amassed enough impressions to suffice for a lifetime. I turned over the savings of a year to Cook's Tours. After fifteen days of these wanderings, I went to Rome and showed up at the embassy.

Yurenev maintained in our Italian embassy a way of life worthy of the early days of the Revolution but which elsewhere had been pretty well forgotten. The ambassador, his family, the typists, and porters all used the same dining room and ate the same food. Outside business hours, the rules of "seniority," the sense of hierarchic distinctions, were reduced to a minimum. In consequence Yurenev was surrounded by an atmosphere of comradely devotion much more precious than the respect to which his official position entitled him.

His diplomatic career, however, nearly came to a premature end some months later. It was at the time when Matteotti was kidnapped in broad daylight in the streets of Rome and afterward found dead somewhere in the suburbs. The very day before this happened, Yurenev had asked Mussolini to dinner, and the invitation had been accepted by the Duce. It seemed after the event of a single night as though the whole Fascist system was going to collapse and be swept away by an outburst of poular disgust and the condemnation of the working-class movements of every country in Europe. Disclaimers and repudiations showed that there was danger even from those supporting the government.

For a whole week Mussolini faced a problem growing hourly more threatening. In diplomatic circles it was thought that his fall was inevitable. If he had gone out of power as the result of a political assassination, he would never have got back. The Italian Liberals and Communists forwarded a request to Yurenev to cancel the dinner. The embassy staff agreed with the Italian Communists. Instructions received from Moscow were to the same effect. Moscow, kept informed by its secret agents, considered that Mussolini's days were numbered.

Yurenev showed himself to be shrewder than most political observers of the day. He estimated the opposition at its true worth, saw that it was poor in resources and lacking in resolution. He perceived that the Fascist regime had built up a party and bureaucratic system strong enough to resist any attack such adversaries could launch against it. He had no intention of compromising Italo-Soviet relations, which were then normal. The Italy of Mussolini and the Germany of the Weimar Constitution were the only two countries with whom we were on friendly terms. (It is generally known that the Soviet Union was seeking to assume the leadership of the states discontented with the Treaty of Versailles.)

The gala dinner, therefore, took place. Yurenev, diplomatic representative of a revolutionary Socialist power, welcomed to his table Benito Mussolini, head of a fascist state. The episode was much talked of in Italian society, and even beyond the frontiers. It showed clearly that Soviet diplomacy would, when necessity arose, prove false to the spirit of socialist solidarity.

As a result of this, Yurenev was soon recalled to Moscow. The recovery of the Fascist regime, however, justified diplomatically the attitude he had taken up. Litvinov's friendship sufficed to save him from serious consequences; he was only deprived of seniority—that is to say, given posts of rather less importance—first in Vienna and later in Teheran. Afterward, when the Matteotti affair had blown over, he was appointed ambassador at Tokyo, a promotion which involved the personal approval of Stalin. From Tokyo he was transferred in 1937 to Berlin. He was invited to Berchtesgaden to present his credentials and accept the Führer's invitation to dinner. Two weeks later he was summoned to Moscow, and there, one night, he vanished.

On my way home from Italy I stopped at the Berlin embassy and attended the celebrations of the seventh and eighth of November. I heard Krestinsky, one of the oldest and most honored Bolsheviks, secretary of the Party under Lenin, make one of his strongly thoughtful speeches. Krestinsky was a genuine revolutionary idealist like Lenin, to whom power and prestige made no difference either in manner or in loyalty. He served the Party and the Revolution with a pure devotion up to his end, which I shall speak of later.

When I reached Moscow I found that the Central Committee had assigned me to the post of consul general in China, but for reasons of health I asked to be excused. I gathered that the climate of Canton was no better for malaria than that of Ghilan. Moreover, I did not regard such a post as very exciting. No one had the slightest inkling of the powerful Chinese Nationalist movement to be set in motion twelve months later with the aid of the Soviets. At that time Sun Yat-sen himself, driven out of Canton, was in hiding. A big movement seemed improbable. Needless to say, I regretted my decision later.

I would have liked to return to the Red Army for General Staff work, but as a Communist official I was not free to choose. The destiny and career of every Party member, even Army officers, was decided behind the walls of the enormous building of the Central Committee on Staraia Ploshchad. There a special Assignment Division shifted Communist officials about like pawns on a chessboard. The final assignment handed them might, as in the case of a friend of mine, transfer a general from his division in Moscow to Central Asia to raise opium or cotton. If he objected that the decision was illogical—that he had no experience in that field—he would be told: "There is no fortress a Bolshevik cannot capture."

I was relatively fortunate. The Central Committee, taking into account my knowledge of languages and of the "outside world," decided to give me a job having to do with affairs abroad. As was customary with senior officials, I was received by Molotov, then secretary of the Central Committee, for a discussion of my future job. I emerged from his office after an hour with a *putiovka* signed by him, which determined my work for the next four years. This printed sheet, on which only name, institution, and assignment had to be filled in, stated that Comrade Barmine, former consul general in Persia, was assigned to the Foreign Trade Department as a member of the board of directors of Mezhdunarodnaya Kniga—the "International Book Company"—in Moscow.

22. The Struggle against Trotskyism and Foreign Stationery

FOR FOUR YEARS my life in Moscow was that of a typical Communist functionary. I devoted my days to my job and my evenings to Party activity.

I lived alone in a small room near the center of the city. My two sons were growing up in charge of my mother in the province of Kiev. Like every Communist official's, even the highest up, my salary was limited to 225 rubles a month, which was just enough to provide the necessities. Non-Party specialists and technicians sometimes received much more. In a few cases they refused to take it. This maximum salary for Communists, which was later abolished by Stalin, contributed to the sense of comradeship which kept the Party together. Entirely absorbed in our work and Party duties, we led scarcely any personal life at all. Romance, amusements, the more delicate aspects of human companionship were all but obliterated.

The business of Mezhdunarodnaya Kniga was to import books and stationery from abroad. While the volume of book imports varied little, the need of the expanding Soviet structure, its schools and institutions, for office supplies, pens, pencils, etc., sharply increased. Our turnover, when I came, had risen to six million gold rubles a year, of which five million went for purchasing foreign stationery and office supplies. Foreign concessionaires, who had been given contracts to manufacture certain of these articles inside Russia, were growing rich under our eyes. The largest of these companies was run by an American, Dr. Hammer. The State Mospolygraph Trust undertook to make cheap pencils, but the quality was so bad that they could not compete with Dr. Hammer's more expensive goods. The concessionaires, who had obtained permission to export their profits in *valuta,* must have laughed at our inefficiency.

Our idea was to get the better of this competition and to free the Soviet Union from a costly flood of imports. Mezhdunarodnaya Kniga decided to manufacture office supplies. A very small part of the sums spent for foreign articles would suffice to import the machinery needed to make them ourselves. In that way we would reduce unemployment, which was still an important problem, and free the country from dependence on outside sources. Our first factory, to make typewriter ribbons, carbon paper, etc., was set up in Moscow. Vladimir Ipatyev, the great chemist, who recently refused to return to Russia from the United States and who is now a professor at Northwestern University, helped us to carry out our scheme. Leonid Krassin, commissar for foreign trade, gave us very efficient support. Full of enthusiasm for the plan, I was put in charge of this factory and entrusted with the building of another in Leningrad to specialize in steel pens.

I found in Leningrad an old chocolate factory which had been taken over by the state—or rather, by the municipality. It was rat-ridden and draughty. The dispossessed owner, who had been kept on as a caretaker, tried to convince me that the building was unsuitable for my purpose, that its adaptation would be very costly, etc. This gentleman, I must say, had the patience of a saint, and what he was after I do not know, but I suspect that he only wanted to keep his empty walls to himself. We disposed of his objections and before long equipped the remodeled building with machinery bought in Berlin and Prague. Under the control of a German technical expert, the Krassin Works were soon employing four hundred young Communists who had been out of a job. The German expert was invaluable to us. His ingenuity and devotion made it possible to achieve a quite unexpected success. In a few months we learned to produce pens which were equal to those of Dr. Hammer, and soon excelled them. Our Russian pencil trust, however, never caught up to Dr. Hammer's standard.

My war against capitalist competition, personified for me in Dr. Hammer, shifted to new ground. The state institutions continued to prefer the products of foreign concessionaires, even though more expensive than ours. We had a long-time struggle to convince our state customers that our product was good. By 1929, however, the Krassin Works in Leningrad and Moscow had succeeded in overcoming foreign competition. Their total annual production amounted to six million gold rubles, and they employed a thousand workers.

We felt that we had won a victory, and won it without encouragement from the bureaucrats of the Department of Foreign Trade, who were always advising us not to meddle in speculative ventures but to be content with quietly selling books and stationery from abroad. We had created a new industry and saved the Soviet treasury a foreign expenditure of five million gold rubles a year. Speaking personally, I felt that running the industrial department of Mezhdunarodnaya Kniga produced more tangible results than any amount of diplomatic discussions with the officials of Reza Khan. I began to forget my career in the Orient.

One episode served to remind me of this and to make me smile at my youthful dreams. Amanullah Shah, king of Afghanistan, paid a visit to Moscow. He was our first royal guest. Soviet Square was ringed off by policemen in white gloves, the Lenin Institute was decorated with flowers, a carpet was laid down from door to curbstone, and a cleaner swept it clear of the last grain of dust—all because a foreign potentate wanted to look at Lenin's manuscripts.

The Shah arrived in a car, with our President Kalinin beside him looking as though he were swallowing a dose of castor oil. Kalinin, always proud of his proletarian past and appearance, was not accustomed yet to such performances. It seemed as though a hundred years must have passed since we had lived in the hope of overturning all the thrones of Asia. Our ambassador, Raskolnikov, who had laid the foundations for the Persian revolution and, unknown to him, inspired me with the idea of working in the East, was just then back from Kabul, decorated by Amanullah with the highest order of Afghanistan and given the title of Royal Afghan Prince! However, he neither used the title nor wore the decoration.

Amanullah Shah asked us for advice, for motorcars, for armaments. His chance to use them was very brief. The following year the nomad tribes revolted, and he had to flee from his country.

In addition to his regular work, every Communist was required to fulfill certain Party duties called *nagruzki*.[1] One's *nagruzka* might range from speech-making before factory workers to soliciting subscriptions for the Party press. What a Communist might be called upon to do depended on his ability and the free time at his disposal.

The Party members in every institution were organized in a cell, which elected its own secretary. There were many popular organizations also—Red aid, sport, culture, volunteer defense, etc.—over which the small proportion of Communists had to exercise control. On the directing boards and committees of such organizations the Communists kept a decisive influence. A handful of Communists was thus able to control the activities of thousands of people in all spheres of life. And we Communists were in consequence overloaded with assignments, some of us sitting on a dozen committees.

It was our duty besides to be a shining example to non-Party people and recruit the suitable elements among them into the Communist Party. Needless to say, overburdened with *nagruzki,* we frequently failed to show an example of anything but perfunctory attendance. The "transmission belts," as Lenin called this method of control, were running, but hardly moving the machinery.

Intra-Party democracy was, during these years 1925 and 1926, still alive, though approaching its end. Discussion among Communists went on without censorship. Questions were freely raised, and "Bolshevik self-criticism" still meant something besides a purge of the lower ranks by those on top. The smallest unit of the Party still possessed a certain amount of initiative. In our own cell at the book company we had twelve Communists out of three hundred employees. Before I left, four years later, we had raised the total number by recruiting to about twenty-five.

The secretary of our cell sent the names of some of the better-qualified Communists to the higher body—the District Committee—for assignment to more responsible *nagruzki*. In this way I was put in

[1] The word means "load."

charge of two evening courses organized by the Communist cell of the textile trust. I lectured on Communist history and theory. I expected to find myself talking to a lot of young people and factory workers, but noticed among my listeners quite a number of old Party militants, who were now on the boards of business departments or directing factories. There they sat, side by side with junior clerks whose membership in the Party was only a few months old. "We must keep ourselves up to date," they said—and not without reason, for everything was beginning to change.

More and more of our time in the classes was taken up with the struggle developing in the top ranks of the Party. On short notice I would be instructed to discuss some current heresy, and the regular lesson would have to go by the board. One day I would be told by the District Committee to discuss an article by Zinoviev against Trotsky which had just appeared in *Pravda;* another day, an article of Trotsky's, written twenty years before, on the permanent revolution. All this was a cover for intrigues going on at the top. We sensed this sometimes in a vague way but did not understand until later that this so-called "ideological discussion" was merely Stalin's method of undermining the authority of his rivals in the Party leadership.

Gradually the interest of Party members in Moscow became entirely absorbed in discussions on the subject of "Trotskyism." Far away in Persia and elsewhere I had heard faint echoes of this quarrel. At first all of us younger people had intuitively simplified the issue. For us it had been merely a question of who was to succeed Lenin, and the majority was strongly of the opinion that one man, and one only, had a right to the position. We knew that Trotsky was head and shoulders above his fellow claimants and could alone depend upon the unswerving confidence of the masses. We knew that he had shared with Lenin the heaviest responsibility in the miraculous feat of saving the Revolution and the Soviet state. For years we had hardly heard Lenin's name mentioned without Trotsky's. "Long live Lenin and Trotsky!" had been a constant refrain. But now the other leaders of the Party were producing charges of heretical doctrine against Trotsky, upon which we were fitted neither by experience nor knowledge to pronounce.

The Communist rank and file at this period were flooded and soon floundering in the quagmire of pseudo-Marxist catchwords. Whatever the truth of these doctrinal questions might be, we were deeply disturbed by these attacks leveled at Trotsky. Were not his fame and his unique authority as a leader invaluable assets to the Party and the country? Apart from all questions of dogma, was not Trotsky marked out by character and intelligence as the obvious head of the movement? We felt something depressing, something disillusioning, in this state of personal rivalry among our leaders. But in 1925 few indeed of the men of my generation realized where these rivalries would lead.

No one at that time foresaw the rise of Stalin to personal dictatorship. Our general mood was one of healthy optimism. We were sure of ourselves and of the future. We believed that, provided no war came to interrupt the reconstruction of Russian industry, our Socialist country would be able, within a few years, to offer the world an example of a society based on principles of liberty and equality. How could it be otherwise? The old capitalist Europe was moving from crisis to crisis, while we were soon to present to the eyes of humanity the spectacle of a steady rise of production and of worker and peasant masses living in happy abundance under a planned economy. This conviction was shared by almost all of us.

In those days the struggle was never presented to us as a conflict between Stalin and Trotsky. Stalin was astute enough to conceal his own intrigues for power behind the mask of a Central Committee majority. A part of his strength lay in his very obscurity in the past. Every other Bolshevik leader had left a complete record of his thoughts for twenty or more years. It was easy to pluck out "heresies" from books, pamphlets, and articles written by any of the others years before the Revolution. And Stalin was an adept at such tricks. A paragraph, a line, even a word, would often serve him to brand some prominent Bolshevik as a "mistaken comrade who has not yet learned from his own mistakes." His victims could not answer him in kind because during a quarter of a century he had written hardly anything except a small compilation on the question of nationalities, published in 1912.

We were impressed at first by the fact that now when Stalin did write or speak, in his bare first-reader style, there did not seem to be a trace of rancor in his attitude. While other leaders freely engaged in personalities, Stalin appeared to be the cool, devoted Leninist, patiently searching out the "theoretical" errors of his colleagues and presenting them in a dispassionate spirit. It was precisely his lack of brilliance, his plainness, which inclined us to believe what he said. We did not know that he was directing and egging on these more personal polemics. We could not see that these artificial doctrinal squabbles he was provoking had as little relation to reality as a debate on the number of angels capable of dancing on a pinpoint.

During the entire early period of the factional struggle, Trotsky kept aloof and silent. A struggle for personal power was beneath his dignity, and on questions of principle his record was there for all to see. Why should he waste his time arguing in the press and in Party meetings? That was his attitude. He did not realize the importance of a political machine.

Had Trotsky made the slightest sign that he was ready to fight, the majority of the Party would have followed him. Instead, he left Moscow at the height of the struggle to take treatments in the Caucasus for a throat ailment. His supporters were abandoned, and as they saw

Stalin slowly take hold of the Party apparatus, sending his opponents on distant "assignments," they lost heart. When Trotsky decided that the time had come to fight, it was too late. Whereas a little while before a single speech delivered by him at a Moscow Party conference would have turned the tide, Trotsky now found that Stalin was in effective control of the Party.

I remember the sense of satisfaction with which I read Stalin's articles entitled "The Permanent Revolution and Comrade Trotsky." Their tone was polite, their object the refutation of Trotsky's theory that only if the Revolution were continuous and international could it succeed; that if it were confined within the frontiers of a single country, or halted at any single stage of its development, it must sooner or later collapse. Stalin, supporting his argument with frequent quotations from Lenin, reproached Trotsky with completely ignoring the part to be played by the peasants. The Party need only win over the peasants, he maintained, in order to attain the socialist goal without awaiting the working-class revolution abroad.

Twenty years later his faked-up arguments with their shoddy logic and his extreme promises, not one of which has been realized, seem to me to have been dictated both by ignorance and duplicity, for Trotsky had not in the least ignored the peasants. No one could have imposed greater suffering on the peasants than Stalin has. He has violated every item of Lenin's doctrine of the proper relations between the Communist Party and the peasantry. The Soviet Union, far from building the great socialist society, has, in fact, established a totalitarian tyranny with greater inequalities and more cruelty and contempt for human dignity than existed in the Dark Ages. In 1925, however, obfuscated by a flood of doctrinal disquisitions, we became convinced that the policy of the Central Committee as expressed by Stalin was the correct line, and that we had to discount our personal feelings. The "permanent revolution" seemed to us a dangerous theory. We felt in the end relieved that we members of the Communist cell could vote for the Central Committee—that is to say, for Zinoviev, Kamenev, and Stalin. We deplored the necessity of voting against Trotsky, but since he remained silent and seemed to persist in his errors, we felt this to be our duty.

Trotsky resigned from the presidency of the Supreme War Council and was appointed to the secondary post of president of the Committee of Concessions. But Stalin's shrewd sense of timing warned him not to come out openly against Trotsky just yet. Trotsky was far too popular. If the Party had had the slightest suspicion that Stalin was aiming at Party leadership by attacking Trotsky, his career would have been finished. Instead, he patiently pushed Zinoviev and Kamenev to the fore. He allowed them to handle the fight against "Trotskyism." He allowed Zinoviev to maneuver with the belief that he was to be the real successor of Lenin. Thus these two men served Stalin's purposes and at the same time discredited themselves. Later on, when he decided to get rid of them, he was able to do it without any large-scale opposition from the Party.

Party discords and bickerings about dogma seemed to die down for eighteen months, and then suddenly, in 1926, burst into new and violent life. At the Fifteenth Conference of the Party an unheard-of, unbelievable thing happened. Zinoviev found himself in a minority, and with him all his friends, including Kamenev, president of the Moscow Soviet and vice-premier.

Naturally questions of theory and policy again appeared to occupy the center of attention. First, was socialism possible in a single country? Zinoviev and Kamenev, now approaching Trotsky's view, said no. Socialism, they argued, is international by definition and necessarily presupposes the suppression of frontiers—if not all frontiers, at least those between the chief industrial countries. Stalin, on the other hand, maintained that "the U.S.S.R. possesses all the resources necessary to enable her to build up a socialist system alone." The official formula was a triumph of subtle phrasing and satisfied almost everybody. It was to the effect that we could *build* a socialist system in a single country, but could not *carry the building to completion* until the Revolution had extended to other countries. This piece of casuistry covered two different mental attitudes—that of those who believed in a revolutionary international policy and that of those who favored a strategy of withdrawal. The same kind of casuistry is now baffling American political writers who try to figure out, on the basis of Stalin's recent speeches, whether he is going to collaborate with the democracies or try to extend the Soviet system throughout Europe.

A second debate raged over the question of the character of the Soviet industries. Stalin called them "rigorously socialistic"; Kamenev called them "state capitalist" and argued that the workers must be given a share of the profits.

Stalin had prepared the ground well. All the delegates, with the exception of those from Leningrad—who were civil servants owing everything to Zinoviev, the political boss of that city—had been appointed by the secretaries of the local organizations, themselves appointed by Stalin, the secretary general. Zinoviev, moreover, had made himself unpopular by the violent and disloyal tone of his attacks on Trotsky. Nor did the defeats incurred by the Communist International under his presidency add to his prestige. In Germany, in Bulgaria, in Esthonia, the Communist parties had suffered bloody setbacks. I was one of those who would not be sorry to hear of Zinoviev's fall from power, and my impression was that the Party militants as a whole shared this feeling. Stalin capitalized on this prevalent mood and defeated the Zinoviev group without too much exposing his own interest in the fight.

After a year in the shadows, Zinoviev and Kamenev managed to forget their previous implacable attacks on Trotsky and openly joined forces with him in a united Opposition. This alliance was another mistake on Trotsky's part. Most Communists regarded Zinoviev and Kamenev as mere opportunists, ready to change their views for personal power. Trotsky, on the other hand, was still held in high esteem, despite the fact that he was in a minority. No one questioned his sincerity or loyalty. Now, by associating himself with Zinoviev and Kamenev, while gaining few followers, he damaged his own prestige. Perhaps Trotsky himself, we thought, was not so objective as he had seemed. We wanted, anyway, to end the factional bickering. Lenin's deathbed plea for Party unity was fresh in our minds. The Opposition thus failed of support in the broad masses of the Party, and Stalin easily crushed them.

How was it possible to see one's way clearly through all this confusion of issues? The young could only take the word of their better-informed elders. Whatever our hesitations and doubts, the sentiment of loyalty to the Party and its unity always determined our decisions. I was one of those who invariably backed up the findings of the Central Committee. We could not possibly know the machinations that were going on inside the committee, and even if we *had* known, the threat of a Party schism would have frightened us into obedience. This argument—that any weakening of Party unity might provoke a crisis of which the forces of counterrevolution would take advantage—was used time and time again to bring to naught all attempts to organize an Opposition. It played the decisive part in causing the final downfall of all Lenin's real companions-in-arms.

While these personal issues were being fought out in the forum of theoretical discussions, economic and social changes were taking place in the country. They produced dissatisfaction among the workers and caused a number of party militants who stood close to them to join the Opposition. The N.E.P.—New Economic Policy—which partly restored private trade, was producing disagreeable results. The various state enterprises were being frequently hindered, despoiled, and cleverly exploited by private merchants—Nepmen, as they were called. As a general rule the products of socialized industry were not reaching the consumer direct but were falling into the hands of these Nepmen, who passed them on at prices sometimes many hundred per cent higher than those they paid. A large amount of private commercial capital was becoming available as a result of such "black market" speculation and of the undercutting of nationalized industries by private initiative, which was freer and more clever than the state concerns and less troubled by questions of public welfare. The importance of money in social life was growing and having a demoralizing effect. Gambling houses and night clubs were making their appearance in the cities.

Workers, dependent on their small salaries, were finding themselves at a disadvantage compared to specialists, Nepmen, and the new "capitalists" who were also making their appearance. The differentiation of wages was also growing apace, a few workers receiving higher salaries and the broad masses remaining on very low levels. The unemployed were as badly off in Moscow as in Berlin, and often worse. The workers, unable to pay the high rents now demanded for the fine flats to which they had been transported immediately after the Revolution, were little by little drifting back to the slums. And many a dwelling that had been handsome and clean a few years before was now poverty-stricken and dilapidated.

Those Party militants who felt this situation, and felt it to be more important than that Party unity which was so assiduously preached to them, joined the Opposition. But, owing to our weariness of factionalism and to Stalin's having flooded the Party with raw masses of new members, young and incapable of critical thinking, they could never muster more than ten or fifteen thousand among the million Party members.

23. *The Triumph of "Party Unity"*

TOWARD THE END of 1927, on the eve of the Fifteenth Party Congress, Trotsky, Zinoviev, and Kamenev, leaders of the "United Opposition," realizing that the bureaucratic machine of the secretary general would give them not even a fighting chance at the Congress, since the delegates had all been chosen by officials who owed their jobs to Stalin, decided to appeal direct to the rank and file of the Party —and from then on to ignore the formal discipline of the machine.

There were ample signs that a wide popular sentiment was still with Trotsky and the Opposition. In October, 1927, the authorities had arranged a demonstration in Leningrad to celebrate the tenth anniversary of the Revolution. Trotsky and a few other Opposition leaders, making the rounds of the city in a car to observe the mood of the demonstrators, happened to be caught in a traffic jam near the Tauride Palace. Trucks had been lined up before the palace to serve as platforms for the members of the Central Committee. A police commander, seeing such prominent figures in the car, innocently offered to escort them to a place on a platform still unoccupied.

Word spread through the crowd that Trotsky was on the last platform. They surged forward, cheering, and surrounded Trotsky by the thousands. The trucks bearing Kalinin and other majority leaders were virtually ignored. Police sent forward to restore order were caught up by the crowd's enthusiasm and did nothing. A number of Stalin's men penetrated the crowd and started whistling and booing in an effort to change the sympathetic tone of the demonstration. But their efforts were drowned out by cheers. Finally, in desperation, Kalinin and the others clambered down from their own official platform, which the crowd had deserted, and took their places in the distant truck beside the Opposition leaders. If the cheering would not come to them, they would go to the cheering. But the demonstrators only continued to shout: "Trotsky! Trotsky!"

Following this event, the leaders of the Opposition called a series of private meetings to be held in the poor dwellings of Communist workers. These men, who had been at the head of the government during the unforgettable years, now had to run here, there, and everywhere, sitting down at little deal tables covered with squares of oilcloth, their notebooks before them, explaining to handfuls of workers the problems of state industry and world politics.

Political passion reached its climax when the Chinese revolution, spurred by the Communist International and by Soviet advisers, began to stride from victory to victory. The Opposition accused Stalin of being in league with Chiang Kai-shek and the Chinese bourgeoisie organized in the Kuomintang against the revolution. Stalin did compel the Chinese Communist Party to subordinate itself to the Kuomintang and to put a brake on the rising of the peasants and workers. He remained deaf to warnings from all sides that Chiang Kai-shek was preparing a military coup against the trade unions and the Communist Party at Shanghai. Radek, who, as rector of the Chinese University in Moscow, was well placed to follow the details of the struggle, joined vigorously with Trotsky and Zinoviev in denouncing Stalin's tactics.

The disastrous effects of these tactics were soon dramatically revealed. Stalin stated before a Party conference in Moscow that he was assured of Chiang Kai-shek's co-operation. His statement appeared in the press almost simultaneously with the news of Chiang Kai-shek's attack on the Communists and trade unionists in Shanghai, which was the beginning of an anti-Communist reaction throughout China. This reaction reached its climax with the bloody suppression of the revolt in Canton, which proclaimed a Soviet Republic in December, 1927, but survived only three days.

Stalin's prestige was sharply compromised. The Opposition redoubled their efforts. And Stalin decided to resort to violent means. In Moscow, the secretary of one of the Party district committees, a man named Riutin, conceived the idea of recruiting gangs of thugs armed with cudgels and equipped with whistles, whose duty it should be to prevent the Opposition orators from being heard at regular meetings of the Party. Other gangs of the same kind, on orders from the Central Control Committee, broke into small private gatherings of Party members and dispersed them by force.

On the eve of the seventh of November celebrations of 1927, a rumor went round that the Opposition would attempt to organize a street demonstration. Until this day the G.P.U. agents and the police had taken no part in such disturbances, because Stalin did not dare call on them for intra-Party conflicts. The gangs referred to above had been sufficient to suppress any probable outbreak. Now, however, these organs of the state were employed to suppress an opposition inside the Party.

A member of the Central Committee supporting the Opposition had a balcony near the entrance to the Red Square, where three columns of the marching demonstrators would converge. He decorated his balcony with portraits of Lenin, Trotsky, and Zinoviev. Oppositionists gathered here and shouted: "Long Live Trotsky! Long Live the Opposition!" The balcony was raided by G.P.U. agents and the police, the portraits were torn down, and the Oppositionists arrested and taken to the police station.

Followers of Trotsky managed to raise a few banners among the marchers reading: "Let Us Carry Out Lenin's Testament!" "Against Opportunism, against a Split!" "For the Unity of Lenin's Party!" The police and the G.P.U. agents also seized these slogans and beat up their bearers.

Trotsky, who had no ticket of admission to the Red Square, instead of joining a column of his sturdy followers and marching there with the rest, drove about rather aimlessly in the streets in an automobile. He was shot at in the confusion his appearance caused, and some firemen smashed the windshield of his car.

I was attending the review of troops on the Red Square and had a seat on the official stand near Lenin's tomb, on which the Party leaders stood. There was a general nervousness in the air. From fear of what the Opposition might do, the tomb and the tribune beside it were protected from the marchers by a double line of police. During the six hours that the demonstration poured through the Square, however, only one small thing happened. A band of Chinese students managed to unfurl beneath the official stand a red banner, which they had carried concealed under their clothes, bearing the words: "Down with Opportunism in the Chinese Revolution!" Almost all these students perished later in China because Stalin, having made his followers submit to the Kuomintang at a time when they were capable of independent action, tried to restore his prestige by ordering ill-prepared insurrections against it—such as the above-mentioned Canton revolt—when the time for action was past.

Meantime, at the regular meetings of the Central Committee, discussion was growing more and more violent. Even here Stalin was afraid to let Trotsky speak and instructed his henchmen to hoot him down. Stalin had constantly added to the Committee until now the meeting hall was filled with new members who owed their posts to him alone. They knew whom they had to serve. The official minutes of the last session attended by Trotsky revealed the enormous pressure exerted to silence him. Amid the noise and catcalls, Trotsky's fiery oratory lashed Stalin like a whip. It was the last time in his life he ever addressed a Party meeting. *Pravda* reported his opening phrases as follows:

> Trotsky: Through the present apparatus, through the present regime, the proletarian vanguard undergoes the pressure . . . (The noise increases more and more. The orator can hardly be heard.) . . . of upstart bureaucrats including the worker-bureaucrats (tumult, whistling) . . . of functionaries, petty bosses, newborn proprietors, privileged intellectuals of city and country . . .

The furor made it impossible to continue. Stalin's lieutenants shouted their answer: "Down with him! Down with the rascal! The renegade!" The hall was in an uproar. Yaroslavsky picked up from his desk the heavy volume outlining the First Five-Year Plan and hurled it at Trotsky. It missed his head by a fraction of an inch. The few supporters of the Opposition rushed forward to protect their leader and surrounded the tribune. Trotsky gazed calmly at Yaroslavsky over the tumult: "Well, if you can't convince people with this book, you can at least use it to knock them down!"

Zinoviev also tried to speak. "Either you will give us an opportunity to appeal to the Party, and speak to the Party, or you will have to put us in prison. . . . There is no other alternative. . . ." The audience laughed. Stalin had already chosen his alternative.

Sympathizers of the Opposition in the lower ranks of the Party were similarly terrorized. They were also systematically deprived of their jobs. Stalin was hitting the Opposition in the stomach. Victor Serge describes how the Communist printers in his unit reacted to the struggle.

"You understand," a printer said to Serge, "there's unemployment in the trade. Besides, I have children. If I join up with you and you are defeated, what's going to become of me and my kids?"

Stalin did not risk the Opposition's getting a hearing at the Fifteenth Party Congress in November, 1927. He decided to act in advance. A few days before the Congress opened, he had Trotsky, Zinoviev, and Kamenev expelled from the Party on a charge of violating Party discipline. I was on the guest tribune when Stalin and his right-wing supporters, Rykov, Bukharin, and Tomsky, complacently mounted the platform—inglorious conquerors! The hall unanimously cheered the "triumph of the Party Line," but there was a touch of consternation in the applause. Like many others, I supported the majority only because I hoped thus to end the sapping struggle once for all. Only as a measure necessary to insure the safety of the state and prevent the splitting of the Party could such a drastic step be justified.

Without consulting the Party membership, Stalin decided to banish Trotsky to Central Asia. News of this fact burst like a bombshell in Moscow. Despite all that had happened, the ranks of the Party supporting Stalin had still believed that matters would right themselves, that repressive measures would be unnecessary.

Thousands of sympathizers gathered at the station from which Trotsky was scheduled to leave, shouting: "Long live Trotsky!" His portrait, set up on the roof of a railroad car, was loudly cheered. Police and agents of the G.P.U. fought the demonstrators, but when the train started they climbed onto the engine and all over the train and forced it to halt. Twice they uncoupled the engine. But Trotsky was not on the train. The G.P.U. had taken no chances.

Trotsky was sent from a suburban station on a different train. A squad of G.P.U. men had appeared suddenly in his apartment and ordered him and his wife to prepare to leave immediately. Trotsky, to thwart Stalin's probable plan to represent his exile as voluntary, decided to resist. If they wished to exile him, they would have to do it by force. He locked himself in a room. The G.P.U. agents called their superiors, asking instructions. They were told to smash the door down. It was not a task they relished. An agent who had been a former officer under Trotsky smashed the glass. But at the sight of his old chief he was seized with remorse.

"Shoot me, Comrade Trotsky, shoot me!" he cried.

"Don't talk nonsense," Trotsky said. "No one is going to shoot you. Go ahead with your job."

Trotsky was carried bodily out of his house and taken to the train and to Alma-Ata.

Once he was safely gone, the G.P.U. got busy, and a weary round of arrests, imprisonments, and deportations of the Opposition began. Rumblings in the ranks of the Communists in the Red Army had to be silenced. But it was too late now for resistance. Trotsky's cause was lost.

In 1928 the difficulties foreseen by the Opposition began to materialize. It became necessary to take exceptional measures to compel the peasants to hand over their produce to the state. Stalin used force against the peasants. Requisition agents accompanied by armed detachments searched everywhere for hidden grain. They plundered the peasants even of their seed. There were numerous episodes of violence and brutality. Thousands of peasants were arrested and jailed.

Bukharin, Rykov, Tomsky, and Uglanov—at that time secretary of the Moscow Committee—insisted on a return to normal conditions in the country districts. They formed the right wing in the Central Committee, upon which Stalin had leaned until now in getting rid of

Trotsky and the left. All of a sudden Stalin turned against this right wing. He was astute enough to draw advantage from the resentment caused by the expulsions and arrests of the left. These measures had been accepted only with great reluctance, and a campaign against the right, whom Stalin encouraged the Party to hold responsible for him, was welcomed.

The right had not even the courage to go openly into opposition. They capitulated almost immediately. I was present at a Moscow Party conference in the course of which Uglanov, who had shown no mercy toward the Trotskyists, made a pitiful recantation and confession of sins, promising with tears to toe the Party line in the future, praising Stalin's clearsightedness, and delivering himself of all the rest of the routine hokum.

I realized then that he and his companions were beaten, practically without a fight. Kalinin and Voroshilov had been more or less on their side, and the country as a whole preferred them to Stalin because they had demanded liberty of production and exchange for the peasants and the right to make money out of their farms. But the leftist elements in the Party were against them. They were for a strong hand against peasant resistance and believed the right wing was surrendering to the kulaks. They supported Stalin's maneuver with real conviction. Bukharin, theoretic leader of the right, was then in charge of *Pravda,* the official Party organ; but Stalin countered this by making it known that the real organ of the majority was the *Komsomolskaya Pravda,* the organ of the Communist Youth, an extremely vital daily paper. Most of the Communist Youth who helped Stalin in his struggle against the right perished later, since they gave signs of "heretical leanings."

The peasant situation was daily getting worse. The Draconian measures enforced by Stalin were having the effect of disorganizing agriculture, and the future looked bad. The right continued to hope. Trotsky and a few thousand other exiles managed to maintain political contact, and this kept the older members of the Party in a constant state of excitement. Ordered to refrain from his activities under threat of imprisonment, Trotsky refused. Stalin did not carry out his threat, and the rumor went round that Trotsky was to be sent abroad. We were profoundly shocked, accustomed though we were to bad news. Up to then we had regarded differences of opinion among Communists, no matter how grave, as nothing compared with those that separated Communists from the capitalist world. But now there was talk of banishing Trotsky—handing him over, that is, to the capitalists. I found myself inwardly condemning this action of the Central Committee. But no one could do anything. The only Opposition then in existence, the right, kept quiet and tried its best not to be noticed.

I felt a second psychological shock of the same kind on Stalin's fiftieth birthday, when the papers devoted a whole page to his praise and gave him the official title of *Vozhd* (leader) of the Party. I had not forgotten what he said in 1924, when his words were obviously directed against Trotsky: "The Party needs no leader—it has but one collective leader, the Central Committee." This argument, set forth by Stalin in a very noble article, had had decisive weight with me and with all of us who had been resenting the attacks against Trotsky.

I began now to suspect that we had been duped. Stalin's statement at that time had been merely a maneuver. The whole business was just a tactic for grabbing the leadership for himself.

My friend Briquet, like myself a naïve supporter of the official Party line, persuaded me only with great difficulty that, since the outlawing, exile, and disgrace of so many of the leaders, the Party was beginning to lack authority and had need of a chief to rally round— a man worthy of confidence by reason of his resolution and his deep knowledge of Lenin's doctrine. It was by such arguments that the worship of a Party leader finally became established. But Briquet left me less than half convinced. It was with a heavy heart and many doubts that I looked back upon the factional struggle in which I had played so confident a part.

Poor Briquet! No man was more sincerely devoted to Stalin or more loyal to the "general line of the Party"—a new term used to denote Stalin's policy. It was a crooked line indeed, which changed its direction on the average of every three months or so. Briquet later became an influential member of the Central Control Commission of the Party. In 1937, however, his name appeared casually in a list of those denounced as "enemies of the people." He found out finally for what the Party needed to have a leader.

During the four years I spent in Moscow, my health returned. I still yearned for the Orient, and when the Commissariat of Foreign Trade proposed that I go back to Persia as trade representative, I was eager to accept. My two sons were living with my mother in the Ukraine, and I had accustomed myself to having no personal life, to living only for the Party and the Soviet cause. But I was on the reserve list of the General Staff, and they countered the proposal of the Foreign Trade Office with the suggestion that, in view of my military and business experience, I go to Paris, where the Soviet Government was buying extensively for our Air Force and new armament industry. After living those four years in the Moscow atmosphere of interminable Party quarrels, I was ready to go anywhere. In January, 1929, I departed for Paris to work with the Soviet Trade Delegation.

24. *Paris, the Great Plan, and the Battle for Gold*

I WAS STRUCK by the austere beauty of Paris. The color of her buildings, a product of smoke, fog, and aging stone, had for me, after the bright tints of Moscow, an effect of noble poetry. In contrast to Moscow, also, life in Paris was rich, luxuriant, and gay. But I was not particularly impressed with this latter contrast. I saw the vast difference here between the rich and poor and thought that when our Five-Year Plan should be completed, the general level of life in Russia would be much higher and would be free to all on equal terms.

At the same time, I became more troubled as I remembered our slums at home. The poorer quarters of Paris were not so bad as ours, and it ought to be just the other way round. After all, slums were to be expected under capitalism. But now that we had achieved the Revolution, the misery of Moscow seemed a reproach to me, an evidence that, for the time being at least, the march of socialism had been slowed down.

What astonished me most of all was the liberty enjoyed by the press —the profusion of papers representing all shades of opinion, laying about them in all directions, sparing no one, however powerful, and freely upholding the most contradictory and audacious doctrines. At that time the Bolshevik Party was afraid of a free press, and quite frankly so. The Party taught us, and we firmly believed, that, even if free expression were extended only to the other left parties, foreign bourgeois influences might filter in through that narrow crack, casting doubt on all our values and sapping the foundations of the regime. Paris showed brilliantly that a free press is not a danger to a ruling class possessing strong support among the people at large, but a condition of security and progress. But I had no time to indulge in doubts or deep reflection on this theme. Work was pressing, and work meant constant fighting.

The character of my work for the next four years, in Paris, Brussels, and Milan, cannot be explained without some account of the dominant factor of this whole period in the U.S.S.R.—the First Five-Year Plan.

Indignant criticisms voiced in illegal pamphlets by the exiled Trotsky Opposition were finding a large response in the Party and had forced Stalin to reconsider his first project of a five-year plan of industrialization—originally laid out on very timid lines. He had decided to outbid his political enemies and now went to the opposite extreme. He adopted a five-year plan with such gigantic increases in production that it could not possibly be carried through. This took the wind out of the sails of the left and at the same time permitted him to marshal the vigorous elements of the Party against the right, who favored an extremely cautious tempo. The Party willingly supported Stalin against the right leaders, Rykov and Bukharin, whom it suspected of wishing to establish an agricultural bourgeois state. There was another hidden reason for this almost fantastic jump in Stalin's mind: the repressions in the Party and the state of siege in which the country found itself, at this period, could be made endurable only by some effort heroic enough to make men forget the unpleasant realities of their lives.

Stalin's battle against the peasants had already driven him to undertake a forced collectivization of agriculture. For this it was essential to build, and build quickly, huge factories for the production of tractors and farm implements. As a result of this, as well as of the continuing struggle against the right, the Five-Year Plan was whipped up still higher every few months by the addition of new improvisations. The officials of Party committees and directors of state industries, in what we called an "administrative ecstasy," all joined in the game of outbidding one another and began proposing all sorts of "super-plans" in various enterprises. To top it off, Stalin announced that the Five-Year Plan, already monstrous enough in all conscience, was to be completed in four years!

The psychology common to all thoughtful Bolsheviks in those days might be expressed somewhat as follows: Stalin's iron fist is hard to bear. His narrow vision is costing the country dear, as are his tyrannical methods. But, in spite of apparently insoluble difficulties, and although each spring the regime has seemed to be tottering on its last legs, the man's indomitable will is giving Russia a new industrial equipment. After a few more years of this terrific, almost superhuman strain, we may, notwithstanding his limitations, see a general increase of prosperity and happiness.

The slogan of all this period was: "Catch up to and surpass America!" We were enthusiastic for rebuilding our country industrially into a new United States. And thus in spite of everything we supported Stalin's policy with determination. This spirit penetrated even the ranks of the Opposition and helps to explain the frequent capitulations among them. "Stalin's work, cruel and clumsy though his methods are"—they would argue—"is more important than our differences with him. He is doing the job brutally and badly, but he is doing it." Few foresaw that the moral and political means by which Stalin was doing the job would change the result and frustrate all the magnificent efforts we were making to build a genuinely socialist industry and a free and prosperous life. The builders in Russia were too completely absorbed by the exhaustive effort they were making to realize until later what was going on. And we abroad, out of touch with real conditions in Russia, able to get information only from the rosy reports of the official press, felt confident that, in spite of tremendous difficulties, the scheme was progressing all right. We did our part with all energy and enthusiasm, not handicapped at first by any doubt.

To put 125,000,000 peasants in the collective farms, to "set the muzhik on the tractor," to mechanize the whole of Russia, was no easy task. It was not only necessary to build great factories for tractors and farm machinery, to set up in the Russian steppes automobile shops worthy of Henry Ford's Detroit. All these giants also had to have steel; they had to have electric energy. New metallurgic foundries, power stations, quarries, mines, power dams, railroads had to be opened up. Millions of new workers had to be housed. Thousands of factory buildings had to be erected. All this demanded millions of tons of cement and other building materials. The innumerable tractors and automobiles would need oil, and the oil industry had to be immensely expanded. The whole business was like a snowball rolling down a mountain, every new construction entailing other constructions.

The thing could be accomplished only by means of tremendous imports of machinery from abroad: heavy machinery, machine tools, installations for power stations, mines, oil wells, and railroad rolling stock. We had to buy all these things and pay for them with hundreds and hundreds of millions of dollars each year. For this the Soviet Union needed gold, and it had very little in the State Bank Reserve. So another branch of Soviet industry had to be speeded up: the neglected gold mines in Siberia and the Ural Mountains. But machinery for them also had to be brought from abroad, and at best the rise in gold production would not be felt for several years.

Desperate efforts were made to raise gold inside Russia. Torgsin[1] stores were opened, where goods unprocurable elsewhere could be bought at prewar prices by anyone bringing gold money or golden jewelry. The G.P.U. arrested the remnants of the new bourgeoisie of the N.E.P. period and tried to extort their hidden treasure. Intourist offered the "Miracles of the New Russia" to curious tourists, provided they would bring foreign currency with them. But these internal devices brought only a minute fraction of what was needed.

The only way to procure the needed precious metal—which Lenin once had condescendingly promised would be used in the socialist future only as building material for comfort stations!—was to sell everything that could be sold to the capitalist world, at any sacrifice and at any price. Then we began exporting everything we could lay our hands on, not only the raw products which Russia had always exported—timber, flax, manganese, ore, etc.—but also foodstuffs of every kind, even those for want of which the Russians themselves were starving. Nothing was spared, not even the most indispensable and scarce supplies such as butter and sugar. Not even fruit or poultry was spared, and the sick in the hospitals had to go without. This wholesale exportation of foodstuffs was one of the causes of the 1931-

[1] Abbreviation for "trade with foreigners."

174

32 famine which raged in the Ukraine and in central Asia, and which was felt in every corner of the country. The famine was carefully hidden from the outside world by the government, despite the presence of foreign correspondents in Moscow. Even we Soviet employees abroad did not know the real gravity of the situation, and so carried on our export work with a free conscience.

The Soviet Union was often accused in these years of "dumping," as a deliberate attempt to ruin the foreign trade of other countries. The truth was much simpler. Foreign importers knew how desperately the Soviet Union needed gold, and offered prices for our exports so low that they were often less than the cost of production. This loss was not considered decisive by Moscow, and we accepted such offers in many cases. But the prime task of the foreign-trade delegates abroad was to try to get better prices, fighting for every dollar of gold that could be squeezed out. We had also to try to get as much advance payment as possible for our goods and as long credits as we could get for the machinery we were buying.

In every European capital a desperate battle was being waged, a battle for credits and a battle for gold; and in this I, too, played my part. It was no less exciting in its way than the fighting I had seen in Bokhara against the Moslem guerrillas.

Very soon our credits were exhausted, and for those given earlier the demand notes were coming in. We played the markets with an air of confidence, though the treasury was counting its last few foreign banknotes. The Soviet Government announced, through the medium of the Communist papers of two worlds and any organ of the press which happened to be sympathetic, that the Soviet currency was the most stable in the world, that the U.S.S.R. had never yet failed to honor its commitments and never would. It is indeed a fact—and a miracle—that there is no recorded case of a Soviet bill's being protested.

I happen to know, however, what superhuman efforts were needed to save us from the catastrophes constantly over our heads. Every time heavy payments fell due, we officials of the foreign trade and our colleagues of the bank lived through a period of nightmare.

This war was waged and won under the direction of a single man to whom his country owes a debt of gratitude for having saved it if not from bankruptcy at least from humiliating and perhaps fatal complications. This was Arcady Rosengolz, the People's Commissar for Foreign Trade. His two deputies, Liubimov and Veitzer, were stationed in Berlin, where they acted as a center for all trade and financial operations. The sums received or paid by us every day, no matter how small, were reported by telephone to Berlin. Weekly statements, drawn up in great detail, were submitted to Moscow. More than once, when, despite all our efforts, we could not raise enough to meet the coming bills, Moscow had to send deliveries of gold from its last reserves by airplane. The Politburo sat in emergency session while

Rosengolz reported. Stalin saw Rosengolz at work; Stalin knew that without Rosengolz everything would have been lost. . . . Rosengolz was shot as an "enemy of the people" on March 15, 1938. His deputies, Liubimov and Veitzer, were both arrested about the same time and disappeared.

Our trade delegation was quartered in a seven-story building at 25, Rue Ville l'Evèque. Its staff consisted of about three hundred persons. When I arrived in Paris, and was appointed director of the Department of Imports, the embassy and the trade delegation had just been completely overhauled. The various nationalities of the Soviet Union were well represented among the high officials. The Ukrainian Dovgalevsky had taken the place of the Rumanian Rakovsky as ambassador. The trade delegation, formerly directed by the Ukrainian Piatakov and the Georgian Budu Mdivani, was now in charge of a former People's Commissar of Finance, the Russian Tumanov—afterward of another Communist, the Jew, Gurevich.[2]

Every week the directors of the different import and export departments would meet in Tumanov's, and afterward Gurevich's, office for a regular "war council." Gurevich would smile slyly and begin thus: "Comrades, I need only two things from you—money, and money."

We would present our statements of the sums received and expected, and of bills to be met. Very often, after exploring every possible source, we would find ourselves short of cash. Michael Ostrovsky, who was in charge of the petroleum export department, more than once saved us in the nick of time. Soviet Russia was the main supplier of oil to France. Although the French society, Petrofina, was paying huge advances against the deliveries of oil, Ostrovsky would go and make an appeal to the good nature of his "capitalists" and get another million or two francs, over and above his contract, for a problematic extra shipment in the remote future. Naturally his fairy godfathers would not do this without compensations in price. At our next conference Ostrovsky would triumphantly show his checks.

At these conferences we were forever trying to think up new items of export from Soviet Russia. Some of the proposals we made were ingenious. At our suggestion Moscow started sending to France Caucasian wines, vodka, wood carvings, toys, all kinds of peasant handicraft objects, and so on. The Russian peasant women were organized to gather for export berries, mushrooms, and medicinal herbs in the forests. I suggested that we try exporting carbon paper, pens, pencils, and other types of stationery from the factories of Mezhdunarodnaya

[2] The policy of racial equality was carried out with the same impartiality in the purge. Dovgalevsky died a natural death, but Tumanov has disappeared in some prison; Gurevich was arrested and disappeared in 1937 or 1938, together with his then chief, the commissar of public health, Dr. Kaminsky; Piatakov and Budu Mdivani were both shot in 1937; Rakovsky, condemned to a long term, was recently reported to have died in prison.

Kniga, which I had been in charge of when in Moscow. Everything that might possibly produce one more cent was mobilized for export in the great battle for gold.

Even our most ingenious minds were knocked flat, however, when we received an Intourist circular telling us of a new scheme that had been conceived in Moscow—the export of human beings!

For many years immigration from Soviet Russia had been virtually closed. Only diplomats, officials, and engineers going abroad on state business had been permitted to leave the country. In France, the United States, and many other countries there were hundreds of citizens of Russian descent—both *émigrés* from prerevolutionary times and White Russians from the Civil War days—who, having established themselves financially, were anxious to have their relatives in Russia join them. Up to now all their efforts, especially those of the Whites, had been fruitless. But under this new scheme devised by Intourist, these *émigrés* had only to put up enough money, and they could get their relatives out. Although normally a Soviet foreign passport and exit visa cost a dozen or two rubles, they had to pay from 800 to 1,500 gold dollars in cash to get a passport and exit visa for their relatives! For these sums Intourist would get busy and dig up, if necessary somewhere in a Siberian concentration camp, some "enemy of the regime" who had given up all hope of ever getting out, or of even freely moving around inside Russia, and export him body and soul in a Pullman car to his rich relatives.

I have to admit that we in Paris, much as we wanted to balance our budget, were not enthusiastic about this item of barter. We did not ourselves develop this side line to the fullest extent. But I heard that in other countries it was quite a "selling line"!

The attitude adopted by the French capitalists, as by the English and in part the Americans at that time, was in marked contrast to that of the Germans. The Germans were ready to grant us long-term loans of three hundred and four hundred million marks, whereas the French either refused long-term transactions altogether or, when some of their capitalists did agree to deal, offered terms extremely unfavorable to us. But for the advent of Hitler, Germany would have been in a position to exercise a very strong economic influence in the Soviet Union for many years. Russia was creating new industries, and if the initial order for machinery was given to Germany, it was a matter of course that the spare parts, replacements, and equipment for further factories would be bought there, too; and the technicians invited to come to Russia and superintend the new plants would be Germans.

I was amazed at the lack of initiative shown by the French in this situation. We succeeded in doing some business in France, but only by paying very dearly for what we bought. The French industrialist who consented to give us a two-year credit would raise his prices, often adding as much as 40 per cent, in order to cover the risk. Even with

177

such a profit he was frightened because the Russian White *émigrés* in Paris kept assuring him that the Bolshevik regime would soon collapse. When they had him frightened enough, these same White *émigrés*, knowing that, whatever happened, we would honor our bonds, would discount our notes at that figure. Later, when our financial situation improved, the Russian State Bank employed discreet agents to buy up these notes secretly, and in this way we managed to recoup ourselves for some of our losses.

Foreigners at this time understood very little of what was happening in Russia. For instance, I was negotiating for the purchase of a quantity of coke furnaces destined for Kuznetsk. We asked for delivery in nine months. The director of the French company protested.

"But I've just come back from Kuznetsk!" he exclaimed. "The place is a trackless desert. What *is* the point of taking delivery of stuff which you can't possibly use until the district has been opened up? And that won't happen for two years at least."

Actually Stalin's ruthless determination had thrown into Kuznetsk gangs composed of Old Bolsheviks, Young Communists, workers' shock brigades, engineers fired by enthusiasm or terrified by threats, convicts condemned to forced labor, and expropriated kulaks. These men lived in huts and ate black bread and stale cabbage. But the factory was ready in a year.

At the end of 1930 I was promoted to the post of assistant trade representative and director general of imports. The legal and social conditions under which we worked, far from improving, had grown worse. The decisions of the French courts would have made existence impossible for us if means had not been discovered of evading them. The former owners of ships nationalized during the Revolution, and now flying the Soviet flag, obtained judgments entitling them to seize moneys, property, and stock belonging to the Department of Foreign Trade. Our ambassador, Dovgalevsky, protested, but did not succeed in keeping the bailiffs from entering our premises to put seals on our furniture. Goods, funds, and payments had therefore to be shipped to us camouflaged as the property of a mixed company, of which the U.S.S.R. held the majority of shares.

Dovgalevsky's personal gifts were daily put to the test. Speaking French perfectly, and familiar with the habits and psychology of the country—he had lived in France as a student—the ambassador distinguished himself by his patience, his courtesy, and a subtlety that lay behind a dignified exterior. He could have passed anywhere for a great French engineer, which indeed by training he was. No one was better suited to carry on the struggle for Soviet influence, and by the time he died at his post the situation had greatly improved.

The French did help us to develop our aluminum industry, the French aluminum company of Louis Marliot giving us technical assistance. I signed with Louis Lumière a contract for the building in

Valerian Dovgalevsky, ambassador to France—died in Paris of natural causes. *Standing, left:* Marcel Rosenberg, later ambassador to Spain—recalled and disappeared in 1938. *Right:* French Premier Edouard Herriot.

Leon Karakhan (*middle*) former vice-commissar of foreign affairs, later ambassador to Turkey—shot in 1937 after secret trial. *Third from the right*: President of Turkish Republic, Ismet Inonu.

Russia of the first factory for the production of cinema film. I bought grapevines for the Crimea and the Caucasus from southern France, cork from Algiers, phosphates from Morocco, watches from Switzerland, machinery from Belgium, and iron from Luxemburg, spending in this way more than eight hundred million francs a year.

But among my diverse duties the first and most important was that bearing on the building of a Soviet air force and airplane industry. I worked with a special commission sent from Moscow composed of Russia's outstanding military engineers. The Commission was led by Jacob Alksnis, Chief of the Soviet Air Force, and it included the famous designer, Andrei Tupolev, creator of the best types of Russian planes, who later designed the plane which flew over the North Pole to the United States. In Russia Tupolev was responsible for setting up our airplane factories, with their remarkable experimental laboratories. Accused of sabotage, he disappeared during the purges, together with the whole group of brilliant constructors who had worked under him. His friends never heard of him until Hitler attacked Russia, when he miraculously reappeared to play again a prominent and responsible role in the Russian airplane industry.

Because of the scale on which we purchased equipment, the airplane manufacturers signed with us technical-aid contracts and permitted our engineers to spend months in their factories studying their methods. Our men worked at the Gnome et Rhône, one of the largest French airplane factories, which had received orders from us for several hundreds of the latest type engines. Foreign specialists also came to Russia and assisted in erecting plants to turn out planes within her boundaries.

These services rendered by French industry in the early days of Russian aviation were great. French manufacturers share with American the credit of helping the U.S.S.R. to build its air power.

25. *In the Bourgeois Encirclement*

THE SOVIET COLONY in Paris was a very peculiar and self-contained body in this cosmopolitan capital of Europe. By the Soviet colony I mean those Russian citizens and their families who were in the service of Soviet organizations functioning there—the embassy, the trade delegation, the bank, the transport and shipping offices, the tourist bureau. The Soviet authorities in Moscow who sent these men abroad impressed on their minds that they were an outpost of the great army of builders of socialism, working in a hostile encirclement. While dwelling in enemy territory, they must show an example of modest living, resistance to bourgeois temptation, and devotion to proletarian duty.

Less than half of this colony were members of the Communist Party. And in the trade organization there were a number of non-Party specialists who had received their training in prerevolutionary bourgeois business.

The colony was a microcosm of the mother country. Although the Communists were in a minority, the Communist cell was the political director of our lives. The secretary of the cell, and his bureau of five elected members, were autocratic legislators. They controlled and directed our doings even more completely than if we had been in Russia.

I was often present at the deliberations of this high body and heard them discuss the problems that cropped up daily. Their psychology was like that of Christian missionaries sent to live in a pagan country. They organized their community almost like a Trappist monastery. And since the pagans in this case were highly civilized, and lived joyfully and in comparative luxury, the missionaries looked upon them as something in the nature of a decadent Rome! The missionaries were not so much worried about recruiting new converts as about preserving their own monastery from disintegration under the surrounding influences.

Besides this little circle of the Soviet elite, there existed in Paris a large Soviet Russian colony in the usual sense of this word—a body of people not connected with any official organization but holding Soviet passports. Part of them were prerevolutionary emigrants who had automatically changed their Imperial passports when the Soviet Embassy arrived, and part members of the White immigration who had recanted early and regained their citizenship through amnesty from the Soviet Government. All these, if not officially considered second-rate citizens, were at least ignored. They were never invited to our meetings or receptions or social gatherings; and we were not interested in their affairs or their way of life.

The population of our little colony of the chosen fluctuated between three and four hundred. The first problem to be solved was that of lodging them in the best way for organizing their lives on the principles established by the Party. For the embassy staff of about fifty persons, this presented no difficulty, for they all had quarters in the embassy building. But the employees of the trade delegation—about 80 per cent of the colony—constituted a real and long-lasting problem. For a time they took rooms in various hotels. But when they began to look around for apartments, difficulties arose. One unwritten law of the colony was that it was unethical for a Soviet employee to buy furniture or household goods. To do this was called "bourgeois over-growth." So they had to rent furnished apartments. But these were very expensive in Paris, and so they looked for cheaper rents in the remote suburbs. But here arose another snag. A Soviet employee could not buy an automobile. That also was forbidden.

Very few dared break the rule about furniture, but there were constant complaints about it to the bureau of the Communist cell. I was present once in a meeting of the bureau when this subject came up. I argued that, although not myself personally concerned, since I was alone and living contentedly in a hotel close to my work, it was stupid to have such a rule at all. My argument was simple: Over a period of two years, which was the average stay of Soviet employees in Paris, a man would pay in the difference in rent three times the price of the furniture he needed. He would go back to Russia with nothing to show for his money, leaving a French landlord that much richer. I asked our legislators to tell me just where lay the danger of "bourgeois overgrowth" if a man saved money by buying furniture and then had the furniture to take back home with him besides. But I could get no reasonable answer—only general remarks to the effect that the Soviet employee abroad is a soldier and must be ready to move anywhere at a moment's notice. The question was raised many times, but always with the same result.

There was a like discussion over the question of buying auto-mobiles. On this point we had a strict order from the Central Committee. Purchasing cars was absolutely forbidden. The reasons were much the same. Buying a car, besides being a "bourgeois overgrowth," would involve the buyer in a long-term credit, and so tie him to his post. The Soviet employee must not only be ready to move anywhere, but he must be ready to move with a light heart. Since he could not, in the present state of the exchange, pay for his car from Russia, he would lose it if he moved, and would therefore be reluctant to go. Moreover, if he had saved any money out of his salary, he ought rather to send it to Russia and so increase the balance of foreign exchange there.

We argued that, if our employees weren't allowed to buy cars, they would spend their money on less useful things. And that, in fact, was just what happened. Many of the employees' wives, because of this rule, bought expensive dresses and fashionable fur coats. Our insistence on common sense in this matter produced an entirely unexpected result in Moscow! The Central Committee decided that, if so many of our people wanted to buy cars, their salaries must be too high. And so it decreed a cut of 30 per cent all round—this 30 per cent to be deposited to the employees' credit in Moscow, in Soviet money, at the official rate of exchange.

About a year after that we found a solution to the housing problem. A huge eleven-story unfurnished apartment house, in the *quartier de*

Buttes-Chaumont, was rented by our delegation. The delegation itself bought furniture and furnished each apartment. The employees were then obliged to rent these apartments from the delegation. Thus the colony was concentrated in one building, and the building was soon nicknamed the "House of the Soviets in Paris." Although this house served well to isolate our colony still further from the "undesirable influences" of the metropolis, it furnished a lot of copy to the White Russian press, who must have had eavesdroppers in our colony. Its gossip columns were full of inside stories of life at the "House of the Soviets." Upon one point in particular they frequently employed their irony.

It was a custom for the members of the colony, in general conversation, whether with the "elite" or with outsiders, to complain a little at being obliged to live in this "awful capitalist encirclement." They suffered at being severed from Russia and were always dreaming about an early return home. These complaints, I myself found, were repeated a little too often and too insistently to be sincere. And the White press, pointing out that material conditions in Russia were pretty rough and the Soviet employees in Paris a lot better off even than average French officials of the same rank, made them look dubious indeed.

In our Communist cell nobody, however, officially questioned the sincerity of these sentiments. A rule established by the bureau that all employees must pass at least one vacation in two years in the Soviet Union was received on all sides with "enthusiasm." No one dared suggest that it might be more simple and more restful to go to the French Riviera. I could not see why we should close our eyes to the evident fact that we were enjoying better conditions here than most of us had ever known before in our lives. To accept this fact openly would not, in my opinion, have cast any doubt on the loyalty of the colony and would have avoided much unnecessary hypocrisy.

I do not wish to give the impression that there was anything exceptional about our salaries or our way of living. If our trade delegation was better off than French business houses, this applied only to employees of low and middle rank. We paid a secretary or stenographer from $75 to $100 a month; a bookkeeper or salesman from $125 to $175. These rates were about 50 per cent higher than those paid in French offices. But our executive personnel—directors of export and import departments, including the top officials—never received more than $200 or $250 a month, although the business they did amounted to hundreds of millions of francs annually. And these salaries, of course, were much less than those of Frenchmen handling half as much business.

I myself lived very modestly in Paris, partly because I had never lived otherwise, partly because I was sending two-thirds of my salary—which was $200, and later $250, a month—to Moscow for my twin boys. The Torgsin stores had not yet come into existence, and the old rate of exchange in Moscow had been maintained artificially despite the depreciation of the ruble; the food shortage had sent prices soaring; and my mother had to pay as much as three dollars to five dollars a pound for the butter she bought for the boys.

I occupied a small attic room in a hotel on the Place de la Madeleine. I did not need an apartment, since I went home only late at night for a short sleep. We all usually worked late at the trade delegation. Especially after the minor personnel had gone home, the executives would stay on. Many of our week ends were also passed within four office walls.

One or two evenings a week there would be a closed meeting of the Communist cell, held at our embassy. There we would discuss the current problems of the Soviet Union and of our work and life in Paris. This Party cell, existing semi-legally, could not work among non-Party men; it had no other activities beyond these meetings. But everyone was full of zeal, and our talks usually went on till 2 or 3 A.M.

As we emerged from the embassy at this early hour, each group still arguing noisily in Russian, the French policemen at the embassy gates would stare at us, both dumfounded and suspicious. "These crazy Russians!" To calm our nerves we would go to Montparnasse for a glass of beer at La Rotonde or La Cupole. Here, my brain still buzzing with arguments about the Five-Year Plan, I would look around at the French Bohemians, chattering gaily in their after-theater supper parties, or at the ladies of easy virtue waiting expectantly at the tables. They would seem to me like unreal shadows of a distant world.

We had very little time left for private life or for amusements, and we were usually too tired to do any creative work of our own. On evenings off, most of the inhabitants of the House of the Soviets, if they didn't go to a near-by movie house to see American Westerns, would gather in one another's apartments and drink and sing and play cards till late.

In the rare week ends that I had to myself, until our Bureau started "collectivizing" our pastimes, I was able, however, to see what I wanted to of Paris. I don't think it is necessary to describe my delight in the unending galleries of the Louvre, the Musée de Luxembourg, the Cluny, or Notre Dame de Paris—though I must mention how deeply moved I was by the force and beauty of Rodin's sculpture as I walked out of the museum dedicated to his works. My admiration was great for the magnificent perspectives—of which the French are unsurpassable masters—such as the vista from the Louvre to the Arc de Triomphe or the *terrasses* of Versailles.

For me the movies were always more than mere entertainment: they were art and education. In Moscow I had not been able to see the ones that were making history in the Western world, such as Charlie

Chaplin's *Gold Rush* and *The Circus*. There was no chance of their being brought to Russia. And when I got to Paris, these pictures were out of date. All Paris was rushing to see the first successful American "talkie" pictures, with Al Jolson in the famous role of the "Jazz Singer." However, I went patiently through the newspaper notices of small suburban theaters until I found revivals of the old masterpieces.

One night I sneaked out of a meeting of our Party cell—an unusual act of abandon—in order to dash in a taxi to an old filthy barracks of a theater in Ménilmontant and see the *Gold Rush*. The film was scratched, the projection was terrible, but it gave me more enjoyment than I have ever had in the most luxurious cinemas on the great boulevards. In this way, too, as revivals in remote suburban theaters, I saw *The Birth of a Nation* and *Intolerance*, the two Griffith pictures which marked a turning point in the art of the cinema.

During my second year in Paris, in my work with imports, I felt that I lacked the technical knowledge necessary to my task. So I went to the Conservatoire des Arts et Métiers and took evening classes in industrial chemistry. This did not leave me much free time to enjoy Parisian life. And, what is more, the bureau decided, just at this time, that the evenings and week ends of our colony members were not well organized—that the comrades, left to their own initiative, were wasting their spare time. For week ends they decided to combine the pleasant with the useful by hiring busses every Sunday to take the colony on collective excursions to famous châteaux, cathedrals, and battlefields. And, to fill our evenings with somewhat lighter amusement, the bureau organized dancing and dramatic soirées in the basement of the trade delegation building, where there was a lot of space and a big stage.

The other and no less important purpose of these soirées was to help establish friendly ties between our colony and the French personnel of the delegation. Out of working hours these French employees—about two hundred of them—were practically strangers to us. Many of them had been recommended by the French Communist Party and were Party members, or relatives of Party members, at the time we engaged them. But the Soviet Government, anxious to avoid any official connection between our business organizations and the French Party, had decided that all French Communists working for us must resign temporarily from the Party and stop all political work. The rest of our French personnel had no interest in politics whatever. In consequence a problem arose about the kind of entertainment to be enjoyed at these soirées.

The French were used to their own ways and naturally suggested inviting a jazz band, which would play the usual modern dances—fox trots, tangoes, etc. But fox trots and tangoes were taboo in the Soviet Union at this time as "signs of bourgeois degeneration." And they were forbidden to Soviet employees abroad also. So here was an impasse.

First the bureau decided to enforce the rule. At the opening soirée the band played only waltzes and polkas. But neither our French guests nor the band got any kick out of that. The evening was a complete flop.

Next time the bureau chose a compromise. The band was allowed to play some fox trots, and the guests were invited to dance them—but not the members of the Soviet colony! We had to sit like mamma's boys and watch the Frenchmen fox-trotting and could only join in when the band played a waltz or a polka. Of course, everybody was embarrassed, guests and hosts alike.

I felt that the world was hardly going to be revolutionized by such childishness and plotted a little surprise for the overvirtuous members of our bureau. I called on our ambassador, Dovgalevsky, with whom I was very good friends, and brought with me Ivanov, director of our metal import department, an Old Bolshevik and one of the more sensible members of the bureau.

"If we really followed the class argument seriously," I said, half joking, "we would ban the waltz instead of the fox trot, because the fox trot was born among the underprivileged Negro race. The waltz, on the other hand, is precisely the dance of aristocratic society—traditional in all the princely courts of Europe!"

The reader who has never seen *Pravda's* Marxian invectives against the fox trot will not appreciate the boldness of this. It did, however, win the day. At the next soirée, when the band started off with a fox trot—to the utter consternation of the guardians of our morals—Ambassador Dovgalevsky, Ivanov, and two other high officials of the delegation, Breslav and myself, invited four French girls to be our partners and sailed off onto the floor. My fox-trotting was not so bad as you may think, either, for during three previous evenings I had taken an intensive course in dancing school for just this purpose!

We all had a lot of fun that evening and did not experience any "disintegration." The whole soirée went with a swing and lasted till dawn. Even the band went home contented.

Our moralists were silenced, but a couple of months later I heard a strange echo of the affair. I received a letter from a friend in the foreign bureau of the Central Committee of the Party. Among other things, he told me, very cautiously, that a report had arrived that, in spite of our serious duties in Paris, certain people, myself included, were giving too much time to dancing. Naturally he didn't really believe this, but he wanted to warn me to be very careful not to injure my reputation.

This letter arrived at a time when I was working from eight o'clock in the morning till one or two at night, keeping my official job and my studies at the Arts et Métiers going at the same time. The letter annoyed me, and I showed it to my chief, Tumanov.

"Never mind," said Tumanov. "I'm just sending to Moscow for approval of your promotion to the post of general director of imports.

I'm giving a full account of your excellent work in the past and right now. That will stop the gossip."

My promotion was indeed promptly approved.

The affair of the kidnapping of General Kutepov, leader of the White Russians in Paris, kept us all thoroughly jumpy for six weeks or so. I have no idea what really happened to Kutepov. If he was spirited away by the G.P.U., as the evidence seemed to show, the thing was carried out in total independence of official Soviet representatives in Paris.

Public opinion, however, saw us as well as the G.P.U. as the villains of the piece. The White Russian *émigrés*, among whom the general had been popular, were furious. The monarchist paper *Vozrozhdenie*, run by an ultra-reactionary gang without scruple or moderation, worked up the *émigré* military circles to a white heat of indignation. *Émigré* officers held meetings in the Rue de Grenelle, and we were warned of a contemplated attack on the embassy. Dovgalevsky declared a state of siege. Most of the Party members armed themselves and slept at the embassy. Camp beds were put up in the larger rooms, and we all took turns at mounting guard. In case of attack we should not have hesitated to defend by force of arms this scrap of Soviet territory in the heart of Paris.

I remember sleeping on the ground floor with the secretary of the embassy, Divilkovsky, who had been wounded at Lausanne when Ambassador Vorovsky was shot. He was a nervous creature who slept badly, moaned a great deal, and had a way of starting awake, grabbing at his revolver. Ambassador Dovgalevsky, by contrast, was possessed of complete self-control. One evening there was an insolent demonstration under the embassy windows, with the French police conspicuous by their absence. I found myself behind the big entrance gate with Dovgalevsky. We expected any moment to see the great door crash down. We released the safety catches of our revolvers. The demonstration did not go that far, however.

The sparse news reaching us from home, besides describing breathtaking successes in the building of new industries, gave a rather grim picture of the background of these successes. Forced collectivization, arrest and deportation of the richer peasants, severe measures against the intellectuals, friction within the Party, a system of bread cards, declining rations, risings in distant parts of the country—all these things made us feel uneasy. A number of non-Party specialists serving on trade missions abroad, recalled to Moscow at this time, refused to return. Many of them took posts with foreign firms. Going back to Russia meant giving up a life of comfort and also rendering an account of their behavior while abroad. These considerations played a greater part in leading most of them to act as they did than any spirit of political opposition. The Central Committee decided to start a *chistka* of all foreign embassies and trade missions.

186

The cleansing commission made the rounds of all the capitals of Europe, interrogating without mercy the staffs of the Soviet missions. Its arrival from Moscow brought fear into all hearts. Private life, amusements, past records, personal origins, contracts—everything was raked up. At the meeting at which we were introduced to this commission, an old, harsh, and domineering member of it began to berate us as though we had all been corrupted by the bourgeois influences around us. I lost my temper and answered him in an angry tone and without mincing my words. The result was unexpected. Shortly afterward I was recommended by the Central Committee in Moscow for election as secretary of our Communist cell and was, it is needless to say, elected. Of a hundred Communists who were summoned before the commission, only sixteen escaped reprimand, exclusion from the Party, or recall.

To keep us free from bourgeois influences, it was recommended that our colony read *L'Humanité*, the French Communist paper. The White Russian papers *Poslednia Novosti* and *Vozrozhdenie* were absolutely forbidden. Comparatively few of us knew French well enough to read *L'Humanité*, and the rest, had they obeyed this order, would have had to depend for current news on the much-delayed Moscow papers. Almost the entire colony, therefore, bought the White Russian newspapers regularly. The restriction was emphasized by a new order, with the explanation that by buying these papers we were practically financing them—even though not influenced by them. This second order did not do much good. Almost all the colony members, except for a few timid souls, continued to buy the papers and read them in secret.

I considered this situation more demoralizing than the contents of the papers, and when I was elected secretary of the cell I decided to end it. I talked the matter over with Dovgalevsky, and we found a reasonable solution. We decided to trust the powers of resistance of our colony against White propaganda and at the same time prevent our employees from buying the newspapers in large quantities. The order forbidding the reading of these papers was canceled, and I instructed our employees' club to buy three copies of both each day and put them in the library for everyone to read.

I was trying my best at this time to dissipate the atmosphere of hypocrisy and petty deceit which had been cultivated by my predecessors. In this Ambassador Dovgalevsky always stood behind me, and he helped me more than once at our Communist cell meetings when I was criticized by some fundamentalist. We became great friends, and I spent many hours at the embassy with him. He was a man of quiet tastes, with a love of literature and art. We sometimes used to sit down to a game of poker, he and I and Muradian, president of the Soviet Bank in Paris, and Ostrovsky of the petroleum trust. Muradian is now in prison or in some concentration camp. Ostrovsky has disappeared. Dovgalevsky died before the purges began.

We were occasionally joined in the embassy drawing room by another veteran of the Revolution, Nicholas Kuzmin, consul general in Paris, whose fate was characteristic of the times. He had lived long in Paris before 1917—a professional revolutionist working under Lenin. After the Revolution he commanded the Red Army which operated in the White Sea and Archangel region against General Miller and the English and American Expeditionary Forces. As a former *émigré*, he longed to revisit his old haunts, Montparnasse and Montmartre, and the Party appointed him to the post on which he had set his heart. Merely to breathe the air of Paris was for him a sustaining pleasure.

On one of his visits to Moscow, Kuzmin was foolish enough to recite to his old friend Voroshilov the stereotyped complaint at having to live as an exile in a bourgeois country. Such remarks were thought proper in Bolshevik circles. A few weeks after he returned I saw him open a telegram, the contents of which appeared to knock him flat. Voroshilov, in the sincere belief that he was doing him a good turn, had wired the happy news of his appointment to a military post in eastern Siberia. Kuzmin put a good face on this piece of ill luck and returned to Russia.

After the Dome and the Rotonde, Irkutsk or Krasnoyarsk were too much for him. In his distant command he got mixed up in an unfortunate affair with a woman. He was sent to Archangel to direct the Arctic Shipping Line. A short time after he came there, the ice breaker *Sibiriakov* was smashed to pieces on an ice floe. In 1936 and 1937 this disaster was raised up against him—his real crime being that, during the Civil War, he had been one of Zinoviev's friends. And so poor old Kuzmin, the most disinterested of Frenchified Russians, was liquidated as an "enemy of the people."

26. *Milan—London—Brussels*

IN 1931 THE POLITBURO appointed me Soviet trade representative in Brussels. Belgium had not yet recognized the U.S.S.R., and so the trade representative there functioned also as a semi-official diplomatic agent. It took months for me to get the necessary visas.

While waiting for them to come through, I was sent to Italy as director general of imports at Milan.

As soon as I arrived I had to leave for Sicily to arrange for the immediate purchase of five million lemons. My arrival at Palermo and Messina, though no one was supposed to know the object of my journey, had the effect of sending up the export price of lemons 20 per cent! This was flattering, but not exactly what I was after. I decided to retire, in the guise of a tourist seeking rest, to a quiet little resort near Palermo and study the conditions of the market. As soon as the exporters were persuaded that I wasn't thinking about lemons, they began to hunt me out. Their prices were once more normal; and I even managed, by means of some picturesque gesticulations, to strike a pretty good bargain. I spoke no Italian at this time, and I was not greatly helped by the fact that the merchants of Messina imagined that they spoke French. Still, we got on well.

Fascist Italy showed itself well disposed toward the Soviet Union. In the course of the First Five-Year Plan it received a number of important orders. The films concerned allowed us long credits, guaranteed by the state, quoted us very reasonable prices—a good deal lower than those of their French and English competitors—and supplied us with first-rate machinery. Soviet technicians came to the conclusion that Italy, which they had always considered a backward nation, had made enormous strides since the war and now possessed up-to-date industrial equipment.

We bought Fiat cars, airplane engines, dockyard equipment, and ships. At Venice, Genoa, and Trieste the naval yards built merchant ships for us. I traveled all over the country and met several leaders of Italian industry. I had to negotiate the purchase of a number of ships with old Admiral Count Ciano. He offered three-year credits, but we wanted five. We could come to no agreement. My dealings with Senator Agnelli, of the Fiat Works, and with Signor Benni, of the electrotechnical industry, were more successful.

The most exciting thing I saw in modern Italy was the great air maneuvers at Milan, in which three hundred "enemy" airplanes attacked the city in pitch darkness, breaking through the powerful lines and bombarding Milan with flares. It was an impressive spectacle, and it made clear to me the fact that in aviation the attacker was in a dangerously superior position. Under a real attack, in spite of an admirably organized defense, the city would suffer terribly. Notwithstanding such demonstrations and the writings of the Italian General Douhet, the prophet of the air blitz, the military leaders of the democracies refused to learn this lesson until thousands, during the first years of Hitler's blitz, had paid with their lives for this die-hard attitude.

Moscow sent the Communist engineer, Puchin, to help me purchase a quantity of machinery. He was a young and very devoted scientist, at that time totally absorbed, under instructions from Piatakov, in equipping our growing chemical industry. In 1936 his name, for the incomprehensible reasons, appeared among the sixteen victims at the Zinoviev trial. He was shot.

My two sons had been placed, at my request, in a model school just outside Moscow. A friend went to see them there while I was in Italy and wrote me an alarming letter. The air was good, certainly, and the place was situated among pine woods; but the children were kept hungry, swore like troopers, and played games with knives. The older boys in the school, my friend informed me, were misbehaving with the girls. While working in Paris I had returned once to Moscow and had been somewhat enlightened on the real conditions of life in Russia. The official press and the "friendly" papers of foreign countries had never tired of describing it as a happy land where the general standard of living was steadily rising. But what my friend wrote, in addition to my own observation, made me decide that Boris and Shura, now almost eight years old, had better join me.

I met them in the station at Milan. What puny little creatures in the wretched clothes that had been all they could get during those hard years! The woman friend who traveled with them told me that when they went into the station restaurant at Vienna they were thunderstruck at the sight of food such as they had never even dreamed of in the whole of their young lives. Boris voiced his amazement by asking: "Have they finished their Five-Year Plan here? Is that why they've got so much food?" A saying that was much quoted in Moscow and traveled far.

After seven months my Belgian visa came through, and I left for Brussels. I settled my sons in a *pension* on the Belgian coast and went to work.

The Belgian authorities, determined to ignore the existence of the U.S.S.R., refused to stamp my diplomatic passport, which also could not exist, and gave me a visa on a separate sheet. This permitted me to remain in the country one month, after which it had to be renewed. While in Belgium I could occupy no official position. I could have only a private office and do business only as a private individual. The banks and important industrial firms boycotted us—their obstinate hostility being due to losses suffered by Belgian concerns in Russia during the Revolution. Several of them insisted on retaining their nominal rights in a number of the confiscated enterprises. As late as 1931 the annual report of one metallurgical company announced to its shareholders that "our inspectors were unable to visit our factories at Yuzovka in the Ukraine, owing to their being temporarily occupied by the Bolsheviks. . . ." [1]

[1] Yuzovka is now named Stalino, and that hardly suggests a better welcome for the Belgian inspectors.

Business is business, however, and the Belgians did buy from us both minerals and wood. They also bought butter and canned fish, both of which we sold cheap. But the members of the government refused to have anything to do with me. Some Belgian politicians, realizing the absurdity of the situation, agreed to act as intermediaries between the government and the Soviet agent, who was not recognized legally. At my request a member of parliament would write to Monsieur Hymans, the foreign minister, to find out whether Soviet ships entering the Antwerp harbor ran any risk of being sequestered, as the shareholders of certain concerns had suggested. Monsieur Hymans would assure me that there was no danger, but his reply would be addressed not to me but to his colleague in Parliament.

Two new friends whom I made in Brussels, the Socialist deputies Wauters and Pierard, helped me get in touch with a former acquaintance, the amiable Dr. Van der Ginst, with whom I had traveled in 1924 from Athens to Naples. At his dinner table we took up again the political discussion begun in the Mediterranean eight years before.

Both of us had, to some extent, changed. Van der Ginst, impressed by the success of the Five-Year Plan—of which he knew neither the seamy side nor the cost—seemed almost ready, I thought, to agree with me that Bolshevik violence, the dictatorship of the proletariat, and Stalin's energy and autocratic methods were showing fruit. Was not one of the most backward countries in the world becoming transformed under our eyes into a socialist industrial power? I, on the other hand, was disturbed by inner doubts. I could see before my eyes a Moscow sucked dry, rationed, ground down by hard necessity and the still harder discipline of the Party. I could see my two boys threatened with anemia and thoroughly devitalized as a result of the privations they had endured. I began, deep in myself, to wonder whether we were not paying too dearly in suffering and exhaustion for our industrial victories, and what would be the ultimate political consequences.

It may be that my companion has now forgotten all that we said in these conversations. I, however, looking back, seem to see in them the first indications of a curious and very widespread turnabout. The old warriors of the Revolution, faced with the Stalinist degeneration —at first morbid, then monstrous—felt, with a sense of death in their hearts, implacably opposed to the dictator and his bureaucracy. The reformists, the moderates, the liberals, on the other hand, after having been relentless adversaries of the Revolution in the days of its great and sincere dreams, now permit themselves to be seduced into enthusiasm by the successes of the totalitarian state. It should be remembered that at the time of our conversation, 1932, the Germany of the Weimar Constitution was in the throes of a mortal illness for which reformist socialists could find no cure, and that illness seemed to be spreading throughout the democratic world. The U.S.S.R., on

191

the contrary, was straining every nerve to build a great industrial future. This contrast in part explained the newborn enthusiasm of many liberals for Stalin's Russia at that time.

Little by little I managed, in spite of difficulties, to get some business going. I signed contracts for the sale of asbestos and manganese. Sales of timber reached such high figures that Moscow soon sent me an assistant, on whom I conferred the title of "Director of the Timber Department." He was a young man named Ershov, a great talker with a fine conceit of himself, but ignorant of French, of trade matters in general, and of the timber trade in particular. His former profession had been that of propagandist for some local committee of the Party. I was not long in discovering why this odd appointment had been made. Ershov was the personal protégé of Tzikhon, the commissar of labor (his name is never heard now), whom he kept in linen, neckties, silk socks, etc., sending him these gifts in the diplomatic pouch.

The more all open criticism was repressed, the more secret favoritism flourished. There was a good deal of talk, it is true, about mutual criticism, but it worked only one way—from the top down. Its main use was to furnish scapegoats for the sins of higher-up officials. I will cite two more examples of the favoritism I mentioned.

Asmus was appointed Soviet minister at Helsinki for no other reason than that, when he was attaché of the legation at Vienna, Lazar Kaganovich, a member of the Politburo, had come there to consult a physician, and Asmus had given him a good time. Litvinov had intended to make him a consul in some minor post, and the order from the Politburo giving him the distinguished position in Helsinki came as a very great surprise.

Michael Ostrovsky, when head of the trade delegation in Paris, deceived by some men of straw set up by a group of Russian *émigrés,* sold them timber on terms that meant a loss of several hundred thousand francs. Rosengolz removed him, drew up an adverse report to his conduct, and submitted it, with supporting documents, to the Party Commission of Control, recommending punishment. Meanwhile Ostrovsky, who was a protégé of Voroshilov, was given the post of ambassador in Bucharest. The Commission of Control was powerless.

The Belgians allowed us no credits; consequently we bought from them considerably less than they bought from us. Their trade balance with the Soviet Union was not favorable. Since it was impossible for the Soviet Union to have an official trade delegation in Belgium, I prepared to start a mixed company operating with both Soviet and Belgian capital, or, at least, counting a number of Belgians among its shareholders. This company was actually formed, but not until after my departure from Brussels, which was not entirely voluntary.

After I had been there some months I had occasion to visit London. The great English city fascinated me. My reading of the English novelists, most of whom were translated into Russian, had given me a preconceived idea of England in which the names of Dickens and Kipling and the thought of poverty, hypocrisy, order, tradition, a certain kind of good nature, and a magnificence unlike anything I had ever known played equal parts. My first sight of the white cliffs gave me a genuine thrill. I lost myself in the maelstrom of the largest capital of the Old World and soon saw that all sorts and conditions floated in it, very good as well as very bad, and that what was most noticeable about these people was a strong sense of discipline in which respect for the rights of the individual played a predominant part.

Soon after my return from London I was called to Paris, but on the train between Brussels and Liége I heard the news of the assassination of President Doumer by a Russian. A Russian? We Soviet officials abroad were so used to suspicion and ill will—to actual misrepresentation, too—that my mind instantly began to consider possible complications. I broke off my journey and returned to Brussels in order to be ready for what might happen. As I expected, the journalists of the right immediately tried to find in this the hand of the Soviets. They were considerably put out of countenance when it was announced next day that Gorgulov was a sort of fascist lunatic or lunatic fascist. Some friends told me that the Soviet Embassy in Paris had felt as I did and had put itself in a state of defense, mounting sentries, as always when there was any chance of a disturbance.

Returning to Brussels, I found that my office and entire apartment had been turned upside down. There is something peculiarly sad and revolting in the sight of a dwelling that has suffered physical brutality. Everything I possessed, no matter how trivial, had been flung about and trampled under foot. Drawers stood wide open and empty; my official ledgers were gone; my clothes and personal papers lay all over the floor, and the locks of my trunks had been forced. Several letters and photographs were missing. The safe was adorned with official seals forbidding me to open it. I found on the table a note requesting my presence at police headquarters, and I went there at once.

An inspector received me very impolitely in a ground-floor room of the Palais de Justice. I noticed that he refrained from offering me a seat. I went, however, to an armchair and settled myself into it before protesting against the housebreaking and looting to which I had been subjected.

The interview opened on a note of strain.

"By using the word 'housebreaking,' " barked the inspector, "you are insulting my men, who were merely carrying out their orders."

"I have no wish to reflect on your men, Inspector," I replied, "but there is no use pretending that my first impression was *not* that a very clumsy burglary had taken place. It was only later that I realized that I had been made the victim of an illegal act of search carried out with quite unnecessary brutality. Since we are living in a civilized country, may I point out to you that there is such a thing as the Rights of Man?"

I began to understand this raid when I learned that the order of search had been issued by the district attorney of Mons, a city which I had never visited and where I had no friends or correspondents. Mons at that time was the scene of a miners' strike which had been full of dramatic incidents. The miners had greeted the moderate socialist minister, Vandervelde, with catcalls, had thrown several police officers into the canal, and had locked a number of engineers and mine managers into their offices. Who was behind these excesses? It never occurred to anyone that the miners might have been sufficiently discontented and overwrought to resort to violence on their own. No, there happened to be at Brussels an official Bolshevik agent who pretended to be concerned only with matters of business but who in reality was doubtless spending his nights manipulating invisible threads which would set in motion a riot in a distant mining district!

That, anyhow, was how the official's mind had worked, and for this reason he had felt justified in ordering a search of my premises. My protest infuriated the inspector and convinced him that I was at least a dangerous agent of the Comintern. While I was awaiting in a neighboring room the return of my personal belongings, several plainclothes men entered one by one. We eyed each other. Two or three of them found it necessary to walk by and brush against me as I stood waiting. When I reached for my back pocket, they made a rush for me, but stopped short when a harmless cigarette case emerged in my hand.

It was necessary for them to come home with me in order to examine my safe and remove the seals. I naturally refused to take them in my official car, and, still more naturally, to get into theirs, which happened to be a prison van.

"All right," I said, "you go in your car, and I'll go in mine."

"Impossible. We must not let you out of our sight."

"Am I to consider myself under arrest, then?"

"Nothing of the sort—but the law forbids us to leave you until the seals have been removed from your safe."

"Well, then, if I am not your prisoner, you must be mine!"

We compromised by making the journey in a streetcar.

My safe was completely empty. Their eyes popped out of their heads. Surprise—disappointment—admiration! Obviously I had managed to empty the safe just after—or just before—the seals were attached. A damned clever trick!

Moscow, informed of what had happened, told me to return and make a detailed report. I was, at that time, giving my attention to the establishment of a shipping line between Leningrad and Antwerp. In spite of the importance of the scheme, and the fact that I employed

an eminent lawyer, Marcel Henry Jaspar, who later became minister of education, the government refused to give me a return visa valid for more than one month. That did not give me time to go and make my report and return. I knew that the police inspector had submitted a detailed report in which he made a great point of the Bolshevik insolence of my attitude.

"Police headquarters have got it in for you," said my Belgian friends.

"Because of the Mons strikes, I suppose?"

"More particularly because you disappointed them. They were pretty sure you were up to something!"

I left my children near Ostend and went back to Moscow. The Commissariat of Foreign Trade approved my project for the Leningrad-Antwerp Line, and, after completing some other business, I started back. But my visa had expired, and I had to get a new one in Berlin. The Belgian consul general there explained, with an air of considerable embarrassment, that he had received categorical instructions to refuse me a visa and inform me that I was forbidden to cross the Belgian frontier.

"But my sons are in Belgium!" I exclaimed.

"I'm sorry, but it is quite impossible."

My two boys were treated with all the honors of war. Their departure resembled an exchange of prisoners. An official of the Soviet trade delegation in Paris went to Belgium to conduct them to the German frontier, where I received them.

I have since learned, more or less, what lay behind all this comic business. A former agent of the G.P.U., Agabekov, who had fled to Belgium after making a mess of various jobs in counterespionage in the Levant, had become the principal informer for the Belgian police in all matters connected with the Soviets. What he didn't know he invented. In order to maintain his status, he would himself recruit Belgians for a fake G.P.U. and then denounce them to the government. To him it would have been a small matter to invent a participation by the Soviets in the strikes at Mons.

Three years later Belgium recognized the Soviet Union, sent an ambassador to Moscow, and received a trade delegation in Brussels. Belgium's distinguished diplomats accredited to Athens paid me friendly visits. We talked of the beauties of Bruges and Ghent and of the architecture of the magnificent Palais de Justice in Brussels, though naturally I spared the feelings of my colleagues by never referring to my inside knowledge of the latter building. Thus the winds of diplomacy veer.

I would like to say here one thing more. At the time when the Soviets were poor and revolutionary, the intervention of their diplomatic and trade representatives in labor movements was much exaggerated and a great fuss made about it. As a matter of fact, the Communist International had its own channels of communication with

Moscow, and the G.P.U. ran its own secret service. We diplomatic and commercial agents confined ourselves as strictly as possible to our own legitimate tasks. While the foreign press continued to discredit us and hold us in suspicion, the real agents of propaganda and penetration abroad were carrying on their work unhindered.

On the other hand, since the Soviet Union has entered the circle of respectable powers, richer than it was before, its production of gold having assumed impressive proportions, and since Stalin's regime, based on no moral principles, is not bothered about the means it employs to extend its influence, foreigners seem quite willing to shut their eyes to extreme irregularities on the part of its official delegations. The G.P.U. has lately been able to use the diplomatic and trade missions, not in promoting strikes or encouraging foreign labor movements, as we were accused of doing, but in carrying out insolent and brutal political assassinations under the very eyes of the foreign police. Such things have been done in France, Switzerland, Spain, and Mexico almost without hindrance.

27. *Realities under the Five-Year Plan*

AFTER MY UNSUCCESSFUL ATTEMPT to re-enter Belgium, Moscow was obliged to recall me. On my return in November, 1932, I was appointed first vice-president of the machine-tool importing trust, the "Stanko-Import," which bought factory equipment from all over the world. A substantial part of the imports were going to the armament and airplane industries now being rushed ahead at a feverish pace.

During my four years abroad I had been in Moscow for an extended stay only once. That was in the summer of 1930, when I was present at the Sixteenth Party Congress, to which the Central Committee had invited as guests the secretaries of the three most important Russian Communist cells abroad—those of Berlin, London, and Paris.

Even then one's Communist convictions had to be pretty deeply ingrained not to admit any doubts. After the improvements of 1922-28, Moscow showed appalling changes. Every face and every house front was eloquent of misery, exhaustion, and apathy. There were scarcely any stores, and the rare display windows still existing had an air of desolation. Nothing was to be seen in them but cardboard boxes and food tins, upon which the shopkeepers, in a mood of despair rather than rashness, had pasted stickers reading "empty." Everyone's clothes were worn out, and the quality of the stuff was unspeakable. My Paris suit made me feel embarrassed in the streets. There was a shortage of everything—especially of soap, boots, vegetables, meat, butter, and all fatty foodstuffs.

I was much astonished to see crowds waiting in front of the candy stores. Fellow travelers after a hasty trip through Russia would return home and tell glowing tales of the socialist paradise where crowds waited in long lines, not for bread, but for candy. The truth was quite different. Famished people sought anything to fill their empty stomachs. Even the revolting sweets made of saccharine and soya beans were gladly consumed, because they were almost the only edible things that could be bought—and even then one pound of them cost an average day's wages.

Manufactured goods and food were much scarcer than money, and money was scarcer than jobs. It was true, as propaganda abroad said, that there was no unemployment; but living on a workman's pay was the hardest thing in the world. The housing crisis had reached a point never before known. In front of the empty co-operatives, long queues stood day and night in the hope of being allotted ridiculously small quantities of foodstuffs. Elsewhere a man who sold food of such miserable quality would have been held up to public execration and gone bankrupt. In contrast to the early days of the Revolution, conditions were even worse in the country districts than in the big towns.

I was struck by these material evidences of crisis, and still more by the nervous tension among Communists, intellectuals, technical specialists, and workmen; in short, among all those who had been most involved in the Five-Year Plan. Faces were marked with anxiety and fatigue, and minds were so exhausted that no one seemed capable any longer of controlling his reactions or of seeing things calmly. Everyone was caught up in a tangle of imperative instructions, resistant facts, constantly recurring difficulties, official lies, nerve-racking needs, fears, and doubts.

I spent a few days at the Central Committee's rest house at Marino, but even there the careless laughter, the air of gaiety which had impressed me on my last visit, had vanished. I saw nothing around me but sullen looks, heard nothing but cautious talk, was conscious only of men utterly exhausted, incapable of making any further effort, their nerves worn so thin that they were always on the verge of a quarrel. I made the acquaintance there of Prigozhin, a young Marxist professor from Leningrad, who while in England had married George Lansbury's daughter. He became the director of an institute of philosophy and history in Moscow, but vanished after the Kirov affair. I am very much afraid that he may have perished along with Zinoviev's friends. What became of Lansbury's daughter I do not know.

I attended a session of the organization bureau of the Central Committee. Legally the Orgburo is almost as important as the Politburo.

The one is supposed to deal with problems of administration, the other of policy. The Orgburo was made up of five secretaries of the Central Committee, the secretary of the trade unions, and the secretary of the Youth Movement. Gamarnik represented the Army. Kaganovich presided at this session. Rosengolz's deputy, who gave the report, had spent two months preparing a detailed document on the personnel of our trade missions abroad and on the causes of the new wave of desertions from their ranks. Kaganovich allowed him six minutes in which to present it! Other speakers had to be content with two; and some were never allowed on the platform at all.

Rosengolz, our foreign-trade commissar, still young-looking and dressed in shirt and boots of pseudo-military cut, read a list of colleagues whom he wanted to have with him in the department. Kaganovich appeared to be shocked by his audacity and brushed him aside with: "We will go into that together." Although formally they had gathered for an exchange of opinion, actually none was to be allowed. He made the final decision, which was to reduce all personnel abroad by 50 per cent and put two hundred approved Communists in foreign service. When I left the meeting I saw clearly what the situation was. There was no longer any discussion on matters of importance, nothing but a pretense for the sake of appearances. Power was entirely in the hands of the men in Stalin's confidence.

Nothing of moment happened at the Sixteenth Party Congress. The rooms and corridors of the congress building were crowded. There were endless wearisome ovations which turned the sittings into something very much like a series of sporting events. There was not a single serious debate. Stalin delivered a survey of the world situation. As always, he spoke poorly, with a pronounced Georgian accent, accompanying his words with angular movements of his arms. He proclaimed the approaching triumph of communism in the world at large, and the coming of the German revolution, throwing in a passing denunciation of the aggressive designs of the French General Staff against the Soviet Republic.

I was profoundly distressed but did not dare show my dismay. The worst aspect of the whole thing was the official enthusiasm and loud acclamations with which his words were received. It was only too clear that what was being said bore no relation to what was being thought. It amounted to no more than a paean of victory, loud glorification of industrial triumphs, eloquent approval of the "general line," while in reality the situation was such that the country was tense and almost at the breaking point, and everyone was wondering what the next day would bring.

The right—Rykov, Bukharin, and Tomsky—were given time to speak in condemnation of themselves and allowed to declare their repentant loyalty to the "general line." If I say they looked defeated, it is an understatement—they looked utterly demoralized. They were men worn out, with no fight left in them, though they might, if they had made the effort, have stirred up an effective opposition. Tomsky tried to strike a note of dignity, when announcing his surrender, by refusing to insist on his own mistakes and on those of his friends. Stalin poked heavy sarcasms at him.

In contrast to the official optimism, an alarming note was introduced by Commissar of Agriculture Yakovlev, who read a report admitting that widespread destruction of livestock had taken place. (Yakovlev later disappeared in the purge.)

Stalin thought to achieve all the wonders of the Five-Year Plan, not by organization and expert direction, but by working the masses up to ecstatic enthusiasm and superhuman efforts. He did achieve some wonders, but the plan threatened to founder in a kind of anarchy. Costs increased, wastage of labor and of human energy became enormous. I got firsthand knowledge of a good many details of this campaign of industrialization. The following incident explains why I use the term "anarchy" in connection with it. It serves also to show the psychological motives lying behind many of the costly errors made as well as the very real victories achieved.

Alexander Serebrovsky, a prominent Communist and a brilliant engineer, famous for his reorganization of the oil industry on American lines after a visit to the United States, was put in charge of a trust of metals. The production of copper had never exceeded 40,000 tons a year, but the Central Committee issued the slogan: "150,000 tons of copper next year for the socialist state!" Serebrovsky's first assistant, Shakh-Muradov, also a Communist engineer, protested against this hopelessly impossible order. An attempt to realize such figures, he pointed out, would mean trying to exploit distant seams, for which it would be necessary to construct hundreds of miles of railroad through the desert, besides building up a whole new mining industry. This could not be done in less than three or four years. The astonishing enthusiasm and energy which had created such gigantic metallurgical plants as Magnitogorsk and Kuznetsk would degenerate into mere rash adventure, squandering of the capital invested, and destruction of the machinery installed—which, indeed, did happen later—if such wild plans were acted upon.

For thus raising his voice against a ruinous policy, Shakh-Muradov, an able engineer, also trained in America, was denounced as "an opportunist of the right," charged with wrecking the plans of the Central Committee, and relieved of his post. Realizing that he could do nothing, since the question had become one of prestige for the Central Committee, he bowed to the verdict, admitting that he had been guilty of not understanding the full profundity of the attitude taken by those who directed the policy of the Party.

His own proposal to bring the annual production of copper up to 100,000 tons was rejected. Other engineers, more terrorized, or perhaps only less conscientious, took his place.

Serebrovsky publicly condemned the opportunism of his disgraced assistant and solemnly promised, in a *Pravda* article, to carry out the order of the chief and bring the production of copper up to 150,000 tons in one year. Himself a good engineer and an organizer of great experience, he knew perfectly well that the promise could not be kept. But the Central Committee and its leader insisted that he make this statement as evidence of his loyalty and obedience to the Party discipline. As a matter of fact, during the whole course of the Five-Year Plan, notwithstanding prodigious efforts, copper production never reached an annual figure of more than 50,000 tons, and it took a long time to stabilize even that.

There were thousands of incidents of the same kind, and the penalties for those who stood up for their true judgment became increasingly severe. No one now can call back to life the technical experts who perished in G.P.U. labor camps or were shot for having too much professional self-respect to endorse an obviously insane scheme. In Shakh-Muradov's case, professional integrity had been at war with Party loyalty, and the latter eventually won the day. As a Communist, he felt obliged to recognize that he was wrong, although as an engineer he knew quite well that he was right. He—like thousands of others—hoped through thus dividing himself to go on helping his country and perhaps to save its industries even in the teeth of mad adventures planned by ignorant politicians.

Such moral sacrifices, however, came to nothing. Both Serebrovsky and Shakh-Muradov, engineers of the highest caliber, experienced in the direction of metallurgical enterprises and known to industrial circles in two continents, are now in prison as "enemies of the people," if they still live. As for the copper industry, in spite of the enormous sums of money and the prodigious efforts sunk in it, the new factories were at the end of the Second Five-Year Plan in a state of extreme disorganization, and the new machinery had deteriorated. Tragically for the country, the same situation was brought to pass in many Soviet factories.

At the price of this prodigious waste, which could continue without bankruptcy only in a state-owned economy, Russia gradually learned a few of the elementary lessons of production and its management. How far she still is from American standards can be seen in the report of William L. White on conditions as he recently found them in the best factories of Moscow and Leningrad. People who think these conditions are due to the war are mistaken. War, by centering all minds on a common purpose, decreases rather than increases the natural inefficiencies of a state-owned economy.

Loyalty to Stalin at the time of which I am writing was based principally on the conviction that there was no one to take his place, that any change of leadership would be extremely dangerous, and that the country must continue in its present course, since to stop now or attempt a retreat would mean the loss of everything. On my return in 1932 the condition of Moscow had changed even more than in 1930, but it took me some time to understand how deep these changes went. It was only by being in the country that one could fully realize how the achievement of even a mere subsistence standard of existence had become for everyone a matter of constant scheming and striving.

The Ukraine and several of the more distant provinces were in the throes of famine. Drought had nothing to do with this. The food shortage was due entirely to the breakdown of agriculture caused by enforced collectivization and the peasants' reaction to it and by the policy of indiscriminate exports. In the cities there was famine, too, but there provisioning was organized from top to bottom, with food cards, categorized rations, Torgsins, and shops reserved for people belonging to favored bureaus or employed in the commissariats. In the special stores reserved for the privileged—specialists, that is, and high officials—such things as food, drugs, and clothes could be obtained with difficulty in small quantities. But in the Torgsins, stores for trade with foreigners—though, in fact, they were patronized chiefly by Soviet citizens, since foreigners were few and far between—anyone could buy anything provided he paid for it in gold, silver, jewels, or foreign currency. The Torgsins accepted dental plates, silver icons, watches, wedding rings, spoons, and even silver currency from China or the Argentine. And one could find there such rare objects as boots, dress materials, aspirin, tea, chocolate, and soap.

An exceedingly small number of persons—very high officials, foreigners, and the top specialists—were able to frequent first-class hotels in the cosmopolitan style, with fine restaurants, orchestras, and bars. Supper for one at the Hotel Metropole cost as much as a minor clerk could earn in two months. As vice-president of Stanko-Import, I received five times that sum—five hundred rubles a month, the wage of a "bureaucrat." Besides that, the Commissariat of Foreign Trade, thanks to the influence of Rosengolz, provided me with a room at the Hotel Novo-Moskovsky, in the center of the city. I could afford to take this room only because the Commissariat paid my rent of thirty rubles a day.

The problem of food was, for me, a very complicated one. In the hotel restaurant a bowl of soup cost five to seven rubles, a plate of meat twenty-two rubles, a glass of tea one ruble. I had to feed my two boys and the maid who looked after them. If I had boarded at this rate I should have got through my month's pay in three or four days. To get a bread card meant weeks and months of red tape. How could I manage to live? By good luck I had developed a passion for automobiles during my stay abroad, and it came to my rescue now. The ban on buying automobiles abroad had been lifted just before I left Brussels, and I had bought a secondhand Buick for one hundred English pounds and had it shipped from London to Leningrad. I sold my Buick to Torgsin, not without a great deal of difficulty in getting the necessary authorization, and received for it five hundred Torgsin rubles, each one worth about forty paper rubles. We lived mainly on this money for a year and a half.

At the hotel we were strictly forbidden to do any cooking in our rooms. But the maid prepared our food in secret, in a little recess just inside the door. Every once in a while the manager came up threatening to turn us into the street, but, like everybody else, we put him off with promises. At the end of eight months like this I got two rooms in an apartment house reserved for officials of our commissariat. Naturally, these two rooms had been fought over by a dozen officials, all as vexingly situated as I was and all pleading special rights, peculiar circumstances, powerful patronage, or reasons of state. Rosengolz snatched the morsel out of their greedy mouths and gave it to me; having gone through the war, he did things with a certain military directness.

My Buick, before being turned into food and shelter, served to enlighten me on some of the results of the Five-Year Plan in the field of communications. Up to that time I had known only what the Soviet press told me on this head, and, on the whole, I more or less believed it. I realized that our motor industry was young and our road system pretty bad, but I had gathered that in this field, as in others, we were making immense progress—"overtaking with giant strides our most advanced neighbors. . . ."

I had promised myself a motor trip through the central parts of Russia. A friend, as keen on motoring as myself, went with me to Leningrad to get his car, which was arriving on the same boat as mine. Our hearts beat fast as we watched the cranes deposit on the quay our two elegantly shaped Buicks, which stood out in such pleasant contrast to the old dilapidated machines most officials had to get along with. But here came our first disappointment: the cars were delivered to us completely stripped, I might almost say gutted. All spare parts and accessories had been stolen on board the ship.

It was a fine, cold day, ten degrees below zero, with bright sunshine and crisp snow. To send our cars on to Moscow and make the journey by train would have appeared to us an act of sacrilege, an unpardonable lack of confidence in our country and its government. Everyone knows that since the days of Alexander I, that is, for more than a century, the Petersburg-Moscow road had been one of the best in Russia. Running in an almost straight line between the two capitals, and maintained with the greatest care, it had been the pride and joy of the Department of Roads and Bridges under the Imperial regime. Let's take that road! The landscape might be melancholy, the fields and woods smothered in snow, but at least we should have the joy of arriving in Moscow like true Europeans. The distance was about 450 miles. We could do that easily in twelve to fourteen hours' driving time.

First we had to get a card entitling us to buy gasoline. We made the necessary requests to the administration of the road and car society, the Avtodor, to the gasoline rationing board, and to the Committee of the Party in the hope that we might be able to hasten the formalities. The business was completed in two days, for we both held high positions. Our gasoline cards gave us the right to replenish our tanks anywhere in the Union, without further explanations.

We were in high good humor when we took the road. The first 150 miles passed pleasantly enough against a background of trackless snow and a mildly Arctic landscape. From time to time we passed trucks standing motionless by the roadside, some empty, some loaded. There was never any sign of their drivers. The heavy vehicles waited there on the white road, looking oddly abandoned. The sight was a strange one and pricked our curiosity. The farther we got, the more numerous became these trucks, until at times it looked as though whole caravans had been abandoned by the roadside. It was only very occasionally that we met one on the move, and when we did so we noticed that the driver stared at us with an expression of surprise mingled with respect.

We began to think about refilling our tanks. We would do it at the next market town, a traffic center of importance, the hub of several roads linking the various big townships of the ancient government of Tver.

The small town was dozing in the cold sunlight. We went into a tavern.

"Where can we find gas?" Some truck drivers seated at a table made ironic faces when we put the question to them.

"Gas, comrades? We've been waiting for gas for two days! There's not a drop anywhere along the road. Didn't you see all the stalled trucks?"

We gazed at each other in amazement, for we had been led to believe that the Soviet Union came second only to the United States in oil production. We would have to look into this mystery later; but what could be done to solve the immediate difficulty? We had a bad quarter-hour cudgeling our brains. Then my friend had a brilliant inspiration.

"There must be a few druggists somewhere in this hole. Let's buy up all their benzine."

We went through that town with a fine-tooth comb, putting our case to every druggist we could find. They were impressed when they learned that we were directors of the Commissariat of Foreign Trade, and we collected several quarts of benzine. We started off again under the surprised gaze of the stranded drivers. It wasn't that they thought us adepts in black magic, but that they assumed that the G.P.U.— the only people still likely to have any gas—had got us out of our difficulties because we happened to be, so to speak, "in the trade."

We counted on being able to fill up again nearer Moscow. But as a result of the delay there was no longer any hope of getting home that evening. We should have to put up somewhere for the night. This new problem was hardly less difficult than our last one. There were no hotels on this road, and the few taverns were already crammed with carters, truck drivers, local officials, and peasants. Their taprooms were suffocating, and most of them had no accommodations. We finally found one with beds in the living room, and sheets, to be sure, but sheets which had already been used by someone else. The manager explained, "We do our washing once a month." We accepted the inevitable, for sleeping in our cars would have meant risking death from cold.

Next day our drugstore benzine carried us another 70 miles and then gave out. We realized with horror that we still had more than 200 miles to go. The white ribbon of road stretched endlessly before us. The abandoned trucks which we passed at intervals reminded us of an army in retreat. Several of them were scarcely visible under their blankets of snow. At every village, at every filling station, we made the same inquiry, always without effect. There was no gas to be had. We began to hate the sight of those cards which gave us permission to replenish our tanks "anywhere in Russia." Wouldn't it have been simpler to tell us there was no gasoline to be had between Leningrad and Moscow—after five peaceful years of triumphant industrialization —or, rather, that the filling stations were there but all bone dry?

"Does this often happen?" we asked.

"It's very remarkable when it doesn't," was the reply.

In Moscow we had seen for ourselves hundreds of persons queuing up for a few quarts; we knew that gasoline was being sold on the black market at four or five times its official price; but we had thought that those in charge of the Five-Year Plan would at least have provided for the needs of people traveling on state business on the main road between the capitals. All these broken-down trucks meant disorganization of work and failure to transport food over vast districts of the country.

We spent our second night at an empty filling station. Whatever happened we'd got to get to Moscow somehow! My eye caught sight of a barrel. "Kerosene?" I asked. The risk was considerable, but we had to take it. We trembled with apprehension as we fed our cars, accustomed to the refined product of Shell, with the awful stuff used for local lighting—black, greasy crude oil, full of foreign bodies. Surely our engines would never be able to digest such food! But they did. To an accompaniment of spitting, kicking, groaning, and jerking, we finally got off.

The road was a road now only by courtesy. Ruts of frozen snow alternated with stretches of ice. There were quite unaccountable holes and lumps in the surface. Our springs broke. We got them mended in a rough-and-ready way at a village smithy. We were frozen and exhausted; we both had streaming colds. My companion went to sleep as he drove, very nearly turned his car over in a stream, and got a nasty jab in the ribs from the wheel, which was damaged in the process! We looked pitiful and sick. We might have been conducting a retreat from Moscow instead of traveling to Moscow in modern cars. At last, at Kalinin, we managed to get some gas. Victory!

Defeat, however, waited for me at the gates of Moscow. Just outside the city, near the race course, the road became a perfect modern speedway. Who could have suspected a trap? Those who passed here regularly knew what to avoid. I, unfortunately, was a stranger. A near-by drain had burst, and the water, having run for some time over the snow, had flooded a downhill slope and turned it into a sheet of ice as smooth as a mirror. I saw it only when it was too late. The Buick slid and skidded, cut a small tree in two, and came to rest against another, smashed and at its last gasp.

A crowd gathered round to look at the wreck. Repairs would cost me 1,000 rubles at the very least. And then, as though things weren't bad enough already, a heavy truck hit the slippery slope and very slowly and quite inexorably came slithering toward us. It would have obliterated the Buick except that some poor fellow who was curiously leaning over my engine acted as a buffer. He was crushed by the impact and hung suspended between the two vehicles. An ambulance took him away; but I could not make inquiries about him, for I ended that pleasure trip in bed with an attack of sciatica. I never knew whether he survived.

As for my Buick, I soon came to the conclusion that I could not possibly keep it. The garage charges alone would have eaten up a third of my salary. I had had enough of our roads. Besides, what was the use of having a car if one couldn't afford to buy food? And so, as I have said, it went to Torgsin.

28. *Bureaucratic Degeneration*

IN 1933 the Politburo decided to send to Poland a special govern- ment mission of good will under the presidency of Vice-Commissar Ivan Boyev, later president of Amtorg, and I was designated a member of it. The Russian flirtation with Poland was developing favorably. For a long time the Soviet Union, bound to Germany by the Treaty of Rapallo and a series of commercial agreements, had regarded Po- land as its most dangerous enemy, calling her the "soldier of French Imperialism and champion of the Treaty of Versailles." Each spring the Politburo discussed the possibility of an offensive by the Poles and worked the country up into a state of war fever. Then somebody had the idea that, since Germany had abandoned itself to nazism, we should attempt a reconciliation with Poland. Stalin, though still cling- ing to the hope of an eventual understanding with Hitler, had made diplomatic approaches in Warsaw, and they had been well received.

On our arrival in Poland we were welcomed with a politeness not far removed from open sympathy. Public opinion there was still re- joicing at the easing of tension between the two countries, and business circles were hoping to find in Russia a badly needed new market. Poland had more fear of Germany than Soviet Russia, having at least three quarrels of long standing with Berlin, concerning the Corridor, Upper Silesia, and Poznań. There seemed to be nothing to estrange her from the Soviet Union, which, besides, could provide an outlet for her industries such as Germany never could. Colonel Beck, to be sure, was a great deal more frightened of bolshevism than of nazism, and he had already begun overtures to Germany. Nevertheless, even of- ficial circles welcomed us in a friendly manner and gave us banquet after banquet.

If I had not already learned from experience how empty and mean- ingless official receptions are, my education on this point would have been completed in the following weeks, which left me with an aver- sion to "toasts." We were overwhelmed with compliments. We were also shown over a number of model factories, most of them idle owing to the crisis.

The port of Gdynia gave me an idea of the power of modern in- dustry. In the course of a few years an entirely new city, equipped to receive ocean liners and serve as a base for a squadron of warships, had sprung up on a stretch of uninhabited sand dunes. It was a spacious, well-laid-out city, logically organized to the last detail, and not built, like some of our new Soviet towns, by forced labor. There were a lot of things about which I had not yet made up my mind, but I could not ignore the fact that the labor of political prisoners in concentration camps had played an essential part in our exploitation of the northern forests and in the building of our great works such as Khibinogorsk and Magnitogorsk and the White Sea-Baltic canal.

Our mission to Poland produced no results except a few minor orders—a small amount of iron purchased in Upper Silesia by my colleague, the president of the Metalo-Import, and a dozen or so machine tools ordered by me for Stanko-Import.

The final ceremony connected with our journey was staged upon our return at Moscow. The Polish ambassador, M. Lukasiewicz, organized a great reception and banquet in honor of the delegation. The reception was attended by the diplomatic corps, officials of the Commissariats of Foreign Affairs and Foreign Trade, and the High Command of the Red Army. Generals Tukhachevsky, Budyenny, and Egorov, soon to be marshals, were present and took an active part in the amusements and dancing as well as in the "serious" discussions which developed in the course of the evening.

The banquet was an intimate affair. The heads of the two commissariats with their more important subordinates were the only guests. On either side of M. Lukasiewicz sat Rosengolz and Acting Foreign Commissar Krestinsky—Litvinov was abroad—and around the table Vice-Commissars Sokolnikov, Eliava, Loganovsky, and, I believe, Radek. Since then, all these men have been either shot or condemned as "fascist spies." Lukasiewicz and Boyev drank to the "important" results of our trip and to the happy future of Soviet-Polish relations.

Suffering from influenza ever since my stay in Warsaw, I went off, a few days later, to the Kremlin hospital, where I was attended by Dr. Levin, who enjoyed the confidence of all members of the government and who was very attentive to his patients. He was shot in 1938 for having—according to his "confession"—shortened the last hours of Maxim Gorky as a result of instructions received from Yagoda, then chief of the G.P.U. Yagoda, to be sure, wielded unlimited power, but he was only Stalin's instrument. And old Dr. Levin, whom I knew to have spent his days in untiring efforts to save human lives and mitigate human suffering, was the last man in the world capable of such a murder. Yagoda, who knew the real facts, was condemned at the same trial with Dr. Levin and also shot.

I was going through a sort of crisis. Up till then I had been one of those Communists who, relying on the wisdom of the Party, had seen in the expected success of the Five-Year Plan the cure for all our ills. Living abroad and entirely absorbed in my work, I had relied on the opinions expressed by Party officials and had allowed myself to be deceived by government lies. I knew that the country was being asked to make impossible efforts and endure excessive sufferings, but I knew it only in an abstract sort of way and felt quite certain that the fruits of the plan would soon be visible. Moscow was now to me a terrible eye opener. Life had improved only for a very few—for the rest, the masses of the people, it had become so much worse that they seemed to have abandoned themselves to despair. They never dreamed of complaining.

The porter of the building in which I lived did a little boot-repairing every evening in his tiny lodge, which swarmed with children.

"Why do you work so hard?" I asked him, knowing that his working day was not eight or ten hours but had no limit.

"Why?" he said. "Because I am starving. I've got seven mouths to fill, and I'm paid a hundred and twenty rubles."

"But now that bread cards have been done away with, there's an increase of 10 per cent in wages to cover the increase in the price of bread. That ought to help."

"You really think so? There are seven of us, counting my wife and five children. We need seven kilos of bread a day, since I can't afford to buy anything else. The price has been raised to one ruble for black bread, and two rubles for white, per kilo. But all the increase I get is eight rubles a month. Don't forget that the raise isn't 10 per cent of my wages, but only 10 per cent of what I was permitted by ration cards to spend for bread. And that isn't seven kilos, but three. So you see, Comrade, I must either work at night, steal, or see my whole family starve."

I found myself literally trembling with indignation when I learned that the workers were in such a desperate state fifteen years after the "proletarian" revolution. I felt ashamed also. We were supposed to be past the worst phase of the effort, and yet even now comfort was possible for only a few. The millions had been deliberately condemned to poverty and misery. The "special" shops, where the workers could sometimes get a bit of cheap food, had been closed down; and, on the theory of general abundance, new free-for-all shops were opening everywhere. But here everything sold at fantastic prices—prices for which "speculators" on the free market had heretofore been prosecuted. This new policy was nothing but shameless robbery of the people in the name of industrialization. The ruble, little by little, had fallen until its purchasing power was ten, twenty, thirty, or forty times lower than that of 1926, according to the articles purchased. Wages had not even doubled during this period. In a statement made at a Party conference in Moscow, Khrustchev, secretary of the Moscow Committee, speaking of wages—a subject which most people in authority preferred to avoid—said that they had risen to two hundred rubles a month for skilled workers and one hundred for unskilled. The ordinary working-class family had to spend 90 per cent of their pay on food. And what miserable food it was, compared with that available in Western countries where I had lived! The standard of living of the Russian workman in 1933 can be estimated by comparing his wages with the prices of foodstuffs in these "free" state shops, which were the only ones that remained.

Meat cost nine to ten rubles a kilo, white bread two rubles, black bread one ruble, sugar ten rubles, rice nine, butter twenty-two to twenty-six, eggs ten to twelve rubles for ten, a pair of shoes 100 to 150 rubles. Thus the worker, receiving, as Khrustchev stated, 100 to 200 rubles a month, had to go almost entirely without butter and eggs (to say nothing of fruit), and could only rarely indulge in meat. Black bread, potatoes, cabbage, and buckwheat were the main items of his diet.

This state of affairs was carefully concealed by the Soviet press, and no one living abroad knew of it. My outraged feelings were not quieted by the constant promises of increased wages in the next Five-Year Plan that kept appearing in the official press. The results of the first plan had made me doubtful of the validity of such promises for the second. But I did experience a revival of hope when, in 1935, Premier Molotov, in the course of an important interview with the editor of *Le Temps*, solemnly declared that, after two more years, all prices would be reduced 50 per cent. This promise was never made good; no part of it was realized; the words were nothing but a lie. The misery of the proletariat—officially the "ruler" of the country—remained unrelieved. Any regard for the conditions of the people was entirely subordinate to the aim of maintaining the dictatorship.

Gradually I began to realize this fact, but only at the cost of bitter inward conflict. At each step toward clearer vision I had to wrestle with the sentiments which had bound me to the Party, its authority, and its proclaimed ideals. I had been brought up in the bosom of the Party; not one single hour of my adult life had been lived outside the Party; my every idea, judgment, and wish had existed in relation to the Party, which in my eyes represented a collective thought, knowledge, and will infinitely superior to my own. But I felt now that, if I could not think my own thoughts and draw my own conclusions, I should go and drown myself. Must I then judge the Party—condemn, perhaps, the Party's policy? I now had to put this question squarely to myself. From this moment my private judgment began to take shape, but several years were yet necessary—years of experience and observation—before it would reach a general conclusion. My case is not unique. For thousands and thousands of Russian Bolsheviks this period, ending with the bloody years 1937-38, was crucial.

With my appointment to Stanko-Import I entered a group of high officials of the Foreign Trade Commissariat at Moscow. For the next three years of my work, under the immediate direction of Arcady Rosengolz, I could observe the internal functioning of the Soviet governmental machine from close at hand, and the changes that had taken place during the years of the plan. Rosengolz, the People's Commissar for Foreign Trade, had changed greatly since the days of "the battle for gold." He had always shown a liking for authority and iron administration. To me he had seemed the perfect bureaucrat, full of energy in his allotted field but fearful of criticism—two traits which usually go hand in hand. I will give some details about a few jobs which I carried out under his direction, since they will illustrate the change I refer to and also illuminate the general setup.

Soon after my return from Poland, we were instructed by the Politburo to countermand our German orders for machine tools and to revise our budget so that preference should be given to Great Britain and the United States. I had been invited by the British Government to attend the great Empire Exhibition of Machinery, but so much had to be done at home that I found it impossible to go or to send anybody. The authorities, besides, were becoming chary of letting specialists out of Russia because, ever since the "Engineers' Trials" and subsequent acts of repression, those sent had shown a tendency to settle down abroad.

The fashion now was to say: "Let the directors of foreign firms come to Moscow if they want our orders!" In this way I made the acquaintance of a Mr. Brown, the manager of a large English machinery concern. I showed him over our new ball-bearing factory, Sharikopodchipnik, which had been built under the supervision of my friend Bodrov, once a commissar in Budyenny's cavalry, later counselor of our embassy in Bokhara, and finally an able director of industry. It was he who, when Switzerland refused to sell to us, organized the first Soviet watch factory with machinery bought during a trip to America.

The manufacture of ball bearings involves much detailed calculation and extreme precision of workmanship. The machinery used for the purpose is very costly and has to be maintained with scrupulous care. When I went through the shops with Mr. Brown, a number of machines were standing idle, since no one had yet learned how to use them. Moreover, my guest noticed that the floors of the rooms where the work of highest precision was being carried out were made of cement. "Cement dust," he said, "will soon deteriorate delicate machinery." Nobody had ever thought of that! Mr. Brown suggested that the floors be covered with a certain oil by-product, and I wrote a report to the Industry Commissariat, mentioning his suggestion.

Two years later I went over the factory again. I found an epic struggle now being carried on against bad work. A higher and higher percentage of the product was being rejected as below standard. Alleged sabotage was being hunted down; there was a never-ending series of investigations; and "shock tactics" had been introduced, with the usual slogan: "Get on with the plan." But I noticed that the floors were still made of cement! There had been no time to halt the machines and make the necessary alterations. The Party chiefs insisted that the plan of production of this much-publicized factory should be "exceeded at any costs."

Bodrov, goaded on by the Politburo, had brought his monthly production of ball bearings up to two million, but only by keeping his machines running without the necessary stoppages for overhauling.

The result was that his equipment was wearing out and constantly stopping, and the nerves of his men were worn to shreds. Ordjonikidze, the People's Commissar for Heavy Industry, was demanding an output of three million. Bodrov insisted that his machines should be overhauled, and was dismissed as a saboteur. He, like others, disappeared. An engineer named Melamed was taken on in his place to carry out the Politburo's maximum program, and he guaranteed the extra million. For three months he achieved that rate, and was lavishly rewarded. When the percentage of discarded products rose disastrously and whole departments had to stop work, he was denounced as an "enemy of the people" because he had allowed his equipment to deteriorate. A certain Yussim, a young engineer known for his *Stakhanovist* enthusiasm, replaced Melamed. I do not know what happened to him.

It is usual for our newspapers to publish "records" of industrial production while keeping a discreet silence about the cost involved. Ordinarily, machinery, instead of being repaired, is used until it is ruined, and then replaced. Thus the real cost of production of Soviet goods is higher than in any capitalist country, despite the fact that the workers are paid extremely low wages. This super-exploitation should make it possible to cover most of the losses and produce cheaply, but the incompetent bureaucratic system, wasting labor and materials, destroys this possibility. I personally observed this same thing in several other branches of industry.

The chief trouble seemed to be that, without competition and without free trade unions, there is no stimulus to the management to use their brains. They can afford to be wasteful and incompetent because they are not under pressure from competitors to produce better and cheaper goods, and not under pressure from the workers to pay higher wages. Their problem is much simpler. When the abolished capitalist profit is not enough to compensate for their wasteful inefficiency, they cover it by cutting down on the workers' wages. That is why, in spite of the fact that workers work as hard and harder than in capitalist countries, the Soviet industries are unable to give them the same decent standard of living. It was a basic principle with Lenin that the socialist economy would justify its existence only if it produced more and better goods at less cost than capitalism, and thus guaranteed the workers better conditions of life. This principle of Lenin's was constantly in my mind during the following years, and out of it grew irrepressible doubts as to whether we were on the right road.

After a year at Stanko-Import, I became familiar at first hand with the workings of the enormous and highly centralized bureaucracy which managed the Soviet state. Naturally, I expected the Politburo to concern itself with the broader aspects of our work at Stanko-Import, which involved tens of millions of rubles in a vital branch of import. But I was astonished at the minuteness of this concern and the interminable red tape which reached directly to Stalin himself.

As a result of overcentralization so much time was spent on relative trivialities that not enough was left for the consideration of really major problems. I saw the Politburo waste hours discussing a small contract made by Stanko-Import.

The contract was with a German house, Stock and Company, to supply us with tools and machine parts. We had had complaints about the quality of the tools, and in addition the accounts were somewhat mixed. The director of a factory we were supplying with these imported tools wrote a letter of complaint to Stalin. Apparently they had met before, and Stalin remembered him. The Politburo ordered a hearing. Rosengolz and his assistants, the industry's commissar and his assistants, the president of Stanko-Import and I, the director and chief engineer of the complaining factory were all ordered to appear. On this little matter involving a couple of hundred thousand rubles, all of us high officials, abandoning other pressing business, had to prepare a brief, explaining the transaction and defending ourselves. It used up three days and three nights of my time.

We arrived at the Kremlin at three o'clock on the day of the hearing. We went into the large hall reserved for those waiting to appear before the Politburo. In this room were gathered many high officials, members of the Soviet and Party administration, and heads of commissariats, companies, and factories. All of them sat around for hours until their "cases" were called, while their departments marked time. This went on whenever the Politburo sat. In this room the current governmental gossip was retailed while the waiting officials munched ham and cheese sandwiches, drank tea, and smoked innumerable *papirossi.*

At seven o'clock our case was called. We filed into the hall of the Politburo. Around the table were Voroshilov, Molotov, and other members of the highest body of the Communist Party. Stalin, his pipe in the corner of his mouth, his hands clasped behind his back, was pacing up and down by the window. He rarely presided at Politburo meetings, preferring to leave that job to Kalinin, Kaganovich, or Molotov. When we entered, Stalin smiled and nodded at the complaining factory director. This sign of favor was immediately reflected in the general attitude. The rest of us already felt guilty.

The director spoke for a long time, accusing our company of every crime on the Soviet calendar, from signing "sucker" contracts with the capitalists to outright sabotage. Now and then Stalin, without waiting to be recognized by Kalinin, who was presiding, interjected a comment or an attempted witticism.

"So Stanko-Import was taken in by the Germans!" he said.

The entire hall roared with laughter at the surpassing humor of the Boss. I looked over at poor Rosengolz. Even he attempted a weak smile.

A couple of hours passed while accusers and accused wrangled and perspired to the accompaniment of inept questions from the members of the Politburo. The issue was technical, relating to the specifications of machine tools. It was clear that neither Stalin nor the other members of the Politburo were following the discussion. Occasionally they asked a question. But in order to understand the problem it would have been necessary, even for a competent specialist, to sit down with the documents, contracts, and catalogues and study them for days.

Finally Stalin, who had taken a seat near Molotov, rose.

"All right," he said. "That's enough. It's easy to see that Stanko-Import made a very poor contract. I propose that Rosengolz be warned, that Stanko-Import send a director to Germany to straighten matters out, that the president of Stanko-Import, Halperstein, be severely reprimanded. . . ."

Kalinin, scarcely bothering to look up, said: "You have heard the proposal. If there are no objections, it is so ordered."

There were no objections, and we were dismissed, to give place to the next victims.

A thin appearance of collective work is still kept up at Politburo meetings. Stalin does not "command," he merely "suggests" or "proposes." The fiction of voting is retained. But the vote never fails to uphold his "suggestions." The decision is signed by all ten members of the Politburo, with Stalin's signature among the rest. Yet everyone knows that there is only one boss. The phrases used, the forms of address, follow traditional Party terminology; but behind them all Comrade Stalin's word is law.

As I heard the other members of the Politburo mumble their approval of Stalin's "proposal," I asked myself: "What would happen if someone got up and said: 'I disagree with Comrade Stalin'?" But the idea was fantastic. Stalin has devised techniques for ferreting out in advance any possible opposition. Any potential strong man is weeded out before he can try out his power—as was done in the case of Sergei Kirov. Stalin not only is generally called "the Boss" by the whole bureaucracy, but *is* the one and only boss.

For this reason among others, the Soviet bureaucracy is a cumbersome and frequently unworkable machine. Initiative on the part of subordinate bureaucrats is stifled. Everyone seeks to avoid responsibility. Everyone looks to the top for a covering order. And since thousands of relatively unimportant, as well as all-important, problems must pass through Stalin's hands for final decision, the top is always jammed. Weeks are spent in waiting: commissars wait in Stalin's office; presidents of companies wait in the offices of the commissars; and so on down the line. I often spent hours waiting for Rosengolz to get a decision from Stalin, while subordinates waited for me to get one from Rosengolz. When Stalin got bored or tired he would go off to one of his villas, giving orders that he was not to be disturbed; the top machinery would practically cease to function, and the whole thing be in a bottleneck.

Why did Stalin insist on this direct control over every single phase of Soviet life, which imposed such a vast burden on him? The answer is that only in this way could a man like him continue as dictator. A genial and brilliant, and less suspicious man, having the confidence of large numbers of self-reliant and intelligent lieutenants, could manage to hold power without personally supervising every petty decision.

This system has demoralized people, and especially the leading executives and the creative intelligentsia, beyond recognition. Men for whom I had had great respect were now sadly changed. Take Shumiatsky, for example, with whom I had worked in Persia. On his return from Teheran he had been put in charge of the Moscow School for Chinese Officers, where cadets were trained for the armies of revolutionary China. After a short time there he was transferred to the Institute of Eastern Workers, and finally ended up as director of motion-picture production. This, surely, would be a fine field for his bubbling energy, his good taste, his background of wide culture. But no; for ever since the first great films of Eisenstein, Pudovkin, and Dovzhenko, the Soviet cinema, though it had magnificent sites available and a whole continent to play with, the folklore of a hundred different peoples to draw on, and a recent historic past crammed full of incident, had been steadily deteriorating. We were producing nothing of importance. I often wondered why. Mutual friends gave me some details of Shumiatsky's work, and I wondered no longer. Any flicker of inventiveness was snuffed out by a pedantic censorship, and the categorical instructions of the central authority invaded even the fields of thought and imagination. Shumiatsky, the man in charge, had no time to see the directors—no matter how famous—who knocked at his door. He could spare his departmental managers but a few hurried minutes once a week. And yet no one dared do anything without his definite permission and approval, because it was known that he was in Stalin's confidence, and that Stalin took an interest in the cinema.

How then did Shumiatsky, the great organizer, the cutter of Gordian knots, the old revolutionary, spend his precious hours? In trying to enlist the favors of the high bureaucrats for his productions? Not even that! Most of his time was spent running round to various villas inhabited by the powerful men of Russian politics—Kaganovich, Voroshilov, Mikoyan, and other friends of the Boss—giving exhibitions, in their private projection halls, of foreign films which the public would never see, which even the movie trade would never see, but which had been imported for gold in order to amuse these aristocrats of the Soviets.

Before any Russian film could be shown generally it had first to be projected privately for Stalin and then for his favorites. Shumiatsky had to listen to advice which was often a thinly disguised command, to make unexpected alterations, to suppress whole films without explaining why, and to sack artists or managers just because the Boss had frowned.

Awards, in Shumiatsky's world, were distributed as arbitrarily as condemnations and penalties. Orlova, a young actress of no particular merit, for no other reason than that she had appealed to the Boss in *Circus* and *The Jolly Boys,* was created "artist emeritus of the Republic," an honor which had been instituted for outstanding performers of twenty and thirty years' service. Imagine the feelings of Stanislavsky, who had to make an epoch in the history of the theater before he received this honor!

Shumiatsky, the director of a great industry, unable to cope with his work, and doing little more than paralyze the best efforts of his subordinates, had become a mere servile factotum of the ruling bureaucracy. He built himself a princely palace just outside Moscow—but he did not enjoy it for long. Except that he was an Old Bolshevik, I do not know what Stalin found against him, for he had never shown the slightest sympathy for the Opposition. But he was denounced for inefficiency and disappeared in 1937. And on the principle that no high Soviet official is ever allowed to retire into private life, I assume that he is now somewhere in a concentration camp, if he has not been shot.

The most trivial incidents showed in what direction things were tending. I remember passing an evening with several well-known Soviet intellectuals, whom I shall not name since I have no wish to get them into trouble. One of them, X, a famous architect, began suddenly to talk of the project to build a vast Palace of the Soviets just below the Kremlin, facing the Moskva River. Already blasters were at work dynamiting the Cathedral of Christ the Saviour in order to clear the site. The competition for the winning design had ended when Stalin chose an immense, heavy, circular building surrounded by a colonade, to which the architectural genius of our leader had added, as a crowning achievement, a colossal statue of Lenin in stainless steel.

"The whole thing," said X, "will look exactly like one of those rich chocolate *Bandkuchen* so dear to the heart of the Berlin confectioner, into which they sometimes stick a candle, a doll, or a little tuft of flowers. From the technical point of view, it is a step back toward the worst kind of decorative building popular at the end of the last century. Most of the rooms will have to depend on artificial lighting; there won't be enough exits; the enormous size of the rooms will present extravagant structural problems. But that's not the worst—the site chosen could only just carry the cathedral; the ground is soggy and frequently subsides; part of the foundations will be in a marsh; it will cost dozens of millions to prepare the ground. And why put up a thing like that anyway just beside the Kremlin? No one with any taste would have dreamed of doing it."

A few days later I was amazed to read in the papers that architect X had expressed himself most enthusiastically about the scheme of the new palace! He had been asked to make a statement, and he knew what he had to say.

That's how things are, then, I thought, and I added a few remarks of my own on the whole project. Why spend millions on building a palace while the entire population of Moscow is suffocating from overcrowding? How explain the fact that not a single working-class member of the Moscow Soviet has got to his feet and said: "Wouldn't it be better, comrades, to use these millions to build houses for the workers?"

But the Soviet has ceased to exist except in name, and any deputy taking himself and his duties in this serious way would have been regarded as a fool, or, worse still, a counterrevolutionary. Didn't Stalin know better than anyone else what ought to be done?

Many people realized the indignity of this, but what could they do? They could only laugh bitterly. A saying current among the Party intelligentsia expressed their mood: "Best of all, don't think; if you can't help thinking, don't speak; if you speak, don't write; if you write, don't publish; if you publish, confess and recant immediately."

In my dealings with my staff I noticed similar changes. Trade-unionism had practically ceased to exist. Formerly the union local had been a power to be reckoned with whenever it came to inflicting punishment, dismissing employees, or in any way altering wages or other conditions of labor. Now neither the factory directors nor we—executives in Soviet institutions—needed to bother our heads about anyone representing the workers. The local existed, but its activities were confined to carrying out the biddings of the Party cell. Apart from this, all it did was to see that the "voluntary" loans to the government—they were, in fact, forced—were duly paid. There had ceased to be any protection whatever for the clerk in the office or the worker in the factory.

The whole atmosphere was so depressing that I began to dream of finding a retreat in some job where I should not have to shoulder any responsibility—as a librarian, perhaps, or a box-office clerk in a theater! I longed for more time for thought; for some occupation which, by establishing me on a different rung of the social ladder, would help me to look at things critically, to reflect, and to find out if my doubts were correct. At the end of 1933 I resigned from the Stanko-Import and asked the General Staff of the Red Army to recall me from the Officers' Reserve to active duty.

29. Old Friends Meet

I HAD HOPED, on returning to the Army, to be sent to the Air Academy for a technical course. There I would be left alone for four years, away from the turmoil of politics and bureaucratism. It would be a kind of haven.

But I was to be disappointed.

The Soviet had begun sending arms on a small scale to a number of Eastern countries, carrying on the operations through various departments. Now Stalin gave orders to concentrate all arms-export business under one head, where it could be directly supervised by the Politburo. The Commissariat of Foreign Trade had a small trust organized for the export of automobiles. Partly as camouflage, it was decided to expand this trust and incorporate the arms-export trade into it.

Just at the moment of my resignation from Stanko-Import the problem came up of selecting a president for the new trust. The General Staff wanted a military man there, and so, instead of recalling me and sending me to the aviation school, it submitted my name to the Politburo for this position. Stalin approved the nomination.

I was summoned to Rosengolz's office, and he imparted the news to me.

"You are an Army man," he said, "experienced in foreign trade and diplomacy. You are an Orientalist. Furthermore, you are interested in cars." Here he winked at me—for my unfortunate auto odyssey from Leningrad to Moscow was a standing joke. "This is just the job for you. You will have a big task in your hands—the conquest of the whole Eastern market."

Party discipline was strict; there was nothing for me to do but forget my dream of quiet study. I became the first president of the new Auto-Moto-Export Trust, one department of which was to deal in cars and the other in armaments—the latter destined to be a prominent item in Soviet politics. The export of motorcars was quite open. But the more important and more difficult part of my work was arranging armament transactions, which had to be kept carefully from the public view.

Up to this period the Soviet Union had been importing both arms and automobiles. Even now we had no idea of competing in Europe with Western producers; but Sinkiang, Afghanistan, Mongolia, Turkey, and Persia offered markets to which our system of communication gave us easy access. I won't go into the strenuous job it was to establish the machinery of so important a trust, nor of the fight I had with rival governmental enterprises to get suitable premises and an adequate staff.

I had the greatest difficulty in getting hold of arms and cars for export. The Politburo had to pass upon all export and import plans. Not a single bushel of wheat or pound of butter, not a bale of cotton, a ton of ore, not one yard of cloth, one car, one machine, beyond the schedule laid down by the export-import plan, could be sent out of or into Russia except under a special ruling of the Politburo signed by Stalin himself. All essential details were discussed by the Politburo. All export lists, sales prices, and terms of payment were submitted to Stalin. His word was final, no matter what decision had been reached previously by the Commissariat of Foreign Trade, the Planning Commission, which drew up the schedules, or the commissariats which directed industrial output. Each individual scheme was revised by these bodies annually and quarterly, with indications of the countries the exports were destined for, and all this regularly submitted to the Politburo.

Not only exports and imports had to go through this process, but also all phases of internal distribution. Trusts and administrative bodies formulated their requirements, after which the Commissariat of Industry drew up a rationing order and submitted it to the Politburo.

After being passed by Stalin as boss of the Politburo of the Party, all these decisions had to be sent on to the Sovnarcom[1] to receive the formal sanction of the government. The Sovnarcom never assumed the responsibility of altering by one jot the decisions of the Politburo. It acted merely as a recording and forwarding office. Premier Molotov served merely as a rubber stamp for Stalin's decisions. When I would receive a sheet containing the decision of the Politburo regarding, say, a shipment of one hundred automobiles to Sinkiang, signed by the general secretary, Joseph Stalin, I would act upon it. When the same decision, word for word, would come along four or five days later, typed on Sovnarcom stationery and signed by Molotov, and thus made official, the cars would be already on their way. This absurd situation continued until the spring of 1941, when Stalin, sensing the war danger, and seeing the greater simplicity of Hitler's position as Reichschancellor as well as Party Führer, decided to dispense with these cumbersome fictions and make himself Premier.

At Stanko-Import I had waded deep in the tangled red tape of Soviet bureaucratization. But as head of the Auto-Moto-Export Trust I was completely submerged in it. I could not make a move without endless conferences with each of the several commissariats concerned in our work. The Foreign Office had to be consulted to make sure we were not conflicting with general foreign policy toward the country involved. Detailed production schedules had to be worked out with the

[1] Abbreviation of the Russian words for Soviet of People's Commissars, the cabinet of ministers in the Soviet Government.

Commissariat of Industry. The question of releasing our latest military models and inventions had to be taken up with the Army; the problem of sales prices and financing, with the Commissariat of Foreign Trade; transportation problems, protection of shipping, etc., with other departments. Woe to me if I did not foresee months in advance how many railroad cars I would need, and in what direction they would be traveling! All this had to be included in the quarterly plan of the Commissariat of Roads and Communications.

I spent frantic weeks scurrying about from one department to another, reconciling their conflicting projects. And not I alone, but all my executives spent most of their days in this nerve-exhausting labor of dashing from one authority to another or sitting in interminable conferences. If we did any collected work on our own proper job, we did it at night.

Finally, before being submitted to the Politburo, all my armament arrangements had to be approved by the Arms Export Commission of the Supreme Defense Council, presided over by War Commissar Voroshilov, with Tukhachevsky and Gamarnik as vice-presidents. I had to keep in close and constant touch with our Army leaders. I hoped that my old chief and friend Tukhachevsky would be able to help me in my new responsibilities—at least as far as the General Staff was concerned. He did what he could, but he could not do much. The Army also had become enmeshed in the ubiquitous red tape.

My first remeeting with Tukhachevsky is vivid in my memory. The marshal came forward to greet me with that spontaneous courtesy which he always showed to his juniors. He had grown heavier; his hair was graying at the temples. His expression, however, was still young and virile. He had the same air of calm assurance and the same attentive manner of listening and speaking.

During our interview the telephone rang. The marshal took up the receiver calmly and then suddenly jumped to his feet, replying in an entirely different, a definitely respectful voice:

"Good morning, Klementi Efremovich. . . . Exactly as you wish, Klementi Efremovich. . . . That shall be done, Klementi Efremovich. . . ." This was the way he took orders from Voroshilov.

The incident made a sad impression on me. Seeing a great soldier take orders in just that fashion helped me to understand why it was that all my questions took days to get an answer. Even Tukhachevsky no longer dared to make decisions; he merely carried out commands. He, too, had to ask and ask; his every action had to conform to instructions, from Voroshilov on the one hand and the Politburo on the other. In my further dealings with him, other details drove me to the conclusion that his will had had to bend; and that, in the vast bureaucratic machine, he, like others, had become one more revolving cog. He had been a leader; now he was reduced to a functionary.

On another occasion a long memorandum which I had forwarded

to Tukhachevsky, dealing with purely technical questions about tanks to be delivered to the Turkish Government, was returned to me with marginal remarks, comments, corrections, and instructions inserted opposite each paragraph in Voroshilov's own hand! I had thought that Tukhachevsky would turn it over to his subordinates to answer. To such an extent had all power become centralized. To such an extent had all initiative, even in the highest circles, been crushed. In most cases Voroshilov himself dared not make a decision without consulting Stalin.

At one time a problem arose about some airplanes which I had delivered to the Persian Government. It was my duty to submit the problem to Tukhachevsky and Gamarnik, since Voroshilov was on vacation. The thing was of no great importance, for the Politburo had already rendered a decision about the planes. Now the problem was merely about delivering certain accessories, the release of which required the approval of the War Commissariat. My discussions with the two Army chiefs lasted for three weeks, the much-needed deliveries being meanwhile held up. The trouble was that Voroshilov, without whom no one would act, had not come back from the Black Sea coast. At my request Gamarnik at last decided to ring him up, but in the Caucasus a secretary replied: "Wait until the War Commissar gets back!"

At this time I often met two other old friends I had made at the General Staff School—Generals Alksnis and Hekker. Their fate comes to my mind. Alksnis, after getting his pilot's certificate and carrying out a number of daring and record-breaking flights, became the Commander in Chief of our Air Force, which he practically put on its feet. He was a strict disciplinarian and had high standards of efficiency. He would himself frequently inspect his flying officers, and woe to any of them who turned up unshaven or carelessly dressed! Not that he was fussy or took the slightest interest in smartness for its own sake, but, as he explained to me, flying demands constant attention to details. It demands rigid discipline. Headstrong he may have been, but he was a man of method and brought a wholly new spirit into Soviet aviation. It is chiefly owing to him that the Air Force is the powerful weapon it is today. Not only was Alksnis, the Commander in Chief, shot, but his principal collaborators also met their tragic end in the purge.

From this blow the recovery of the Air Force was difficult and took a long time.

General Hekker was acting at this time as Voroshilov's chief of protocol, in charge of all dealings with foreign military attachés, a job that demands great finesse. The soldier in him was pushed into the background to make room for the diplomat. I invited him several times to receptions I held for Turkish and Lithuanian military delegations arriving for the purchase of arms. He gave me tips about this and that individual, initiated me into the secrets of this rather subtle branch of psychology, and made sure that I lived up to the formal refinements. When I raised my glass to propose a toast, I would see his piercing eyes watching me from the far end of the table with a vague anxiety. I felt then that I was still for him the "Benjamin" of the War College. Although twelve years older now, I was indeed still the "Benjamin" among the thirty-odd presidents of trusts in our foreign-trade system, for I was only thirty-four. But I did not disgrace him.

When, in 1935, I was leaving for Greece, I went to pay Hekker a farewell call. He had just been made corps commander and was wearing for the first time the new, heavily braided uniform of his rank, corresponding with that of a three-star general in the American Army. This reward for so many years of blameless service delighted him. He was surrounded by friendly colleagues who joked with him on his promotion. He begged me to send him from Athens two yards of better-quality gold braid, which I solemnly promised and did. It was nontarnishable goods; and he received it a short time before his arrest and disappearance. . . .

I want to include in this chapter of my memoirs a mention of the last Congress of the Soviets that I attended, and the last review of the Red Army that I saw.

At the Congress of the Soviets, held in the great palace of the Kremlin, when Tukhachevsky appeared on the platform, the whole room rose to its feet and greeted him with a storm of applause. The ovation was marked out from all others by its force and sincerity. Tukhachevsky's speech was also distinguished from others by the fact that he never glanced at a note. That had been the oratorical style of all the Old Bolsheviks in the heroic days, but since the heresy hunts that followed the expulsion of Trotsky, the dread of a slip was so great that practically all speeches were read from a manuscript.

Tukhachevsky was a good orator, and his speech stirred the audience to its depths. The percentages of increase in armament and recruiting which he quoted showed the enormous might of the Red Army. He was listened to in silence as though his words had woven a spell around his listeners. I saw Stalin applaud Tukhachevsky ostentatiously.

The review was the last of a long series of such majestic spectacles I had attended, first as a marcher with the other students of the War College, later as a spectator. Tukhachevsky, as acting war commissar in the absence of Voroshilov, reviewed the troops. On this occasion an incident occurred which subsequently acquired an ironic significance. Admission cards to the stands were extremely difficult to obtain, and I was particularly anxious that a Turkish military mission which had just arrived as my guests should have an opportunity to appreciate the military might of the Soviet Union.

After some unsuccessful attempts to secure cards, I was advised, as a last resort, to apply to Pauker and Volovich, two high officials of the G.P.U. whose special duty it was to see to the personal safety of Stalin.

Wherever Stalin was to be present, I was told, these two men had complete discretion as to admissions. I went up to see them and secured the cards immediately. It was obvious, if I had thought of it then, that Pauker and Volovich carried Stalin's life in their hands. Either one of them could have organized his assassination with ease. Notwithstanding this fact, in the purge of 1938 both Pauker and Volovich were denounced as terrorists who had plotted to kill Stalin. The real reason was that as G.P.U. executives they had conducted the "investigations" of leading victims of the purge trials. It is not generally known that, together with the chief, Yagoda, everyone in the directing staff of every department of the G.P.U. was shot in 1938. In order that no one should be left to tell how the famous "confessions" were obtained, all the purgers were purged. Dead men tell no tales.

On the stroke of ten the sound of a trotting horse broke the tense silence on Red Square, where the troops were drawn up. Tukhachevsky, mounted, came through the Gate of the Saviour and beneath the high Byzantine tower. Kork, commander of the Moscow garrison, his friend and companion-in-arms, rode to meet him, saluted, and in a few words rendered his report on the garrison. The stands were full to overflowing. Stalin was standing on Lenin's mausoleum, with his hand upon the granite balustrade. Tukhachevsky and Kork, surrounded by their staffs, took their stations beneath him, and the troops began to file past these two doomed generals—infantry, rifles with fixed bayonets; cavalry; trucks mounted with antiaircraft guns; tanks, small, large, and amphibian. Planes under the command of Alksnis covered the sky. It was a day of supreme glory. Who but a lunatic could have imagined that the man watching it all from just above Lenin's mortal remains would soon be massacring and branding as traitors the men who had created such strength and now commanded it?

In Western countries the general public and many statesmen actually believed the tall stories of plots against the Soviet regime between the Red High Command and the Nazis. Stalin possesses enormous powers of propaganda throughout the world. Intelligent readers, however, when these fabulous charges appeared in the columns of foreign papers, merely asked the question: What facts are they being used to conceal? Two years later the Stalin-Hitler pact made obvious the answer. That pact was plainly the result of long secret negotiations between Stalin and the Nazis. Stalin himself was guilty of the acts of which he accused and for which he executed his own generals.

The idea that Tukhachevsky's group had political sympathies, if not direct contacts, with Germany; and that, while trying to impose its views on the government, it had sent up a few trial balloons to ascertain what the German reaction would be, is as absurd as the formal charges. Only those who knew nothing of the part played by Stalin and Voroshilov in the control of the Army could believe it. Questions affecting the Army's political orientations, and indeed all practical questions, even those of minor importance, could be decided by Gamarnik, by Tukhachevsky, or even by Voroshilov only after detailed and precise instructions had been received from the Politburo—that is to say, from Stalin. This general procedure applied with still greater force to questions involving relations with foreign powers—even where confined to the limited field of technology. Every contract necessitating technical military assistance from abroad was discussed line by line at more than one session of the Politburo. All correspondence on such matters was rigidly supervised and controlled. To a person professionally occupied, as I was, with such matters, it is perfectly obvious that the other heads of the Army could not possibly have carried on conversations or exchanged letters with representatives of foreign powers without Stalin and Voroshilov being privy to every word.

The execution of these generals, the finest flower of our leadership, who would have formed the High Command and the General Staff in the then-expected war with the fascist powers, struck a terrible blow at the Red Army. This was proven later by the inept Finland campaign and the first disastrous year of the present war.

Let me insist with all the earnestness I command that these men, profoundly devoted as they were to their Soviet fatherland, and employed, as they had been for long years, in preparing the Red Army for a decisive trial of strength against fascism and nazism, not only could not have committed the crimes imputed to them had they wished, but were psychologically incapable of it.

The Stalin-Hitler pact, and Stalin's subsequent international policy, have exposed the imposture which dishonored the name of Marshal Tukhachevsky. Stalin knew that Tukhachevsky and the other Army leaders were implacably opposed to Nazi Germany and favored a united front of the democracies and the Soviet Union against Hitler. He had to get them out of the way before consummating his own pact with Hitler.

Vozrozhdeniye, the Russian monarchist organ in Paris, published the statement of a certain Alexeyeff, accusing Tukhachevsky of having intimate connections with the German General Staff at the very moment when the Soviet marshal, attending the funeral of King George V in England, was carrying on negotiations with the French and British military authorities. Later Alexeyeff was tried behind closed doors by a military court in France on the charge of being a German spy.

Stalin obtained this fabrication through agents working not only for the G.P.U. but at the same time for the Gestapo. The interest of the Gestapo was twofold: they were getting rid of the most brilliant generals in a powerful army which Hitler intended to strike at the favorable moment; they were helping Stalin to fool the democracies with his pretended anti-fascist zeal. Having acquired these forgeries, Stalin used them first to convince the Czechoslovak statesmen, and through them the French and the British, of Tukhachevsky's guilt. Only thus could he continue to play his double-crossing game up to the very moment of his pact with Hitler.

A clear light is thrown on the question of whose interest really demanded the execution of the Red generals and other leaders of Soviet life by a dispatch which appeared in the Nazi newspaper *Frankfurter Zeitung* on August 29, 1939—six days after the signing of the Stalin-Hitler pact. Here is the text, published under the caption: "As to the Pre-History of the Germano-Soviet Russian Pact—From our Moscow Correspondent."

Moscow, August 27.
. . . It took months to achieve the rapprochement between Germany and the Soviet Union. As for the Soviet Union, during recent years essential changes have taken place both in its structure and in its personnel. We must now regard them as unavoidable premises of the historic development. The removal from the social life of the Soviet Union of that upper layer who go by the name of Trotskyists, and were on that ground removed, was indubitably a very essential factor in the rapprochement between the Soviet Union and Germany. . . .

The disastrous beginning of the German-Russian war, due almost entirely to the Red Army's lack of capable leadership, shows how Hitler used, in the interests of Nazi Germany, the criminal stupidity and blind vindictiveness of Stalin. The Russian people paid for it with millions of dead, the devastation of their richest territories, and the torture of two years of retreat and Nazi occupation. New commanders trained in the school of disaster had to grow up from the young officer ranks in these bloody years before Hitler could be thrown back. This is the truth concealed and belied by the fable of Joseph E. Davies that, in executing the leaders of the Red Army, a farsighted Stalin was removing "fifth columnists" in preparation for the war with Hitler.

30. *Trials of an Arms Exporter*

ONE OF MY TRUST'S big armament deals was with Turkey. It accounted for most of the credit of 8,000,000 gold dollars put at the disposal of the Turkish Government by the Soviets. The purpose of this twenty-year, noninterest-bearing loan was to weld Turkey and Russia more closely together, politically and militarily. After prolonged negotiations I signed the contract with the Turkish ambassador, Vassyf-Bey. Tanks, armored cars, artillery were packed in huge cases, disguised as consignments of trucks, and loaded aboard Turkish transports. The Politburo had given orders to send the best-quality equipment, and we surpassed ourselves in carrying out the instructions. The factories involved gave special attention to quality, so that our exports should compare favorably with those of the Western powers.

Curiously, while Stalin and Voroshilov concerned themselves with the details of this transaction with Turkey, discussing it several times at Politburo meetings, the most important question—what quantities of tanks or armored cars were to be sent—was practically overlooked. This because the antecedent problem was overlooked—on what principle the prices were to be established. The total amount of credit being limited, the one question depended on the other. I went to Rosengolz.

"How much in our project to the Politburo are we to charge the Turks per tank, armored car, cannon, and gas mask?" I asked him. "Here are our production costs, and the official Red Army prices, but as you know, the prices paid by our own Army are artificially low. It will depend on the price how many machines the Turks will get."

Rosengolz thought for a moment. This was a heavy responsibility which he wasn't eager to take. He fidgeted, hands in pockets, looking away.

"You know what to do," he said. "You have the prices of our competitors, Krupp and Vickers. Figure it out for yourself."

"Yes, Arcady Pavlovich," I said, "but on what general principle shall I make my calculations?"

He waved me aside. "Use your own judgment," he said.

It was the Turks who helped me to a decision. The Turkish war minister sent a commission of military experts headed by an old general whom the others addressed as "Pasha," although Kemal Ataturk had abolished that title. These experts surprised me by inquiring whether the machine guns we were installing for them on tanks and armored cars, and also the reserve cartridges, could not be of *German* caliber.

What was the meaning of this? German caliber machine guns would make them dependent on Germany for the regular supply of ammunition. "Whom do they intend to fight, then?" I asked myself. More vaguely I suggested to Rosengolz that possibly the equipment we were sending Turkey might one day be used against us. I told him that officers I had sent to Turkey with samples of the tanks had reported a noticeable influence of Germans in the Turkish General Staff. He made no answer. I remarked that, when the Turks had cash to spend on armaments, they preferred to deal with the Germans, Swedes, or French rather than with us. He pretended not to hear.

Thus left to my own resources, I decided to make the Turks pay high. I increased the prices a good way above my original intention, and consequently reduced the quantities to be sent. My proposed schedule of prices and quantities was approved by the Politburo. I sent the schedule to Vassyf-Bey, and within two days Ankara had cabled its approval. It apparently made no difference to the Turks. They had twenty years in which to pay, and who knew what would happen in twenty years?

Among the things I sold on credit to the Turks were several hundred trucks for the Army and a hundred busses for the municipality of Ankara. This last figure was amusing. The capital of a backward country like Turkey was providing one hundred busses for its 150,000 inhabitants; whereas Moscow, with 3,500,000 people, had fewer than four hundred busses, a third of which were always under repair. Obviously the Turks were regarding my exports as a gift.

The tanks we were delivering to the Turkish Government were to be made in the Leningrad Tank Factory. I learned that the factory was overhauling its machinery and had temporarily stopped production, but still had some tanks ready for the Army. I went to see Marshal Tukhachevsky to talk over the possibility of having some advanced to me for delivery to the Turks.

"I would give them to you gladly," he said, "but I don't think you should deliver them. Here, read this report."

I read a report from the commander of the Far East Army. It was an analysis of the recent fighting between Russian and Japanese troops on the Mongolian border. There had been several frontier incidents, sufficiently violent to involve tanks, artillery, and aviation. By both sides these clashes were regarded as a testing ground for new types of armament and munitions. The report stated that the worst experience of the Red Army was with riveted tanks. Not only were these tanks extremely vulnerable to antitank artillery, but the impact of exploding shells would drive the rivets into the tank with such force that they became as fatal to the crew as bullets. The report recommended that in further production riveted tanks be replaced with welded ones.

"That's why we've stopped the production of this type of tank," said Tukhachevsky. "I suggest that you tell the Turks to be patient."

Although we were not giving the Turks all the tanks they wanted, our policy was, as I said, to give them the best quality. So the Turks had to wait, but they received welded tanks.

I tell this story because seven years later I read with astonishment in an American newspaper that the American tank factories, among them that of Chrysler, had to stop production at the time of the most critical battles in North Africa, for a change of blueprints and retooling, at a cost of several million dollars and months of precious time. The riveted tanks they had been producing, the dispatch said, were vulnerable to artillery and dangerous to the crews. By the impact of exploding shells, the rivets were transformed into deadly bullets, etc., etc. Briefly, what I read was almost word for word the same story I had read seven years earlier in the study of Marshal Tukhachevsky in Moscow. It seemed to me incredible that the Russian experience with tanks had remained a secret throughout the first years of America's desperate effort at rearmament.

The news was especially sad to me because there had been a chance that I might learn about this state of affairs and tell my new countrymen of the Russian experience. The chance was lost through circumstances beyond my control. Upon my arrival in the United States I had been recommended by a distinguished American whom I knew in Paris, Walter Lippmann, to Byron Foy of the Chrysler Corporation for work with his concern. Our negotiations dragged along until I was compelled to take another job.

But to return to my Turks, after months of delay, all the tanks, armaments, trucks, and busses they ordered were assembled on the wharfs at Odessa. At the very moment when a Turkish ship, dispatched in haste from Istanbul, was preparing to take them on board, Rosengolz telephoned me to stop loading.

"But why, Arcady Pavlovich?"

"The License Control Board has just informed me that this shipment does not appear on the quarterly export plan approved by the Politburo."

"But it was approved in the annual plan, and there has been a special decision of the Politburo concerning all deliveries to Turkey! The Turkish ambassador has urged me to speed up the shipment. We may be penalized."

"Nevertheless, it's impossible! You know as well as I do what strict instructions there are on this point. Draw up a project of decision for the Politburo, showing an addition to the quarterly export plan, and bring it to me immediately. I will take it to the Boss at the first opportunity."

The Boss was busy with other things. The heavy bureaucratic machine was dragging. The Turkish ship returned half-empty. We lost almost two months, which cost money both to us and the Turks. But the quarterly plan was deemed more important than considerations of trade, good sense, or commercial reliability. Without a decision of the Politburo to include this item in the plan, Rosengolz could not let me execute the contract. Even if he had agreed, the customs authorities in Odessa would have forbidden me to load the ship.

Much precious time was lost in such formalities. I have already said that Rosengolz, trying to save a little of it, would often communicate to me the texts of urgent decisions of the Politburo before they came from Molotov's office copied on government stationery. With the same idea of skipping red tape, Rosengolz often went with important problems direct to the Politburo, over the head of the formal government.

"Draw up a Politburo project, Barmine," he would say to me. And this he would correct and take to the Boss on one of the days when he was holding audience. Stalin's magic signature was necessary for everything. It appeared not only on all decisions affecting our sales and financial operations, but even on our freight plans.

I stress this point of Stalin's minute control of our work, because, during the third Moscow trial, the broken Rosengolz was forced to confess himself a Trotskyist, a saboteur, and a fascist agent. He was made to admit that he had embezzled sums of money, appearing on his departmental budget for the purpose of financing Trotsky plots abroad, and that he had deliberately exported to Japan huge quantities of pig iron, knowing that the machine factories of the Soviet Union were standing idle because (or so it was said) they could not get deliveries of metal. The operations to which he alluded in his "confession," and about which the court was careful not to demand details, were, to us who knew the facts, quite obviously impossible without Stalin's approval. I leave my reader to guess what must have been my state of mind, and, generally speaking, that of all officials in industry, commerce, and finance, and of the Party, who, reading the account of the trial, knew offhand and at once that the "confessions" could not possibly be true.

As for myself, I was filled with a sense of revolt and disgust when I read Rosengolz's "confession" that he had intentionally increased the export of pig iron to Japan in order to sabotage Soviet industry and help the cause of fascism. I recalled the number of times I had been summoned to Rosengolz's office to read the latest decisions of the Politburo about exports to be made by my trust, and to append my signature, thus making myself, as was usual, personally responsible for the execution of the decisions. I often used to meet there my colleague Polishchuk, president of Techno-Export. This newborn trust, the outcome like my own of successes in the industrial field, exported rails, agricultural machinery, pig iron, etc., chiefly to the Orient. I recalled that on the directive bearing Stalin's signature after the paragraph instructing Auto-Moto-Export to send a new batch of arms and trucks to Sinkiang, I had read an item relating to Techno-Export which ran, almost word for word, as follows:

"The quarterly plan for the export of pig iron presented by Techno-Export has been found insufficient. It has been decided to increase the amounts shown by x thousands of tons, and to instruct the Department of Foreign Trade, on the personal responsibility of Comrade Rosengolz and the president of Techno-Export, Comrade Polishchuk, to place the supplementary quantities herein mentioned on the foreign market within thirty days. In arranging for this, note should be taken especially of the particularly favorable prices now prevailing in Japan, Turkey, and Persia. Comrades Ordjonikidze and Piatakov are hereby instructed to see that the necessary deliveries are made by the factories concerned, after consultation with Comrade Rosengolz, within the period named. The president of the Party Control Commission, Comrade Yezhov, shall superintend the execution of this decision and shall report results to the Politburo."

Poor Polishchuk, who appended his signature to this paragraph, can hardly have foreseen that his chief, Rosengolz, and probably he himself, would pay with their heads for this "categorical instruction" issued by the Boss. The name of Polishchuk, actually responsible for executing these "traitorous and pro-fascist" decisions, was not included among the list of victims at the trial, but his knowledge of the matter makes it probable that he, too, disappeared.

Had Rosengolz cared to defend himself, he could have cited issues of *Pravda* for that period containing triumphant declarations of the editor, Mechlis—also a secretary of Stalin's—the gist of which was that the success of Russian industrialization might be seen by the increased exports of pig iron to many countries, and, in particular, to Japan.

As the work of my trust grew, I often had difficulty getting necessary armaments for export because my requirements clashed with those of the Red Army. Our industry could not fill both orders at the same time, and I had frequently to seek the help of my friends in the General Staff, and, on the very tough cases, go to Gamarnik or Tukhachevsky. We would agree upon some compromise, at times postponing their orders, at others my deliveries abroad. When we were unable to come to an agreement, my chief, Rosengolz, would have to fight it out with the Army chiefs in the Politburo or get a decision from Stalin.

The General Staff was co-operative, although my exports only brought them additional headaches. Several times the arms and munitions I needed urgently were lent me from the Army depots. And when sometimes the ordnance officers would try to "unload" on us old, questionable stocks of powder charge for shells, or outmoded gas masks, the controversy would be decided in my favor by the marshal or his assistants. The best experts among the officers of the artillery and tank departments of the staff were working with my trust, helping to prepare technical specifications, participating in parleys with foreign purchasing missions, conducting tests on the Army grounds. I remember that once at a reception, the chief of the tank forces, Khalepsky, jokingly complained to Tukhachevsky that "Barmine wears out my officers with overtime work," and begged the marshal to stop this "exploitation." But the Army experts were extremely helpful and did a first-class job. The only department with which I had a tough time was that of my old friend and classmate, the chief of the Air Corps, Alksnis. He was up to his ears in a tremendous expansion of the Red Air Force and kept his aides on such a rigorous schedule that they were unable to do much for me.

But on the whole I worked with the Army staff smoothly, each understanding the problems and difficulties of the other. In spite of the obvious advantages to the Foreign Trade Commissariat of these cordial relations, Rosengolz grew suspicious that I was sometimes too considerate of the viewpoint of the General Staff.

"As president of the Auto-Moto-Export, you must forget that you are a reserve officer. Never mind *esprit de corps*. You must stand up to your friends in the General Staff. Don't be soft with them."

He was even more annoyed when, in the middle of the year, with the work of my trust going full swing, I was suddenly called up by the Army for three months' retraining. I pointed out to him that several dozen General Staff reserve officers occupying high executive posts in the government, in industry, and in the foreign service were called at the same time.

But Rosengolz had his own idea, typical of his stubborn and persistent bureaucratic mind. One day a couple of months after my return from the retraining course, he received me with a smile of satisfaction.

"Now you're a civilian," he said. "At my request the government has just ordered your retirement from the Officers' Reserve Corps. The General Staff protested, but it went through. You can get your discharge papers. You can stand up to them now as a one hundred per cent foreign-trade official. So that's that."

This unexpected turn hardly brought any advantage to us or made my work easier. But it brought me at least a partial compensation which I did not think of at the moment. The Red Army provided a discharged veteran with a bonus in proportion to his years of service, doubled for the time spent in combat units at the front. For me, on the basis of almost sixteen years' service and the salary of a brigade commander, it amounted to several thousand rubles. This gift from the sky came at the moment when the problem of better food, new clothes, and a rest in the south for my children and my mother was a pressing one. It solved the problem for awhile.

At the end of 1934 I was instructed by the Politburo to negotiate with the Afghan ambassador for the export to Afghanistan of a number of planes, mountain artillery, and other armaments, to be delivered on generous credit terms.

Because Afghanistan is a buffer state between Russia and India, the British looked with disfavor upon the increasingly cordial relations between the Amanullah Shah and the Soviet Union. Bacha-Sakow, a nomad chieftain, was gathering forces about him to fight Amanullah. The British gave him their support, and Bacha-Sakow marched on the capital. Word reached Moscow that Amanullah's power was menaced. The Politburo decided to send the crack troops of the Red Army to his assistance. Two divisions entrained for Afghanistan to fight for Amanullah. The Afghan war minister accompanied our commanding general. But just as they were preparing to enter Herat, word came that Bacha-Sakow had beaten Amanullah's army and that the valiant Shah had deserted his men and fled to Italy. Moscow ordered our troops to return at once. So secretly were these maneuvers conducted that the outside world never knew how near Russia came to going to war in Afghanistan.

However, the British soon found Bacha-Sakow too proletarian for their tastes. A naïve herdsman, he actually attempted to pursue an independent policy. It would have been to our interest to win his confidence, but Stalin stubbornly refused to deal with this peasant who had overthrown a prince of the old royal family. Subsequently the British supported another member of the royal family, Nadir Shah, and enabled him to seize power. Bacha-Sakow was captured and executed. Stalin decided to deal with Nadir Shah. I was instructed to reach some favorable understanding with the Afghan ambassador for new armaments. He seemed extremely stupid and helpless, and the endless negotiations bogged down. It occurred to me later that perhaps Nadir Shah's ambassador was not so stupid but was merely playing the British game.

The great province of Sinkiang in western China was another object of our attention. Separated from the rest of China by wide deserts and bordering on Russia, Sinkiang seemed a logical area for Soviet penetration. At the moment when I started the new trust, the Politburo decided to give full aid to the governor of Sinkiang, who was besieged in his capital by a number of rebel Moslems, incited, in our opinion, by the British. The job of sending arms to Sinkiang was left to me. It turned out a very difficult task.

The capital of the province was already menaced by the rebels. The Politburo ordered two brigades of G.P.U. troops with air units of the Red Army to clear the roads and liquidate the rebellion. Meanwhile, on the order of the Politburo, we shipped a number of planes and bombs to the borders of Sinkiang. There they were stuck for some time, as the road to Urumchi, capital of Sinkiang, was blocked by the rebels. Finally the command of the Red Army Air Force operating there took charge of this shipment. They "delivered" our cargoes, consigned to the governor, by dropping the bombs on the rebel forces gathered round the capital, and by landing the planes right on the airfield of the besieged fortress. I was instructed to send the bill for the bombs, as well as the other goods, to the governor.

Breaking through to Urumchi, the Soviet troops swept the rebels before them. Soon the pro-Soviet governor of Sinkiang was firmly established in power.

According to Stalin's plan, Sinkiang was to become a sphere of exclusive Russian influence and to serve as a bulwark of our power in the East. We had to equip 10,000 Sinkiang troops completely, from boots to

231

Kuomintang insignia. Soviet advisers, who actually exercised the authority of ministers, were placed at the governor's elbow. A commission headed by Stalin's brother-in-law, Svanidze, was sent to Sinkiang to draw up a plan of reconstruction for the province. My trust was instructed to send engineers to build roads, airdromes, and hangars all over Sinkiang.

Sinkiang was soon a Soviet colony in all but name. The Soviet Government had guaranteed her currency with a huge loan of silver, dominated her trade, and was directing her politics. Although nominally a part of China, Sinkiang sent her own consuls to Russia, and the Chinese ambassador, understanding the situation, raised no questions. At this same time, 1935, Chiang Kai-shek addressed a request to us through his air ministry for a delivery of airplanes. I was instructed to refuse. Stalin did not want to strengthen Chiang Kai-shek's government.

I had a slight squabble with the G.P.U. over some artillery sent to Sinkiang. The governor informed us that the artillery was secondhand, although it was listed as new. An investigation disclosed that the G.P.U. troops, on returning to Russia after helping to put down the rebellion, had decided to exchange their old cannon for the new ones we had sent. They had made the exchange without bothering to inform Moscow. I brought my complaint to Rosengolz. "Don't start anything with the G.P.U. men," he said. "Give Sinkiang a discount and forget it."

In general I tried to keep my work free of intervention from the G.P.U., and I learned only a good deal later how closely they watched me. As my work grew heavier and I had to stay at my desk late at night, I asked the Foreign Trade Commissariat to send me an extra stenographer. In response a young woman appeared with a letter of recommendation from the commissariat. She was very smartly dressed in clothes obviously bought abroad, had a well-tended skin and lacquered nails, and wore jewelry—in marked contrast to the usual simply and shabbily dressed Russian girls. She told me that her husband, Grozovsky, was an employee of the Central Executive Committee, and that they had come back from abroad some time ago. Her recommendations were very high, and I put her to work on secret correspondence. Indeed, she had charge of all my correspondence for three or four months. She did not show overmuch zeal or exactitude, however, and when at the end of this period she asked my permission to resign—giving as a reason that she wanted to spend more time with her child—I let her go without regret.

I would have forgotten this small episode had not her name appeared in the Paris newspapers four years later when I was living in France as a refugee. The papers were full of the sensational details of the kidnapping of General Miller, the leader of the White Russian *émigrés*. The police and the French newspapers accused the Soviet Embassy of arranging the kidnapping. They mentioned a high official of the G.P.U., covered by diplomatic immunity, who had left suddenly for Moscow right after the crime. The police suspected this official's wife, who was secretary of the trade delegation, of a share in the plot. She was subpoenaed and forbidden to leave Paris until the investigation was over. She was living in the embassy building, and when she went out she was always driven in a luxurious embassy Cadillac, accompanied by members of the staff. The French police agents would follow her at a distance in a small Citroën.

One morning, at the height of a newspaper campaign demanding her arrest, she came out for the usual drive and was followed as usual by the Citroën. She drove out of the city, and when clear of the traffic her driver stepped on the gas and sped away so fast that the police could not keep up. They never saw her again. The next day the newspapers could only state the sad fact that "Madame Grozovsky as well as her husband" was now out of reach of French justice. I realized then that, while working at Auto-Moto-Export, I had been under the closest scrutiny of the G.P.U.

My work brought me often in contact with members of the diplomatic corps, especially those from Eastern governments. Not only did I get to know the details of their work, but I saw something of the social life they led in Moscow. The fifteen years which had passed since my association with Chicherin had brought many changes. All the great powers now had their representatives in the capital of the world revolution. The most outstanding personalities were, undoubtedly, Bullitt, Vassyf-Bey, and Lukasiewicz, ambassadors, respectively, of the United States, Turkey, and Poland. The most original figure, however, was the Lithuanian minister, Baltrushaitis, who had been a famous Russian poet before the war.

Diplomatic life in Moscow during these three years was rich in colorful details, both personal and political, but I will turn from them to an incident which, quite unexpectedly to a great many people, has now acquired historical importance.

31. *The Birth of Parachute Troops*

IN 1934, while still a reserve officer, I was called up for a retraining course, as I have said before. I spent these three months working in the headquarters of the chief of the General Staff in Moscow. During this period I had a chance to watch at close range the development of a new and daring weapon conceived and created by the Red Army—parachute troops.

Many people have expressed their surprise that this advanced military technique should first have arisen in an industrially backward nation. The story of its origin, which I happen rather accidentally to know, has never been told. It is interesting because in a roundabout way the idea came from the United States, although from its amusements rather than its industries.

There had been many serious accidents in our Air Force, the death rate among students, pilots, and observers being higher in Russia than anywhere else. And in 1929 General Alksnis, head of our Air Force, decided to send an observer to the United States to study the work done in the parachute field. He chose Sergei Minov, a young, energetic major in the Air Force, whom I had come to know through a mutual friend, General Alexander Fradkin, later a head of the Soviet military purchasing agency in the U.S.A. Minov stopped off in Paris on his way to the United States. I was in Paris at the time, and Fradkin was then my assistant for the purchase of aviation material, and the three of us spent several hours together. Minov was a little dubious about the value of his trip. How much would he be permitted to see? And was there much he could learn anyway? "Still," he said, "if there's anything new in parachuting, the Americans will have it."

He spent almost a year in the United States. On his way home he passed through Paris again, full of enthusiasm for what he had seen. Although Russia was not then officially recognized, he had been courteously received. He had visited airplane factories, airdromes, and training schools. He praised highly the quality of American parachutes and the instruction given to pilots. He had made his own first parachute jump in America.

"But you know," he went on—sticking to the official Soviet line even over drinks in a Paris café—"I saw some things which were scandalous. In order to make a living during the depression, first-rate pilots have to resort to making jumps as a show business. I saw one man doing it to amuse the crowd at a county fair! Think of it! An invention which we regard as a lifesaving device, almost a clinical instrument, is used to give onlookers a thrill!"

Well, that was capitalist America, we agreed. We did not know that crowds at American county fairs have been amused this way since the invention of the parachute. Happily, in Soviet Russia, we thought, where human energy is distributed by plan, a skilled airman does not have to make his living stunting at a county fair.

Fradkin and I were ready to go on to other topics of conversation, but Minov kept turning this matter over in his mind.

"Still," he said, "you should have seen the interest of that crowd. Such excitement must have a propaganda value."

When Minov submitted his report to the chief of the Air Force, Alksnis, he mentioned the interest which parachute jumping could arouse as a sport. He suggested that the interest of the Soviet population, and particularly the young, could be turned toward aviation by using this sport as an instrument of propaganda. Alksnis passed the comment on to the Politburo. Stalin agreed that it was a good idea. That set the wheels of the bureaucracy in motion. Articles appeared in the Soviet press describing parachute jumping in glowing phrases. Parachute clubs were formed. Parachuters were given nation-wide publicity. Youths, lost in the anonymity of the mass, discovered that they could get into the spotlight by participating in the new pastime. Girls as well as boys joined in.

The radio and the newspapers told of the exploits of parachuters. Every official organ of propaganda beat the drums for parachuting. It soon became what baseball is for the youth of America. There were competitions in delayed yanking of the ripcord. Jumps were made under varying conditions—at night, in winter, over forests, onto lakes, alone, in groups, with military equipment, and without. The radio would announce that Ivan Petrov, son of peasants, was returning to his *kolkhos* for a visit. He would not go by railroad or on foot but would drop at his father's door from the skies. Ivan's parachute jump to his home town would keep the peasants talking for weeks. Soviet parachutists established world records, and many were decorated by the government—both boys and girls.

The result was that tens of thousands of young Soviet citizens became expert parachutists. Many developed a passion for flying and enlisted in the Air Corps. This had been the aim of the propaganda campaign. Others, however, in the course of their compulsory military service (a two-year period which begins at eighteen) turned up in the infantry. The High Command discovered that, in addition to the regular air arm attached to each division, they had thousands of infantrymen with experience as parachutists. It occurred to them to separate these parachute jumpers into detachments for special training.

That was how parachute troops developed from an idea born in the mind of a Soviet airman watching the crowd's response to a parachute stunt at an American county fair.

The Red strategists no longer believed that revolution would come in the West through the spontaneous action of the workers. It would come as a result of war between Soviet Russia and the capitalist world. When this war occurred, Soviet parachute troops, dropping from the skies into the industrial centers behind the lines, would organize the workers to fight the capitalist armies in the rear. This idea gave the parachute troops a very lofty mission. They became a sort of elite in the Red Army ranks.

The 1935 Red Army maneuvers, which I attended, although now a civilian, as a guest of General Yakir, were conducted in the western Ukraine. Military observers from a number of foreign powers were there. General Jonah Yakir was in charge, and the maneuvers were attended by Marshals Voroshilov, Tukhachevsky, and other high-rank-ing Soviet officers. From a platform erected on a high hill we watched the armies engage in mock battle.

We saw the first use of parachute troops to capture a field suitable for the landing of troop transports. The operation, which all told was a matter of minutes, was extremely impressive. An entire brigade of 3,500 men with light tanks and artillery descended from the skies. First 1,200 parachutists landed within an area the size of an average American airfield. In ten minutes they had established control of the area, and then great transport planes appeared, landing under the protection of machine-gun fire from the parachutists. Out of these poured some 2,300 air-infantrymen. From between the wheels of the giant planes rumbled motorized light field guns and baby tanks.

All the foreign observers expressed their admiration of this new arm. It was clear that here was something of the greatest importance to military strategy. I am certain that no military observer failed to point this out to his government.

Seven or eight similar maneuvers took place in different military regions in 1936, ending with one in the Moscow region in the presence of Premier Molotov and War Commissar Voroshilov, in which five thousand parachutists and air infantrymen participated.

After the maneuvers in White Russia, a banquet was given by General Uborevich to honor the foreign military delegations which had attended. The delegations represented countries which, many people thought, might join Stalin in a front against Hitler. The climax of the banquet came when Uborevich toasted the guests. "I raise my glass," he said solemnly, "to the English, French, and Czechoslovak armies, and to their representatives, our highly esteemed guests."

To reply in the name of the British delegation, there arose the commander of the Second Aldershot Division, a stocky English officer, who returned the compliment in excellent Russian.

"We were impressed," he said, "by the enormous technical achievements of the Red Army. We much admired the work of the parachute troops. I drink to the health of the Red Army and Marshal Voroshilov."

This man was General Sir Archibald Wavell, who today, after his experience in Crete, must have a vivid sense of the significance of this technical achievement of the Red Army. I have no doubt he made an urgent report on it then. But at that time the British and French High Commands apparently regarded the whole development as a new-fangled gadget without real importance. The Germans were first to appreciate its meaning.

Hitler wasted no time in building a parachute army of his own. Applying German efficiency and organizational technique to this brilliant idea of the Russians, he soon far surpassed their achievements. It suffices to recall Oslo, Rotterdam, Eben-Emael, and Crete. From the fiords of Norway to the isles of Greece, the parachute troops of the German Army have made military history. Each of these fallen citadels was taken by this new arm, conceived and first developed under the guidance of Marshal Tukhachevsky and his aides, Generals Yakir, Uborevich, and Alksnis. Meanwhile, however, Stalin had shot all these men who built the parachute force, dealing almost a death blow to the whole instrument. The result was a complete failure of the first attempt to use it in a real war in Finland. Not only had the organization been deprived of its leadership, but the cause in which it was used was opposite to that for which it had been planned. Instead of being welcomed by Finnish workers waiting to break the bonds of capitalism, the Soviet parachute troops dropping behind the Finnish lines were shot down by indignant Finns of all classes defending themselves against the army of Soviet totalitarianism.

The Germans, more skillful and organized for brigandry from the beginning, had better luck—for awhile. But a powerful Anglo-American parachute army is paying them back now with dividends for the lesson it learned.

32. *An Automobile Executive in the Meshes of Bureaucracy*

IN MY AUTOMOBILE DEPARTMENT, the chief article of export was to be a three-ton truck, named "ZIS," built to American specifications in the Stalin Plant at Moscow. We were also producing a smaller truck and a passenger car in the plant at Gorky (formerly Nizhnii Novgorod), built with the technical advice and according to the blueprints of Henry Ford. The farsighted Mr. Ford had concluded a contract with us by the terms of which we could not export these cars, although as late as 1934 we were still producing his 1930 model. In order to offer passenger cars as well as heavy trucks to my oriental customers, therefore, I had to get them outside Russia. I made agreements with the English Vauxhall Company and the Ford Company of Egypt, designating my trust as their sole selling agents in Mongolia, Sinkiang, and northern Afghanistan.

In order to draw attention to our motor industry, we sent a few of our Moscow "ZIS" trucks, loaded to capacity, on a race through Persia and Afghanistan. Driven by powerful engines, built more for strength than economy, these trucks made a record trip over the difficult terrain. Their drivers and engineers were welcomed by local dignitaries and given much-advertised banquets. At one place in Persia our trucks drew up to a shallow stream, where the bridge had been washed away. A number of British and American-made trucks stood waiting to be ferried across. With their less powerful and more economical engines, they dared not tackle the stream. But our drivers simply stepped on the gas, churned through the water, and disappeared over the slope on the other side. We sold many trucks to Persia and Afghanistan on the strength of this performance.

I suggested that we organize a similar race through Finland and send two cars to the Paris motor show. Rosengolz took my scheme to the Kremlin, but Stalin decided against it.

There was a balance of about £4,000 to £5,000 standing to the credit of my trust in a London bank. This represented commissions paid us by English and American firms for selling their cars in Eastern markets. In view of the impending arrival in Moscow of several Afghan and Persian buyers, I asked leave to spend a small portion of this sum—which did not appear on the balance sheet of my plan—in buying a really good American passenger car to use during their visit and afterward retain as the property of the trust. Rosengolz could not give me this permission; it required the say-so of the Boss, and the Boss said no. So, in order to get my guests about—guests of an automobile trust at that—I had to hire cars from Intourist!

Foreign trade was no easier for me than my work in Moscow had been, and for the same reasons. On one occasion I sent my assistant to Persia to sign a contract for 250 trucks. At the same time the vice-commissar for foreign trade, Eliava, an Old Bolshevik of Georgian origin, made a journey to Teheran and returned so satisfied with what he had seen that, on the strength of his report, the Politburo issued "imperative instructions to the Auto-Moto-Export Trust to raise the sales of trucks in Persia to 400." Negligence on the part of somebody in Rosengolz's office left me in ignorance of this decision. I never knew of it until I was summoned before the Party Control Commission, a formidable institution, which kept a watchful eye on Communist executives.

The president of the Commission at that time was Yezhov, who later, when Yagoda was executed, replaced him as head of the G.P.U. Yezhov headed the G.P.U. during the maddest years of the purge, 1937-38. One day he was suddenly removed and disappeared. Not a word as to the fate of this man who had occupied the highest offices, including that of secretary of the Central Committee of the Party as well as president of the Control Commission, was ever published. It is rumored that he ended his days in an insane asylum, and that rumor seems plausible to me.

Zhukovsky, one of Yezhov's assistants, catechized me severely.

"The fault was not mine," I said. "The instructions were never passed on to me. Who is to blame if such an important decision is sent to everyone except the man supposed to carry it out?"

"Ignorance of the law excuses no one. Instructions issued by the Politburo have the force of law."

"In any case the instructions couldn't have been carried out because the Soviet-Persian Bank could not give us further credits."

At this Zhukovsky flew into a passion. He was not accustomed to being argued with. As I learned later, officials called before him for investigation were expected to plead guilty at once. "Can't be carried out" is a phrase simply not to be used in connection with Politburo decisions. On this occasion he chose to give his ill-humor the appearance of surprise.

"What's that? Are you telling me that our exports are financed by our own bank? Who gets all the profit then?—some capitalist firm, obviously. I suppose you realize that you are committing a crime!"

Clearly he was quite ignorant of the workings of trade with the Orient. There all exporting countries set up banks with the primary object of facilitating their own commercial transactions. Our contract in Persia was with the Ramazanov firm, which, in order to pay us on delivery, while giving credit to Persian dealers, borrowed the necessary funds from the Soviet-Persian Bank. There was no risk in this. The bank kept the owner-rights until the credit was repaid. The firm of Ramazanov, moreover, had a solid reputation.

I tried to explain this, but Zhukovsky did not wish to understand. Another detail increased his fury. My assistant, Nodel, whom I had sent to Teheran, was not a Party member.

"Barmine, you have been guilty of gross irregularity. The whole thing smacks of negligence. We shall take steps against you."

I knew well that I stood little chance of being exonerated. The only thing I could do was try to carry out the Politburo's decisions now. For that I should have to get a supplementary credit from the Moscow Foreign Trade Bank. The director of the bank, Svanidze, seemed agreeable to what I asked. But when it came to getting the money, something was the matter. A telephone call from the Control Commission had put a stop to it. The bank officials looked extremely apologetic. I could see that the shadow of the Control Commission over this whole transaction was frightening them. They were so frightened that they even cabled the Soviet Bank in Teheran to cut off all credits for Ramazanov, making it impossible to execute even the original scheme for the export of 250 trucks. When I reached home I found an order to report to the Economic Department of the G.P.U. That meant two investigations for the same "irregularity," and in the same unreasoning spirit. The G.P.U., however, when they heard of the other inquiry, dropped their own.

When the Control Commission met to announce its decision, I ran into Loganovsky, who was then acting as assistant to Rosengolz. He said: "I think you're going to be reprimanded." A reprimand is the second measure of discipline inflicted by the Party. The order of these chastisements is as follows—warning, reprimand, severe reprimand, expulsion from the Party.

The chairman at the hearing was Shkiriatov, another assistant of Yezhov's. One circumstance seemed to bother the Commission and count in my favor. The firm of Ramazanov, finding its credits with the Soviet Bank cut off, had gone to the Bank of Iran and got a sufficient advance to make it possible to pay me cash for the remaining deliveries. However, the stipulated date of delivery was now past; the negotiations had been interrupted, and there was no hope of increasing the total of our exports to Persia, as the Politburo desired. This failure was caused not so much by the neglect to let me know of the Politburo's decision in the first place as by the clumsy and ignorant intervention of the Control Commission in my business with the bank. In order to punish me for a "crime" I had not committed, the Control Commission, in the person of Zhukovsky, was actually sabotaging the country's important export plans and also damaging our reputation for financial reliability in Persia. Rosengolz and Loganovsky knew this, but who would dare to tell the truth in the face of my Party judges?

Zhukovsky's reprimand report accused me of negligence in having entered into contract with and given credits to a financially weak firm which offered insufficient guarantees, and having thus put the state in the way of material losses. I pleaded Eliava's favorable report, and argued that Ramazanov, although refused credits by our Soviet Bank, was paying regularly. The Persian State Bank had backed him up and demonstrated the solid financial position of the firm. Consequently no material damage had been incurred by us.

I could feel that my defense had only the effect of irritating the Commission, since it put them in the wrong. Shkiriatov changed his line of attack.

"But the Politburo's decision has not been executed."

"I was not informed of that decision. I have done my best right up to now, and it is not my fault that I didn't succeed."

"No one has any right to be ignorant of the decisions of the Party."

At the same hearing Levsky, one of the directors of the Soviet Oil Export Syndicate, was brought up on a similar charge. He made no attempt to defend himself, but pleaded guilty and begged the indulgence of the commission. During the adjournment Loganovsky, who had not dared to speak in my favor, said:

"You're behaving like a child. Why not admit that you're wrong, as everybody else does? If you do that, you'll get off with a mere warning."

Levsky did get off with a warning, but I was reprimanded. This was the first disciplinary action taken against me in seventeen years spent as a Party member, and it hurt me the more for being utterly unjust. Rosengolz refused to interfere. When I pointed out to him that in similar circumstances Ordjonikidze, the commissar of heavy industries, had not hesitated to defend his collaborators against Yezhov, he told me dryly to take my complaint to his assistant, Eliava. Eliava agreed to ring up Yezhov in my presence and try to get the reprimand rescinded. But when he did so he spoke in such deferential terms and in a tone of humility so unworthy of an Old Bolshevik that I realized at once his intercession was useless. Stalin's new favorite, Yezhov, already wielded great power behind the scenes, and was feared even by the most prominent members of the Party.

Business took me frequently to the Stalin auto works in Moscow, and sometimes to the Gorky works at Nizhni Novgorod. Both places were in a constant state of siege. Their atmosphere was one of feverish excitement. Work never stopped night or day; Party inspectors were everywhere; the directors seemed overtired and no longer able to think straight about anything; they had no adequate time to shave, sleep, or eat, to say nothing of resting. At any moment some new dangerous crisis might crop up. Sometimes it would be the men, sometimes the raw material, sometimes the administrative staff. At every hour of the day or night something was always going wrong at the critical moment. Whatever happened, the plan of automotive production had to be carried out. Every individual felt personally responsible and knew that he might pay with his life if it failed.

I can still see Likhachev, the director of the Stalin works, rushing about, his face purple, in a little group of engineers and foremen— shouting, threatening, swearing. He got as good as he gave; the place was a veritable hell. Suddenly an office boy would run up: "Central Committee on the telephone," and Likhachev would jump to meet a new trouble. In such appalling conditions he had to direct the labor of more than 25,000 men, of whom over 10,000 were occupied in constructing additional shops. His task was complicated by the fact that the industries which ought to have supplied his, practically did not exist. He had to create them, get them into running order, and himself manage, somehow or other, to produce everything that he had need of.

At Gorky, in similar conditions, Diakonov was in control of 25,000 to 27,000 workers as well as an additional 15,000 occupied in new building operations. He was in his office day and night, but it was with the greatest difficulty that his department heads managed to see him once a week for a serious talk. He sat there up to his eyes in papers, instructions, plans, blueprints, or swamped with interminable conferences and discussions, frittering away his energies on the innumerable details and trivial breakdowns of routine. He put heart and soul in his work and completely wore himself out—only to disappear and give place to a new director. His fate was shared by thousands of heads of trusts, factories, state farms, machine depots, and the like during the great purge of 1937-38. They just vanished into the void. New men have come forward. But the system remains the same.

In the general hierarchy of the automobile industry, Likhachev and

Diakonov were under the orders of Dybets, a former anarchist workman who had emigrated to America. He had returned to Russia in 1920 and, sponsored by Bukharin, whom he had known in New York, joined the Party. He was energetic and capable and played a great part in the building of our automobile industry. He ended his career in prison, condemned with his assistant, Mayers—also returned from the U.S.A.—in 1938. Bukharin's testimonial to his character, found among the Central Committee's records, was by that time fatal. So far as I know, all the men who were sponsored by Bukharin or his fellow victims over a period of twenty years have suffered a similar fate.

In marked contrast to the management of Soviet industry, I remember my surprise when in 1932 I made the acquaintance of the director of the Ford works in Antwerp and saw how his factory was managed. He received me in a comfortable glass-partitioned office situated in the very middle of the factory. For me the mere appearance of his office was sufficiently striking. Instead of the mass of papers, files, drawings, plans, and sealed envelopes which would have littered the desk of any director of a Soviet industry, I saw before me a perfectly smooth surface broken only by a white scratch pad. The man himself was calm and cheerful. During our interview he sat quietly at his table, saying a word over his telephone from time to time. For one brought up in the Soviet system, it was incredible to see a factory operating under such calm direction. I left his office filled with respect for the American way.

It happened, on another occasion, that I was detailed to show the Citroën works in Paris to Obolensky-Ossinsky, a prince of the old Russian family of Obolensky, but also an Old Bolshevik. He was a man of wide erudition who had been the first to propose that the Soviets build an automobile industry. M. Citroën was interested in our plans and in the results we were achieving. Ossinsky recited the latest boast of the Five-Year Plan. "Our works at Gorky," he said with a smile, "will have an output greater than all of yours put together."

The substance of M. Citroën's tactful reply was this: "I admire the efforts you are making, but it seems to me that an industry as concentrated as yours needs superb technical efficiency, a tradition of production, and an uninterrupted flow of material. So long as such conditions are not realized, I should say it would have been better to build several factories on a rather smaller scale. The administration of gigantic industries is a very difficult problem."

This intelligent capitalist and experienced engineer was more than right, and we knew it. Our uncritical transfer of American-scale factories to Russia, with its very different conditions, did often prove disastrous. After a very sad experience, Stalin changed his mind. He decided, in his usual brusque way, that what formerly had been the magic "American system" was now criminal "gigantomania." And, of

242

course, the usual number of scapegoats was found to shoulder responsibility for his own earlier mistake.

I was never to see Ossinsky again. He was later in charge of the Central Statistical Office, and from there was taken to prison—denounced, like others who had greatly served the republic in its earliest days, as an "enemy of the people."

One day Ordjonikidze, paying a visit to the Moscow automobile factory, stopped in front of a shining truck destined for export. I had insisted on an elegant finish for these trucks, quite different from that employed on the vast mass of trucks destined for the home market.

"I want all production to be of this quality!" he said to Likhachev, as though merely to give the order was tantamount to getting it carried out.

Likhachev never batted an eye. "Right! It shall be done," he said.

Nothing, of course, was done, or could be, because the technical equipment of the shops and the constant race after quantity—"Always go one better than the plan" was another of Ordjonikidze's slogans—made it impossible.

I was told of this imperial ukase while busy on a related problem. My three-ton trucks had proven so strong that Persian drivers, using them for their own private business, would add a yard to their length by contrivances of their own and carry loads of five to seven tons. Reckoning on the state of the Russian roads, we allowed ourselves 150 per cent margin on power and load capacity. Our model was too heavy and had too much power. I suggested a slight modification of construction which would have provided a more economical truck, capable of carrying five to six tons—twice our advertised load. But this would have demanded greater accuracy in the shops and more precision in certain details.

Armed with letters from a number of Persian drivers, I succeeded without difficulty in convincing Likhachev and his chief, Michael Kaganovich, the brother of Lazar. The motor journal, *Za Roulem,* published my article on this subject. But Ordjonikidze shelved the matter with the words: "No! Better wait until we build a new factory. We can always find money and labor." He imagined he could increase the total output merely by giving an abstract order, but at the thought of creating a new and more economical model, his initiative failed him. In a word, he preferred squandering capital on unnecessary new plants to improving the technical methods of those already existing.

As I have said, we were sending the limousines and graceful torpedo bodies of the Ford and Vauxhall companies into Mongolia and Sinkiang at the same time as our far cruder trucks. The cases loaded by Ford in New York had to cover several thousand miles by sea to Leningrad or Odessa, and thence almost another 7,000 miles by rail to Siberia and Kirghizia. In Verkneudinsk the Fords, shining with blue lacquer and nickel-chromium, would be taken out of their cases,

243

and they would ultimately arrive at Ulan Bator, the capital of Mongolia, by way of roads deep in mud and across numerous small rivers and extensive marshlands.

The Mongol government would distribute them to its high dignitaries and the heads of the People's Party. These officials are all ardent hunters and soon found a new way of using these triumphs of modern engineering technique. Having a chauffeur drive them at full speed across the flat, hard surface of the immense steppes, standing on the seats, they would shoot the terrified hares and wild birds that were put up in their course.

Cars so roughly treated very soon became unusable, and enormous quantities of spare parts had to be ordered, and forwarded by us, taking many months to reach their destination.

Persia and Turkey, being more civilized, presented a different problem. Trade with these two countries necessitated greater elasticity of handling and greater speed. We were able to succeed here only by modifying our methods of trade. In Russia we could, if need be, sell cars without spare parts and keep the customer waiting weeks if he wanted any. In Persia and Turkey, what we could not provide, others could, and that meant that we would lose our customers. At a meeting of the heads of all our trusts, with Rosengolz presiding, I proposed that we start spare-parts depots at Ashkhabad, Baku, and Odessa, so as to be able to carry out orders with expedition. The commissariat officials put up a passive resistance which was insurmountable.

I spoke some pretty harsh words. They were received in icy silence, and my proposal was turned down. Rosengolz, up to that moment always cordial to me, became deliberately unfriendly. I had presumed to comment on the bureaucracy! He would stomach no such remarks. His oversensitive temperament interpreted them as an attack on the spirit of the hierarchy in which he had his place.

Rosengolz's coolness toward me became more and more marked as time passed. His staff was quick to notice it, and it hindered my work. My struggle to get the technical specialists I required became hopeless, and my reports had a way of remaining unanswered. I finally sent in my resignation. I know that Rosengolz got the letter, but for two months he made no reply, though we saw each other frequently. When I saw that he had no intention of mentioning it, I brought it up myself and kept insisting on it. After my two years' experience with Auto-Moto-Export I had lost all ambition to keep my place among the high-ups of the Soviet foreign trade. Political conditions and the life of the Party had grown so sickening that my old longing for quiet study again obsessed me. I hoped again now that I might find my way, with the help of the General Staff, to the Aviation Academy. Thus, when Rosengolz at last gave in and I bade him farewell, my feelings toward him were almost friendly. Neither of us had the slightest idea that it was our last handshake.

244

Seven presidents of the Soviet Union, *left to right*: Khodjaev (Uzbekistan)—shot in 1938; Musabekov (Azebaijan)—shot in 1938; Petrovsky (Ukraine)—disappeared in 1938; Kalinin (Russia)—alive; Cherviakov (White Russia)—suicide in 1937; Rakhimbayev (Tajikistan)—shot in 1938; Aitakov (Turkestan)—fate unknown. *Standing*: Yenukidze, secretary of the Soviet Union—shot in 1937.

© *International News Photos*

© *Wide World*

Sergei Kirov, member of Politburo and secretary of the Central Committee of the Communist Party—killed in Leningrad in December, 1934.

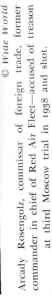

© *Wide World*

Arcady Rosengolz, commissar of foreign trade, former commander in chief of Red Air Fleet—accused of treason at third Moscow trial in 1938 and shot.

Arcady Rosengolz was then a little over fifty—a bulky-shouldered, handsome Jew, with a heavy jaw and iron character. I had known his daughter by his first marriage, a girl not unlike him in looks and strength of will. It happened that I was staying in the rest house of the Central Committee at Gagry in the Caucasus in 1935 when she arrived there on her way to the villa of Lakoba, a friend of her father's. We danced that evening on the terrace of the rest house, and I felt in her a strained and artificial gaiety. I was told that something was going wrong in her marriage. Two days later news arrived that she had shot herself during a stay in the mountains.

Her father lived a retired life in the government house close to the Kremlin, devoting his evenings to work. He was a forceful executive, with a strong feeling for authority, a born bureaucrat, and, when I knew him, devoted to Stalin. He had known Trotsky, however, during the years of fighting, and had belonged to the Opposition from 1923 to 1928, when it stood some chance of success. Since then he had served Stalin punctiliously and without a murmur of doubt or hesitation.

He had married quite recently a young woman who worked in his office, a jolly red-haired girl, very imperfectly educated, and brought up in a religious household. Frightened by the spreading shadow of the purge, she gave him for good luck a religious medallion to carry in his pocket. It was found on him and brought into court during his cross-questioning at the Third Moscow trial. What had been a gesture of affection on the part of a frightened and bewildered woman was turned into a matter of ridicule. The man was mocked and derided by Stalin's prosecutors before being condemned.

His last word after confessing himself a miserable traitor and saboteur was: "Long live Stalin!" The next day he was shot.

33. *"Life Has Become More Joyful, Comrades"*

THE THREE YEARS of my work in Moscow, 1933-35, were years of a critical change in Stalin's policy—the most momentous change since he had risen to power. In them the whole future fate of the Soviet state, and to a great extent of modern European history—although we did not know it then—was determined. This change was not fully understood by the foreign correspondents or literary visitors to Moscow. It could not very well be understood by anyone not in touch with ideas and processes in the inner circles of the Bolshevik Party. Therefore it seems best to me to reserve for a separate chapter of my book an account of this change and the effect which it had on our views and feelings.

Let us turn back, then, to the year 1933.

It was only by great exertions that Stalin had overcome the consequences of the famine of 1931-32 which followed his enforced collectivization. He knew during that famine that his leadership was at stake. Another poor harvest and disaster might descend on him. He put all the Party's energy into the spring sowing of 1933. Thousands of Communists were sent into the countryside. They were recruited from all branches of the government. Strict political and police supervision was established over the peasantry. The G.P.U. went grimly to work to weed out the discouraged and the unwilling. The nerves of the country were stretched to the breaking point. But the effort succeeded.

Toward summer, reports started coming in that the harvest of 1933 would be a good one. Tension in the Party relaxed. Many who had doubted began to think that, despite Stalin's authoritarian methods —or perhaps because of them—the country would, after all, overcome its difficulties. I myself saw with renewed hope how economic conditions slowly improved. As was to be expected, Moscow was the first to give signs of this: one by one, long-forgotten delicacies began to enliven the store windows, and it became easier to get foodstuffs and clothing—though, to be sure, only those with full purses were very largely benefited.

Feeling in the Party was more optimistic than it had been for years. With successes in the economic sphere, we hoped for an easing up in the Party regime, an end to expulsions and repressions. The terror in the country, we thought, was no longer necessary. Life must assume an even keel. We wanted unity in the Party and peace in the nation. The foreign situation, as well as the internal strain, required it. Instead of the revolution in Germany which our leaders had predicted, the Nazis had seized power. Germany was arming, apparently without hindrance from either England or France, and it looked as if her arms would be used against us. The Russian people must be prepared for war. This demanded a policy of conciliation both within the Party and between the Party and the country. Such a policy would assure an increase in production as well as an improved morale and would extend the support of the governing regime among the population. It would also make it easier to achieve in the international field that rapprochement with the democratic nations demanded by the new program of "collective security" proclaimed at Geneva by Litvinov.

This policy really began to be adopted. Many Bolsheviks who had been expelled for oppositional views were readmitted. Thousands of them again found their place in Soviet industry. Ordjonikidze, commissar of heavy industry, even recruited some of them for key posts in his department.

The great role in these changes was played by Sergei Kirov, member of the Politburo and secretary of the Party in the Leningrad District. He partly revived the old "liberal" spirit that had made Leningrad in the postrevolutionary period a cultural and scientific center, carrying the policy of conciliation as far as he could in his own district. In the Politburo he had been a stanch supporter of Stalin's "general line," and there could be no question about his orthodoxy. This fact, together with his energetic work on the first Five-Year Plan and his talents as an organizer and brilliant orator—here he was second only to Trotsky—soon made him the outstanding spokesman of the reconciliation policy.

Kamenev and Zinoviev were among the Old Bolsheviks readmitted into the Party. And as an indication of the extent to which Stalin seemed to be pursuing the conciliatory policy, both of them were permitted to address the Party Congress in February, 1934. Discussions everywhere became livelier. There was less dread of the mailed fist of the G.P.U. Kirov went the furthest in restraining it. He gave orders that dissidents in Leningrad were not to be hounded. It was well known that in 1933, when Stalin proposed the death penalty for Riutin, an oppositionist who had issued a program explicitly demanding his removal, it was Kirov who persuaded the Politburo not to shed the blood of a Party member because of his opinion. Stalin had maintained that the program really instigated his assassination. But he did not insist. He allowed Kirov to carry the day, and for the time being Riutin's life was spared. It was also known that in 1934, when the G.P.U. unearthed some alleged "terrorist" moods among young workers and students, Kirov favored a moderate policy in dealing with them, saying that their revolt had not gone beyond the stage of hotheaded talk.

At the Party Congress in February, 1934, Kirov was greeted with an ovation. The entire Congress rose to its feet at the conclusion of his address. There was discussion in the *couloirs* as to whether his applause had not exceeded that given to Stalin. Kirov was elected one of the secretaries of the Central Committee, which meant that he would have to move from his own district of Leningrad to Moscow, where he would be working beside Stalin at the heart of the Party apparatus. At a great mass demonstration in the Red Square in honor of the Party Congress, Kirov was designated to speak in the name of the delegates. His fiery speech, a veritable ode to the new era that was dawning, was loudly acclaimed by the people.

Stalin appeared to be favoring the new policy of conciliation eulogized by Kirov. Indeed, he soon took the apparent lead by announcing a project for a new Soviet constitution, which he declared would be "the most democratic in the world." Not only that, but he appointed the best minds in the Party, including former leaders of the Opposition like Radek, Bukharin, and Sokolnikov, to sit beside himself and his lieutenants on the extraordinary commission which was to draft the new constitution.

It seemed to us that the years of quarrels and repression had been left behind. A new era was indeed dawning.

It is impossible to say at what point Stalin began to fear the consequences of the new course. The prodigiously rising popularity of Kirov and his policy obviously alarmed him. He had no illusions about the true feelings of those who chorused from day to day their adulation of him. He began to fear that the new policy of democratization so rapidly developing would end by posing the question: Do not new methods require new leaders? The question of the dictatorship and of the dictator himself might arise. As this more humane and democratic regime developed, would not he, who represented ruthlessness and dictatorial oppression, be forced to give place to other leaders? Kirov in his eyes personified this danger.

Signs of Stalin's displeasure were visible to the inner circle soon after the Congress. Kirov was not summoned from Leningrad to certain Politburo meetings, and his permanent departure for Moscow to take up his new duties was postponed from week to week. On the plea that conditions in Leningrad demanded his expert attention, Stalin in fact kept Kirov from assuming his new duties for nine months. Kirov's influence, however, continued to grow, and at a plenary session of the Central Committee in November, 1934, he submitted a report urging still further conciliatory measures, which won enthusiastic applause and approval. He was the man of the hour, and the question of his transfer to Moscow was again taken up and decided upon as urgent. He was to return to Leningrad only long enough to hand over his job to his successor.

A few days later, on December 1, 1934, as Sergei Kirov stepped from his office into the corridor of Smolny, he was shot and killed instantly by a Young Communist named Nikolaiev.

The news stunned the Party. Who, we asked, could possibly want to kill the foremost supporter of the conciliation policy? It was inconceivable that any group within the Party could have this wish. And at first the official report took this fact into consideration. We were told that Nikolaiev had been the agent of a "fascist power," that he had confessed to receiving money from a foreign consul in Leningrad. In accordance with this report, and by way of retaliation, 104 anti-Soviet "plotters," who had been in prison since long before the assassination, were shot. This sudden outburst of terror shocked me. I was filled with horror at what seemed the evidence of Stalin's rage and panic at Kirov's assassination. But I hoped that it did not foretell a new era of terror. There was no reason to think that the new policy of conciliation would be abandoned because of this isolated act.

In a few days we were called to attend a Party meeting of our Moscow District. I thought it would be the usual memorial meeting at which orators would commemorate our dead leader and his comrades would tell of his work. I entered the hall with Abram Prigozhin, son-in-law of the English labor leader, George Lansbury, whom I have mentioned before. Prigozhin was then director of the Philosophic Institute in Moscow. Many years before he had voiced for a brief time an agreement with Zinoviev or some other oppositionist, but that was long since forgotten—or so he thought.

We found an extraordinary tension in the hall. The district leaders looked exceptionally stern as they moved about nervously on the platform. I interpreted this as due to the solemnity of the occasion. Still there seemed to be more here than solemnity. Before long the secretary of the district started speaking in a harsh, strained voice. The death of Kirov, I thought, had affected him deeply. But, after touching hastily on the merits of the dead man, the secretary's speech took a sharp turn. We listened in amazement:

"Vigilance and more vigilance is necessary within the Party . . . thousands of masked enemies within our ranks. . ."

What was going to happen now? We had thought all this was over.

"Comrade Stalin personally directed the investigation of Kirov's assassination. He questioned Nikolaiev at length. The leaders of the Opposition placed the gun in Nikolaiev's hand!"

In this way we learned that fifteen Young Communists, accused of having connections with Nikolaiev, had been executed with him, and that the former Opposition leaders, Zinoviev and Kamenev, had been secretly tried and were now in prison.

All of us knew what this meant. Conciliation was over. A new terror had begun. I looked at my friend Prigozhin. His face was white.

When the speaker had finished, others rose to endorse the new line. "The Central Committee must be pitiless—the Party must be purged . . . the record of every member must be scrutinized. . . ."

Nobody alluded to the "fascist agent" theory, on the basis of which 104 prisoners had been shot. Nobody recalled that Kirov stood for the very things that the Opposition had most wanted. Each tried to outdo the other in denouncing the Opposition and demanding pitiless measures against them. It all seemed forced, and behind it we sensed that the motive power was fear. The implications of this new turn were indeed frightening to think of. We could only hope that Stalin's hour of rage and panic would pass. It meant war in the Party, implacable war against all who had ever disagreed with Stalin.

When we walked out into the cold air, Prigozhin was dead white—and trembling. "It is all over with me," he said. "None of us will escape."

Three days later he came to my apartment. "I am expelled from

249

the Party," he said. "I've lost my job. They found deviations in my lectures."

He looked forlorn standing there, his shoulders bent forward. "I don't know what to do. Each day I wait for them to come and arrest me. What will become of my wife and baby?"

I felt sad and helpless. What could I say?

I suggested that he try to get a position remote from Moscow. "The farther off you are, the better chance you have," I said.

What he did, I do not know. I never saw him again. When I tried to phone him, I was told that the line was disconnected.

An iron broom now swept through the Party, dragging thousands to their doom. No corner of the country was exempt. Everyone who had ever voted for the Opposition, or expressed sympathy for it, was included. To make it plausible to base such a reign of terror on the murder of Kirov, the old Opposition leaders, Kamenev and Zinoviev, weak men demoralized already with an abject recantation, were induced to confess that they were "morally responsible" for the murder. It was a sacrifice they must make for the Party—so they were told— a means of restraining their followers and welding the Party into a unit against the rising tide of terrorism.

This was no new departure in official morals under Stalin. Truth had long been held subordinate to the interests of the Party. They did what was demanded of them—under what pressure is not known. But their first comparatively mild "confessions," admitting themselves responsible for a crime which had blasted their own hopes and benefited no one but Stalin, gave Stalin and the G.P.U. a good start toward those subsequent and more prodigious "Moscow confessions" which astounded the world.

In some regions deportations of entire sections of the population were instituted to cleanse them of "enemy remnants." It was estimated that between fifty and a hundred thousand people were shipped from Leningrad alone to the prison camps of the Baltic, the Volga, and Siberia. For weeks the railroad stations were jammed with victims of this new policy of ferocity.

No one dared discuss what was happening. We received news of the fate befalling our best friends and acquaintances without comment. I remember, on the day after our district conference, learning from Rosengolz that my colleague Herzberg, president of the precision instruments import trust, had been arrested. Herzberg and I had been taking language lessons from the same teacher. She had been loud in her praises of his scholarship—no matter how busy he was, he never missed a lesson. She now told me with surprise that Comrade Herzberg was not at his office for the regular lesson. Could anything be the matter? She was still more surprised the next day. But it would have been imprudent for me to enlighten her. Any mention of the purge was imprudent; it might lead to some avowal of emotion or opinion. When at last the names were published of those condemned with Zinoviev and Kamenev, and Herzberg's was among them, our teacher, too, sank into a ghastly silence about her star pupil.

Several weeks after the district meeting, our Communist cell at Auto-Moto-Export received a circular letter from the Central Committee "to be read in closed conference." The letter was a "hymn of hate" against the former oppositionists and a call to new repressions. It was couched in bitter and ferocious language. We learned from it that, since the purge started, many thousands of Party Communists had torn up their Party cards and fled. They had gone underground. They were living under assumed names in distant towns and cities. Many had attempted to escape over the frontiers. It did not occur to the authors of this letter that they were painting a picture of triumphant counterrevolution—that this was exactly what had happened in Hungary and Bavaria when the Soviet regimes were overthrown. They only argued that the Party was filled with traitors, that the fury of the purge must be redoubled.

It seems strange now that we did not realize at that time what was happening. Stalin was starting the destruction of the old Communist Party, which had been the foundation of the Soviet regime in so far as it honestly strove for a better world. I think it is indubitable that the idea of accomplishing this by the physical extermination of the leaders was born in his mind when he saw that the Hitler Blood Purge of June, 1934—when men were shot in their homes without trial—was not only successful internally but did not bring to the Führer contempt and boycott from the civilized world. For years after that, English and French statesmen continued to treat Hitler with respect. It was said that later, when Litvinov warned Stalin of the risk he ran with his wholesale executions, of alienating sympathizers in the democratic world and frustrating the policy of the Popular Front, he said: "They'll swallow it."

What made it difficult for us to realize, in those tense and confusing days of 1935, that Stalin was choosing the road of totalitarian counterrevolution was his command of the press and the platform and of every channel of information. The papers at the time of Kirov's death were filled with his praises, and with expressions of grief, actually far exceeding those which followed the death of Lenin. For at least twelve days all Soviet newspapers were devoted from the first to the last line to the life and death of the beloved leader Kirov. In pages surrounded with great black bands of mourning we were told of the dreadful grief that had seized our country, our leaders, and, most heart-stricken of all, Stalin.

We learned at the same time, or soon after, that Nikolaiev, the assassin, had been well known to the G.P.U. as a neurotic young man with inclinations to terrorism. He had openly talked of his murderous intentions toward the Party bureaucracy. Stalin had found the Leningrad branch of the G.P.U. negligent. Its heads had been tried and sentenced to prison—one of them for ten years. All this was told to us, but its significance was drowned in a sea of recrimination against the Opposition, the Party traitors, who had "placed the gun in Nikolaiev's hand." With the two weapons of the dictator, fear and propaganda, Stalin swamped the judgment of the Party altogether.

In the atmosphere of gloom and confusion we failed to notice what was most important: that Stalin alone profited by the death of Kirov, who was the sole man strong enough in the Party to resist him.

We failed to notice that the negligence of the G.P.U. in protecting such a high Party official was without precedent in the Soviet Union.

We failed to notice that the light sentences imposed on the negligent G.P.U. officials, when compared with the summary execution of 104 prisoners not even implicated in the crime, and of sixteen Communists, all but three of whom denied any knowledge of it, were equally extraordinary. (The officials were not actually imprisoned at all, but transferred to executive posts in concentration camps—that is, in fact, only demoted.)

It also escaped our attention that the attempt to direct public grief and indignation at Kirov's death against the Opposition was artificial and absurd. Kirov was the one man in the Politburo upon whom the Opposition was pinning its hopes of a conciliatory policy, which would give it a chance to work permanently in the Party and help in the building of a socialist state.

It could not be affirmed on the basis of these facts that Stalin instigated the murder of Kirov. It is entirely probable, however, that the negligence of the Leningrad branch of the G.P.U. had the tacit sanction of the Boss. It is not necessary to believe that he gave explicit instructions to Yagoda, who was then head of the G.P.U. It is more likely that Yagoda complained to Stalin that Kirov's lenient policies were making it difficult for the G.P.U. to take strict measures against discontented Party elements in Leningrad. Kirov, Yagoda may have said, was making the efforts of the G.P.U. to guard him difficult. He had ordered the release of a number of suspects merely because there was no certain evidence against them. There was right now, for instance, a young man in the Leningrad Party apparatus, close to Kirov, who was known to be critical of the Party leaders and to advocate terrorism.

Stalin may have made the significant reply: "If Kirov insists, leave it at that. . . ."

Yagoda's own subsequent confession concerning his deeds as a poisoner and secret assassin while working under Stalin in the G.P.U. —perhaps the only true confession in all the Moscow trials—makes it certain that he would have understood the meaning of such a remark.

Something of that kind seems to me the probable explanation of the mysterious negligence of the Leningrad G.P.U. in protecting the hero of the conciliation policy and Stalin's only rival since Trotsky in the reach for Party leadership.[1]

Certain it is that Kirov's death marked the beginning of the end of the Communist Party. It was the heralding sign of the bloodiest counterrevolution in history.

What made this whole process unintelligible to foreign observers was that Stalin, in entering upon a policy of bloody repression *within the ruling regime*, did not overtly abandon the "policy of conciliation" *in the country at large*. On the contrary, he used that policy, or the semblance of it, as a cover for his systematic destruction of everybody, within the cadres of the Soviet state, who could oppose or question his totalitarian power. He had to have support somewhere, and he found it in the politically unconscious masses of the population. The situation is symbolized in the fact that by the time his new constitution—"the most democratic in the world"—was solemnly promulgated, the ablest of the men who had drafted it had been seized and imprisoned without process of law and were soon to be shot.

The good harvest and the improvement of the food situation facilitated this maneuver. Early in 1935 bread cards were withdrawn and bread was made available on the market. To strengthen further his position, Stalin gave the peasant on the *kolkhoz* the right to farm a patch of land for himself and own some livestock. The collective farmers were also permitted to sell their surpluses on the open market.

At the same time Stalin flooded the population with decorations, honors, and awards. Explorers as well as *Stakhanovites* were made

[1] Some readers will inevitably think that a personal "hatred" for Stalin dictates the foregoing opinion. I want therefore to point out that Boris Nikolaevsky, a socialist scholar of international reputation who has no personal reason whatever for an animus against Stalin, has arrived independently, after exhaustive study, at the same conclusion. Initiated readers will know that I am quoting one of the most erudite and dispassionate students of the revolutionary movement:

"The Party convention in February, 1934, decided that Kirov, as pointed out in a previous article, should become the principal party-political leader of the new course and that, in line with this decision, he was to move to Moscow from Leningrad and take charge of the chief political divisions of the Communist Party. This could not mean anything else than the beginning of Stalin's end. . . .

"The main danger that confronted Stalin in 1934 was the danger of losing control over the party machine. This danger was personified in Kirov. . . .

"The history of Kirov's assassination constitutes within its consequences one of the most significant pages of the history of Bolshevism, and, at the same time, one of the darkest and most puzzling. . . .

"One thing is certain: *the only man who profited by the Kirov assassination was Stalin.* (Walter Duranty declared that the beginning of Stalin's personal dictatorship came after the Kirov assassination.) There was no longer any possibility of limiting his power by means of legal and intra-party action. Stalin, thereupon, began to prepare the liquidation of all his intra-party opponents, *especially those who had favored reconciliation and agreement with the democracies. . . ." The New Leader,* August 23, 1941

"Heroes of the Republic." Officer titles and privileges were restored in the Red Army; marshals were created; Orders of the Red Star, of Lenin, of the Red Banner, of the Red Banner of Labor were generously bestowed on soldiers, sailors, workmen, and engineers. Titles of National Artist, Artist of Merit, and Scholar of Merit were distributed among the intelligentsia. Thus, while beginning the destruction of the Party, Stalin was assembling a host of new supporters who should be dependent on him for a suddenly acquired eminence in Soviet life.

In one of his speeches the dictator declared:

"Life has become better. Life has become more joyful, comrades."

Everyone took up the refrain. The press brimmed with eulogies of the new Soviet constitution in the making. It was to be the highest triumph of man's reason up to that date. It would guarantee freedom of press, speech, and assemblage, universal manhood and womanhood suffrage, the secret ballot, freedom from arrest and search without warrant. It would even guarantee the "right to work." It was described as "a monument to Stalin's wisdom" and compared to Beethoven's Ninth Symphony. Stalin, in an interview with Roy Howard, stated that, in the elections under the constitution, "lists of candidates will be presented not only by the Communist Party but also by social organizations of all sorts outside the Party."

The real significance, and real use, to Stalin, of this "democratic" constitution were shown at the first election held under it. Voters who had taken seriously the promises contained in it were surprised to find, when they entered the booth to cast a "secret ballot," that the name of only one candidate was printed on it, and there was no space in which to vote for anybody else. This one candidate was often endorsed not only by the Communist Party but also by various "social organizations," etc.; that is how Stalin's boast to Roy Howard was fulfilled. Moreover, since Stalin's purge in the ruling cadres began almost simultaneously with the election to the new "democratic parliament," many of the candidates originally designated on the ballots, and glorified to the "electorate" in press accounts and campaign speeches, were imprisoned by the G.P.U. on the very eve of the election and other names substituted on the ballot, so that the voters found themselves voting at the last moment for some totally unknown and unexpected person. Other candidates, though elected, were purged in the interval between the elections and the assembling of the parliament—for to mention "parliamentary immunity" in such a situation would be a crude joke—and thus the voters often found that the candidate they had elected, besides being the only one they could vote for, was not permitted to represent them after all.

Moreover, as the purge continued after the first session of the "Supreme Soviet" (the new parliament), it was discovered at its second session that almost a quarter of the members had been removed by the

254

G.P.U. in the interim. No trouble was taken to fill their places with a by-election: it would have seemed a waste of time.

Finally the parliament, at its first session, had elected a presidium to sit upon the platform and guide its deliberations, and at the second session even some of the members of this presidium had mysteriously disappeared. Their absence was not explained; it was merely announced by the chair that nominations were in order to "complete the presidium." In the general atmosphere of fright it was tacitly understood that sudden absences of this kind had better not be discussed. As to the personnel of the parliamentary residue, I believe it is the first and only time in history, not excluding the original achievements of Hitler in the same line, when as many as 15 per cent of the members of an "elected" parliament were high officials of the secret police—in this case district and departmental heads of the G.P.U.

Such was the manner in which the "voice of the people" expressed itself while Stalin was consolidating his totalitarian power. Americans should remember this when they read that "democratic elections" are being held in the countries "liberated" by the Soviet armies. There is no reason to suppose that the procedures differ essentially from those described above.

In the outside world, among liberal and sympathetic circles, the constitution was a huge success. It embellished the popular front policy and made plausible Stalin's gesture toward an alliance with the democracies against Hitler.

In the Party we realized that the constitution was used chiefly for show purposes. But we nevertheless hoped that its promulgation might bring an end of the terror that had followed Kirov's assassination. We did not ourselves then see clearly that the policy of conciliation, the whole pretended turn to "democratic" forms of government, had become in Stalin's hands a ruse by which he eliminated his rivals in the real government, which was the Communist Party, and entrenched his own dictatorship. In its six years this so-called "most democratic constitution" has been nothing but a cynical camouflage for the most perfected totalitarian tyranny in the world. It seems to me that foreign observers are still far from understanding this fact.

IN WRITING about these years in Russia, I have refrained from saying any more about Stalin's personality than seemed relevant to my story. Primarily my relations were with the regime and not the man. However, since 1941, when Hitler rejected Stalin's frantic attempts at appeasement and forced him into the camp of the democratic Allies, a sentimental disposition to excuse and even admire his brutal force of character has arisen in England and America. It is a mistake, and I think perhaps it may be useful if I say what manner of man he was to those who worked so long and hard under his leadership and received a largess of death sentences in reward.

I met Stalin many times and saw him during a period of thirteen years, not only as he is on dress parade before delegations or admiring audiences, but in his office at work. I happened also to be on close terms with his second wife's brother and sole confidant, Pavel Alliluyev. From Pavel I learned in casual conversations the story of his sister's bitter married life and of her sudden death in 1932—that crowning "mystery" which has given rise to the wildest rumors. I was also on friendly terms with several of Stalin's secretaries, and I shared a room for a long period of years with one of them. The man may be dead now, but I do not know his destiny and am compelled to withhold his name. We conversed intimately as an everyday matter of course about Stalin's ways and doings. I knew, for instance, days before the news was communicated to Party members that the decision had been made to exile Trotsky.

I mention these things, not with the idea that hearsay evidence even at first hand is a substitute for personal knowledge. I merely want to explain that my personal impressions of Stalin are supplemented by innumerable conversations with those people who stood in a close relation to him. Their conversations are hardly separated in my mind from my own experience, which they reinforce. I feel that I know the man pretty well, and I will not say anything here that I am not sure of.

I had my first glimpse of Stalin in 1922 at the Fourth Congress of the Communist International. He was then still a mortal. Indeed, he was not even considered an outstanding leader of the Communist movement or the Soviet Government. He was one of the secretaries of the Party's Central Committee, a technical post of secondary importance, which, to be sure, he was soon to transform into a focus of higher power than belonged to the autocratic czars. In those days, however, it occurred to none of us that a secretary of the Central Committee, even the senior of the three secretaries, who simultaneously occupied the second-rate government post of commissar of workers' and peasants' inspection, might become a leading political figure in the next two years and almost a deity in the subsequent decade. His relative unimportance seemed obvious to all those at the congress. While first-rank leaders like Trotsky, Bukharin, Zinoviev, Radek, Rakovsky, and half a dozen others would be surrounded by delegates from all corners of the globe the moment they stepped into the corridors, and their every word eagerly listened to, Stalin walked alone.

He was about to leave the imposing Hall of St. George, where the Congress was held, when I first saw him. As he approached the head of the stairway, wearing a military greatcoat over his semi-military tunic and boots, an obscure young clerk employed at the Comintern office stopped him and asked him a question. I was sitting on a near-by bench, smoking, idly watching the delegates go out. The Comintern clerk was undersized, and, as frequently is true of people of very short stature, he was inordinately active. Although Stalin himself is not above five feet six, the little clerk hardly came up to his shoulders. Stalin towered over him, nodding occasionally or dropping a word, listening impassively. The little fellow hopped around, tugging at Stalin's sleeve, lapel, or button, talking incessantly and with what would be to me an irritating ardor, as though burning up with more enthusiasm than he had room to contain. What held my attention and made me remember the scene was Stalin's amazing patience. He struck me as an ideal listener. He was on the verge of departing, had one foot on the edge of the stairs, yet he stood there for almost an hour, calm, unhurried, attentive, as though he had all the time in the world to give to this agitated little clerk. There was something monumental about his manner.

That first impression remained always in my memory, an impression of stability and patient force. Patience is a rare trait in men of action. It it not usually found in conjunction with "capriciousness," "disloyalty," "rudeness," and a dangerous thirst for power—the four traits with which Lenin, in his deathbed letter to the Party, his *Testament*, characterized Stalin. That rare combination is the principal key to his character.

In the flesh Stalin looks very different from the retouched photographs and chromos that convey his image to the world. He looks more coarse and common, and also smaller. His face is pockmarked and sallow. His jet-black hair has turned a darkish gray, and there are gray streaks in his bushy mustache and thick eyebrows. His eyes are dark brown with a tinge of hazel. His expression tells nothing of what he feels. There is to me a curious heaviness and sullenness about him. The man seems neither European nor Asiatic, but a cross between the two.

The semi-military costume in which I first saw him became his invariable dress, until it blossomed into the imposing uniform of a marshal. There may be several reasons for this. One, I think, is his power complex. Owing to physical defects—a withered arm and two toes grown together—he was found unfit for service in the Czar's Army. An element of overcompensation probably enters into his inclination to the soldier's uniform.

But the main reason for not changing his costume is probably more subtle. In the totalitarian system it is necessary to the stability of society that a prevailing mass of the people deify the leader. For this they need a constant image. Changelessness is one of the attributes of deity. Stalin is shrewd enough to sense this fact.

At public meetings Stalin never sits in the center, but always at the side or back. When he rises he waves away the applause as though it were an annoyance, although obviously he enjoys the tribute, and the life of a Russian orator who got more applause than he did would not be worth two cents. At state receptions, when playing the gracious host to *Stakhanovites*, Heroes of Labor, Arctic flyers, etc., he behaves with studied simplicity—an unassuming friend to all, especially the diffident provincials. When entertaining at his home with his phonograph, Stalin himself selects the records and places them on the disk. Although he never dances, he urges others to dance, overcoming their shyness in the presence of the leader. He even goes to the trouble of finding a likely partner for a young man.

At party sessions or business conferences Stalin usually listens quietly, smoking his pipe or a cigarette. While listening he is jotting aimless curlicues on the pad before him. Two of his personal secretaries, Poskrobyshev and Dvinsky, once stated in *Pravda* that on these occasions Stalin sometimes writes on his pad: "Lenin—teacher—friend." They asserted: "Often at the end of a working day we would carry away from his table sheets of paper covered with these words." It is not beyond Stalin to give his approval to this sort of publicity. But it is not necessary to believe that he is sentimental.

Stalin seldom traveled before the war except on vacation trips to the Caucasus. His trip to Leningrad at the time of the Kirov assassination was an epochal event. The triumphal processions indulged in by his czarist predecessors are foreign both to his nature and to his policy. He is a cautious person and he feels safer at home. He also knows that he does better by allowing distance to lend him an aura of mystery. With the exception of funeral processions, when he proceeds along a short route cleared hours in advance by G.P.U. troops, and when he appears on top of Lenin's mausoleum in Red Square on anniversary celebrations, Stalin, so far as I remember, has ventured to walk in the streets of Moscow only once. This short spontaneous walk, from the Bolshoi Theater to the Kremlin, created a sensation, and the following morning the Soviet press made a great display of the event.

Stalin is widely regarded as a "man of mystery." There are several not very mysterious reasons for this. One is that he cultivates the idea as a part of the technique of modern absolutism; he wears mystery as the czars wore purple. Moreover, he does keep his own counsel. Any man who sends to death, one after another, his closest friends has to keep his inner thoughts to himself.

But to us who worked under him, he did not seem mysterious; he seemed a man with a sense of inferiority which made him touchy, vindictive, and suspicious. He seemed a ruthless and unscrupulous man, concentrated on problems of personal power, and, partly for that reason, partly because of natural limitations, lacking in statesman-like vision. We knew him as a slow and plodding thinker, cautious and suspicious. Bela Kun, the inept leader of the abortive Bolshevik revolution in Hungary, said of him rather aptly: *"Il ne sait pas aller trop vite."* [1] Henri Barbusse, his servile French biographer, an assiduous collector of legends about him, said less aptly that Stalin is as cautious as a lion. Stalin himself remarked on one occasion: "Healthy suspicion is the best basis for collaboration." That is no mere aphorism with him. It is an expression of his temperament and a working rule of conduct. It has permeated the social relations of the entire Soviet Union; it has twisted the lives of 180,000,000 people.

Trotsky used to denounce Stalin as a "mediocrity," and from the standpoint of talent, taste, knowledge, or intellect, that is not untrue. But the fact remains that this "mediocrity" ousted Trotsky from his supreme position, banished him from Russia, sentenced him to death, and executed the sentence upon him in exile. In certain qualities he is far from mediocre: strength of will, patience, slyness, ability to perceive human frailties and play upon them with contempt, and the supreme gift of pursuing a chosen goal inflexibly and without scruple. With these talents Stalin is generously endowed. If he is a slow and cautious thinker, he is swift and ruthless once he begins to act.

Many outsiders have wondered why, in a political document like his *Testament,* Lenin should have mentioned, in warning us against Stalin, so superficial a quality as "rudeness"—almost a virtue, one might think, in a proletarian revolutionist. It is because they do not realize the heights to which Stalin, in his want of fellow feeling, can carry the art of being rude. His remark when he first read that same *Testament* of Lenin is a good example of it, which unfortunately I cannot quote in print.

Although Stalin is probably no less cultured than the average politician, he was an ignoramus by comparison with Lenin's other lieutenants. That was one source of his sense of inferiority. The top leaders of the Bolshevik Revolution were middle-class or aristocratic intellectuals, steeped in the culture not only of their own country, but of Europe as a whole. They spoke two or more foreign languages. Most of them were also trained to use their own language with literary skill, and many with artistry. Stalin was the exception among

[1] Freely: "He's a slow-goer."

them. He was the least distinguished of all—neither orator nor writer nor theoretician. He had never stayed long, as the others had, outside Russia. Even as a Russian his horizon was bounded by a provincial background.

He began to learn Russian at the age of nine and never fully mastered it. He uses it like a blunt and clumsy tool. Not only is the foreignness of his accent obtrusive, but his written style is stilted and dull. Notwithstanding his many years of prison and exile—the "university of revolutionists"—he never obtained a thorough grounding in literature and social science, as did the other Bolshevik leaders. Not even his dogged persistence could master the difficulties of German, which he tried hard to learn and gave up as a bad job. Nor did he fare better with Esperanto, to which he turned as a short cut, persuading himself that it was to be the language of the future International. This leader who has made the boast that there is no fortress a Bolshevik cannot capture has never crashed a single linguistic bunker. And the sense of that defeat haunts him. Knowing no foreign languages, he has never been able to gain a firsthand insight into the non-Russian world.

Stalin speaks in a slow monotone which is tiresome to the ear. At Politburo and Central Committee meetings during Lenin's lifetime, both before and after the Revolution, he used to sit apart, sulky and silent, unable to participate in the rapid fire of ideas and seeming to despise the whole thing as idle chatter.

The fact that a man with these qualities of mind and heart has risen to absolute power over one-sixth of the earth's surface, controlling the destinies of 180,000,000 people, and utilizing to what ends he will the knowledge and brains of others, should be a warning to all who tend to disregard cavalierly the spirit and the statutory safeguards of democracy.

Henri Barbusse's biography of Stalin, a contribution to legend rather than history, declares that, unlike Lloyd George, who had thirty-two secretaries, Stalin is assisted in his superhuman labors by only one, Poskrobyshev. Poskrobyshev is actually, or was in my day, Stalin's head personal secretary, and as such held the official post of chief of the Central Committee's Secret Department. Previously this post had been held in turn by Tovstukha and Bratanovsky. In addition Stalin had a dozen personal secretaries, each of whom did the Boss's research and his letter writing in a particular field: military and naval affairs, trade and industry, agriculture, finance, foreign affairs, international press and information, the Soviet apparatus, the Party apparatus, etc. Each such personal secretary had a couple of assistants and had at his disposal for all practical purposes the entire apparatus of the Commissariat that corresponded to his sphere of activity. His reports and opinions were usually far more decisive than those of a People's Commissar or minister of the formal government. Officially, however, these secretaries were entitled "Assistant to the Secretary of the Central Committee." As a group they were called the "Secret Department"—an amusing comment on the nature of one-man government.

Another department of Stalin's secretariat is his personal correspondence with the Soviet masses, which is enormous. My guess is that Stalin's correspondence with the common people is greater than that of any other ruler in history. A special secretary with a staff of assistants attends to this mail. Not a single letter remains unanswered, and many thousands of the answers bear Stalin's personal signature. Since he is omniscient and omnipotent, everybody appeals to him—collectivized peasants, students, school children, scientists, engineers, soldiers, industrial workers—asking his advice in practical matters and in matters of Marxist-Leninist theory, on political problems, scientific problems, literary questions, and ticklish personal enigmas; sending to him engineering and scientific projects, inventions, books, pictures, sculptures, pieces of handicraft, everything. Complaints against local Soviet and Party leaders, against farm and factory and office managers, form an important part of this correspondence. Another important section consists of personal greetings and expressions of good will, usually in the form of verse or in concrete gifts. Henri Barbusse insisted that Stalin personally reads every single letter! He would be God indeed if he did, but he does convey that impression to the masses.

Here are two examples as reported in *Pravda:* An old peasant woman from a collective farm, after thanking the leader for her happy life under his stewardship, begs him to accept her most precious possession, a cow, as a gift from her heart to her "beloved comrade." The reply from the Kremlin, bearing Stalin's signature in his own handwriting, thanks the old woman for her generous gift, explains that he cannot use the cow, and begs her to keep it in memory of Comrade Stalin. Another: A *Stakhanovite* pace-setter, decorated for his work in a factory, offers his medal, his most precious possession, to the leader, arguing that Stalin is more worthy of wearing it than he. The leader modestly replies: "Medals are not for those who are already famous anyway. They were designed principally for those worthy ones among the unknown who deserve to be rewarded with fame and honor."

Many of the personal secretaries of Stalin were acquaintances of mine. His chief secretary Poskrobyshev—a roly-poly, red-cheeked, baldish little man, whom I first met in 1923 during one of my vacations at Marino, taught me to play billiards. He grew in importance and pomposity during the fifteen years that I knew him. For many years the personal secretary in charge of Party cadres was the Old Bolshevik and old alcoholic Selitsky. Dvinsky had charge of watching the G.P.U. Grishin, once in charge of finance and foreign trade in the Secret Department, was later transferred to the Commissariat of Finance. Stassova, herself once a secretary of the Central Committee like Stalin, an

Old Bolshevik conspirator of the underground days, had charge of Comintern, Profintern, International Workers' Aid, and other international organizations. Radek had charge of international politics and press. He was assisted by Tivel, one-time head of the Indian Revolutionary Committee of the Comintern, later shot on the charge of attempting to assassinate Stalin. Litvinov, after his resignation in May, 1938, as foreign commissar was reported to have occupied Radek's post in the Secret Department for three years. These were some of the secretaries personally known to me.

Some of Stalin's secretaries subsequently rose to the highest positions in the hierarchy. Mekhlis, once in charge of the press, became editor of *Pravda* and later vice-commissar for defense. Yezhov, another personal secretary, rose to be head of the G.P.U. and disappeared at the height of his power.

Stalin's favorite among the secretaries was a very young brown-haired lad named Kanner, who came to him almost as a child. Stalin despised his own eldest son, but he loved Kanner—or at least cherished him—like a son. He made Kanner his secretary for industry while the young man was still finishing his schooling. After more than ten years of devoted confidential service, Kanner asked permission to resign and study engineering. News of that created a minor sensation. Stalin refused to let him go. This happened two or three times to my knowledge. Then came a bigger sensation—Stalin yielded, and Kanner matriculated at the Industrial Academy. An altogether extraordinary act of grace! And, moreover, Kanner kept his warm place in the Boss's heart all through his engineering course. When he graduated, still relatively young, he was given one of the highest posts in the Commissariat of Heavy Industry—a position comparable to that of president of the Bethlehem Steel Co. He seemed to be almost a kind of crown prince in the new totalitarian aristocracy. His abilities were genuine, too, and his brilliant future seemed assured. Kanner was denounced in the purge as an "enemy of the people" and disappeared. My guess is that the young man's only crime was to argue sharply with Stalin in defense of the heads of the trusts under him against fantastic accusations.

Stalin has been married three times. He has three children, two sons and a daughter. His first wife was a simple Georgian woman who died in 1907. His son Yasha (Jacob) by that marriage detests his father, and the feeling seems to be reciprocated. I have heard Stalin refer to him, in the presence of his secretaries, as "my fool." When Stalin married for the second time, he took Yasha to live with him at the Kremlin, and there Yasha led a miserable life. Stalin beat him as he himself had been beaten by his father, a shoemaker who was often drunk. (According to Emil Ludwig's not too brilliant theory, this experience was the decisive factor in making a revolutionist of Stalin.) Yasha, who is not very bright and has no special talents, attended engineering school. When he grew up he drifted about Russia on orders from his father to stay out of Moscow. For some years nothing was heard of him, but early in the German-Soviet war the newspapers announced that a son of Stalin, a junior artillery officer in the Red Army, had been taken prisoner by the Nazis.

In 1917 Stalin met the sixteen-year-old girl who was to become his second wife. Nadia Alliluyeva was a lovely girl with large black eyes like her Georgian mother's. Her father was an Old Bolshevik worker who harbored Lenin when he was in hiding. In 1918 she joined the Communist Party. Soon after that, Nadia became one of Lenin's junior secretaries. A year later, when she was eighteen, she was sent in line of duty to the Tzaritsyn front, where Stalin was political commissar. The forty-year-old veteran fell in love with the young beauty, and they became husband and wife. Of this marriage Stalin had two children, a son Vassily and a daughter Svetlana, his favorite.

Vassily is now a colonel in the Red Air Force, many times decorated and holder of the title "Hero of the Soviet Union." He is married and has two children. This last fact never appeared in print to my knowledge, and reporters have not been permitted to cable it abroad. Stalin perhaps does not like to be known as a grandfather.

Beginning in a haze of ardent romance at the front, life for Nadia soon turned into a dismal existence, and with Stalin's rise to dictatorship it became actually painful. As I have said, I knew well Nadia's brother, a simple and splendid fellow and a very able executive. He was working in the Commissariat of Foreign Trade at the same time I was. Whenever his sister's name was mentioned, his face would become overcast. He was painfully reserved about her life, but from him I learned how unhappy she was. An intelligent and sensitive woman, serious and reserved, she was surrounded by sycophants and flatterers, and she despised them. Even after having two children, she attended for three years an industrial engineering school, preparing herself for an independent career as an industrial executive. This gave her a life and an interest of her own.

The growing brutality of Stalin's regime and his attitude toward his old fighting comrades weighed heavily upon her. Herself an active militant in the Party, she was also deeply hurt by Stalin's contemptuous treatment of her. Accompanied by Voroshilov, he would disappear for days at a time into one of his country estates, spending his time in more congenial company provided for him by his servile G.P.U. chieftain, Henry Yagoda. On several occasions Nadia happened upon her husband in these festivities, and there were ugly scenes during which the Dictator treated her rudely.

I saw her with her brother during the celebration of the Fifteenth Anniversary of the Revolution in November, 1932. In three weeks she was to receive her diploma as a chemical engineer. She looked pale and worn, little interested in the proceedings around her. I could see that her brother was deeply concerned.

Two days later, on November 9, 1932, Nadia Alliluyeva's sudden death was announced. The cause was never officially divulged. There was a rumor that she had been killed. The rumor gained some credence, especially among those who had in mind a certain precedent: Budyenny shot his old wife in the back during a quarrel and later married a young actress. Budyenny's prestige as a military hero was so great that the whole affair was hushed up and he could go unpunished for that and later become one of the five marshals of the Soviet Union. If Budyenny's prestige is great, Stalin's is infinitely greater—that is the way the rumor spread. But I know from the lips of her own brother the true story of Nadia Alliluyeva's death. That evening at Voroshilov's villa neighboring Stalin's, she made some critical remarks about the peasant policy, which doomed the villages to famine. In answer, Stalin insulted her before his friends in the obscene manner which Russians call *matershchina*. Nadia returned home and shot herself through the head. The official communiqué in the press said only that she had died a "sudden and premature death."

Soon after Nadia's death we learned that Stalin had married a sister of Kaganovich. Up to now, however, not a word has been published in the Soviet press about this marriage.

The incident which most strikingly proves how unerring was Lenin's aim when he called Stalin disloyal is the murder of Yenukidze. If Kanner was like a son to him, Yenukidze was over longer years a brother. At the very beginning of his revolutionary career, when young Djugashvili (Stalin) was known as Koba, Yenukidze had been his teacher of Marxism and of its application to Russian problems. That was some forty-five years ago. From then on they were the closest of comrades and friends. They plotted and worked together for the overthrow of czarism; they dwelt together in prison and exile; they rose together to pre-eminence in the councils of the Communist Party and the Soviet Government they had helped to found. If Kalinin's office as chairman of the Central Executive Committee of the Soviets is roughly equivalent to that of president of the republic, Yenukidze's as its secretary was equivalent to that of vice-president, and as Stalin's closest friend his unofficial power was almost limitless.

As often happens in friendships among men, Yenukidze and Stalin differed diametrically from each other in character. Where Stalin is callous and brutally rude, Yenukidze was the very soul of kindness and sensitiveness toward the needs and feelings of others. He remained after his rise the same simple friend and comrade he had always been—human, responsive, sympathetic. He often overstepped the rigid Bolshevik doctrine that there can be no division between personal and political friendships. He would visit old friends and come to their rescue when in need, even though they were in the opposite camp. Everyone knew this, Stalin best of all. He also knew, as everyone did, that Yenukidze, who had been an unflinching Bolshevik every day and moment of their life together of forty-five years, could not be party to any anti-Soviet action, no matter how much he might help personally the companions of prerevolutionary days who went into opposition.

I know one such family who owed much to the generosity of Yenukidze. Together with the father of that family—Kalistrat Gogua, a Menshevik—Yenukidze and Stalin had founded the Tiflis branch of the Social Democratic Party in 1900. The three of them had been arrested and imprisoned together. They had also loved the same girl. The Menshevik had won out. He married the girl, and they had a daughter. Although the father was ostracized for his Menshevik conviction, Yenukidze could not forget old friends. He arranged to have the wife and daughter live in Moscow. He gave employment to the daughter, Irina, at the International Book Company, where I worked.

I met Irina Gogua there in 1925. She was twenty-three years old. We became friends and saw a good deal of each other until 1935. Since her father was in exile, I never met him. But I knew her mother, with whom she lived in Moscow on Mashkov Lane. I knew their circle of friends who lived in the same apartment house, the chief of whom were Gorky's wife, Ekaterina Pavlovna Pyeshkova, and Gorky's publisher, Ladyzhnikov. These people had been close sympathizers of the Bolshevik movement prior to the Revolution, but shrank back from bolshevism in power. My friendship with Irina had its inception in hot discussions over that issue, but despite our political quarrels the Goguas and their friends liked me and welcomed me to their home.

It was in this family that one evening in 1925 I ran into Abel Yenukidze. He was received affectionately, as an old friend of the family. It was evident from their conversation that this was one of his periodic visits, and that he was solicitous about their welfare. Indeed, Irina confirmed this impression after his departure. The family, like very many others of the kind, owed its very existence under the Soviet regime to the generosity and humanity of Abel Yenukidze. Only one thing Abel could not accomplish—he could not bring back from exile the father, the man who had been a successful rival of Stalin in love. That man was never permitted to live again with his wife and daughter.

When I returned from abroad in 1932, Irina was married and had been transferred from the International Book Company to the office of the Central Executive Committee under Yenukidze. Being directly under the wing of the vice-president of the Soviet Republic, she was in the safest possible situation. But in 1935, in the panic and terror that followed the Kirov assassination, the impossible happened. Stalin removed Abel, his closest and oldest friend, from office and appointed him to an obscure post in the Caucasus. One day toward the end of that year a packet was brought to me. It was in a large envelope bearing the return address of the Central Executive Committee. I opened it with curiosity. There was no line of writing in it, only a bundle

265

of old photographs. They were snapshots of me, alone or with Irina and her friends, taken at various times during the last ten years. My heart sank, for to me this was an unmistakable signal. It meant that Irina was expecting arrest and a search of her premises by the G.P.U. She was protecting me from incrimination.

As the news of Yenukidze's disgrace had not yet been made public, this was utterly incomprehensible to me. I was in bed with influenza at the time, and worry over Irina enhanced my feverish condition. I telephoned her home time and again, but there was no answer. Finally the news was published of Yenukidze's disgrace. It was accompanied with scurrilous attacks upon the man whose decrees on behalf of the government the same papers had been printing practically from the inception of the Soviet Republic until two weeks before. The following day I ran into a woman friend of Irina's and learned of Irina's arrest and exile to a place unknown. I will probably never know more.

Abel Yenukidze was shot as a traitor in 1936. The friendship of Yenukidze and Stalin had become a legend in the Party. Those who knew of the lifelong association between the men said that Cain had slain his brother Abel.

That Stalin is vindictive to an extreme degree is too obvious to need remark. He himself once confided to Kamenev that his highest idea of pleasure was to plot a sweet revenge upon an enemy, spring it successfully, and then go home and peacefully sleep. His purges have proven the truth of this. He has probably enjoyed a wholesale revenge upon all who ever uttered a slighting word to him, or, except in strictest privacy, about him. His personal enemies, so far as he could identify them, are all dead. But to us who lived through these years of death, vengeance upon enemies does not adequately describe them. It is my opinion that Stalin finds a perverse pleasure in sending his own friends to death.

Archbishop Michael Curley, of Baltimore, remarked in 1941 that Stalin has sent more human beings to death, to report the statement mildly, "than any other man the world has ever known." To get the full measure of the man, it is necessary to add that in a keynote speech at a Congress of the Party, held in the midst of the purges, Stalin blandly declared: "Of all the treasures a state can possess, the human lives of its citizens are for us the most precious."

35. *The One Precious Life*

MANY THINK that Stalin's own life is one of Spartan simplicity and self-consuming devotion to the cause of the suffering Russian people. That Spartan simplicity is a skillfully kept-up appearance. Until the end of the twenties, Stalin did live modestly, like other Bolshevik leaders. He occupied a two-room apartment in the Kremlin. He now lives like an oriental potentate and, while tossing hundreds of thousands to their death with a careless hand, strives to preserve and prolong his own life with a fabulous expenditure of the money and time and labor of others.

Stalin, when I knew him, was paid as secretary general of the Party about 1,000 rubles a month—which amounts to $190 or, in actual purchasing power, about $40. By such reckoning a W.P.A. employee in the United States, or even a family on relief, received more than the dictator of one-sixth of the earth. One of his dozen secretaries accepted this salary for his master and disposed of it. On the first of each month the superintendent of the Kremlin sent a small bill to Stalin's secretary for the rent of his apartment. A similarly modest bill was sent for his board. When the Boss left for a vacation in the Caucasus, his secretary would send to the Health Department the customary payment for a stay in a house of rest. The secretary sent 3 per cent of his salary each month to the Party treasury as membership dues. As a member of the government, Stalin had a pass entitling him to travel free on any train. He owned no automobile or conveyance of any kind. He owned next to nothing. He had no bank account and no savings deposit. He carried no checkbook or pocketbook. Like the Mikado or the Dalai Lama, Stalin's hands never touched money. But that does not mean that he lived thriftily; it means only that he was free from any accounting for what his absolutely unlimited whims might cost.

As the leader of a "workers' state" with a very low standard of living, he is obliged to hide this fact. He is obliged to keep up the camouflage of "simplicity." For that reason you will never find in the Soviet press a description or photos of his family and home, as you do in the American press of American statesmen.

Even in absolute monarchies, civil lists of the royal expenses are published. The people at least know how much the king is costing them. But no information as to how Stalin spends the wealth of the Soviets has ever appeared in the press. The Russian people, who ultimately pay for it all, have absolutely no control or even knowledge of these expenditures or their amount. His various residences are "rest houses" —the property of the State Rest Administration. The roads built for his convenience are paid for by state disbursements for improvement of communications. The cars he rides in come from the state garages. Everything he does or uses is incorporated in the state budget as overall expenditure in the public interest. That is what gives point to a remark sometimes spoken in a whisper by people in Moscow when they read Stalin's declarations that he has built "socialism in one country": "Stalin is right—not only in one country, but for one man."

A central government garage full of dozens of Rolls-Royces, Packards, Cadillacs, and Lincolns, with chauffeurs on duty day and night, is at his disposal. When he travels he rides in a special train preceded and followed by other trains. Guards are stationed at regular intervals along the route. Instead of a suite in a sanatorium, four palatial residences along the Black Sea are reserved for his exclusive use and maintained all the year round with a complete staff of servitors. The one at Sochi, listed officially as "Government Summer House No. 7," which I visited in 1935, is the oldest and least pretentious of them. In appearance and appointments it does not exceed the residence of a prosperous American businessman in Florida or California. It stands on top of a hill near the famous Matzest sulphur springs, from which water is conducted to a special bathhouse belonging to the villa. The whole hilltop is organized into a park and protected by a special detachment of G.P.U. troops. Dwelling houses for them, and for the servants, abut on the driveway just inside the gates. Next, as you ascend the hill, comes the garage, with room for twenty-five or thirty cars. Higher up and nearer the home of Stalin are three villas for the Dictator's guests, equipped with tennis courts, squash courts, a special house for billiards, etc. In the few sunny days I passed in one of these houses in November, 1935, my fellow guests were Ivanov, People's Commissar for Agriculture—shot after the Third Moscow Trial in 1938; Ghikalo, secretary of the Central Committee of White Russia—afterward purged as an "enemy of the people"; Zakhar Byelenky, vice-president of the Commission of Soviet Control—disappeared during the purges; Nestor Lakoba, president of the government of Abkhasia, and his brother. One of the brothers was shot in the purge and the other died at about the same time.

Another of Stalin's villas, in Abkhasia, high up on the mountain near the road to Gagry, was built, I suspect, in imitation of Hitler's "Eagle Aerie" at Berchtesgaden. Stalin was not pleased with it, and recently, at Zelyony Myss on the Black Sea, he carved out a vast park area with a tremendous sea front, permanently closed it to the public, and there built another home. This estate with its landscaped parks and preserves is kept a careful secret from the Russian people. I cannot quote figures on the exact cost of landscaping, building, and the like, but from the expanse of the grounds I doubt if Hearst's San Simeon is much more costly than the palace of Zelyony Myss. Stalin has a fourth small vacation home on the shore of the Crimea.

All these residences, I was told, were completely equipped, like the one I saw in Sochi, for the most exacting tastes in recreation. They contained everything from billiard room to motion-picture halls and stables of thoroughbred horses. Stalin's special delight is automatic musical devices. He has a full assortment of pianolas, phonographs, and radios and loves to spend an evening exhibiting his treasures to his guests. The Commissariat of Foreign Trade had a standing order to its representatives abroad to pick up the latest models for use in the Dictator's various homes. I remember the trouble I had in 1931, while working in our trade delegation in Italy, filling an order for records of different Italian singers.

Stalin's chief outdoor amusements are hunting and sea bathing. He used to bathe in the Black Sea after the beach had been cleared for fully a mile around. He also indulged in an occasional game of *gorodki*, an ancient Russian game somewhat similar to skittles, in which he was joined by Voroshilov and other intimates. He seldom loses a game. More active sports are barred to him because of his withered left arm.

The homes provided for Stalin near Moscow are less sumptuous. Years ago he lived in a modest country place at Gorky, a house once occupied by Lenin, having evicted Lenin's widow in order to move in himself. Now, however, Gorky has been converted into an historical shrine, and Stalin has built himself two other country estates, his favorite being at Borvikhi. These residences are surrounded by the villas of his satellites.

Foreign visitors sometimes express surprise at the strides made in Moscow in the matter of civic improvement. They know nothing about the historic monuments, such as the Sukharevka Tower, destroyed, with no good reason, in this process. It never occurs to them to ask whether, from the point of view of progress, it wouldn't be better to tear down Moscow's pestilential slums and replace them by workers' dwellings worthy of a civilized country.

They also do not notice that these improvements opened up first of all certain arteries for fast motor traffic and made it easy for the police to guard them. The avenues in question are those which lead from the center of the city to the Mojaisk road, the Vosdvizhenka, and the Ar- bat—those, in short, which Stalin's car takes when he goes to his Borvikhi house from the Kremlin. Twelve model motor roads radiate from Moscow to a distance of twenty-five miles in twelve different directions—and they are the only really good roads in the whole of Russia! They serve those outlying suburbs in which the villas of the government officials are situated. The villas passed, one finds oneself again on the old czarist roads, which are not engineering feats of which a Russian can be proud.

By a decree of the Moscow Soviet, a zone of wooded country and river land has been set apart at Borvikhi in which both building and bathing is strictly forbidden—the ostensible reason being that the waters that flow through Moscow must not be polluted. Hundreds of people who happened to live in villages in this zone were cleared out. Citizens are not even allowed to walk there. Why, I wondered, this wealth of precautions at Borvikhi particularly, while both above and below that point, people are allowed to bathe and sleep on the river bank? On inquiry I learned that the whole district is reserved for the villas of the officials of the Central Committee and of the G.P.U., which surround, at a respectful distance, the Dictator's home.

I had occasion to visit a friend of mine in one of those villas. Our car entered an area which looked like an immense estate, perfectly kept and still more perfectly watched. At every crossroads policemen in white gloves and impeccable uniforms examined our passes. Even my friend was forbidden to enter the most private zone of all. The roads were immaculately clean—and quite empty. From time to time we passed a luxurious car. The landscape looked as though it had been carefully ventilated, swept, and trimmed to perfection. My friend's villa would have stood comparison with any of the rich houses which dot the neighborhood of Western capitals. It had been most carefully designed and was equipped with terraces, verandas, tennis courts, lawns, and a private park. True, it did not "belong" to my friend, but was known as Villa No. X of the Central Executive Committee. The happy tenant, however, could enjoy it until the end of his days— or until he should fall into disgrace, an eventuality which would certainly hasten that end—just as fully as though it were his own.

The fabulous manner in which a man grown accustomed to absolute power spends the funds of the state on his own impulses, concealing them behind the loudly proclaimed interests of the people, is well illustrated in the grandiose story of the Institute of Experimental Medicine. Even the Rockefellers or the monarchs of former times would not be able to organize the scientific resources of a great country in their personal interests. And yet in a sense that is what Stalin has done.

Stalin was approaching his sixtieth year, a time when cautious men become seriously solicitous about their health. His friend Gorky was still older, and still more solicitous about his health. Accordingly, one day *Pravda* published an article by Gorky raising the question how to keep men from getting old and dying so soon. In conclusion he proposed the creation in Moscow of an Institute of Experimental Medicine, the principal object of which should be to conduct research into the preservation and prolongation of human life. Gorky pointed out that such an enterprise would be unique in its kind, that only in the Soviet Union was there enough regard for human life and enough money for such an institute.

Gorky's proposal was followed up with a series of enthusiastic articles by scientists and physicians. Several hundred million rubles were appropriated by the government. A huge tract of land near Serebryanny Bor, one of the choicest suburban spots in the Moscow region, was set aside for the institute's grounds. Construction work on laboratories, clinics, libraries, living quarters for a tremendous personnel, etc., began and proceeded at unprecedented speed. Moscow buzzed with the epoch-making news. To those in the know, it was clear from the very urgency with which the institute was being pushed to completion that its object, the prolongation and preservation of human life, was of primary interest to the leader himself. It was not a mere accident that at the head of this institute were placed Stalin's personal physicians, Professors Preobrazhensky and Speransky. The famous Ukrainian scientist, Professor Bogomolets, was also invited to take part in the work of the institute.

Then something else happened. The newspapers suddenly announced that the Academy of Sciences, a gigantic institute with scores of buildings and an annual budget of hundreds of millions, which had been in St. Petersburg for two hundred years and had remained in Petrograd and Leningrad for twenty years of the Soviet regime, was to be moved as a body to Moscow. The reason given, that the academy ought to be in the capital, seemed valid. But why had not that idea occurred to anyone during the preceding twenty years? And why was a prodigious sum of money to be spent on this gigantic transfer of institutions, and construction of duplicate buildings, at a time when funds and building materials were so badly needed by Soviet industry, by the Army, by housing projects in overcrowded Moscow, by a thousand and one more urgent undertakings? It was because the leading authorities in experimental medicine, physiology, biology, endocrinology, etc., who worked at the institutes of the Academy of Sciences in Leningrad, were needed for the new institute. Some innocent people protested, but they were soon discreetly silenced. Since the specialists in the field of medicine could not very well be removed from their laboratories in the academy, the entire academy, with all its departments, libraries, institutes, museums, even including the huge paleontological specimens, had to be brought to Moscow at a tremendous cost. And here further millions had to be spent in the erection of new structures occupying several blocks on the Moskva River. Unfortunately the duties of Professor Bogomolets, as president of the Ukrainian Academy of Sciences, required his presence in Kiev, the capital of the Ukraine. You cannot find any good reason to move a Ukrainian academy to a Russian capital. But this problem, too, was quickly solved. A branch of the Moscow Experimental Institute, in fact, in its size a new institute, was built for him and his staff in Kiev. The atmosphere in which this undertaking was carried out is suggested in the greetings to Stalin published in the press at the time. For example: "May you live a thousand years!"—originally offered by the Central Committee of the Turkmen Communist Party and published in *Pravda*. And this from Papanin, the famous North Pole explorer: "You are immortal, our beloved Leader! May you live three times as long as you have lived!" This motif of the dictator's longevity was repeated in subsequent years in both poems and public addresses.

Today from the Institute of Experimental Medicine, staffed by the best scientists in Russia and managed by Stalin's personal physicians, come prescriptions for the Dictator's daily regime, his dietic and exercise program—everything that may help to preserve his health and prolong his life. And while these well-paid experimenters work feverishly for a clue to the riddle of longevity, Stalin waits patiently. He has conquered Russia and is the sole ruler of 180,000,000 people. Does he hope to conquer death itself?

So far the most important result of the research subsidized by the Institute of Experimental Medicine is the discovery by the above-mentioned great scientist Bogomolets of the famous A.C.S.—a rejuvenating serum.

Dr. Martin Gumpert, a noted American physician, tells rather enthusiastically in a recent book[1] the story of Dr. Bogomolets's discovery. He says that, when the Nazis occupied the Ukraine, Bogomolets and the members of his Kiev Institute, described by Dr. Gumpert as "one of the most modern and most elaborate in Soviet Russia," were evacuated to Ufa in the Urals and continued their work without cessation during the tragic years of war. Dr. Gumpert writes:

When the miracles of the A.C.S. and the experiences of hundreds of Russian physicians are confirmed . . . Dr. Bogomolets will join the ranks of those few heroic figures who have moulded the fate of mankind for the better. Trustworthy reporters have stated that Joseph Stalin and Kalinin, the aged president of the Soviet Union, are among the people who have benefited from the Bogomolets serum. If science at this critical stage of history could protect and prolong the life of our worthy and experienced leaders, we might well be at the start of a new era. . . .

Dr. Gumpert adds:

On January 5, 1944, Professor Bogomolets . . . won the rank of of Hero of Socialist Labor; he was also decorated with the Order of Lenin and the Hammer and Sickle Gold Medal. . . . His book, *The Prolongation of Life,* has been read by millions of Soviet citizens and probably plays an important part in the defiant optimism which leads the suffering Russian masses to victory. . . .

The hospitals and maternity homes of the U.S.S.R. are still short of drugs, antiseptics, medicated gauze, and the most rudimentary necessities for the care of the sick and the dressing of wounds. Whole regions

[1] *You Are Younger Than You Think,* New York, Duell, Sloan & Pearce, 1944.

devastated by war lack hospitals and elementary medical help; those infested by malaria are deprived of quinine. To provide elementary medicines, hygienic surroundings, and adequate diet for the people, to stop shooting them, and to release twelve million from concentration camps, would be the simplest method of prolonging human life in Russia. But there is not a man or woman in the country who would dare to make that obvious comment on the story I have told.

36. A Diplomat's Paradise

IN OCTOBER, 1935, when my resignation from Auto-Moto-Export was finally accepted, I went on vacation to the Caucasus, staying at Sochi in the new rest house built for the senior officers of the Red Army by Voroshilov. A foreign trade official named Vlassov, who took my place as president of the trust, was called up for negligence within a very few weeks. He had allowed a number of parachutes required by Turkey for her national holiday celebration to be dispatched via Germany—where they disappeared en route. Stalin, informed of what had happened, had Vlassov put on the mat while a new consignment of parachutes was sent to Ankara by airplane over the Black Sea. Vlassov received a "severe reprimand."

The officers' rest house where I stayed is a group of eight magnificently luxurious five-story buildings, each with a complete plate-glass façade toward the sea. The opulence and comfort of the several buildings is graded according to the rank of those assigned to them. The highest generals have a whole building to themselves, an up-to-date manorial mansion, a model of technical ingenuity designed to provide the best possible advantages of light, sun, air, and quiet, with terraces which can be adjusted to admit or keep out the sunlight by a system of movable partitions. A specially constructed funicular railway takes the guests down to a private beach in such a way that they are spared the slightest fatigue.

This magnificent building was constructed at the cost of dozens of millions of rubles on a high bare rock. It is significant that Voroshilov at that time gave strict orders that the public should not be allowed to look inside the buildings or enter the grounds. I was rather embarrassed by an unexpected visit from my former client, Captain Enver Bey, the Turkish military attaché at Moscow, accompanied by a newspaperman. It was impossible to refuse access to a foreign guest, but the director did not conceal from me that he was having the jitters about what might happen to him as a result of this act of disobedience.

The rest house had just been completed when I came there in 1935. Readers who are made envious by my account of the luxury in which the Red Army generals and colonels rested may comfort themselves with the knowledge that fully 90 per cent of those who stayed there in the next three years were either shot or disappeared in the purge.

On my return to Moscow I asked again to be sent to the Aviation Academy, and my friends in the General Staff supported me. But Stalin, who decides everything for Soviet executives, said no. "He's had enough education," were his words as reported to me by the head of the Foreign Service Bureau. Litvinov, hearing that I had left the Commissariat of Foreign Trade, asked that I be attached to the Foreign Office. I was appointed first secretary of our legation at Athens and left in December of that year for Greece.

I broke the journey at Sofia, stopping to see my friend Raskolnikov, our minister to Bulgaria. I found him looking still young, living well, and in good spirits. He was doing useful and astute work in Bulgaria and was enlisting Slav sentiment in the Balkans on the side of Russia. During his hours of leisure he was also writing a novel—for this former commander of Red flotillas on the Volga and the Caspian was a fine dramatic author. His *Robespierre* had been produced with success in a Moscow theater.

Raskolnikov and his wife and I, as we walked together in the garden of the legation, little imagined that our lot would soon be comparable to that of the followers of Robespierre, the last Jacobins—proscribed and compelled to flee from the guillotine. The conqueror of Kazan and northern Persia, when recalled in 1938, refused to return to Russia and went into hiding. In July, 1939, after more than a year in hiding, he sent me for publication, from somewhere on the French Riviera, an open letter denouncing Stalin's dictatorship, an eloquent and able letter. He died in delirium a few weeks after its publication—in the opinion of friends, poisoned. I had, during my visit, the pleasure of telling him that the fame of his military operations at Enzeli in 1920 had influenced my life by turning my thoughts toward the East.

My train stopped for a few minutes in a very shabby little station. There was nothing to be seen but a newsstand and some posters on the wall. But my eyes caught a magic name—Thebes! I had left Sofia under snow, but here it was warm and bright with sun.

Our minister, Kobetsky, met me at the station at Athens, and we drove to our legation. It seemed placid and restful after the noise and bustle and tense routine of Moscow.

Greece was then going through a period of sudden changes. Within a few years several regimes had come and gone. A year before I arrived, General Kondylis, a forceful soldier, the son of peasants and a former friend of Venizelos, had made himself dictator. Against him his old friends organized the Venizelist insurrection of March, 1935, which he put down. The country, at that time, was almost equally divided between the Monarchists, under Tsaldaris, and the Republicans, who still stood by Venizelos and Sofoulis.

In November, 1935, Kondylis, thinking that he controlled the situation, proclaimed the restoration of the monarchy and recalled the exiled king, George II, from London. The king, brought up in the English liberal school, and an abler politician than Kondylis, saw that the best chance of stabilizing his throne lay in a general pacification. He insisted on granting an amnesty to the Venizelists, re-establishing political liberty, holding democratic elections, and coming to an agreement with the Republicans—in other words, putting an end to the dictatorship of Kondylis. The latter tried to frighten him by threatening to resign. The king very coldly accepted the general's resignation and conferred the presidency of the council on a prudent old lawyer, Professor Demerdzis.

Demerdzis proclaimed the restoration of democratic liberties. The exiles returned from the islands; the Communist Party came into the open, and its daily paper, *Rizospastis,* reappeared. Kondylis died suddenly—perhaps of a broken heart. Venizelos, tired of public life, remained in self-imposed exile in Paris, where he, too, died the next year. Tsaldaris and Demerdzis were soon also cut off by death. In the course of a single year Greece lost its three most representative statesmen. In the empty space they left, the shadow of Metaxas, the future dictator, slowly emerged.

At the moment of my arrival in Athens, in the last days of 1935, the newly restored monarchy seemed anything but solid. Kobetsky and I went to the palace to offer the king our New Year's greetings. The building gave the impression of being not yet really inhabited. A master of ceremonies, Count Merkatis, introduced the members of the diplomatic corps. The king shook our hands and spoke a few words to each. Very English in his appearance and manners, he impressed me as a man of calm and solid character. He was clean-shaven, with well-chiseled features, and wore a monocle. In less than a year I was to see him establish the monarchy, which then seemed so precarious, on a much firmer basis. Little by little he turned a royalist dream into a reality. The palace was freshly furnished, royal equipages drove again through the streets, a mounted guard dressed in the national costume reappeared, a number of impressive reviews were held, a court took form, the crowds were inducted into the habit of cheering the king in the streets. In short, the king did his job seriously and effectively.

I followed with interest the work of the first parliament in the new monarchy. The Tsaldarist and the Venizelist members were in about equal strength, and the Communists, with fifteen seats, held the balance of power. They were in a position to swing a close decision whichever way they liked. Here as elsewhere they had abandoned the class war and gone in for the Popular Front. Their votes determined the election of a Venizelist leader to the presidency of the chamber.

The king, following the rules of constitutional procedure, invited this leader, M. Sofoulis, to form a government drawn from the two chief parties. But after a month's effort Sofoulis was still unable to bring them together. There were too many die-hards, and the memory of past battles was too fresh.

Discussions dragged out until the very existence of parliamentary government was jeopardized. In the huge hall of the ancient palace, where sat the parliament, the best orators of all parties, Sofoulis, Kafandaris and Papanastasiou, poured out their brilliant eloquence. Leaning with his elbows on the government bench, Metaxas, who had been made acting premier on the death of Demerdzis, listened with obvious irritation and boredom to the accusations and counteraccusations of the various speakers. The members of the diplomatic corps, who had been present at the solemn opening, soon tired of the debates. I was almost always alone in the diplomats' box, where I sat day after day accustoming my ears to the new musical language and grasping with difficulty the fine points of the deputies' oratory.

On August 4, 1936, the king, persuaded by Metaxas, who made the most of labor troubles of a deadlock between the two major parties and of the growing influence of the Communists, suspended the constitutional regime. Metaxas, with the king's consent, proclaimed himself dictator.

Although, besides my diplomatic work, I supervised our trade delegation and negotiated its commercial agreements with the Greek Government, I had less work to do here than I was accustomed to in Moscow. We missed an excellent opportunity to exchange Soviet wheat for Corinth raisins, offered on exceptional terms, because of a strict rule of our Foreign Trade Commissariat forbidding barter. Moscow categorically refused to sanction the transaction, and so, thanks to bureaucratic rigidity, a good bargain was lost. By this time I was beyond feeling surprise at anything like that.

I regarded my diplomatic appointment as an escape and was pleased to find it unexpectedly agreeable. Kobetsky was a charming man who hated complications, sociable and loquacious, and was able to appreciate comfort and the beauties of the Hellenic scene. We made a number of excursions together by car, never tiring of the landscape, the ruins, and the blue heavenly sea. Our diplomatic labors left us plenty of time to savor these delightful trips.

Another thing that made my job unusually pleasant for a diplomat was that Kobetsky turned over to me the whole business of "cultural relations" between Greece and the Soviet Union. This included all contacts between the legation and the Greek intelligentsia. It brought me into the world of Athenian literature, scholarship, painting, sculpture, architecture, the theater—all the things I had so loved in Moscow during my young days at the War College and again in Italy and France. I found the Greeks affable, friendly, and hospitable. Very soon the doors of many of the most cultured Athenian homes were open to me. And I was proud when toward the end of the year other members of the diplomatic corps expressed their surprise in seeing, at our receptions, not the usually stodgy assemblage of dignitaries, but three or four hundred of the liveliest and most interesting people in Athens.

Better than all this, my duties in the matter of cultural relations brought me an encounter which was to be of the highest importance in my life.

Two weeks after my arrival from Athens, a group of Soviet architects arrived from Moscow. They were touring Europe, studying both modern and ancient architecture. Naturally Greece came first on their itinerary, and it was my task to present them, on January 8, 1936, to the Society of Greek Architects. Fifty or sixty men awaited us in the hall of the Industrial Chamber of Athens, and among them one woman—almost a young girl, rather, with hair of rosy gold and a gay and graceful way of moving. Our architects were besieged with questions about Soviet architecture, and as only one of them spoke French, and bad French at that, I had to translate both questions and answers. Soon I found myself elaborating the answers, and naturally, since I had the floor, I ended up by making a speech on the principles and trends of Soviet architecture. When the company split up into small groups, the president of the society came up to me.

"May I introduce you to one of my colleagues who would like to meet you?"

And he brought me face to face with that small golden-haired girl. She had the classic Greek forehead and intelligent and lively eyes. I had assumed that she was the wife or daughter of some member, but the president said:

"Mr. Barmine, this is Màri Pavlides, my eminent and successful colleague."

After the usual greetings she asked: "Are you leaving Athens soon, Mr. Barmine? Where do you all go next?"

"I'm not leaving," I said. "I'm staying in Athens, at the Russian legation."

"Oh, that's fine," she said, and then laughed as though slightly embarrassed. "I thought by your speech that you were an architect," she added.

"Thank you, mademoiselle. That's extremely flattering, but I am only a diplomat. I'm ashamed to say that I had not taken you for an architect. Please accept my apology."

"Please accept mine for not recognizing you as a diplomat!"

We both laughed. My Russian colleagues joined us, and after mutual presentations we parted.

Much as I was absorbed by my cultural contacts, I do not want to imply that I did no diplomatic work at the legation or took no interest in politics. We certainly kept at it quite as much as the other legations in Athens. But I shall have to disappoint readers who expect me as a former Soviet diplomat to make sensational revelations about secret activities involving the G.P.U. and the Comintern. The legation as such had nothing to do with the work of the G.P.U., and neither Kobetsky nor I knew anything about it—except that its agents, naturally, were in the staff watching us.

Of the Comintern's activities, also, I have little to say. We had no connection with its work at all. The Foreign Office still kept aloof in those days, strictly adhering to the principle that the Soviet Government and the Communist International were distinct entities. In obedience to this principle, we even abstained from contact with the Communist members of the Greek Parliament, though often meeting other members.

It did happen once, however, that I broke this rule and engaged in a "secret activity." I was holding, in addition to my legation job, the post of consul at Athens, and in this capacity I received visitors at the consulate twice a week. Most of these visitors were either Greek businessmen seeking visas to the Soviet Union, or Russian emigrants asking to be readmitted to citizenship. As an occasional distraction, some sly person would come in with a daring project for revolutionary activity —and naturally he would need money and "Comintern literature" to carry it out. These fellows were crude enough, and their association with the *asphalia* (Greek secret police) could be smelled a mile off. They were indefatigable in their provocations, and we had such visits regularly, although just as regularly we showed them the door.

One morning the consulate porter let into my office a young woman, tall and blonde, leading a small child by the hand. She looked calm and self-controlled when she sat down, but I could see that she was deeply disturbed.

"What can I do for you, madam?" I asked.

First she glanced round to make sure the porter had gone. Then she began to speak in broken French, slowly and with difficulty. She was the wife of Zachariadis, general secretary of the Greek Communist Party, and a Czech by nationality. Since the Party had gone underground, she had lived in a small isolated cottage in the suburbs of Athens. She never saw anyone and almost never went outside the door. Her husband came home very seldom, and only for brief visits; then he would disappear for weeks. Another Party member, however, one of his aides, met her regularly and remitted enough money to keep herself and her child alive.

"You probably know from the papers," she said, "that Zachariadis was arrested ten days ago. Since then I've waited for his aide at our regular meeting place twice, and he hasn't appeared. All my money is gone. I hesitated to come here, but I don't know anybody in the town —and I have a child."

In response to a question she gave me the name of the aide, and it happened that I had read it that very morning in a list of arrested Communists.

"I'm afraid you will hear no more of him," I said. "Do you have any plans? What do you ask us to do?"

She wanted to go to Moscow. She had an out-of-date Czech passport and wanted me to give her a visa and the funds for the journey.

I went to Kobetsky. He looked annoyed and alarmed when he heard the story.

"You know very well that we have no right to do anything in such cases," he said. "We cannot compromise the legation."

"But you can't just leave this woman and her child on the street. Her husband is in prison, and she has absolutely no one to help her. We could give her a visa easily enough, and some money from the legation. Nobody would know about it. It is a shame to turn her away with nothing."

"Don't insist, Alexander Grigorievich. I can't do anything of this sort, and I won't," said Kobetsky very nervously.

The discussion was long and unpleasant and fruitless. I just managed to control my anger and went back to the consulate.

"Here is our minister's answer," I told the woman, whom I found waiting patiently. "The legation can do nothing, absolutely nothing, for you. But now I want to talk with you as a private individual. Have you any friends or connections in your own country? If you got as far as Prague, would you be able to shift for yourself then?"

"Yes, I think I would," she said slowly.

"Then, here's enough money for the journey to Prague and food for you and the child. I want you to understand that I'm giving you this out of my own pocket, without authorization from my chief. Nobody must know about it. I'm doing it secretly, because if I told him he would forbid it. Go to the Czech legation and ask for your visa. If you have any difficulty, tell them to call me."

The men at the Czech legation were understanding and human. After a couple of delicate conversations with me by telephone, they agreed to give her a visa. She came back to thank me. I never heard of her again.

There is one other "secret activity" to which I must confess—one formally forbidden to all officially accredited diplomats. I acted as foreign correspondent for the official Soviet news agency, Tass, taking over the job from my predecessor in the diplomatic post. Before leaving Moscow I had been told by the Foreign Office that Tass had this job for me. The Foreign Office would give me no official authorization to take it, but also made no formal objection. I went to see the director of Tass, Doletsky, our Russian Roy Howard—small and rosy and affable, although not Irish—and we quickly came to an understanding.

I had already done some magazine writing, but this was my first experience in the newspaper field. It added tempo to my quiet diplomatic work and gave point to my interest in the exciting political life of Greece. My dispatches were stamped "Tass Agency in Athens," but they were always delivered to the Greek censorship office by the legation porter.

The Greeks were tactful enough not to inquire about the mysterious person behind this stamp, who was sending news, objective, to be sure, but at times rather unpleasant to the new dictatorship. I doubt very much if my identity was really a secret to them. But the members of the diplomatic corps had no idea that all "Tass, Athens" dispatches during those two years were from the pen of one of their colleagues. I know this, because they repeatedly asked me why I sat so patiently through every session of parliament. I casually brushed their questions aside with a jest, but on one occasion I was sorry I could not unveil this mystery. I fear I was the cause of the recall from Athens of the Japanese chargé d'affaires.

On the occasion when a gang of terroristic officers assassinated the government ministers in Tokyo, this chargé d'affaires gave an interview about it to the Greek press. Forgetting the usual discreet and noncommittal manners of the Japanese diplomat, he declared that such events were not surprising on the part of the Japanese Army, and that those who understood the internal situation in Japan had to expect them. I quoted this interview quite incidentally in one of my dispatches, but *Pravda* and *Izvestia* played it up on their front pages. This may not have been the only reason, but the Japanese diplomat was promptly recalled.

Not long after my arrival in Athens we received from the British legation an engraved invitation to attend the religious ceremonies to be held in mourning for the death of King George V of England. The Soviet Union was officially an atheist government, and neither Kobetsky nor I had been inside of a church for many years. He hesitated about going and finally telegraphed to Moscow for instructions. Litvinov telegraphed back: "Do as the other diplomats do." So Kobetsky and I put on our tails and top hats and drove to the cathedral in considerable solemnity—not, however, removing the Red Banner with hammer and sickle from our car. A curious and amused crowd gazed at it as we drew up in front of the cathedral, and at us, as we imperturbably ascended the steps.

A few days later we received from the British minister, Sir Sydney Waterlow, the thanks of his new sovereign, Edward VIII. The same post brought us English magazines containing photographs of the funeral ceremony in London. Marshal Tukhachevsky figured among the generals and princes who followed the royal coffin. He was walking beside a small plump general whose name I remembered—Franco, representing the young Spanish Republic.

About a month after the meeting of architects I have described, I met in a photograph shop the girl architect whose golden hair had remained in my memory. We smiled at each other, and she showed me the photographs she had called for—pictures of herself dressed in the national costume, dancing on a penthouse terrace. Pointing to the penthouse, she said proudly:

"I designed it and built it for my mother. You can see the Acropolis and the Parthenon from its windows."

We were planning alterations in our legation building at this time.

"Providence must have sent you to me," I said. "We are just looking for an architect. Maybe you can bring the Parthenon to our windows, too!"

She agreed to look at the place, and our first rendezvous was a professional one. We examined the rooms when she came, but our conversation soon wandered from the subject of properly locating a secretariat to the differences between ancient and modern architecture. She was soon explaining to me how the pillars of the Parthenon are accurately curved to make a majestic straight-lined harmony. Her discourse was so enthusiastic, and her interest so vivid, that it seemed wasteful to be talking in a prosy office of the legation when the Parthenon itself was only a mile away. We finished our conversation on the Acropolis.

I told her that I intended to visit the famous ruins of Mycenus and Epidaurus and asked if she could suggest someone to guide me round these places. She would be glad to do it herself, she said.

On week ends after that we drove into the country to the places that history has made famous through all the world: the majestic amphitheater of Epidaurus; the severe tombs of Clytemnestra and Agamemnon; the somber cleft of Delphi; the field and ruined moss-grown walls where centuries ago the village of Tanagra stood.

I could have been perfectly happy had I only been able to keep my mind off the dreadful trend of events at home. I tried not to let the shadow fall on our wanderings along dusty roads, under the hot sun, with the sea always shimmering in two or three places along the horizon. I was full of admiration for the genius of Hellas and for this beautiful and intimately understanding child of it.

Gloomy thoughts hung over me in the workday evenings when I was alone in my rooms. I tried reading and taking long walks, but I could not shake off the gloom. I sought the company of other people, going out with my friends in the Greek intelligentsia. We visited cafés and the small taverns in the suburbs of Athens. But these dinners, although my friends were gay and the food and music good, seemed dull to me in comparison with my archaeological week ends. I felt that I would be more at ease with Màri.

I suggested to her one day that, after giving so much time to art and history, we had a right to some diversion. Would she go out with me one evening? We could dine at some quiet restaurant along the coast.

We drove out to Glyphada, a small summer resort on the Gulf of Phaleron. Going beyond the fashionable hotels, we stopped at a neat little inn that sat right on the sandy beach. We ate alone on the terrace; the air was still and balmy, and the full moon was reflected in a tranquil sea. The waiter, solemn and mustachioed, brought us *barbunia* fresh from the sea and a bottle of *Retzina* wine. We finished with white country cheese.

I filled our glasses.

"Here's to your happiness, Màri," I said. "Do as I do—this is the custom in our country."

In one slow drought we emptied our glasses and clinked them loudly together. Then I carelessly tossed mine over my shoulder. She laughed and did the same.

The waiter and the proprietor both jumped up when they heard the glasses break. But we did not seem to be drunk or quarreling. The proprietor sat down again. The waiter came across to our table and looked inquiringly at our smiling faces.

"Bring some more glasses," I told him, "and put the others on the bill."

"When two people do that in Russia," I said to Màri, "it brings good luck to both of them."

We wandered out along the beach, took coffee at another neat restaurant, and danced together under the evening sky to the music of a Greek jazz band. The floor was crowded, but it seemed to me that the music played for us alone. I felt lighthearted and joyful for the first time in years.

We went back to the beach and sat on the rocks. Neither of us spoke. I looked into Màri's face. Her blue eyes seemed dark and shining as they looked back into mine. I took her in my arms and kissed her.

37. *Living through the First Moscow Trial*

THE SOVIET PAPERS reported so little of what was really happening at home that the first half of the sinister year 1936 passed for us in conditions of almost idyllic calm. Life in Russia, I told myself, was probably finding its normal level. It would take time, of course, for old wounds to heal and for the people to forget the bitter privations of the First Five-Year Plan. Doubtless I deliberately deceived myself. I deliberately forgot the things I had seen. I escaped from my own thoughts.

One day in August the storm burst on us from a clear sky. The radio and then the Moscow papers announced that the trial of Zinoviev, Kamenev, and fourteen other members of an "anti-Soviet terrorist center" was to open in five days. The two former party leaders, on the theory of a vague "moral responsibility" for the murder of Kirov, had already been treated with implacable harshness. They had been sentenced to prison for ten years, and their political friends had been imprisoned or deported in thousands. The holocaust demanded by Kirov's dead body had been, it seemed, sufficient. I at least was sick and horrified of it, and so I believe were all my comrades. But there was to be no end. Stalin was going to drag that cadaver out again and use it to get rid of some more of his disarmed and repentant critics and rivals. The articles in the Moscow papers seemed to leave no doubt about the outcome of the trial. Every line pointed to the death penalty. But none of us at the legation could believe it. Kobetsky, once Zinoviev's secretary and protégé, grew visibly older day by day. He, who was usually so voluble, maintained a gloomy silence, spending the hours smoking alone in his study and listening to the radio. During the progress of the trial the emotional atmosphere of the legation became that of a bad dream. We went around without speaking of a thing which seemed mad, incredible, disjointed from all fact and reason.

We read with astounded eyes that Zinoviev, Kamenev, Smirnov, and thirteen others had, in a glare of publicity, confessed themselves guilty of atrocious and quite obviously impossible crimes. The "confessions" were shot through with fallacies and contradictions and consisted entirely of general statements of intention. No acts were reported and no documents adduced. Nobody in touch with the facts and the methods of "justice" that had already been followed in the Kirov murder could regard as anything but a grim comedy the talk that came so glibly from the victims' lips about a "Leningrad center" plotting Stalin's assassination and the overthrow of the Soviet regime with foreign aid. It became even more sickening when for a moment the tragic truth burst through the shameless spectacle.

Smirnov steps abruptly out of his assigned role and, in reply to the prosecutor's question: "When did you leave the center?" answers: "I never thought of leaving it because there was nothing to leave."

Vyshinsky, surprised and insistent: "Didn't the center exist?"

Smirnov, wearily: "What are you talking about?"

But such brief human interludes were rare. The nightmare would begin again, the half-mocking and half-maniac dialogue go on. To us older Party members these trials were fantasies. There was no question of believing the confessions. We knew the men; we had worked with them from the time of the Revolution and the Civil War. We also knew that in Soviet conditions the things they confessed were quite simply impossible. But these fantasies were not put on for our benefit. A new generation, ignorant of the past, was the audience. They were the ones who had to believe—and they had no other reading matter but the confessions themselves and the inane denunciation of the victims which was a part of the general nightmare. No critical comment in the papers, no articles in magazines, no public discussions, no private conversations—except in whispers and behind locked doors. It was apparent to us, who had lived under this system, that the younger Soviet generation, by and large, would believe these ignominious tales.

What did seem impossible to us, however, was that the outside world would take this fantastic exhibition seriously. Surely there were enough grown men, and enough political commentators of realistic mind and training, to tell an obviously tendentious, police-invented pipe dream from a fact. But we were wrong. With the aid of "liberal" journalists and "sympathizers" eager to be deceived, Stalin was able to sell the world his war of extermination against all rivals in the grab for power as a defense of the "socialist fatherland" against a sudden and heretofore unheard of crop of fiendish traitors. "The riddle of the Moscow trials" was explained with cynical simplicity: Trotsky, desperate for personal power, had entered into arrangements with the Nazis, Fascists, and Japanese aggressors to overthrow the Stalin regime. Stalin, new friend of the democracies, had discovered the plot in time. He should be thanked for blocking the "sinister" plans of Trotsky.

But to return to Athens: I read the dispatches and listened to the radio during the trial of the sixteen with a constant question in my mind. It was not whether to believe the confessions or not. We all knew that the confessions were dictated by Stalin and the G.P.U. But we did not then know, we could not then understand, the purpose of this monstrous business. To what end was Stalin again raising up this hurricane of fear and hate, demoralizing the Soviets and damaging their cause throughout the world?

We all thought that the unbelievable depth of self-abasement to which the sixteen had sunk would at least save them from the firing squad. After all, had they not been Lenin's friends and Stalin's comrades? One could not put them out of the way like "mad dogs."

I went over the various precedents in my mind. The great trials of our Revolution had almost never ended in executions. In the first years many anti-Bolshevik Socialists were merely expelled from the country. The trial of the Socialist Revolutionaries in 1922 produced only conditional death sentences, though the accused had actually fought with arms in their hands in a time of civil war and had organized an attempt on Lenin. The trial of the Shakhti engineers, accused of sabotage, had sent only a few to their deaths; the rest received short sentences and soon were allowed to work in industrial enterprises in Siberia. The heroes in the Ramsin trial, who pleaded guilty to plotting armed intervention in Russia with the French General Staff, had been after a brief imprisonment pardoned and were reinstated. The Russian Mensheviks, convicted of similar crimes in the next big trial, had got off with long terms of imprisonment. The trial of Thornton and other English engineers in 1933, which was a suspicious business—I was in court at the time—ended in very mild punishments. No, Stalin would never bring himeslf to spill the blood of his former comrades, of men with whom he had worked for years and who ranked with the oldest leaders of the Party and the October Revolution. Such an outcome of this mad exhibition was unthinkable.

One piece of news strengthened us in this conviction. The right of appealing for mercy to the executive head of the Soviets, abolished after the Kirov affair, had been restored on the very eve of the trial—quite evidently, we thought, in the interest of Zinoviev and his fellow prisoners. It never occurred to us that this may have been a lure to induce them to "confess."

A ghastly silence fell upon us when news of the verdict and executions came over the radio. None of us dared speak even in a whisper. We lacked the courage to look one another in the eyes. I was stunned. I knew that this was the end of a whole epoch in Bolshevik history.

Poor Kobetsky, whose close bonds of work and friendship with Zinoviev were known to all of us, sat white and silent. He was crushed. He had a duty to perform, however. He had to summon his staff, read them a statement on what had happened, and tell them to pass a resolution approving the sentence of the court. He locked himself in his study to write out that statement, and he read it to us in a quivering voice. All the terms officially required were there—"scum of humanity," "shot like mad dogs," "the wise leadership of our beloved chief," "extermination of the Trotskyist vermin." It was torture for him to read; it was torture for us to listen. Nobody gave a sign of what he thought or felt. The resolution was adopted unanimously without a show of hands; and each of us was left to his own deep feeling of remorse.

A few days later the Greek papers published a dispatch from Moscow announcing the forthcoming recall of several Soviet diplomats whose reputations were alleged to have been compromised—Davtian, Raskolnikov, Kobetsky. I brought Kobetsky the paper. He said nothing. A tense expression came into his face. He sent a telegram to Litvinov demanding to have the offensive statement officially denied or be recalled at once. Litvinov replied: "Remain at your post and await orders."

The normal course of our days was resumed, but the weight that hung upon our spirits was something that I cannot describe in words.

Each mail from Moscow brought us lists, drawn up for the guidance of librarians and Party secretaries, of books which must be immediately burned. In all cases they were those which contained references to the theorists of Marxism or the men of letters who were presumed to have been compromised, no matter how remotely, by the recent trial. Since every man of first- or second- or even third-rate prominence throughout the past fifteen years was already involved in some heresy, I asked myself in amazement what there would be left for our libraries to put on their shelves! It was enough for a classic work to have a preface by Bukharin or Radek or Preobrajensky—to the flames with it!

"At this rate," I thought, "we shall burn more books than the Nazis —and more by Marxist authors!" Which, in fact, we did. Indeed, a large number of Marx's own books were condemned because they had been edited by Riazanov, famous Marxian bibliophile, the creator of the Marx-Lenin Institute, who had been deported some time before. The first edition of Lenin's works, edited by Kamenev and containing praise of today's "traitors," was withdrawn from circulation.

Stalin himself expurgated and republished the sole volume of his own "works"—a compilation of articles and speeches—and quietly withdrew the earlier edition from the bookstores and libraries. His reasons for doing so may be seen in these quotations from his earlier writings:

"All the work of practical organization of the [October] insurrection was carried out under the immediate direction of the president of the Petrograd Soviet, Comrade Trotsky. We can say with certainty that it is above all to Comrade Trotsky that the Party owes the rapid coming over of the garrison to the side of the Soviet and the good organization of the work of the Military Revolutionary Committee."

"Comrade Trotsky maintains that in the persons of Zinoviev and Kamenev we had a Right Wing in our party. . . . How then explain that the Party was able to avoid a split? . . . There was no split and the differences lasted only a few days, because Kamenev and Zinoviev were Leninists, Bolsheviks."

". . . Bukharin . . . has not violated a single decision of the Central Committee. You demanded Bukharin's blood? We shall not give it to you, know that well. . . . We are against the policy of amputation. . . . We are for unity. . . . If we begin this, where will it end? We will chop off Bukharin today, then another tomorrow, until the party is destroyed!"

Nobody would have been foolhardy enough to recall at the time of the trials any of these three statements of Stalin's.

Throughout that summer Màri and I had gone together on many beautiful trips, which I shall hardly forget. We visited the islands of the Aegean Sea, among them Samos, the home of her family—dreamlike in its peace and beauty. But the events of August cast me down completely. Neither our love nor the splendor of the Greek landscape could lift me out of my depression and dark gloom. We ceased to visit the ancient cities of Greece. Occasionally we took long walks through steep and narrow streets in the suburbs of Athens. Most of the time I would be silent, and I know that Màri's mood was as low as mine. She, too, was going through a period of sorrowful stress.

We had planned a future together: she would close her office in Athens and come to Russia with me. We would find work together there, doing our part in the gigantic rebuilding of the country. But when she told her family about this plan, it roused a storm. They would not hear of her marrying a Russian. Their frail girl, who had spent her whole life in warm and sunny Greece, would perish in the snowy wilds of Russia where bears were said to wander at large through the icy streets! She would be sick and miserable there! She would be lost forever!

Màri did not believe in the terrible pictures they drew and held firmly to her decision. She told me about the arguments in her family with a smile and made light of them. But I myself was worried—about things more trying to sensitive nerves than bears walking in the street. I knew how difficult it would be for her, who had spent all her life in comfort and plenty, to go up against the hardships of our daily exist-ence in Moscow. I had no doubt about her courage: I was keenly aware what determination and persistence had been required to enable a young girl of Greek leisure-class society, defying teasing of friends, the skepticism of professors, to study hard for five years and become an engineer-architect. This she had done; and for that reason her family, knowing her character, tried all the harder to crush out this new "ec-centric idea." What worried me and made me feel sad, even more than the hardships she would have to endure, was the inevitable disillusion-ment which I knew awaited her in Russia. I had wanted her to love Russia and be happy there.

One afternoon, as I was preparing to leave our legation for an official reception, my telephone rang. I heard Màri. Her voice was trembling: "Shura, I know you have an engagement to keep, but I must see you at once—just for five minutes."

I went off quickly to a small café near the Stadium. Màri was already there. She clung to my hand; her eyes looked tired and anguished.

"I just needed to be near you for a minute," she said, half apolo-gizing. "Just to get my courage back—I felt I was losing it."

She was going through the crucial moments of her fight. Her mother had appealed to her in tears: Màri was her joy; her sons would be leaving home for good; she could not live without her daughter; she would never see her child again. This emotional appeal had been almost too much for Màri after the long barrage of intellectual argu-ments she had stood up against.

We sat at the table. I held her hands.

"*Anaskhomen tas kardias* (Raise high your hearts)," I said, quoting an inscription that she had translated to me on one of our trips.

She smiled, and her eyes brightened. She was brave again when she left me. As I watched her get into a taxi I felt at the same time tender and proud.

After the tragedy of the August trial, our ordinary diplomatic duties slowed down considerably or stopped altogether. We received no letters of information on the general political situation. We were sent no analysis of any current event or governmental action. I had been amazed to see how, during the Italo-Ethiopian conflict, the Soviet Union, although officially in sympathy with Ethiopia, kept on supplying oil to Italy without offering to us the slightest explanation for this action. The civil war broke out in Spain, and our government abstained at first from any act that could be interpreted as definitely throwing in its lot with the defenders of the republic. Of this also no explanation arrived.

When Stalin did decide to give aid to the Loyalists and sent as ambassador to that country the unfortunate Marcel Rosenberg, formerly chargé d'affaires in Paris, I received from Krestinsky a telegram announcing my appointment as consul general in Alicante. That was on November 3, 1936. The appointment was canceled in a few days, however, for this consulate was suppressed when the Spanish Government, and with it the Soviet embassy, moved to near-by Valencia.

In December I decided to drive to Moscow for my vacation. The Balkan roads are impassable in that season, and so I planned to go via Italy, Austria, Czechoslovakia, and Poland—the whole distance from Brindisi to Moscow amounting to three thousand miles. As a sporting adventure the idea had been in the back of my mind for a long time. My winter Odyssey from Leningrad to Moscow had not cured me of my passion. And now I needed to set my teeth into some tough effort as a brief escape from the dreadful gloom of my thoughts.

Kobetsky and my other friends at the legation did their best to dissuade me, pointing out the risks I would run, especially in Russia and Poland. No one, it was true, had ever made that particular trip in winter. They prophesied that I would never get there; that I would only smash my car to pieces and find myself snowed up in the mountains. But I regarded these dire prophecies as a challenge to my prowess as a sportsman, and anyway the worse it turned out, the better it would suit my mood.

To calm my friends I pointed out that the Soviet road plan provided for a highway from the Polish frontier to Moscow. This was due to be finished in November. The worst part of my journey, therefore, would be on brand-new pavements. I was not so sure of this, but it sounded convincing. And I also told them I would pick up a companion at one of our legations along the way.

Owing to the risks of the trip, I did not like to make use of the lega

288

tion car, and, by saving rigorously for a year, 1 had managed to buy a new Ford, which arrived from New York a few days before I planned to start.

On the eve of my departure I drove out with Màri to the seashore. We spent our evening again at the same restaurant where we had broken our wine glasses together. We drank to our future. Màri was full of plans for her work in Russia, and I promised to do my best to arrange my recall from Greece. I would leave my new car there, I said, and we imagined her driving through the Moscow streets to her work.

We took a last look at the Gulf of Phaleron, shining calmly in the moonlight just as it had on our first happy evening there. The air was warm and still. I reminded Màri that at this very time the Russian roads were deep in snow, and icy winds were howling over the countryside. I promised to be back at the end of January.

The next morning, on my way to the port of Piraeus, I stopped at a florist's and ordered a bouquet of red roses to be sent to Màri on the eighth of January with a small card saying: "To remind you of the meeting of architects a year ago."

I mention this because three years later a thing happened which gave to this anniversary an added meaning for both of us. On Christmas Eve of 1939, after living two years as hunted refugees in Paris, we sailed away from the foggy, blacked-out docks of Le Havre to start a new life in a new world. Our ship, the *De Grasse,* was scheduled to arrive in New York ten days later. But she waited several days in Southampton for a convoy and then slowly zigzagged across the Atlantic, avoiding enemy submarines. We were more than two weeks at sea and came ashore in New York on a cold sunny day—the eighth of January.

As we walked from the Hudson across the West Side of Manhattan, the snow was melting in the streets. The taxis rushing by spattered us with mud. We had to thread our way at first through empty fruit crates stacked up on the sidewalk. It all was dirty and untidy, and the noisy crowds jostled us. But we thought we had never seen such a beautiful city in all our lives. We went hand in hand. We felt light and happy. We felt like singing.

We now celebrate this day every year as our own double Thanksgiving. It brought us together; it gave us a new country and home.

38. My Last Trip to Russia

ON THE FOURTEENTH of December, after feverish preparations, my Ford equipped with numerous spare parts but without a heater, I embarked for Brindisi at the Piraeus.

Very early in the morning I went up on deck to take a last look at Hellas. The sky was overcast; now and again weak flashes of sunlight pierced the curtain of gray cloud, touching the mountainous coast line with those soft, tender, and translucent colors which, of all the sights I had seen in Greece, I loved and wondered at the most. But the sunlit hours were few; most of the day, as we passed through the Gulf of Corinth and up the west coast of Greece, the mountains were dark and melancholy. At midday we entered the Gulf of Ithaca—home of Ulysses—and cast anchor close to a lovely town built on the edge of a great bay, in which stood a tiny island fortress that reminded me of Bourdzi in the Gulf of Nauplia. The name of the town was Vathy. From Ithaca we set our course for Corfu, where we arrived that evening. I was struck by the town's similarity to the Italian cities of the Mediterranean, except that here the wild picturesqueness of the landscape was modified by a calmness and a purity of line and feature characteristic only of the Hellenic scene. Next day our ship steamed into the huge harbor of Brindisi.

I covered the five hundred miles between Brindisi and Rome in a single day. It was rather cold, but the sun was bright and the landscape stimulating in its variety, especially in the mountain district beyond Foggia. Small country cottages, built in a style I never saw before, alternated with wretched tenement buildings, the peeling walls of which were covered with the usual slogans proclaiming the greatness of the Duce and of the new Roman Empire. I did not pause until I reached Naples, and there only for ten minutes to swallow an *esprèsso* and spend a moment admiring the Bay of Naples by night. Approaching Rome toward midnight, I got into a fog so thick that I had to slow down to ten miles an hour to avoid running into great wagons loaded with vegetables for the Roman market, which loomed constantly out of the murk. Here the driving became dangerous and unpleasant.

After fourteen hours at the wheel I suddenly found myself in the Roman streets. They were silent and ominous. The fog seemed thicker than ever. The Eternal City was wrapped in a shroud through which showed vaguely the vast bulk of the Coliseum.

At the Soviet Embassy a sleepy porter showed me into the guest room where, after a hot bath, I slept like the dead. My two days in Rome were like the dream of a happy meeting with an old friend. At Milan I attended a conference called by our ambassador, Boris Stein, to discuss a meeting of the League of Nations from which he had just returned and the foreign policy of Stalin and Litvinov. Stein spoke as a loyal and enthusiastic official. He was full of rather ponderous praise for the leaders. I realized once more how completely the "proper way of speaking" had replaced the rough and self-dependent candor of earlier days.

I fed the pigeons on the Piazza San Marco and crossed the Brenner Pass in heavy snow. The journey became more severe, but also more exciting. The Alps and the great Austrian motor road are not the safest places in avalanche time, but the views were splendid. The spiral descent from Semmering after dark, when frost has turned the road to ice and the driver is new to the locality, is not made for weak brakes or weak nerves. I came through all right, thanks to my chains. Later I was to bless them even more fervently on the roads of Poland and White Russia.

At Vienna, in the house of our minister, Lorenz, I met a number of Red Army officers and high G.P.U. officials, gay and excited, on their way to the battle in Spain. They were among those, I imagine, who paid later with their lives for Stalin's failure there. Even those who tried to buy their safety by arranging the murder of some Spanish Republican who did not love Stalin, had to serve with the rest as scapegoats.

At Vienna my hope of finding a traveling companion vanished. I heard much again about danger and the impossibility of motoring through Poland and Russia in winter and was advised, in the most friendly fashion, to finish my trip by train. But I went on.

Road conditions in Poland were, in fact, very bad. During the two days it took me to get to Cracow, and from there on as far as Warsaw, I encountered a terrific storm of melting snow accompanied by gales. In one place the road would be covered with wet ice, in another a foot deep in snow. Beyond Cracow my headlights refused to function, and I drove on in darkness, pulling out of the road when a car approached. It was exhausting and at times almost dismaying, but it kept my thoughts at least from what I wanted to forget. My fear was that I should not reach Moscow by the end of the month, for I had promised to spend New Year's Day with my sons.

The landscape here was beautiful if unexciting—the hills in silent white, the fields abandoned. Now and again I would stop to savor the vast loneliness. Before me and behind nothing was to be seen but the long road between its rows of great trees, and on each side the spreading white fields. The wind whistled and lifted the snow in fine eddies. The road was empty of life, save for a few crows hopping clumsily before the car. I turned on the radio, and the muffled sound of orchestral music mingled strangely with the cold and quiet scene.

On Christmas Eve I arrived through gusts of wind-blown snow in Warsaw. I was the guest of our self-important Ambassador Davtian and his wife, the actress Maksakova. Like many other Russian officials, this slick and ungracious ambassador to Poland was, without knowing it, enjoying his last hours of liberty, actually his last days of life.

After leaving Warsaw next day I passed through a series of Jewish villages which seemed to have lain there crushed for all eternity by a weight of abject misery. The roads now became worse, but the weather, despite the extreme cold, remained pleasant. Two days out from Warsaw I began to be conscious of extreme fatigue, but I held out, for I hoped to cross the Russian frontier before dark.

Two Polish sentries hidden in a ditch beside the road jumped out and ordered me to stop. A few hundred yards farther an officer emerged from the frontier guardhouse. He was affable but firm. There was no possibility of my going through that evening. The regulations were very stringent—no one must cross the frontier after sundown. Besides, the Soviet guards would not show up, no matter how loudly they were called.

The upshot was that I had to go back twenty miles and spend the night in a village.

I found a room in the house of a Jewish woman on the market place. Space was made for my car in a barn among farm wagons, cows, and goats. The local constable came to have a look at me and spent a long time poring over my papers. Next morning, in a temperature of several degrees below zero, I started off again. The Polish officer, with a sentry, accompanied me to the frontier. The wind cut us to the bone, making the cold seem ten times as intense as it was. I stopped the car in front of a small bridge over a frozen stream. The bridge was closed by two bars of wood. The one on our side was painted in the Polish colors—pink and white. Behind the farther one, which was a rich red, stretched the endless territories of the Soviet Union. Nothing was to be seen but an empty desert of snow, and a mile away on a rise of ground a small shack of new-sawn lumber which housed the Soviet border guards.

At an order from the officer, the sentry fired twice into the air. We waited five minutes, ten, a quarter of an hour. Not a sound from the Soviet Union! The distant shack seemed uninhabited.

The Polish officer was now quite blue from the cold. In an irritable voice he said:

"Your fellows ought to repeat my signal and then come down. But it's always this way. When wanted, they prefer to stay in their shack."

We kept on firing, and at the end of an hour, by which time we were all practically frozen, we heard a faint rifleshot in reply. Two figures in military greatcoats emerged from the shack. It took them another half-hour to reach the bridge. The young Soviet officer, as he came slowly along, cast a surprised glance at the car and saluted the Polish captain, who handed over my passport and seemed inclined to hasten the formalities. The Red officer, visibly embarrassed, turned my passport over and over in his fingers.

"My commander is absent, and I don't think I can let you through until he comes back. I think it would be better to wait."

He hesitated. The Polish captain turned to me, making a clucking sound with his tongue. An ironic smile was just visible on his lips.

"You see—always the same story!"

"We'll send for the officer in command," stammered the young subaltern, turning very red.

I cut through his hesitations.

"Open the barrier at once, comrade!" I said. "My papers are in order, and it's your duty to carry out instructions without keeping these neighbors of ours waiting. Don't make this gentleman hang around all day. Any explanations you want from me can wait until we've reached your headquarters."

The tone of my voice produced its effect. I got back into my car and crossed the bridge. On our way to the shack the young guard began to excuse himself. The arrival of a car in the middle of winter was an entirely unexpected event. The last car they had seen—belonging to an English diplomat—had come during August, and in that case Moscow had warned them by telegram of its impending arrival. They had never dreamed that anyone would undertake such a journey at this time of year.

At the frontier shack my reception was more cordial. The commanding officer turned up after a while, the little misunderstanding was cleared up, and I left almost at once. But I had received a piece of bad news: the new highway, which should have been completed, was hardly more than begun.[1] I had to follow a series of older roads, excellent in spots but in general bad beyond despair. Neither the good spots nor the long bad stretches seemed to have any reason for beginning or ending.

I slept in Minsk, a guest of Ghikalo, then secretary of the Central Committee of White Russia, a powerful figure, famous guerrilla leader in the Caucasus during the Civil War, who was shot next year in the purge. A few miles out of Minsk my Ford got into a drift more than a yard deep. It was five o'clock in the morning, and snow was falling steadily. I could see nothing. For two hours not a car, not a cart, not a man came near me. My feet, in their thin shoes, seemed to be completely frozen. I could no longer feel them. Taking my shoes off, I rubbed my feet hard with snow to get the blood moving. At the end of an hour I had to do this again.

I had really begun to despair when a figure at last appeared upon the road. It was a poor man of middle age, a pack on his back,

[1] According to statements appearing in the Soviet press, this highway was finished in 1941 instead of November, 1936, as planned.

293

trudging through the snow. He told me there was a *kolkhoz* about two miles across the fields. I set off to get help and succeeded in finding the place, a huddle of stuffy hovels swarming with children and heavy with animal smells, an abandoned air about the stables. But the men were capable of doing the job I wanted. They managed to connect the car with a team of emaciated horses, though they had some difficulty in making up a full set of harness.

"There's a shortage of straps," they explained. "You know how difficult it is to get a piece of leather."

I spent the next night at Roslavl. On the afternoon of December 31, I reached Moscow by the Podolsky road. I remembered the accident that had ended my journey of four years before and drove with exaggerated care through the Moscow streets. Policemen and passers-by looked with curiosity at the foreign license plate on my car.

I rang up the Foreign Office and parked my car an hour later in the garage of the famous Spiridonievka House where Litvinov was living.

I think I was the first man who ever drove from Warsaw to Moscow in the winter season, and I was proud of it. I understood now why travelers often prefer dangerous routes to the regular tourist roads—an attitude which till then I had put down to snobbery. The only damage to my car was a broken ceiling lamp, which I had banged with my own head. Otherwise it was as good as when I had taken delivery of it in Athens. I left it in Litvinov's garage and never saw it again, as it was confiscated by the government along with all my other Moscow property when I was condemned to death after my break with the Soviets.

I arrived in Moscow just three weeks before the second, or Piatakov, trial. I found that no one, even in the most intimate conversations, would mention politics. Many of my friends, well-known figures, had disappeared mysteriously—arrested, of course. Even their names referred to by mistake in the course of a conversation would produce a feeling of awkwardness, those present pretending not to have heard. Just as men afflicted with mortal illnesses cling, up to the last moment, to empty hopes, so the influential Communists kept believing in an ultimate return to normal conditions and buried themselves in what they happened to be doing.

I was anxious to get some information about the Zinoviev trial, but I had to use extreme caution about it. I put my question at last to a man whom I had known pretty intimately, a journalist well in with Stalin's immediate entourage, who had access to the Dictator himself. He told me that a formal promise of reprieve had been given to the sixteen victims on condition that they make the confessions demanded of them, sacrificing their personal honor as a proof of their loyalty to the Party and readiness to fight Trotskyism. To convince them of the genuineness of the offer, they were informed of the decree promulgated five days before the trial authorizing an appeal for clemency. Knowing Stalin, they felt skeptical, but they had no real choice in the matter.

When the trial began, they soon saw from the atmosphere of the court, the campaign in the press, the innumerable meetings at which everyone, from children under twelve to scholars grown gray in the service of science, demanded the death penalty against "these fascist mad dogs," that they were lost if they accepted the bargain. But it was too late then; they had already confessed. There was nothing left but to drain the cup to the dregs—in other words, take a last gamble by obeying Stalin's orders.

Trotsky has expressed surprise in his book on the trials (*The Crimes of Stalin*) that the accused found it possible to confess that their only motive had been a "lust for power." "For the Party of the proletariat," writes Trotsky, "power is only a means to the transformation of society. To seek power for power's sake is proof of stupidity and vulgarity beyond words. . . ."

My friend from *Pravda* put this apparent act of stupidity and vulgarity in a new light.

"They denied that they had ever had any political platform different from Stalin's. . . . All they had striven for was power—get that clear!" he said. "And the judges, State Prosecutor Vyshinsky, the journalists, all swallowed it. We all loudly proclaimed that they had no political differences with Stalin, that the lust for power had landed them in the last indignity—the loss of all ideals. It was a clever trick, and it became the *leitmotiv* of the whole trial."

I did not understand.

"But don't you see? If they had no political differences with Stalin, and had striven only for power, that meant that Stalin himself had no political differences with them and was fighting solely for his personal power. What they were saying was that they no longer believed in him as a leader of the Party, and that Stalin was ready to send the friends of Lenin to death simply to defend his own position.

"This line of talk completely upset the Boss. He had felt so sure of the outcome of the trial that he went off for a holiday in the Caucasus. Informed by telegram and by the newspapers of the maneuver staged by the accused, he was furious. He wired back, emptying his wrath on the court, the G.P.U., on Yagoda, who had been fooled by this trick, on us of *Pravda* and *Izvestia,* because we had fallen into the trap.

"We all trembled for our skins, and of course instantly changed the tune. *Pravda* hastened to inveigh against the villainy of traitors who had sold themselves abroad, who were preparing a restoration of capitalism and then pretended that they were actuated only by a personal lust for power. The state prosecutor took the same line. But it was too late now to get out of the accused another version more satisfactory to the Boss. To his mind the trial had missed fire; and the doom of Yagoda, who had been chiefly responsible for staging it, was sealed. Eight years ago, you know, Yagoda was in sympathy with Bukharin. The Boss forgets nothing. Yagoda has now been relieved of his post and replaced by Yezhov."

I learned from my friend that the librarians of Moscow were more closely watched than any other class of citizens. The libraries were constantly being raided and purged. The files of official newspapers— there are no others—covering past years had become forbidden reading matter. If a librarian refused to show some inquiring visitor the back numbers of *Izvestia* he might be accused of sabotage. But those back numbers contained signed articles by men now branded as enemies of the people. If he did show them, he ran the risk of being accused of counterrevolutionary propaganda. If he referred the matter to his superiors, he could always be accused of trying to put *them* in a hole. . . .

And I had once thought of becoming a librarian because it would mean a peaceful job!

As a result of the new line taken in regard to the Zinoviev trial, and the need to avoid a similar debacle in coming trials, it was necessary to pretend that foreign governments were making prodigious efforts to overthrow the Soviets by conspiring with and bribing members of the defeated Opposition. The people had to be convinced that the country was full of foreign spies, that anybody and everybody might be in league with the enemy and secretly preparing the restoration of capitalism. In consequence, on orders from above, the papers and the radio, the theater, the bookstores—every instrument of propaganda—was turned into a medium for the propagation of spy stories. Almost every issue of *Pravda* and *Izvestia* contained some article on the hidden enemy, always ending in an appeal for vigilance. A veritable spy mania was set going, and people began to regard all foreigners, even Communists and revolutionary refugees who had been living in the Soviet Union for fifteen years, as spies. People grew afraid to know foreigners. Even to receive a postcard from abroad was dangerous. Many tourists in Russia noticed this phenomenon, but none of them realized its source. It rose out of the necessity of preparing the atmosphere for the fantastic show trials and forced confessions with which Stalin covered his bloody extermination of the old Bolshevik Party.

To show the lengths to which the government went in propagating this spy mania, let me cite the case of Pavlenko, a young Communist novelist of ability. Pavlenko had written a novel called *In the Orient*, dealing with the Chinese Communists. The story begins in the following way: On the banks of the frontier River Amur, a Chinese Communist is shot by Japanese soldiers. Just before the fatal volley the victim lets himself fall alive into the stream. Swimming under water, fired on by the squad, and covered with blood, he succeeds in reaching the Soviet bank. Help comes, he recovers, studies in a Soviet military school, becomes a Red officer, returns to his own country, and covers himself with glory fighting at the head of a Chinese guerrilla detachment against the Japanese. The novel had a certain success.

One day a cinema poster with the title *In the Orient* caught my attention. "A film," I read, "based on a scenario by Pavlenko." The film began in the same way as the book, but the end was quite different. The Chinese Communist, welcomed by his Russian brothers and admitted to a military school, is suddenly unmasked as a Japanese spy! Pavlenko is a novelist of some note, his book having been translated into French, but he was not above converting his idealistic revolutionary story into a scenario of exactly opposite tendency at the bidding of the authorities. The very character whom he had created as an example of revolutionary internationalism becomes an example of the danger of trusting any foreigner, even those apparently most devoted to the Soviet Union.

39. *The Arts Flourish under a Dictator*

WITH EVERY YEAR the shadow of the dictatorship upon the creative arts grew heavier. This process was shockingly apparent to me after a year of absence. The atmosphere was stifling. The almost daily laying down of dicta as to the policy to be followed in creation was emasculating and demoralizing the whole artistic life of the country. Self-abasement took the place of pride, and mediocrity climbed to the seat of genius. A career in the arts became inconceivable without at least a nod of approval from the Kremlin.

Writer after writer, once famous, has been cast down to oblivion at the whim of the leader. Pilnyak, once proclaimed the "father of Soviet literature," was no longer published. A mere reference to him some years ago in a survey of Soviet literature was severely punished. The official opinion now is that Pilnyak was not a writer. The same applies to several others whose books once sold in hundreds of thousands and even millions. On the other hand, writers once under a cloud have been lifted to absolute pre-eminence. The famous poet Mayakovsky had a double fate. The attitude of the official critics was a main factor in the frustration that drove him to suicide. But some years after his death Stalin suddenly proclaimed him the greatest Soviet poet. One of the squares in Moscow was named after him and also a theater and a collective farm.

Count Alexis Tolstoy was castigated up to the early thirties as practically a literary provocateur engaged in dragging an alien ideology into Soviet letters. By Stalin's order this was forgiven, and he suddenly sprang into favor, and after Maxim Gorky's death replaced him as the number one Soviet writer.

Tolstoy's rapid rise from obloquy to supreme heights is typical. An illegitimate son of the noble Tolstoy family, Alexis received his right to use the family title after demonstrating his loyalty to Imperial Russia by stories about the lives and customs of the landed gentry. As a patriotic subject of the Czar, he was further rewarded by appointment to a delegation of Russian writers who went to England in 1916 to promote cordial relations between the House of Windsor and the House of Romanov. He was opposed to the Bolshevik Revolution, and for five years after its advent remained an *émigré*. Only in 1922, with the advent of the N.E.P., did Alexis Tolstoy return to Soviet Russia. His works were printed then, but they were invariably subjected to critical chastisement as ideologically harmful. Perhaps the most resounding of such public thrashings was administered to his major opus, a novel and a play entitled *Peter the First.* Tolstoy got tired of the strain. I have it from the lips of a close friend of his that once late in 1930 he said to another writer not among the favored few:

"You know, my friend, you and I are awful fools. All we have to do to win acclaim is read the stenographic report of the latest Party Congress and faithfully follow its political line."

That, in any case, is exactly what he did. And his subsequent works appeased the critics and won the approval of the Supreme Leader himself. Even his *Peter the First,* edited now to accord with the Party line, was given enthusiastic praise when it became known that Stalin had identified his own labors on behalf of Russia with the career of that czar.

During the mass purge and hysterical spy hunt which followed the Moscow trials, Alexis Tolstoy gave an interview to the Soviet press in which he announced that he proposed to rewrite his now-famous play *Peter the Great.* The play already contained a possible parallel between Peter's struggle against his son Alexis, a tool of the die-hard Boyars, and Stalin's struggle against the Communist oppositionists, who represented "petty-bourgeois influences." But now Bukharin and others were declared to be agents of foreign powers. So Alexis Tolstoy discovered new historic data supposedly in the archives of Peter, on the basis of which to rewrite his play. In the new version, Prince Alexis is a spy and foreign agent in the pay of the King of Sweden and the Sultan of Turkey!

Having by these means become laureate, receiving the Stalin Prize of 100,000 rubles, Alexis Tolstoy published a trilogy on the dictator's career as leader of the Red Army and winner of the Civil War. In this he exposed, in strict accord with the latest official school of history, the criminal role of Trotsky, who, when he was supposed to have been organizer and chief of the Red Army, was actually the secret agent of foreign interventionists. At the extreme point of his career as a bootlicker, Alexis Tolstoy wrote, in what sounds like a transport of religious ecstasy:

"I want to howl, roar, shriek, bawl with rapture at the thought that we are living in the days of the most glorious, one and only, incomparable Stalin! Our breath, our blood, our life—here take it, O great Stalin!"

On another occasion he addressed the Dictator:

"Thou art the bright Sun of the people, the Sun of our times that never sets, and more than our Sun, for in the Sun there is no wisdom."

It would be misleading to infer from Alexis Tolstoy's case that the candidate for literary fame in Soviet Russia must at least have talent. Alexis Tolstoy does happen to be a gifted writer. But that is accidental. The competition is not primarily in good writing, but in adulating the Dictator. Talent no longer counts fundamentally, nor does dignity or good sense. The question is, who praises the Dictator loudest? Take, for instance, the case of the "famous poet," Kolchev. The man has never written a readable poem and probably will never write one in his life. Yet he was suddenly one day acclaimed by all critics as the greatest poet in the Soviet Union. Why? The masterpiece that won him this overnight glory was recited in all the 167 languages and dialects of the Republic. It was committed to memory by street-sweepers and polar explorers, by beardless youths and bearded professors. It was broadcast by radio and distributed in millions of printed copies. Here is a faithful translation of Kolchev's masterpiece:

When Budyenny smiles,
    The ice breaks on the Don;
When Budyenny smiles,
    The maple's bloom is on.

When Voroshilov smiles,
    The sun begins to shine;
When Voroshilov smiles,
    Then spring falls into line.

When Stalin smiles,
    What might a poet dare?
When Stalin smiles,
    It is beyond compare!

Here is another tribute to Stalin, composed by one Sergei Makhalkov and published in all newspapers all over the country, including the official *Izvestia*, on the sixtieth birthday of the Dictator:

Moscow sleeps, nocturnal city
Where the late stars shine on snow.
Only Stalin, out of pity
For us, sleeps not, all aglow.

For the brave, the true, the hardy
Who abound throughout our land,
Thinking of us, never tardy
With his kind, protective hand.

Far beyond the hills and valleys
Where a boy herds flocks with pep,
Through his *kishlak's* narrow alleys,
Stalin guards his every step.

Stalin even hears the chatter
Of the shepherd by the pond.
Should the boy write him a letter,
Stalin will himself respond.

In an *izba,* ill and lonely,
You might groan 'midst Baikal trails.
Have no fear, for Stalin only
Knows about you, never fails. . . .[1]

The poet Bezymensky, a man of mediocre talent but a Communist Party member, wrote an ode for the Pushkin centennial which he read at a solemn celebration in the Bolshoi Theater. It concluded—or should have—with a quotation of Pushkin's famous line:

Long live the Sun! May darkness perish!

But Bezymensky added:

Long live Pushkin! Long live Stalin!

It brought the audience of poetry lovers to their feet in a storm of applause. These acts of literary prostitution were imitated by Professor Luppol, a *member of the Academy of Science,* who wrote on Pushkin's hundredth anniversary:

The celebration of Pushkin is the celebration of the Leninist-Stalinist national policy. For Stalin and the Stalinist Constitution have given Pushkin to his people.

Fortunately there were at that time persons in Russia who still dared to laugh at this obscene sycophancy occupying the place of literature.

[1] These two translations are by Charles Malamuth.

A story current that year in Moscow told how a monument to the great poet Lermontov was erected on the occasion of his hundredth anniversary. The Soviet dignitaries gathered for the unveiling; speeches were made; music was played; and finally the audience strained forward to see the unveiling. As the curtain fell, they saw to their amazement a gigantic statue of Stalin.

"But what has that got to do with Lermontov?" a surprised functionary whispered to his neighbor.

"Don't be a fool," the other replied. "Look! Don't you see that he is holding a volume of Lermontov's verse in his hand!"

In his youth and early manhood Stalin's taste in music ran to homely folk tunes. When he became dictator he developed a devotion to the opera and ballet, of which he is a patron, as he is of almost everything in Russia. Unlike patrons in capitalist countries, whose contributions seldom exceed a few hundred thousand dollars, Stalin's donations, taken of course from the state treasury, run into many millions. The gratitude of the artists is invariably conveyed to him personally. At Kremlin banquets to *Stakhanovites,* polar explorers, and other heroes, as well as to foreign guests, full ensembles of artists appear, rendering complete operas, ballets, and dramatic productions. An entire hierarchy of ranks for actors and artists has been invented, the titles ranging from "Deserving Artist" to "People's Artist of the Republic." In addition to such honorary awards, Stalin "suggests to the government" concrete largess in the form of special subsidies to theaters, millions of rubles for new buildings, and personal awards of tens of thousands of rubles to individual artists whom he likes—all taken, of course, from the public treasury. The press, in announcing such donations, always reports that the action was taken "upon the initiative" of Comrade Stalin.

Stalin is often to be seen at the opening night of a new opera or ballet. Wherever he goes, the old "Imperial loge" is always reserved for him. He usually sits in the second row on the inside chair, allowing his companions to occupy the front seats. G.P.U. agents both in uniform and plain clothes occupy the neighboring seats. During intermission the theater management sets a lavish table in the anteroom of Stalin's loge, for the Dictator never ventures into the foyer for refreshments. Quite often the audience does not even suspect his presence, but finds out about it from the newspapers on the following day. When an audience does catch a glimpse of him in his loge, there is always a stormy ovation in which the entire cast participates from the stage, stopping the performance and shouting itself hoarse with greetings of affection to the Dictator.

To gratify a whim of Stalin's, the Georgian Opera was once brought to Moscow. Its performances were mediocre, but they were lauded without reserve by the foremost critics. Were not the performers Stalin's fellow countrymen?

If the Boss dispenses largess with an oriental lavishness, he expresses his displeasure with a cold brutality. The Second Moscow Art Theater once produced a play of Jacques Duval with the playwright in the audience. Indeed, Duval had come from Paris expressly for this opening. It was followed by a banquet in honor of the dramatist, at which, according to reports reaching Stalin, the director of the theater, Ivan Bersenev, complained to Duval that he could not secure from the Soviet authorities permission to take his company for a tour abroad. Whether Bersenev actually said this to Duval or not is beside the point. Stalin credited the report and forthwith ordered the Second Moscow Art Theater to close its doors and remove itself to the provincial town of Rostov-on-the-Don. When the company refused to go "voluntarily" into this exile, the Soviet press opened a vicious campaign against it. The Second Moscow Art Theater was discovered to be out of tune with the epoch of great socialist deeds and utterly useless to the cause of art. This was climaxed by an express order dissolving the entire organization and scattering its ensemble of actors among the other theaters. Thus ended the Second Moscow Art Theater, eldest child of Stanislavsky's celebrated Moscow Art Theater, founded by Michael Chekhov (now a voluntary exile in the United States).

At a joint session of Party and government leaders in the Bolshoi Theater during the time of the purges, the keynote was sounded by a solemn performance of Beethoven's *Eroica*. The following day the leading music critics announced that this composition of Beethoven's is in tune with the Stalinist epoch. In fact, they discovered in the *Eroica* a prophecy of Stalin's role in history.

This at least helped to popularize the works of one of the world's greatest composers. It also gave a lift to the most talented of contemporary Russian composers, the world-renowned Dmitri Shostakovich. For years prior to the Dictator's conversion to Beethoven, this famous artist languished under an official boycott. This was tantamount to a sentence of death to his art. No composition of his could be performed anywhere in the Soviet Union, nor could it be published. The composer himself was practically deprived of a living and eked out a miserable and furtive existence cheered only by the few truly brave men and women among his friends.

This had been the result of another whim of Stalin's. It so happened that the Dictator had not attended the first performance of Shostakovich's celebrated opera, *Ekaterina Izmailova,* which had established the world reputation of the young composer. The opera grew in fame, however, on its own merits. Nemirovich-Danchenko's Musical Studio was always crowded whenever *Ekaterina Izmailova* appeared on its boards. Finally came the night when, without previous warning to the management, the Boss appeared at the theater. He was accorded what was regarded as the very best place—the director's own loge. But unfortunately Nemirovich-Danchenko's Musical Studio was located in a place not designed originally for operas, and certainly not for such sonorous ones as *Ekaterina Izmailova*. Prior to its conversion into a theater it had been a businessmen's club, and its acoustics had never been properly adjusted. Since the director's loge is virtually on top of the orchestra, the brasses were annoying to the Dictator's ears. Moreover, he had come there that evening to dissipate an ugly mood, and the loud noises aggravated it. In a huff Stalin got up and walked out on *Ekaterina Izmailova* before the end of the second act.

The next day *Pravda* set all the dogs baying against Shostakovich. The keynote article was signed by no less a personage than Kerzhentsev, chairman of the Government Art Commission, who suddenly discovered that Shostakovich was a species of musical counterrevolutionary, a "diversionist" of bourgeois musical standards, and in fact hardly a composer at all. In short, Shostakovich became almost an enemy of the people in the field of music. The sensitive young man of genius, one of the greatest Russian composers since the days of Tchaikovsky, Borodin, and Glinka, suddenly found himself denounced by the very critics who had been praising him to the skies. The Soviet press printed retraction after retraction by these critics, confessing their mistake and making up for it now by condemning Shostakovich as a charlatan and a corrupter of revolutionary tastes.

In *Izvestia* of February 27, 1936, the head of the Union of Soviet Composers wrote: "The articles of *Pravda* are a lesson not only for Shostakovich, but for the whole art front. . . . We have on the musical front three events of primary importance. They are: the conversation of Comrades Stalin and Molotov with Composer Dzerjinsky, author of the opera, *The Silent Don*, and the two articles in *Pravda*. If we understand these three events as we should, we shall draw from them the clearest indication of the road to be followed by Soviet music."

The Proletarian Musicians Association declared: "In the light of Comrade Stalin's letter, new and great tasks present themselves on the musical front. Down with rotten liberalism in relation to bourgeois influences and the theories of the class enemy!" The Association demanded a revision of the canonization of great composers, beginning with Beethoven and Moussorgsky. The letter of Stalin, it declared, ought to make of every Soviet orchestra a collective warrior for authentic Marxism-Leninism. (The letter in question had, by the way, nothing to say about music or any other art, but was concerned with the teaching of Russian history.)

It looked as though Shostakovich was through. His life as a composer seemed to come to an abrupt end. From the greatest heights he had been catapulted in one night into darkest oblivion. How he endured the next few years is hard to imagine, for he is exceedingly frail and sensitive. But relief came with Stalin's discovery of a passion for Beethoven. A clever friend of Shostakovich's suggested that he compose a symphony along the lines of the *Eroica*. Other friends meantime undertook to smooth down the Dictator's ruffled feathers. Shostakovich wrote his own heroic symphony, called it *The Golden Age*, and secured permission to have it performed in the Dictator's presence. With the aid of subtle suggestions from Shostakovich fans, it was discovered that *The Golden Age* was a peerless musical expression of the Stalinist epoch, a veritable fulfillment of what the *Eroica* had only prophesied. Shostakovich was saved. The same critics that had printed self-abasing retractions of their previous praise now retracted their retractions and discovered the grandeur of Shostakovich and his genius.

In the field of the cinema, Stalin is not only an all-powerful patron, but absolute and direct boss. As films are supposed to be important vehicles of propaganda and might disclose to the Russian people the desirable facts of capitalist life, every foreign film shown has to be passed upon by the Politburo, and that means in actual practice by Stalin. Boris Shumiatsky, the head of the Soviet Film Industry, an old friend of mine, himself told me that the Boss ordered that he be privately shown every one of the few foreign films chosen as suitable for the Soviet public. Many of them he condemned as ideologically dangerous. Only such masterpieces as the innocuous fairy tales of Walt Disney and such examples of peasant revolution as *Viva Villa,* or of the critical condition of capitalism as King Vidor's *Our Daily Bread,* managed to pass muster. This does not say that Stalin disliked the forbidden films. On the contrary, he is quite a Hollywood fan, his favorites being Clark Gable, Wallace Beery, and Paul Muni. Shumiatsky told me that the Boss liked gangster films but had issued a standing order that they should not be shown to the Soviet public.

Notwithstanding Charlie Chaplin's popularity with the Soviet public and the reverence for him among our cinema specialists, he was long barred from Soviet Russia only because the Boss has no great liking for comedy. When Alexandrov produced the first Soviet film comedy, *The Jolly Boys,* the critics, knowing this fact, castigated it as a bourgeois deviation in imitation of American art and almost drove poor Aléxandrov to distraction. But subsequently Shumiatsky showed the film to Stalin, who was amused. Word got round immediately that the Boss liked the picture and also liked the young actress, Liubov Orlova, who was starred in it. The critics took up their pens again—the same critics—and praised the picture extravagantly. Alexandrov became one of the greatest film directors of Russia. At Stalin's behest he was decorated with the Order of the Red Star and given, together with Orlova, the exalted title "Artist Emeritus of the Republic." In 1939, after their third film, Stalin's favorites, Alexandrov and Orlova, were decorated again, this time with the Order of Lenin. In the end, Charlie Chaplin, too, was restored to favor, and his films are now shown all over Russia.

Stalin's role as dictator of the arts, however, did not satisfy his sycophants. They had to proclaim him a scientific genius, too, and a great philosopher and writer. In an article in *Pravda* of May 27, 1938, entitled "Stalin, Standard-Bearer of Science," we read:

> . . . Russia has given men of genius to science in the past: Lomonosov, Lobachevski, Mendelyeev, to whom is due the classification of the chemical elements. Another celebrated Russian, Pavlov, has glorified Russia in science. But the greatest of the great *coryphees* was Lenin. Lenin not only blazed the trail for science in our time, but he prepared his pupil and successor, Stalin, who has never yet been surpassed. Lenin and Stalin— these are the standards [*sic*] of science. There are in the history of science no greater victories than those achieved under the direction of Lenin and Stalin. . . .

According to a contributor to *Revolution and Culture,* Stalin is counted among the "profound connoisseurs and critics of Hegel"; he belongs "to the most authoritative experts on the problems of contemporary philosophy." One reads in the *Cultural Front:* "At bottom certain prognostications of Aristotle have been incarnated and deciphered in their full amplitude only by Stalin." And later: "Socrates and Stalin are the summits of intelligence." A professor declares in a meeting of the Communist Academy: "The position of the thesis of Kantism in contemporary science can be definitely understood only in the light of the last letter of Comrade Stalin." (This is the same letter which revealed its proper course to Soviet music.) "Each paragraph of Stalin's speech," we learn on another occasion, "is the most fertile theme for works of art."

The literary *Gazette* goes so far as to praise Stalin as a stylist. "It is the business of the linguist and the critic to study the style of Stalin." A speech of Kalinin, president of the Soviet Republic, ends thus: "If you ask me who knows the Russian language best, I will answer Stalin." Demian Biedny, famous poet, exclaims at a meeting: "Learn to write as Stalin writes!" The editor of *Izvestia* declares at another meeting: "At the threshold of the new era stand two unequaled Titans of thought—Lenin and Stalin." And he concludes, "Can one at the present time write upon any subject whatever without knowing Stalin? Absolutely not. One can neither understand nor write anything interesting without Stalin." A woman of letters sees in Stalin the direct continuer of Goethe.

To such depths the Russian intelligentsia have fallen! Anyone who imagines that Stalin believes this praise, or laps it up in a mood of egotistical willingness to be deceived, is sadly mistaken. Stalin is not deluded by it. He regards it as useful to his power. He also enjoys humiliating these intellectuals, watching them write and sign idiotic statements suicidal to their minds and spirits. He debases them in the same spirit of vengeful glee in which he debased the minds and spirits, and destroyed the bodies, of those who "confessed" in the Moscow trials. He is taking out his spite on those who possess superior gifts. The American fellow-traveling intellectuals might well ponder this fate which has befallen their Russian colleagues.

In rebuking Stalin once for his spite against the socialists, Lenin remarked: "In general, spite plays the worst possible role in politics." Of all the personal factors that have played a role in Russian politics during the last twenty years, Stalin's spite against all men of superior talents is, in my opinion, the most baneful. It has brought, and is bringing, tragic misfortunes to Russia.

40. *The Socialist Dream Ends in Firing Squads*

THE LAST DAYS that I spent in that land of suspicion and abject sycophancy were extremely painful. I found myself avoiding both friends and acquaintances, seeing only those whom I had to see on official business.

On two different occasions, separated by an interval of about three weeks, I saw Krestinsky, the vice-commissar of foreign affairs, and Doletsky, the director of the Tass press agency. On the first occasion they were still both of them normal men, preoccupied naturally, but capable of smiling, joking, making plans, giving advice. Three weeks later they were gloomy and nervous, so absorbed in their inward thoughts that they spoke in dismal tones, stared inattentively, and hardly understood what I said to them. They knew themselves to be doomed men. They knew that the Piatakov trial, not yet announced in the papers, was to take place in a few days' time. Hundreds of arrests were being made daily of those in positions of authority. A few days later Doletsky, several of whose colleagues figured in the Piatakov trial, was actually arrested soon after I saw him. If rumor speaks truly, he killed himself in prison. He was a Communist of long standing, a conscientious official, and the kind of man who never got involved in political quarrels.

I went to take leave of Krestinsky the very day of my departure from Moscow at the end of January. It was two days before the opening of the trial. He was so tired and depressed that, in talking of my tasks in Greece, he would forget to finish his sentences. He begged my pardon, saying that he was overwrought, and bade me farewell. A few days later the Central Committee relieved him of his duties as vice-commissar of foreign affairs.

The last time Krestinsky spoke in public was at a meeting of the Communists of the Foreign Commissariat. Speaking very slowly, and obviously deeply moved, he said that, although he was wholly devoted to the Party which he had served conscientiously for years, he realized that his record as a member of the Opposition in the past made it advisable that, in the present circumstances, he should be retired. Men at the head of foreign affairs, he said, should enjoy the absolute confidence of the country and should be able to show a stainless Bolshevik past. He knew that, nine years before, he had committed the grave fault of joining the oppositionists who had set themselves up against the Leninist wisdom of our chief, Stalin. He approved, without reservation, the decision of the Central Committee, which for that reason had given him a new position in the Department of Justice. The loyal Communist must learn, he concluded, to serve his country where the Party thinks best to send him.

Krestinsky thanked his former colleagues, old and young, assured them that he would never forget them, and asked them to devote all their energies to the service of the Party. He must have known that his change of employment was but a stopping place on his way to prison, and from there to death. There had been too many examples to leave him in doubt. It was one of Stalin's regular methods of procedure to separate his intended victim by some new appointment from his customary surroundings—from those, that is, who know him and could vouch for his innocence—some months before striking him down.[1]

My conversations with Krestinsky concerned an idea I had for drawing Greece away from the economic subjection to Germany into which she was being led, together with the other Balkan States, by Dr. Schacht's ingenious "clearing system." The system grew out of the fact that Germany was in desperate need of foreign exchange and could not spare any gold for financing imports from Greece. The Nazis, giving as their reason that Germany would be a good outlet for certain Greek exports which had few markets at this time of crisis (for instance, Corinth raisins), concluded an agreement between the German Reichsbank and the Greek State Bank according to which the Greek bank put at the disposal of German importers large amounts of Greek *valuta* destined to pay Greek producers. The equivalent in German marks was put at the account of the Greek bank in Berlin, but these

[1] Krestinsky was arrested shortly after his appointment to the Commissariat of Justice. Similarly, Antonov-Ovseenko, consul general of the U.S.S.R. in Barcelona, was promoted to the post of People's Commissar for Justice and told to return to Moscow in order to take up his new functions. He took ship and may have landed in Odessa, but he never arrived at his new post. He was arrested somewhere in the course of the journey, and that was the end of him. The portfolio of justice was merely bait for the trap.

marks could be spent only on German manufactured goods. Thus, for general purposes, they were frozen.

Having lured the Greeks into this agreement as a means of getting rid of things they had difficulty in placing elsewhere, the Germans proceeded to buy all sorts of products, including those, such as tobacco, which Greece was selling for gold to English, American, and other importers. Inasmuch as they paid with practically worthless frozen marks, the Germans could offer higher prices than their English and American competitors and soon crowded them out. They bought everything they could lay hands on, in larger quantities even than was needed for consumption inside Germany. Being in need of foreign exchange, they resold Greek tobacco for gold to England.

The Greeks, not realizing the danger involved in this agreement, were surprised when at the end of the first term they found that the Germans owed Greece many millions of Reichsmarks, which they could not collect except by buying German goods. They tried to stop this worthless credit from increasing, but under pressure of Greek producers anxious to keep on with these sales at favorable prices, and of the German Government, they did not succeed. The balance unfavorable to Greece grew larger every month.

The rate of exchange fixed by the agreement was also unfavorable to Greece. And, moreover, having such a large amount frozen in Berlin, the Greeks were obliged to import almost all their machinery from Germany in order to get a part of their assets back. The Germans, realizing that the Greeks were trapped, set artificially high prices for this machinery. Thus the Germans got back many times over what they had overpaid on the goods imported from Greece. As a result the German stranglehold on Greek economy grew tighter and tighter. Belatedly the Greek economists and statesmen became aware of the situation and appealed to the Western powers, France and England, to take measures to offset it. But it was peacetime; the French and English were going easy and did nothing.

I believed that German economic penetration in the Balkans was as great a danger for Soviet Russia as for the Western democracies and that we ought to oppose this penetration by any means we could. The line of thinking I presented to Krestinsky was this: The Soviet Government holds a monopoly of foreign trade. What the other governments cannot do, even if they want to, our government can do by a simple order to the Foreign Trade Commissariat. It is our only buyer abroad, and Russia is an enormous market which can absorb without difficulty all the exports that Germany is dragging out of Greece, paying for them either in cash or with wheat, which Greece is in real need of. As the Germans cannot pay in either of these ways, a decision of the Politburo would be enough to upset the whole German scheme and greatly increase Russian influence in the Balkans.

I had prepared in Athens a very detailed report on this subject, including a program of carefully planned action. At our first meeting Krestinsky was obviously impressed by my report and promised to back up my plan in higher circles. I got the same warm support from David Stern, director of the German and Balkan Department of the Foreign Office. When I called at the foreign bureau of the Central Committee of the Party some days later in connection with another matter, the head of the bureau unexpectedly mentioned my report. He asked me to give him a copy of it. He had already heard about my plan: he thought it very important, and said that he was entirely for it and would do his best to see it through. I was optimistic. By the way things were going I expected the question would be put before the Politburo and a decision made so that I could return to Greece with new possibilities of action. But I did not know that at this time (January, 1937) Stalin was already beginning to play the game which was to lead to his pact with Hitler.

At my last meeting with Krestinsky, he answered my inquiry about the report with an embarrassed silence. In the foreign bureau of the Central Committee it was answered with a gay slap on the back.

"All right, Barmine. You go to Athens; we'll take care of all that."

I never heard any more about the fate of my report. Krestinsky and Stern soon disappeared in the purge, and I was left to guess that perhaps my scheme had been found too expensive. Only later, when I got wind of the mysterious conversations between Moscow and Berlin, did I realize why the whole idea was buried. It was not convenient to irritate Hitler in that delicate situation.

I left Moscow with mixed feelings of sadness and relief. Sometimes in a dream you find yourself in familiar surroundings, and yet they are also alien and unreal; they are not the same; they oppress you. That is the way I had felt in Moscow, and to leave the country was to lose the old familiar scene and yet also to retain reality. It was like waking up from a gruesome dream of that kind.

On my way to Athens I met two more men who were to be purged shortly afterward. One was our new minister in Lithuania, Podolsky, who was on the same train with me, getting off to take up his duties at Kaunas. He disappeared some months later and is believed to have been shot. At Budapest I stopped for a day with our ambassador, Bekzadian, an old acquaintance and an excellent fellow, a tasteful collector of illumined manuscripts and rare editions. He had, too, a cellar full of the very best Hungarian wines. Soon after I left him he was recalled without any explanation and disappeared.

At Athens I found Kobetsky in a state of heavy depression. The execution of Zinoviev had broken his spirit. He was impatiently awaiting my arrival, to hand the post over to me and leave for Moscow.

When I went to see Màri I was torn by a painful inward conflict. After what I had seen in Moscow, I realized that in taking her to Russia I would be involving her in danger. No amount of loyalty

309

or devoted work on her part could save her if the maniacs of the G.P.U. decided to include her in their witch hunt of foreigners. All my efforts and those of my influential friends would avail her nothing. All I could do then would be to share her fate, but that would not help her. Ought I to warn her against this danger and say good-by to her forever? Every time we met, this tormenting question assailed my mind. I did not speak of it but it preyed on me continually. Instead of bringing happiness to her with my love, I might be bringing her into trouble. Often after an evening with her I went back to the legation feeling lonely and desperate. Have I the right to keep my love when it means such a risk to her?

Finally one day I spoke my thoughts. I told her that foreigners were not well received in Moscow now, and, although I still longed to take her with me, I was anxious about what might happen to her.

She was not much impressed by this, except as an opportunity to say that she too had been worrying about our plan for a very different reason.

"Is it true," she asked me, "that Soviet officials lose favor with their government if they marry foreigners? People have told me that in Moscow they strongly disapprove of this, and that such a marriage almost always ruins a man's career. If that is so, I would not want you to do it."

I told her that I did not think it was so, but in any case I was not disturbed about my career.

"We can get along with any kind of job," I said. "There is plenty of work crying to be done."

Màri insisted that she could not bear to ruin my career.

Her future was the only thing to worry about, I answered.

Finally we agreed on a simple solution—not to worry at all. Whatever fate had for us, we would meet together.

"So long as I have your love, I am ready for what may come," she said.

But I cannot honestly say that I lived up to my side of the agreement.

I had hardly finished taking over my duties as chargé d'affaires when we began to receive the reports of the Piatakov trial. It plunged us into the same state of anxiety and anguish as had the Zinoviev trial in the previous August. Now a new pleiad of our most brilliant and trusted men were to be dragged to disgrace. But this time, surely, Stalin would refrain from shedding blood. Piatakov had been his faithful colleague since the early days of the First Five-Year Plan. He was one of the two men Lenin had recommended to the Party in his *Testament*—the only man he recommended without reserve. All Russia knew what a debt the finances and industrialization of the country owed to this talented statesman. And then Muralov! Ordjonikidze, a member of the Politburo and People's Commissar for

310

Heavy Industries, would surely not let his friend and assistant, Muralov, be shot! The records of Serebriakov and Boguslavsky were of epic stature. Drobnis, a hero of the Civil War, had already been shot once by the Whites and had recovered from his wounds by a miracle. Surely these men, too, were not going to die!

But the appalling news duly arrived—all shot with the exception of Radek, Sokolnikov, and one unknown defendant. Why had these three been spared? To offer a lure to those from whom confessions were wanted in future trials?

In the course of the proceedings, the name of Marshal Tukhachevsky was mentioned by Radek. What Radek said was harmless enough, but merely to see a friend's name mentioned in these carefully prepared confessions made one shudder. General Putna, Tukhachevsky's colleague and our military attaché in London, was convicted of having conspired with the Trotskyists. That meant the end for Putna—whose anguished wife and child heard of his arrest only in Warsaw on their way home. And that also was an omen of evil for Tukhachevsky. Further warning of his approaching end reached us in the news that his appointment to attend the coronation of George VI in London had been canceled and that the much less distinguished Admiral Orlov would go in his place.

All the defendants confessed to incredible crimes. The world has puzzled over the question: Why, if they did not commit the crimes, did they confess? I think the explanation is not difficult. Here were men whose entire lives had been inseparable from the Bolshevik Party, its methods and ideals. Bolshevism was for them the only method of social progress. They had no faith in democracy or social reform. A happy series of circumstances—which may not be duplicated for generations—had enabled the Bolshevik Revolution to succeed in Russia. Now these men who had given their lives to it saw that revolution fail to fulfill their hopes. A crass dictatorship and a worse than feudal reaction ruled in the Party as well as the country. What was there left to live for? It has been suggested by certain Western commentators that the Old Bolsheviks confessed as a last duty to the Party, taking upon their shoulders responsibility for its mistakes. But that cannot be true, for in their eyes the Party no longer existed. They had seen it destroyed by Stalin.

These unhappy men, tormented for endless months by the G.P.U. in its ruthless determination to break their wills, seeing their friends and associates sent to futile death, were in the last stage of demoralization. They had no new vision to cling to. With the collapse of the Party, every vision had been lost. They could only scrabble for their lives, or—what is much the same thing—purchase death as an end to their persecution. That, I think, is the explanation of their confessions.

It must be remembered that for every one of them there were a hundred Party leaders who did not confess. These went to silent and unheralded, but heroic, death behind prison walls, after standing up under months and years of pressure and torment from the G.P.U. What new dream, or what old loyalty, upheld these brave men in their last hours?

We on the outside knew only that the old Bolshevik Party was in process of destruction. Our sole hope was that we might still serve our country since the Party and the dream of socialism had perished.

I continued my work, planning, as soon as Minister Kobetsky returned, to put before Moscow the question of my recall. Thus things stood when a telegram came from Moscow announcing that Kobetsky had died suddenly in the Kremlin Hospital after an operation. I was deeply saddened by this. I was distressed, too: probably several months would pass before the new minister would be appointed and arrive in Greece.

Màri, meanwhile, was getting ready for our departure to Moscow, releasing herself from obligations in connection with her work.

"I'm not taking any more orders for new buildings," she told me one evening. "I don't want to leave anything unfinished behind me when I set off for Moscow. I hope to have my orphanage completed just in time. That's the only job I'm keeping on with."

"You see! Now you're paying the price for not listening to your family's warnings." I smiled. "It's a total loss to marry a Russian."

"I only hope we won't leave before the orphanage is ready," she said. "I don't want to disappoint old General Melas and leave a bad professional reputation when I go."

Màri had won an architectural contest for designing a new orphanage and school and had secured the job of supervising the construction as well—and this although General Melas, the chief donor of the building, had grumbled his disapproval of a woman architect. He had no faith in the emancipated woman, he said. So Màri was putting all her efforts into this one job, and the building was going ahead rapidly.

Alas! I brought her bad luck in this enterprise. Just as the orphanage was nearing completion she was chosen to represent Greek architects at the International Architectural Congress in Paris. She left in June, 1937, handing over the temporary supervision of the orphanage to her assistant and thinking to return in three or four weeks.

"I will be waiting for you," I told her at the gangway of the ship. "Don't succumb to the temptations of Paris and forget us. There's not only me waiting for you, but General Melas as well!"

The old general waited in vain. He never saw her again, and no doubt felt vindicated.

"I was right, after all," he probably said. "What can you expect of a woman? They always put love above business."

One month later, just when Màri was ready to start back to Athens, I joined her in Paris instead—a refugee without a country, hunted and in despair.

312

Alexander Barmine and his wife, U. S. A., 1941.

Alexander Barmine as a private in the United States Army, 1943.

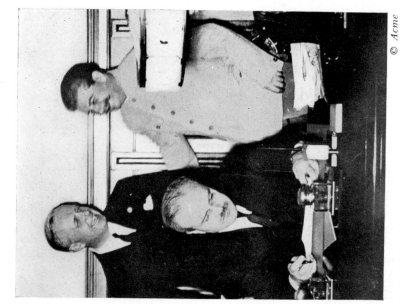

Stalin-Molotov-Von Ribbentrop. Stalin-Hitler Pact, August, 1939.

Scene of the Moscow Trial, the big "Hall of Columns" at Trade Unions House during the hearing.

Epilogue

DURING THE YEARS since the Moscow trials of 1936-38, I have spent many days and many sleepless nights thinking deeply about the whole problem of the Russian Revolution. I have tried my best to see clearly to what result, after all these years of effort and sacrifice, it has arrived.

Lenin's idea of socialism rested upon two major assumptions: that under a collectivized economy production would rise very much higher than it can under capitalism; and that the exploited wage workers would get the main benefit of this increased production, exploitation having ceased. The Soviet economic system, together with Stalin's totalitarian political regime, have refuted both these assumptions.

Having worked actively in both industry and commerce during the two five-year plans, I know by firsthand experience that the despotic and bureaucratic administration of Russia's economic life canceled out the benefits that we expected a collectivized economy to bring. More, not less, could have been accomplished by ordinary individual business-like enterprise, without the merciless driving of workers and clerks and the shooting of honest executives and engineers by political taskmasters and G.P.U. gendarmes—experts in nothing but ruthlessness. The extra energies expended under the persuasive name of "planning" only led to fresh wastage, breakdown, and renewed equally ill-considered experiments, the cost of which must be reckoned in billions of rubles.

The other basic assumption of socialism—that in a collectivized economy the exploitation of the workers would cease—has been even more appallingly refuted by reality. The Russian workers receive a much smaller share of the product of their toil than the workers in any capitalist country—smaller than the workers under the czar. And it is so small, not only because the capitalist's share is taken by those occupying a privileged position in the state, the new bureaucracy, but because an even greater share is used up in the sheer waste and inefficiency of bureaucratic mismanagement.

Nobody in the outside world, even those who have penetrated beneath the faked Soviet statistics, knows to what a state of abject slavery the Russian workers have gradually been reduced. It is necessary to have lived in Russia during recent years to realize this. Leon Trotsky, who left Russia in an early stage of the process, was unaware of it when he wrote *The Revolution Betrayed*. "The nationalization of the land and the means of industrial production," he said, "constitutes the basis of the Soviet social structure. Through these relations, established

313

by the proletarian revolution, the nature of the Soviet Union as a proletarian state is for us basically defined."

Despite his extreme criticism of the Stalin regime, Russia remained for Trotsky to the day he was murdered a "workers' state," no matter how distorted by bureaucratism. State ownership, he thought, made it so. Had he stayed in Russia he would have seen with his eyes how little formal ownership amounts to. The essential question is: How much of the social produce is returned to the worker through wages and the social services of the state? Judged by this criterion the Russian workers, on the eve of the war and after twenty-five years of the socialist experiment, could only honestly be compared with the pariahs of India or the *fellahin* of Egypt. Indeed, their condition is worse than that. For, if the workers of Egypt and India receive miserable wages, they also pay meager prices for what they consume. The Stalinist price and labor policies not only keep wages at incredibly low levels, but keep prices for the goods consumed by the worker's family inordinately high. Thus the pariah of the "workers' state" is robbed not once but twice.

In the early days of the Revolution, unheard-of privileges were extended to the wage workers: comfortable rooms and houses to live in, exemption from taxes, vacations on pay, free rest houses, free schooling, free theater tickets, free medicines, the right to buy food at special reduced prices, etc. As the dream of a high socialist production turned into the nightmare of bureaucratic inefficiency, and the "workers' state" into totalitarian serfdom, these privileges, one by one, were withdrawn. Instead of enjoying the new life so triumphantly extended to them by Lenin after the seizure of power in their name, the Russian workers, a quarter of a century later, have the greatest difficulty in keeping themselves in food and clothing. Except for a favored few, it is no better in regard to lodging. To top it all, in 1939, when the five-day week was abolished, the hours of labor were increased with no corresponding increase in the week's wages. The war brought still worse conditions, but I am not speaking now of emergency measures. *Before the war began,* the real wage of the Russian worker was very much lower than it was at its worst under the czarist regime.

I have not been able, like so many, to hide these facts from my mind. I see plainly what has happened: The state ownership of the machinery has been a failure and the working class, instead of gaining freedom, has paid in increased misery for this failure.

These two factors formed a vicious circle: the more the state-owned machinery failed, the more the workers suffered, and the more the workers suffered the more surely the machinery failed. To put it more simply: Exhaustion, next to bureaucratic inefficiency, was the chief cause of the low factory output. And this cause was visible to the eyes. The workers were badly fed, badly housed, worn out by overwork, and weakened by continuous semi-starvation.

These facts which so impressed me have recently been confirmed by an acute American observer, William L. White, who accompanied Eric Johnston on a tour through Russia. He said:

> *The standard of living here is less than was that of our poorest on W.P.A. . . .*
>
> Although they work so hard, they produce so little that their living standard is less than was that of our jobless on work relief. During our depression as many as 5,000,000 of our people were for a few years down to this low W.P.A. living standard. But in the Soviet Union *about 180,000,000 people have been on an even lower living standard for twenty-five years.*

Mr. White also said that he found "one marked difference between inmates of the Soviet Union and of the Kansas State Penitentiary" at Lansing where he visited a friend.

> Food and clothing in both places are about the same, maybe a little better in Lansing. But should my Kansas friend decide that his penitentiary was not well run, and express the hope that there might be a change of wardens, he would run no danger of being shot if he were overheard by a stool pigeon.

In the Soviet Union, Mr. White wrote:

> . . . competition with the State is outlawed, hence inefficiency is protected. The people accept it because they know nothing better. . . . Over everything rests the dull, unimaginative hand of a bureaucracy which produces only a dreary mediocrity.[1]

The apologists of the Soviet regime will, of course, say that these conditions were produced by a prolonged war, and that Mr. White is prejudiced in favor of American capitalism. It may be well, therefore, to recall the judgment of another American, notably friendly to the Soviet regime, who visited Russia in the summer of 1941 before the war had produced any change whatever in the condition of the workers. Mr. Ralph Ingersoll, then editor of *PM*, summarized his report in these terms:

> . . . *A dishwasher in an American hashhouse would not trade his life for that of an average Soviet workman. Not on the basis of what he would get to eat, where he would live, how well he could clothe himself, and what he might be able to buy with the money left over.*

After a personal investigation of prices, Mr. Ingersoll concluded that the purchasing power of the wage of the average Soviet worker would

[1] *The Reader's Digest,* December, 1944, and January, 1945.

amount, in American currency, to two dollars a week. He comforted himself that the worker's income was really more than that—it amounted, he thought, to ten dollars—because of the special privileges he enjoyed: "special rent reductions to which he is entitled, his vacation, his children's education, etc." Mr. Ingersoll, like other eager visitors, had not been informed that most of these special privileges, including both the children's education and the "etc.," had been, as quietly as possible, withdrawn.

In contrast to this picture of the life lived by the masses in Soviet Russia, we have, in Mr. White's report, some glimpses of that lived by those in power. I will quote two of them.

. . . A table for about 15 is set with immaculate linen. Before each napkin is the tall white-wine glass, the shorter-stemmed red-wine glass, the tubular champagne glass and the squat vodka glass. In the center is a dazzling array of Russian hors d'oeuvres on about 20 platters: smoked salmon, delicious Volga sturgeon, spiced ham, cold roast chicken, salami and countless kinds of sliced sausages.

Gnarled old waiters in baggy dress suits pass around bowls of cold caviar resting in cracked ice. I take what would be several dollars' worth in America. With it are served little pastries and a great slab of unsalted butter.

This initial course of caviar, sweet butter and pastries precedes the smoked sturgeon and sausages, and with it goes white wine. We were to find out that the same course also preceded every meal—including breakfast—which our hosts served us during our stay in the Soviet Union. . . .

Now comes the usual preliminary course of butter, caviar and pastry, during which we are supposed to nibble also the cold smoked and jellied meats. Then the meal, course by course, wine by wine. A soup with sherry. Sturgeon with a sauterne from the Crimea. After it, broiled grouse with a chilled white hock from the Caucasus.

The meal pauses for grilled filet mignon and then comes the climax of all Russian state banquets: cold, shaved, boiled suckling pigs—four of them, each on its platter. With the pig we are given a rich purplish burgundy from the Ukraine.

Mr. Ingersoll thought that the absence of "millionaires" in Russia made it more endurable to the worker to live on cabbage soup while the bureaucrats are feeding in this fashion. It is true that some Russian workers are deceived by the camouflage of "social ownership." They find a little consolation in the fact that those who live millionaire lives are not called millionaires, but "high government officials." But they are not half so gullible in these matters as are the visiting fellow travelers, yearning for something to believe in. These fellow travelers enjoy being impressed by the artificial simplicity and hypocritical pretenses to proletarianism which they find fashionable in the ruling classes. Of course, the whole level of life in Russia is so low that even those who live in luxury cannot command all the riches familiar in the Western world. But the gulf between their lives and those lived by the workers is wider, not narrower, than in America. And the workers, facing starvation, are not so easily forgetful of this gulf as the visiting foreigners.

Let me recall in more detail the life lived by a member of the Soviet privileged class as I observed it before the war. In Moscow he is quartered in the government building, where he has a flat of eight rooms, luxuriously furnished, and two servants. For holidays he has "Villa No. X of the Executive Committee" with a personnel of two, three, or four servants paid by the state, a private cinema if he so wishes, guest rooms, and equipment for all sorts of games—the whole also paid for by the state. He has an "order formula" which he has only to fill out and lavish meals will be supplied for his family, servants, and as many guests as he likes. The government will foot the bill. One or two cars, with chauffeur, are at his disposal. If he wants anything, no matter how costly, he has only to use the telephone. His son is treated as though his father were a millionaire, with state servants at his beck and call, toys imported from abroad, famous doctors to attend him when he is ill. He knows he has only to ask for what he wants and Papa will put through a telephone call. Should this high official feel like taking a holiday for his health in the Caucasus or the Crimea, he will find everywhere the same luxury, will always travel with his family in sleeping-car compartments, in special coaches, or even in special trains, at the public expense.

If any change has occurred in these matters after four years of war, it is an increase in the misery of the toiling masses, not any decrease in the luxury of those who live as I described above. The war has only widened the already vast gulf between the privileged bureaucracy and the masses.

There is a *new kind* of class rule and exploitation in this supposedly classless society, and anyone who imagines that it is *less* crude and violent than in democratic countries is dangerously deceiving himself. It is *more* crude and violent, and is made still more repellent to the moral sense by the all pervading hypocrisy of the "workers' state."

The worker in this workers' state has not only insufficient food and clothing to sustain his life energy, but he has no means of improving his lot. In his individual capacity he dare not protest. In his corporate capacity, as a trade union, he cannot strike. His union is a "company union"; and the company, the owner of his job, is the state. The state is the boss, the strike-breaking agency, and the police all rolled into one. And, besides that, it is in direct and absolute control of the unions, which are simply a part of the police machinery. At a wave of the hand, by some decree or some tricky manipulation of prices, real wages can be (and have been) reduced and hours increased without compensation. But the workers have no power to resist. They have no press, no platform, no single soapbox from which *even to remind the boss of a promise.*

To a casual visitor like Rickenbacker this state of things may seem enviable. But to people who take the socialist or planned society seriously, and are expecting it to deliver us from our troubles, I can say only one thing: The Socialist experiment has miserably failed.

The Soviet bureaucracy has become in every essential respect an exploiting class. Although it nominally owns no property and holds no title to the means of production, it controls the state which does hold such title. The state, nominally the owner of industry and nominally socialist, is actually the instrument of a new and more efficient, and more dreadful, system of degrading and robbing the toiling masses.

Abolishing private property in the means of production does not abolish the exploitation of man by man—Stalin at least has taught us that!

His regime has proved that socialism as the society of the free and equal is unattainable through "proletarian dictatorship." It leaves me also certain that such a society is unattainable through any scheme involving monopoly ownership of a nation's economy by the state. The failure in Russia is not only due to the growth of a regime of privilege out of party dictatorship, but to an organic contradiction between human character and the proper operation of such an economy. I could cite thousands of facts which prove this assertion and prove that the Russian experience is not peculiar, but teaches a general lesson to the whole world. A real betterment of life conditions for the masses can be best achieved under a democratic system, with private enterprise and competition, held within reasonable bounds by a progressive social administration, but neither owned as in Russia, nor strangled as in Germany, by the state.

After the experiences of the five-year plans, those Soviet leaders who had any realism or flexibility began to sense the impossibility of achieving socialism through dictatorship, and to turn their minds toward political democracy. Stalin himself, in my judgment, became convinced of this impossibility. Although his idea of socialism was far from what most of us meant by the term, I think that, such as it was, he worked for his idea sincerely for some time. But gradually he lost his faith. And he abandoned it definitely in the period ending in the Kirov assassination.

Stalin was enough a pupil of Lenin to know that the nationalization of industry and agriculture would justify itself, and socialism succeed, only if production rose higher in Soviet Russia than in the capitalist states, and only if the Russian workers and peasants enjoyed a higher standard of life than that enjoyed by workers of other countries. The frenzied effort of the five-year plans, and their essential failure, demonstrated to Stalin that, without individual competition, without the motive of individual gain, production can never be raised so high as in the capitalist states. It placed before him a momentous choice: whether to relax the dictatorship and let the Soviet state develop somewhat along the lines of Western democracy, or to abandon, together with the socialist idea, all ideas of liberty and equality and follow the example of the Fascists and Nazis.

Stalin encouraged for a while, or consented to, the democratic tendency as advocated by the best of the Old Bolsheviks. He played for a while with the fiction of a democratic constitution. But, when Kirov swam into prominence as its true leader, Stalin realized that democracy would spell the end of his power. With the example of Hitler's Blood Purge before him and the knowledge that at that game no man could outdo him, he decided for dictatorship as against democracy. From that date he deliberately discontinued his efforts to improve the lot of the working classes or decrease their exploitation. He bent his will toward organizing a society based upon the ruthless exploitation of masses of men deprived of all rights in the interest of a privileged minority which is to serve as the backbone of a totalitarian regime.

All this does not mean that Stalin has withdrawn his support from the so-called "communists" who are maneuvering for power in other countries. If he wanted to do that, he need only speak in the right quarters a single word. But it does mean, in my opinion, that he is using their maneuvers only to weaken these countries and enhance his own and Russia's power. He will extend his totalitarian caste system to as many other countries as he can, and it is fantastic to pretend that he is "fostering democracy" or "going back toward capitalism" in Russia or anywhere else. He cannot do that without weakening his own position. His instinctive drive is toward power, and he will defend Russia's power in the world by undermining the democracies, just as he defended his own power within Russia by killing all those who began to see that democracy was the true solution of her problems.

That is the cause and meaning of the great purge of 1936-38. It was no liquidation of a plot, however fantastic; no destruction of hostile parties; no repression of an opposition. It was the systematic extermination of all those who had intelligently served the socialist cause and would resist the deliberate conversion of their country into a totalitarian slave state. It was a counterrevolution. Baron Wrangel, or Kolchak, or Denikin, had they reached Moscow in the Civil War, would not less ruthlessly—not half so thoroughly—have exterminated all those who had played a brave and vital part in the Revolution, or who cared in any active way about life and freedom for the exploited workers.

They were a generation of revolutionary leaders who sought nothing for themselves, who possessed nothing, who as government officials, army officers, members of Party committees, lived the life of the humble, thinking only how best they might serve the good of mankind. They fought to abolish exploitation and build a freer and more just society which should assure to all its members the maximum of possible well-being. Some of them realized their failure and sincerely tried to return to democracy; others clung to their dream. They all are dead. Stalin had them shot. The regime which they worked to establish exists now only in name.

But Stalin needed a new support and, like all dictators, sought it in the Army. At the expense of the rest of the population, he reorganized and equipped the Army as a highly privileged group. But, in order to keep this instrument securely in his hands, he needed a fresh officer caste completely devoted to his person and devoid of any ideological relics of the revolutionary past, or any new "dangerous" notions of democracy. That is why the purge in the Army was even more drastic than among the civil functionaries.

When he had destroyed the brains of the Red Army, its General Staff, making it impotent to wage a victorious fight against the Nazis, Stalin made a pact with Hitler. He hoped by this maneuver to be able, in friendly collaboration with Hitler's Germany, to keep his place as tyrant of Russia. As he told Harry Hopkins: *he trusted that man!* [2] But he should have understood better the logic of a gangster pact. Hitler beat him at his own game. Scorning all his attempts at ingratiation and appeasement, Hitler, knowing that Stalin's army was at the moment headless, attacked him. Thus the Russian people had to pay with their blood once more, and more terribly, for the stupidity and power-greed of this visionless tyrant.

We are now so exultant about the Red Army's victory over our common enemy that we forget how near Russia came to defeat and how much the victory cost her people. It is very important that we should set aside these natural but transitory emotions and see the whole event as it will appear in history. The first year of the war was for Russia a year of bloody and appalling defeat. At the end of that year the enemy was at the gates of Moscow, Leningrad, and Rostov. His weapon was in the country's heart. Even in the worst days of the postrevolutionary invasion and the Civil War, the foreign armies never came so far. The Russian territory occupied by the Germans in the first six months was three times as large as Germany. Its population exceeded Germany's. It contained almost two-thirds of the Soviet industries, created with such pain and sacrifice under the five-year plans. In the second year the German armies pushed clear through to the Volga and into the Caucasus Mountains. Hitler's Alpine detachments planted the Nazi flag on the top of Mount Elbruz. In the third year, when new commanders had emerged, trained in the school of defeat, the Russians rallied and

[2] See Harry Hopkins' article, "My Meeting with Stalin," in *The American Magazine,* December, 1941.

drove the Germans out. But the cost in blood and suffering continued, and the territories which had been industrialized at such sacrifice during the five-year plans are totally devastated.

In the First World War, under the rotten and hated czarist government, with an army ill-equipped, without adequate arms and ammunition, and without Allied help—the first Western munitions arrived in Russia in 1917—the Russian soldiers stopped in the Pripet Marshes the asssault of the great modern armies of Hindenburg and Mackensen. In three years of savage fighting, when the czarist troops had often no more than sixty or one hundred shells to a division, the Germans never broke into Great Russia. They never got past Poland, Latvia, and Lithuania. Yet Hitler's newly created army overran in one year over half of European Russia, and in three months more went to the Volga. Even Charles of Sweden and Napoleon never got so far, the first thrown back from Poltava, the second from Moscow. Is it necessary to point out that the chief cause of the initial disaster was the state of the country and Army as the result of a wholesale purge? *Hitler's army, though only seven years in existence, had preserved all its old officer cadres. The Red Army, though trained for twenty years to meet this attack from the west, had just been purged by Stalin of its commanding staff.*

The Nazis put Russia's total losses in soldiers and civilians at thirty million; the Russians say eight million. If you double the Russian figure and cut Hitler's in half, you have fifteen million—a moderate estimate. Out of these at least six million would be soldiers, and that means that more than half of the Red Army was destroyed. Undoubtedly more than half its equipment was destroyed.

The victory is glorious, but the catastrophe of the first years was gigantic. And there is no other explanation of this gigantic catastrophe than the lack of strategic leadership and organization in the Red Army when the war began.

In other respects besides strategic leadership and organization the two armies were about equal. Stalin had many natural advantages over Hitler. He had had twelve years in which to arm, assuming that he started with the five-year plan in 1928—although Soviet Russia has been building an army ever since 1918. In 1935, when Hitler started with almost no army, Stalin had already the biggest army in the world. He had also built Russia's machinery of arms production up to the level of Germany's. He had twice the population. He had ten times the resources. *He lacked no raw materials.* He concentrated as fiercely on the job. He had trained the nation from infancy in a war psychology.

Moreover, he had absolute control of the economy—no Junkers or capitalists to contend with. He could starve his people to build armaments as Hitler could not. And he did so. In Russia it was not "cannon instead of butter," but "cannon instead of bread."

With these advantages, he should have been many times stronger than Hitler when they met. He was, as a matter of fact, in aviation and ammunition just about equal, and in number of tanks and cannon superior. In spite of this superiority, which should have been still greater, Stalin's army, though double in number of trained soldiers, could not in the first year wage effective modern warfare against Hitler. Such warfare demands skillful strategy and perfect organization of supplies and rear communications. It demands exact co-ordination of the parts of a complicated war machine. With all their enormous equipment, Stalin (who was commander in chief) and his three servile but talentless marshals, Voroshilov, Budyenny, and Timoshenko, were not able to carry out a large-scale counteroffensive. They attempted no strategy. They put in operation no plan. All they used their gigantic manpower and equipment for was to stop successive holes in the dike through which the Germans were pouring. At the beginning of the war they could themselves have been pouring well-armed troops and *Panzer* divisions through Poland, Hungary, and the Carpathian Ukraine into Germany and Czechoslovakia. They could have been there before the Germans reached Minsk, if anybody in the High Command had had the independent force and strategic imagination to undertake a bold maneuver.

(This is not the place to prove this assertion, but it is obvious from the distribution of the major forces of the two armies when the war began.)

There is not a doubt in my mind that that is what Marshal Tukhachevsky would have done—or Blukher, Yakir, Uborevich—any of the trained and brilliant generals whom Stalin shot to safeguard his own power.

The shooting of those generals, and of thousands of lesser officers who had to be put out of the way to keep the Army under heel, is the first and most obvious cause of the large-scale disaster we have described. If Stalin had not shot this "fifth column" in 1937, the battles which saved Russia would have been fought on the Vistula and the Nieman instead of the Volga and the Neva. Three peacetime years is not long enough for a beheaded army to grow a new brain. This simple physiological fact is ignored by the wishful thinkers who are now bent on making a world hero of Stalin. The former United States ambassador, Joseph Davies, even discovered (after he left Russia!) that it was a benefit to the Red Army to shoot all its authentic leaders. No military man needs to be told the contrary.

Here is a rough tally of those who disappeared in the purge:

Three out of five marshals.

Eleven vice-commissars of war.

Six out of eight generals who formed the court-martial alleged to have condemned to death Tukhachevsky and seven others of the High Command.

Seventy-five of the eighty members (all generals and admirals) of the Supreme Military Council of the Red Army, including all the commanders of military districts, the commander in chief of the Air Force, the commander in chief of the fleet, and all but one of the commanders of the different sea fleets.

Ninety per cent of all generals.

Eighty per cent of all colonels.

Approximately thirty thousand lesser officers.[3]

According to figures agreed upon by authorities as wide apart as Souvarine, Krivitsky, and Ciliga (Yugoslav former Communist leader imprisoned in Russia), and confirmed by a great many others, there were in two years approximately one million civilians imprisoned and three hundred thousand executed. Those deported to forced labor and concentration camps amounted to another ten million. To these may be added a million and a half Polish civilians found in Russian concentration camps by Polish officials sent to recruit troops against Germany—this according to the report of the Polish Premier, General Sikorski.[4]

Few people, if any, in America realize the extent and devastating effect of this general massacre of loyal citizens—for that is the only way to describe it. The assertion of Ralph Ingersoll that they shot ten innocent men in order to get one guilty one—a way of administering justice that he thinks the Russian people enjoy—shows how far the mania for justifying and explaining everything Soviet Russian has deceived people over here. It was not a massacre either of the innocent or the guilty, and it was not to be counted in tens but in hundreds of thousands. It was a systematic extermination of men who combined independence with competence, intelligence, and sincerity. It was a destruction of all conceivable opponents or critics of the Dictator, above all every man who wanted Russia to move with Kirov toward democracy instead of with Stalin to totalitarian autocracy.

Stalin conceives the whole problem in terms of force and will, and of these he has an abundance. As a personal trait his force of character is imposing. But what lies under this personal phenomenon is Russia's tragic inability to fight economically—an inability due to the regime of bureaucratic and naked police rule which he represents, and on the top of which he so calmly sits.

Stalin has one superb talent—ruthlessness. He has one and only one method for getting things done—ruthlessness as a system. It worked wonders in his single-handed war against his political opponents and against the Russian people who were disarmed. It put

<hr>

[3] From figures reported to the French General Staff, endorsed by Boris Souvarine, authority on Soviet Russia for *Figaro* (Paris), confirmed by my own computations, and by Walter Krivitsky, who left Moscow after the climax of the purge.

[4] *New York Times*, November 13, 1941.

him in his place of supreme power. It made him premier, dictator. It may make him master of Europe. What will this "success" mean to European civilization?

There is no space to answer this question, except as my whole book is an answer. But today's papers bring to mind one suggestive example. The defense of Leningrad was a military success; but Leningrad might, without altering the fortunes of war, have been declared an open city. When Manila in 1942 was declared an open city by the American Army, the act was sneered at in the Soviet press as though the Americans did not know how to fight. This is one of the primary contrasts in the whole conduct of the war: Where the Americans, while careful of human lives, are reckless of materiel, Stalin is reckless of human lives. Today's *New York Herald Tribune* confirms, from pro-Soviet sources, the fact that one and a half million inhabitants, mostly women and children, died of starvation in heroic Leningrad alone during its two years of siege. Were all these millions of dead an absolutely inevitable cost of victory? How many of them were victims of incredible callousness, contempt for human suffering, and poor organization—victims, rather, of a system and a method of waging war which takes no toll of human lives? Now, in the euphoria of victory, these are "small details." Will history judge as lightly?

My harsh words about *Stalin's regime* are dictated by deep sympathy and love for our gallant ally, *the Russian people*. It is easier just now, as so many "liberals" do, to sing praises to the tyrannical regime and denounce every criticism of it as a violation of unity and an attack on "Russia." It is easy to justify this policy of praise and appeasement, as a prominent American liberal did privately not long ago, by saying that "fewer American boys will have to die if more Russians do." It is a question whether in the long run this new Munich policy will not bring the opposite result.

I must repeat that the tragic position of the Russian people makes all the more glorious their bravery and determination. In the First World War, under the despotic czar, they marched into the battle by hundreds of thousands unarmed—hoping to pick up a weapon from a fallen comrade and carry the fight on. They are not only heroic; they are inured to heroism. No words that can be spoken, even by the eloquent Churchill or the ecstatic Beaverbrook, will give too high praise to their valor.

But it is both an injustice to them and a danger to world democracy to put this heroism of the Russian people to the credit of the Stalin regime. The Stalin regime is totalitarian to the last fiber. To give it the credit for a victory won and for deeds performed by the Russian soldiers serves only to increase the respect for totalitarianism throughout the world. "Stalin succeeds—dictatorship succeeds." The reasoning is obvious. But the premise is exactly wrong. The Russian people would have fought better and won a less costly victory under a democratic government. That is the truth. And it is a truth absolutely vital to the world struggle of democracy.

Some will ask: Why remind us of Stalin's defeats and weaknesses at the beginning of the war, when these things are now past and forgotten? It is just because they are so soon and easily forgotten that it is necessary to stress them, if we are to think straight on present problems. Too many people, deluded by Stalinist propaganda and the spectacular events in Europe, are developing an inferiority complex in the face of a victorious totalitarian state. If this complex begins to influence public opinion and guide our foreign policy, the result will be that, instead of standing firm for democracy, we shall adopt a policy of appeasement.

Chamberlain and Daladier, hypnotized by the aggressive totalitarianism of the Nazis, tried this policy of appeasement. To everybody who dared criticize it (including Churchill) they said: You will bring war. The truth is that *the policy of appeasement brings war inevitably.* And this is as true today as it was then. At root the appeasement policy consists of underestimating your own force and, under the influence of propaganda, vastly overestimating the force of your partner. This permits him to bluff and bully you into a more and more untenable position, until finally you have to fight a "war of survival."

The foremost Allied military experts are of the opinion that without American aid the Soviet giant would have been defeated by Germany. Amid the elation of the hour of Russian victory, this cold fact is too easily forgotten. And the totalitarian apologists, now so inordinately active on the American radio and in the press, are doing their best to keep it forgotten. Let us listen, by contrast, to a journalist who is close to the most authoritative sources, including the White House, Ernest K. Lindley: "In total military power now applied throughout the world, both directly and through Lend-Lease indirectly, neither Russia nor Britain can compare with the United States. . . . Without the other two, none of the three big powers could have hoped to win the war, and *Britain and Russia would have suffered complete defeat."*

This means that without the help of the world's greatest democracy, one totalitarian state, the more efficient, would have crushed the other, which, though much bigger, was weaker. Stalin's totalitarian regime owes its survival in a war with Hitler's to two factors: to the great Russian people who hate the dictatorship so much that even through the hour of greatest danger Stalin had to keep twelve million of them in concentration camps; and second, to the help of the democracies. These facts should be repeated again and again. They should be dinned into the ears of the enthusiastic converts to a "planned society" who, blinded by superficial information and propaganda fairy tales, are ready to discard the "old," the "rotten," the "outlived" American system, and take the totalitarian road.

In conclusion—not to be misunderstood—I must say that I stood

325

for all-out aid to Russia in 1942—advocating it three years ago[5] when many Americans were still hesitating—and I stand for it still. I am an older enemy of German fascism than Vansittart. In building up Russian industrial and military power, we of my generation gave our whole lives to preparation against this deadly enemy. This is not the first time German rulers have led their obedient people against Russia. As the reader already knows, my two brothers were killed fighting in the First World War against Germany. During the German invasion in 1918, I myself was arrested by Germans in Kiev and shot at when escaping. Two years later I received two wounds in the battle of Gomel, where Polish generals were leading German-trained Silesian veterans against our ragged troops.

Besides that, like millions of Americans of Russian, Polish, or Norwegian descent, I hate the Nazi invader more bitterly than Americans who have no ties of this kind in their native countries. We have felt more the tragedy of what was happening. For us each day of heroic Russian and Polish resistance, each day of their sacrifice, meant not only a day gained for English and American preparedness, it meant another fifteen thousand of our brothers killed, another fifty thousand wounded. It meant women and children starved, homes devastated, towns burned, dams and factories destroyed in the land of our birth. With Hitler's depredations added to Stalin's failures and brutalities, I know that what little bit was left of the achievement of the Russian Revolution has in great part disappeared. The tragedy of the Russian people is my own tragedy. Like all other Americans of Russian descent, I am deeply grateful to America for the lend-lease aid, even though it must go through the hands of the tyrant. But I want also to warn the American people.

For three years the fellow travelers and "realistic" appeasers of Stalin made it almost impossible to speak the truth about the Soviet regime. Under pretext of a zeal for Allied unity they cried down as an "attack on our gallant ally in her hour of danger" even the modest appeals of real and consistent democrats to Stalin to release millions of Russians from prisons and concentration camps and let them join in the fight against Hitler.

To be sure, neither the vociferous champions of "unity" nor the Russian press and radio ever hesitated to attack other Allied governments such as Britain, Poland, Belgium, or Greece, in their hour of danger. Nor was the idea that truth about Russia should be hushed up in the interests of mutual understanding always upheld by the facts. Nevertheless, Russia was in real danger, and for three years I abstained from any public utterance whatever against Stalin's totalitarian regime. The publication of this present book was postponed throughout these

[5] *The Reader's Digest*, February, 1942.

years, and except for the above-mentioned statement in favor of Lend-Lease, and one or two military analyses published at the peak of Hitler's advance on Leningrad and Moscow in 1941, in which I predicted that he would be unable to take these cities, and that he already saw the writing on the wall—except for these, I remained silent. But today, when Stalin's empire is not only out of all danger, but is choking in bloody terror such allies as Poland, and when the events in Greece and the communist policy in other countries are challenging democracy, it is the duty of every man who knows the truth to speak out.

I know the Stalin regime in Russia. I have lived my life under it. I know that it is tyranny in its most total and most devastating form. President Roosevelt was absolutely right when he said on February 11, 1940: "The Soviet Union, as everybody knows that has the courage to face the fact, is a dictatorship as absolute as any other dictatorship in the world." As an experiment in a new form of social life it has dismally failed. Those who, in their enthusiasm for a powerful ally in the struggle against Hitler, blind themselves to this fact are doing a terrible injury both to civilization as a whole and to the Russian people.

We need a truer faith in democracy. The democracies are now proving to all those not blinded by the totalitarian "light from the east" that they also can achieve great military victories, and do it more efficiently and with less waste of human lives.

The miracle of victory in Russia happened not because of the genius of the Dictator or the advantages of a totalitarian regime, as fellow-traveling propagandists want Americans to believe. It happened because of the vast spaces, the snow, the mud, the lend-lease aid, and most decisive, the fierce resistance of the Russian people.

The Russian people have fought heroically in a war for a democracy and a freedom which they do not possess. They have fought with the hope—all of them who are politically conscious and still bold enough to think—that they might achieve democracy at the end of the war. But what now is promised them by these English and American diplomats and journalists who come home singing the glories, not of them, but of the Stalin regime? A perpetuation of their slavery! a making fast of totalitarian oppression in the name of democratic victory!

"You fought so well for freedom because you are enslaved," the admirers of Stalin's regime are saying to them. "As a reward we will consecrate your slavery. We will even consent to call it democracy."

That is the position of those who put the heroic victory of the Russian people to the credit of Stalin's totalitarian regime. They are endangering the future of world democracy, and they are stabbing the Russian people in the back.

There are no points where the interests of the United States and Russia clash. These two great peoples have a natural liking for each other, and their relations are logically peaceful and friendly. The main obstacle in the way of making this friendship sure and durable is the stone wall of the totalitarian tyranny surrounding and strangling Russia. Walter Lippmann writes in his book, *U.S. War Aims:*

> While Russia has insulated herself internally against the propaganda of the Western constitutional system, we are not insulated, because of our principles of toleration, against the totalitarian propaganda. . . . As long as this inequality exists, there cannot be true collaboration between the Soviet Union and the Western world. There can be only a *modus vivendi,* only compromises, bargains, specific agreements, only a diplomacy of checks and counterchecks. . . . The Russians simply cannot expect the rest of the world to believe in the democratic principles of their new foreign policy if they do not practice those principles at home.

I only want to add that, if the Russians could practice those principles at home, the friendship of these two peoples might be everlasting. To this ultimate end, every thinking and honest American ought to reject the insulting notion that the Russians enjoy their slavery, and ought to understand that they have the same aspiration, and the same right, as Americans and other peoples of the world to a way of living based on "liberty and justice for all."

Index

Bialystok, 79
Biedny, Demian, 305
Birth of a Nation, The, 184
Blukher, Marshal Vasilli K., 6, 87, 322; purged, 8n.
Blukhov, Michael Ivanovich, 62-3, 65, 71, 77
Blumkin, Jacob, 110-11, 140
Bobritshev, Gen., 152
Bodrov, 210-1
Bogomolets, Prof., 271, 272
Boguslavsky, 311
Bokhara, Emirate of, 97-108, 143; Communist Party of, *see* Young Bokhara Party
Bolshevik (Communist) Party, 37-8, 40-4, 50; Army and, 62-7; Barmine joins, 20, 53; bureaucracy in, 213-9; *chistkas,* 109-11, 127-8; and Civil War, 52-9; Constitution, 247-8; famine under, 94-5, 109, 122, 174-5, 201; favoritism in, 192; and free press, 172; and gold, 174-5; ideals of, 311; inequality in, 58; organization of, 159-60; origin of name, 53n.; in Paris, 180-7; and peasants, 170, 173; propaganda, 64-5, 75; purge of, 245-55; Stalin controls, 159-64, 245-55; and trade unions, 91-2, 124, 127; and Workers' Opposition, 94-5
Bolshoi Theater, 300, 302
Born, Georg (David Stern), 3, 9, 309
Borshchevsky, Gen., 95
Boyev, Ivan, 206, 207
Brannitzkaya, Countess, 29, 48, 96
Bratanovsky, 260
Breslav, 185
Brest-Litovsk, 42, 79, 118
Briquet, 111-2, 171
Britain, 86, 97, 100, 143-4, 147-50, 210, 230-1, 308
Brockdorff-Rantzau, Count, 116
Brown, Mr., 210
Brussilov, Gen., 126
Bubenetz, 87
Bubnov, Andrei Sergeyevich, 127, 128
Budyenny, Marshal Semyon Mikhailovich, 8n., 21n., 78-9, 87, 207, 210, 299, 322
Bukharin, Nikolai Ivanovich, 56n., 91, 92, 113, 124, 125, 127, 147, 150-1, 168-70, 173, 198-9, 242, 248, 257, 286, 296, 298
Bullitt, William, 233
Byelenky, Zakhar, 268
Byelotsky, 128-9
Byron, George Gordon, 153

Chamberlain, Neville, 325
Chapayev, 87
Chaplin, Charlie, 183-4, 304
Charles of Sweden, 321
Cheka, *see* G.P.U.
Chekhov, Michael, 302
Cherkasky, Prince, 86
Chiang Kai-shek, 57, 87, 166, 232
Chicherin, George Vasilievich, 97, 115-7, 119-20, 129, 233
China, 166, 167, 231-2, 243-4; Revolution in, 166
Churchill, Winston, 66, 93, 324
Ciano, Admiral Count, 189
Ciliga, Anton, 323
Circus, The, 184, 215
Citroën, M., 242
Civil War, Russian, 41-4, 52-61, 66-73, 93-5, 124
Clinic for the Newborn, 135
Clausewitz, Karl von, 84
Cloches de Corneville, 83
Communist Academy, 151
Communist International (Comintern), 80, 100, 101, 123, 139, 166, 256, 278
Communist Party: of Bokhara, 97, 100, 103; Chinese, 166; French, 184; Greek, 275, 278; Russian, *see* Bolshevik Party; Turkmen, 271
Conservatoire des Arts et Métiers, 184
Cooper, James Fenimore, 31
Crimea, 44, 93, 129
Crimes of Stalin, The, 295
Cultural Front, 305
Curley, Archbishop Michael, 266
Curzon, Lord, 100

Daladier, Édouard, 325
Dan, Theodore, 22
Davies, Joseph E., 224, 322
Davtian, Ambassador, 8, 16, 285, 291-2; purged, 19
De Grasse, 289
Demerdzis, Prof., 275, 276
Denikin, Gen. Anton Ivanovich, 5, 52-3, 56-7, 61, 66, 69, 93, 129, 319
Diakonov, 241-2
Dickens, Charles, 32, 77, 193
Disney, Walt, 304
Divilkovsky, 118, 186
Djankoy, 129
Doletsky, 306
Dolivo-Dobrovolsky, 85
Dormoy, Marx, 21
Douhet, Gen., 189
Doumer, Pres., 193

330

334